Unbounded Dependency Constructions

OXFORD SURVEYS IN SYNTAX AND MORPHOLOGY

General Editor
Robert D Van Valin, Jr,
Heinrich-Heine University and the University at Buffalo,
State University of New York

Advisory Editors
Guglielmo Cinque, University of Venice
Daniel Everett, Illinois State University
Adele Goldberg, Princeton University
Kees Hengeveld, University of Amsterdam
Caroline Heycock, University of Edinburgh
David Pesetsky, Massachusetts Institute of Technology
Ian Roberts, University of Cambridge
Masayoshi Shibatani, Rice University
Andrew Spencer, University of Essex
Tom Wasow, Stanford University

PUBLISHED

1. **Grammatical Relations**
Patrick Farrell

2. **Morphosyntactic Change**
Olga Fischer

3. **Information Structure**
The Syntax-Discourse Interface
Nomi Erteschik-Shir

4. **Computational Approaches to Syntax and Morphology**
Brian Roark and Richard Sproat

5. **Constituent Structure**
(Second edition)
Andrew Carnie

6. **Processing Syntax and Morphology**
A Neurocognitive Perspective
Ina Bornkessel-Schlesewsky and Matthias Schlesewsky

7. **Syntactic Categories**
Gisa Rauh

8. **The Interplay of Morphology and Phonology**
Sharon Inkelas

9. **Word Meaning and Syntax**
Approaches to the Interface
Stephen Wechsler

10. **Unbounded Dependency Constructions**
Theoretical and Experimental Perspectives
Rui P. Chaves and Michael T. Putnam

For a complete list of titles published and in preparation for the series, see p. 308

Unbounded Dependency Constructions

Theoretical and Experimental Perspectives

RUI P. CHAVES AND MICHAEL T. PUTNAM

OXFORD

UNIVERSITY PRESS

OXFORD
UNIVERSITY PRESS

Great Clarendon Street, Oxford, OX2 6DP,
United Kingdom

Oxford University Press is a department of the University of Oxford.
It furthers the University's objective of excellence in research, scholarship,
and education by publishing worldwide. Oxford is a registered trade mark of
Oxford University Press in the UK and in certain other countries

Published in the United States of America by Oxford University Press
198 Madison Avenue, New York, NY 10016, United States of America

British Library Cataloguing in Publication Data
Data available

Library of Congress Control Number: 2020949498

ISBN 978-0-19-878499-9 (hbk.)
ISBN 978-0-19-878500-2 (pbk.)

Printed and bound by
CPI Group (UK) Ltd, Croydon, CR0 4YY

Contents

General Preface

Oxford Surveys in Syntax and Morphology provides overviews of the major approaches to subjects and questions at the centre of linguistic research in morphology and syntax. The volumes are accessible, critical, and up-to-date. Individually and collectively they aim to reveal the field's intellectual history and theoretical diversity. Each book published in the series will characteristically contain: (1) a brief historical overview of relevant research in the subject; (2) a critical presentation of approaches from relevant (but usually seen as competing) theoretical perspectives to the phenomena and issues at hand, including an objective evaluation of the strengths and weaknesses of each approach to the central problems and issues; (3) a balanced account of the current issues, problems, and opportunities relating to the topic, showing the degree of consensus or otherwise in each case. The volumes will thus provide researchers and graduate students concerned with syntax, morphology, and related aspects of semantics with a vital source of information and reference.

Unbounded Dependency Constructions: Theoretical and Experimental Perspectives examines one of the central topics in syntactic theory over the past half-century, namely the displacement of linguistic expressions from the position in which they would normally appear and be interpreted. The authors give a thorough account of the phenomena which fall under the heading of unbounded dependency constructions, present a critical evaluation of the theoretical approaches to describing and explaining them, and examine psycholinguistic and acquisition studies relevant to them. The result is an important contribution to the series which will be of great value to scholars investigating these phenomena.

Robert D. Van Valin, Jr
General Editor

University at Buffalo,
The State University of New York

Heinrich Heine University,
Düsseldorf

Preface

One of the most challenging facets of the study of human language is that attaining even an inkling of a better understanding of its nature and properties requires collaborative effort from scholars in multiple disciplines and traditions. It can be a daunting task to incorporate and synthesize research from various perspectives, however, it is simultaneously also one of the many attractive facets of current research in linguistics and its relation to cognitive science, broadly construed. The present volume was written from this perspective. Here we have attempted to integrate and evaluate theoretical claims and experimental evidence brought to bear on Unbounded Dependency Constructions (UDCs). The end result is a volume that challenges a host of claims and assumptions in light of new data and experimental evidence. We do not presume to completely settle any of these important debates in the pages that follow, but we do hope that this volume provides a step forward in the current state of research on UDCs from multiple perspectives. Our goal is for those engaged in the study of UDCs—as well as those who may take an interest in this topic after reading this volume—to find our treatment of this topic stimulating and helpful in sharpening their own research, moving forward.

In the course of writing this book we benefited from the expertise of various people who were kind enough to assist us. First, we would like to thank Robert Van Valin, Jr, for the opportunity to write this book for this series. The book benefited substantially from the comments and queries from two reviewers, for which we are very thankful. We would also like to thank the following individuals for discussions and/or suggestions at various stages of this project: Anne Abeillé, Doug Arnold, Ash Asudeh, Emily Atkinson, Marc Authier, Hanno Beck, Robert D. Borsley, Seth Cable, Matt Carlson, Cristiano Chesi, Barbara Citko, Ashwini Deo, Giuli Dussias, John Hale, Phillip Hofmeister, Holger Hopp, Carrie Jackson, Mike Johns, Alan Juffs, Jean-Pierre Koenig, Robert D. Levine, Terje Lohndal, Eric Matthieu, Gail Mauner, Laura A. Michaelis, Akira Omaki†, Lisa Reed, David Reitter, Martin Salzmann, Thomas S. Stroik, Robert Van Valin, Jr, Gregory Ward, Thomas Wasow, Steffi Wulff, and Masaya Yoshida. None of the above has any blame for any errors, omissions, or shortcomings remaining in this work.

We also thank and acknowledge Andrey Drinfeld, Anastasia Stepanova, and Yanwei Jin for assistance with various non-English data, and Adriana King and Corey Wright for contributing to the design of various experiments that made their way into this monograph. Maike Rocker helped us with editing an early draft of this work, Stephanie Richter painstakingly proofread a later preliminary version, Ashley Pahis combed through a near-final version, and Louise Larchbourne meticulously copy edited the final manuscript. Thank you all for this tremendous help.

Portions of the research carried out and discussed in this book were presented at the *Long-Distance Dependencies Workshop* (Humboldt-Universität zu Berlin), a colloquium at the Department of Linguistics of the University of Rochester, a symposium at the Center for Language Science at Penn State University, an invited talk at the Laboratoire de Linguistique Formelle (Université Paris Diderot), and a colloquium at the Linguistics Department of the

Ohio State University. We give our thanks to the audiences and participants for stimulating questions which improved our work. We in addition would like to recognize and thank the College of the Liberal Arts at Penn State University for generous financial support in connection with the experiments in Chapter 6.

Mike would like to thank his colleagues affiliated with the Center for Language Science at Penn State University for creating such a supportive and stimulating environment to work in. During the 2016–17 academic year, Mike was a Visiting Scholar in the Department of Linguistics at Buffalo SUNY, which was a wonderful opportunity. The participants in Mike's graduate seminar on *Long-distance relationships* (Fall 2019) provided invaluable insights and thought-provoking comments on these materials—thanks for your questions and comments! Lastly, Mike would also like to acknowledge Rothrock Coffee and Good Day Café in State College, PA, for providing stimulating venues to write. Mike is grateful to his friends, Ron & Sarah, and his family, Jill & Abby, for their unyielding love and support. He is certain that Jill won't miss frequently being subjected to on-the-fly acceptability judgment requests.

Rui wishes to dedicate this work to two people whose roles were particularly invaluable to this volume: Jeruen E. Dery, for his dedication and insight in earlier stages of this line of inquiry, and Jillian K. Da Costa, for her unwavering support, love, sharp insights, and inordinate hours of discussion about data and everything else besides.

Rui P. Chaves
Michael T. Putnam

List of Figures

List of Abbreviations

ATB	Across-The-Board
BLR	Bayesian Logistic Regression
BNC	British National Corpus
BR	Brown Corpus
CCG	Combinatorial Categorial Grammar
CED	Condition on Extraction Domains
CFG	Context-Free Grammar
CG	Categorial Grammar
CNFICC	Clause Non-Final Incomplete Constituent Constraint
CNPC	Complex NP Constraint
COCA	Corpus of Contemporary American English
CrI	Credible Interval
CSC	Coordinate Structure Constraint
ECP	Empty Category Principle
EPP	Extended Projected Principle
ERP	Event-Related Potential
fMRI	Functional Magnetic Resonance Imaging
HPSG	Head-driven Phrase-Structure Grammar
IP	Inflectional Phrase
L1	First Language
LFG	Lexical-Functional Grammar
LMER	Linear Mixed-Effect Regression
MLC	Minimal Link Condition
MOC	Missing Object Construction
MP	Minimalist Program
PF	Phonological Form
PIC	Phase Impenetrability Principle
pMTG	Posterior Middle Temporal Gyrus
POS	Poverty of the Stimulus
PSG	Phrase-Structure Grammar
RRG	Role and Reference Grammar
SAI	Subject-Auxiliary Inversion
SB	Switchboard
SSC	Sentential Subject Condition
TP	Tense Phrase
UG	Universal Grammar
WSJ	Wall Street Journal
YNQ	Yes/No Question

1

Introduction

1.1 Unbounded dependency constructions

This book is about one of the most peculiar features of human communication systems: the fact that words which go together in meaning can occur arbitrarily far away from each other, across clausal boundaries, as illustrated in (1). In all of these examples, the phrase between brackets is somehow interpreted as if it were instead realized immediately after the verb *likes*.

(1) a. The doctor$_i$ [who]$_i$ I think Ben said he really likes $_$$_i$ has retired.

    b. [Who]$_i$ I think Ben said he really likes $_$$_i$ is THAT DOCTOR.

    c. It's THAT DOCTOR$_i$ [who]$_i$ I think Ben said he REALLY LIKES $_$$_i$.

    d. [THAT DOCTOR]$_i$ I think Ben said he REALLY LIKES $_$$_i$.

    e. [Which doctor]$_i$ do you think Ben said that he really likes $_$$_i$?

The symbol ' $\_$ ' indicates where the fronted expression between square brackets would have been realized, were it not fronted, and the subscript *i* indicates coreference. We refer to the ex situ phrase within square brackets as the **filler**, and refer to the syntactic position where the filler would ordinarily occur in situ as the **gap**. This choice of terminology is merely a matter of convenience and should not be taken to mean that we are committed to the actual existence of gaps anywhere in syntactic structure.

We use the term Unbounded Dependency Construction (UDC) to refer to the type of syntactic construction that hosts filler-gap linkages, such as relative clauses, cleft clauses, topicalization, questions, etc. Despite this terminology, we should stress that there are UDCs without overt fillers, like (2), as well as UDCs without gaps, like the **resumptives** in (3). The last are uncommon in English, but quite standard in certain languages.

(2) a. The doctor$_i$ I think he really likes $_$$_i$ has retired.

    b. Properly taken care of $_$$_i$, iguanas$_i$ can live up to twenty years.

    c. A: Is there a dress code?
       B: No, not that we were made aware of $\_$.

(3) a. This is the girl [who]$_i$ I think her$_i$ dog cries all night when it storms.

    b. [Which girl]$_i$ did you say that you think of her$_i$ whenever it rains?

Other than working-memory limitations, there is no limit to how many clauses a UDC can involve. In (4a) the extraction crosses three clause boundaries, and in (4b) it crosses four.

Unbounded Dependency Constructions: Theoretical and Experimental Perspectives. Rui P. Chaves and Michael T. Putnam, Oxford University Press (2020). © Rui P. Chaves and Michael T. Putnam.
DOI: 10.1093/oso/9780198784999.001.0001

(4)   a.   [What]$_i$ do you think [the students will say [they believe [the TA was trying to do _$_i$]]]?

   b.   [What]$_i$ do you think [the students will say [they believe [the TA claimed [he was trying to do _$_i$]]]]?

The absence of any overt signaling of the gap site causes local ambiguity and, in some cases, global ambiguity. In (5), the correct gap is the last one in the sentence, but many intermediate gap positions are likely to be attempted and rejected during the incremental process of sentence comprehension.

(5)   [Which teacher]$_i$ do you think I should ask someone to persuade John to help me write an anonymous email to _$_i$?
   (i.e. [*Which teacher*] *do you think* _$_x$ *I should ask* _$_x$ *someone to persuade* _$_x$ *John to help* _$_x$ *me write* _$_x$ *an anonymous email to* _$_✓$?)

Comprehenders may sometimes never be absolutely certain that the gap position has been correctly identified. This is most clear in cases where the ambiguity is global, such as in (6).[1] In each of these examples there are two possible gap sites, each yielding very different interpretations, contingent on the prosodic phrasing and the context in which they are uttered.

(6)   a.   Here are ten people who I'd like to remind you are still single.
      i. Here are ten people [who]$_i$ I'd like to remind _$_i$ [you are still single].
      (= *I'd like to remind these ten people that you are still single.*)
      ii. Here are ten people [who]$_i$ I'd like to remind you [_$_i$ are still single].
      (= *I'd like to remind you that these ten people are still single.*)

   b.   How long was the extension cord in the garage?
      i. [How long]$_i$ [was [the extension cord in the garage] _$_i$]?
      (= *What is the length of the extension cord located in the garage?*)
      ii. [How long]$_i$ [[was [the extension cord] [in the garage]] _$_i$]?
      (= *For what amount of time was the extension cord in the garage?*)

   c.   I forgot how good beer tastes.
      i. I forgot [how]$_i$ [[good beer] tastes _$_i$].
      (= *I forgot the taste of good beer.*)
      ii. I forgot [how good]$_i$ [beer tastes _$_i$].
      (= *I forgot that beer tastes good.*)

In (6a) either *ten people* is interpreted as the complement of *remind* or it is interpreted as the subject of *are*. A brief pause at the gap site is crucial to cue the correct parse. Similarly, in (6b) the phrase *how long* can be the complement of the copula (characterizing the size of the cord in the garage) or a modifier of the verb phrase (characterizing the duration of time in which the cord was in the garage). Similarly, (6c) obtains very different interpretations depending on whether *good beer* is a unit or whether *how good* is a unit. Since the gap site is

---

[1] The classic example of such **doubtful gaps** is *Who do you want to succeed?* (Fodor, 1979), where the gap can be the subject or object of *succeed*. See also Sag (1992).

sentence-final, the correct parse is contingent on the stress patterns of the aforementioned expressions.

In spite of the arbitrary distance, the filler phrase is usually required to satisfy the same morphosyntactic constraints that it would have to satisfy had it not been extracted. For example, a plural subject phrase must agree with its subject, even if the latter is extracted. Hence the ambiguity in (6a) vanishes in the counterparts in (7) because the noun *John* imposes singular third-person subject-verb agreement.

(7)   a.   Here are ten people [who]$_i$ I'd like to remind __$_i$ John is still single.
       b.   Here are ten people [who]$_i$ I'd like to remind John [__$_i$ are still single.

The fact that agreement is still enforced is clearer in minimal pairs like (8). We use '*' to indicate low acceptability, regardless of the cause being syntactic or otherwise.

(8)   a.   [Which students]$_i$ do you think __$_i$ know/*knows the answer?
       b.   [Which student]$_i$ do you think __$_i$ knows/*know the answer?

Various other morphosyntactic constraints are likewise unaffected by extraction. For example, the verb *rely* requires PP complements headed by the preposition *on*, and this constraint is still in effect even if the complement is extracted, as in (9).

(9)   a.   It was [ON ROBIN]$_{ON-PP}$ that I relied [__]$_{ON-PP}$ the most.
       b.   *It was [TO ROBIN]$_{TO-PP}$ that I relied [__]$_{ON-PP}$ the most.

It is clear then that the dependency between the filler and the gap is both semantic and syntactic. Further evidence of this comes from so-called **reconstruction** effects like those in (10a,b). Here, the fronted reflexive *herself* is bound to the nominal *Mary*, as if the former were in situ, after the verb. Normally, a reflexive cannot precede its binder as in (10c), or be bound to an antecedent in a different clause, as in (10d).

(10)   a.   It was HERSELF who$_i$ Mary$_i$ didn't trust __$_i$.
        b.   [HERSELF]$_i$, I think Mary$_i$ would NEVER nominate __$_i$.
        c.   *Herself$_i$ would never nominate Mary$_i$.
        d.   *Mary$_i$ thinks I nominated herself$_i$.

Filler-gap dependencies are very much part of linguistic structure. In **extraction pathway languages** there are specific morphosyntactic phenomena which only occur in structures in the domain of a filler-gap dependency. For example, Irish has several different types of complementizers (McCloskey, 1979, 2002)—or verbal particles (Sells, 1984), depending on the analysis. The complementizer *goN* occurs in ordinary non-gapped clauses, as seen in (11a), but *aL* has a complementary distribution as it only occurs in the presence of a UDC, as in (11b).[2]

---

[2] 'N' indicates nasalization, and 'L' indicates lenition. *GurL* is the past form of *goN*.

(11) a. Dúirt mé **gurL** shíl   me **goN** mbeadh   sé ann.
said I   c+past thought I   c   would-be he there
'I said that I thought that he would be there.'

b. an fear$_i$ **aL** dúirt mé **aL** shíl   mé **aL** bheadh   __$_i$ ann.
the man c said I   c   thought I   c   would-be   there
'The man that I said I thought _ would be there'   (Irish)

Crucially, if a complementizer appears after a gap, outside the UDC, then the form must once again be *goN*, as shown in (12). In this example both types of complementizers appear, explicitly signaling where the UDC is. Thus, *goN* can only attach to clauses that do not involve UDCs, whereas *aL* can only attach to clauses that involve a UDC.

(12) an fear$_i$ **aL**   dúirt sé **aL**   shíl   __$_i$ **goN** mbeadh sé ann.
the man COMP said he COMP thought   COMP would-be he there
'the man that he said _ thought he would be there'   (Irish)

In Swedish, for example, otherwise obligatory expletive subjects are not realized inside the extraction domain (Engdahl, 2013), but in Kikuyu, the extraction pathway marking is phonological (Zaenen, 1983; Clements, 1984). The verb in an affirmative declarative sentence causes the low tones in subsequent words to become high tones (tone downstep). This downstep skips over the phrasal category immediately after the verb and applies only to the following expressions. The examples in (13) serve to illustrate. Although *ate* ('that'), the proper name *Karioki* and *mote* ('tree') have ordinarily no high tones (represented below with acute accents), they suffer a tonal shift because of the downstep tone '!' in the verb, as seen in (13a).[3] But this downstep rule is crucially suppressed inside UDCs, as shown in (13b).

(13) a. Kamaú ɛː$^!$ríré   Ka:náké **áté** Káriók$^!$í **átɛmíré**   **mótɛ**
Kamau SUBJ.tell.PAST Kanake that Kariŭki SUBJ.cut.PAST tree
'Kamau told Kanake that Kariŭki cut the tree.'

b. [nóo]$_i$ Kamaú ɛː$^!$ríré   Ka:náké **áte** __$_i$ **otɛmíré**   **mote**
who   Kamau SUBJ.tell.PAST Kanake that   SUBJ.cut.PAST tree
'Kamau told Kanake that Kariŭki cut the tree.'   (Kikuyu)

Other languages exhibiting extraction pathway marking include Romance languages (Kayne and Pollock, 1978; Torrego, 1984), Yiddish (Diesing, 1990), Ewe (Collins, 1994), Paulan (Georgopoulos, 1985, 1991), Adyghe (Caponigro and Polinsky, 2011), Chamorro (Chung, 1982, 1994), Icelandic (Maling and Zaenen, 1982), and no doubt numerous others. We therefore use terms like 'extraction' and 'gap-filling' not only for ease of exposition, but also because it is difficult to escape the conclusion that the relation between the filler and the position where it would otherwise occur is a part of sentence structure.

---

[3] The first high tone of *áte* is spread from the final high tone of the preceding word *Káriók$^!$í* by a rule independent from downstep.

There is also a different sense in which UDCs are unbounded: there can be multiple gaps linked to the same exact filler. We illustrate this with the attested sample in (14), from the Brown (BR), Wall Street Journal (WSJ), and SwitchBoard (SB) treebanks (Taylor et al., 2003), and from the Contemporary Corpus of Contemporary American English (Davies, 2008, COCA). In all these examples the fronted phrase is interpreted as the argument of multiple verbs in the same utterance.

(14)   a. There was no weapon$_i$ that Early could not take $\_{i}$ apart and reassemble $\_{i}$ blind-folded.
          [BR]

       b. It was a case of human error, [which]$_i$ we found $\_{i}$ almost immediately and corrected $\_{j}$.
          [WSJ]

       c. Now, some see Mr. Bush trapped in a position [which]$_i$ he is neither comfortable with $\_{i}$ nor able to escape $\_{i}$.
          [WSJ]

       d. [Who]$_i$ will we play with $\_{i}$, learn from $\_{i}$, love $\_{i}$ unthinkingly, and fight with $\_{i}$ ferociously, knowing all the while that we can do these things because we are linked together by an indissoluble common tie?
          [COCA]

       e. There was the Hungarian Revolution [which]$_i$ we praised $\_{i}$ and mourned $\_{i}$, but did nothing about $\_{i}$.
          [BR]

       f. Fairbanks reached for a towel, a clean one and not the scarcely crumpled one$_i$ that Comore himself had used $\_{i}$ and left $\_{i}$ thriftily on the ledge below the mirror rather than consign $\_{i}$ to the linen basket.
          (Huddleston and Pullum, 2002b, 1096)

Although multiple gaps are usually found in coordination constructions like (14), it should be stressed that almost any construction allows for multiple gaps. Although (15a) exhibits a mix of coordinate and non-coordinate gaps, (15b) does not.

(15)   a. It is the sort of place$_i$ troops complain about $\_{i}$ while stationed there and brag about $\_{i}$ in equal part after leaving $\_{i}$.
          [COCA]

       b. I don't know what you would call them. Knickknacks, I guess. Stuff$_i$ that you hang $\_{i}$ on the wall to put a mirror on $\_{j}$
          [SB]

The reader may sometimes find that more unusual UDCs are harder to process, especially if they are complex and the correct prosody is not obvious. Otherwise, there seems to be no grammatical limit to the length of a UDC or to the number of gaps it can host. Thus, sentences with even more gaps are possible, like (16).

(16) There's no engine [which]$_i$ Geoff can't disassemble $\_i$, clean $\_i$, and put $\_i$ back together without disparaging $\_i$ or complaining about $\_i$.

Although gaps that are linked to the same filler are usually co-referential, this need not be the case (Postal, 1998; Munn, 1998; Chaves, 2012a; Vicente, 2016). In (17) the filler phrase refers to a plurality that is composed of distinct extracted referents i and j. We refer to these dependencies as **cumulative**.

(17) a. A: [What]$_{\{i,j\}}$ did Sam eat $\_i$ and drink $\_j$?
          B: Sam ate sushi and drank beer.

      b. A: [Which stocks]$_{\{i,j\}}$ did Sam buy $\_i$ and Robin sell $\_j$?
          B: Sam bought Sony stocks and Robin sold Facebook stocks.

In (18) multiple gaps are linked to different fillers. Whereas the two filler-gap dependencies are independent in (18a), in (18b) the filler j contains a gap $_i$ from a completely different dependency.

(18) a. [Which problem]$_i$ don't you know [who]$_j$ to talk to $\_j$ about $\_i$?

      b. This is the form [which]$_i$ I can't remember [how many copies of $\_i$]$_j$ we have to print $\_j$.

As we shall see, gaps can be located almost anywhere in the sentence, and all of the aforementioned types of filler-gap dependencies can compound and mix with each other. For example, a UDC can be embedded in another, as in (19), where the fronted phrase j itself contains a relative UDC.

(19) a. [Everyone [who]$_i$ the Queen has been CROSSED BY $\_i$]$_j$ she has found a way to MURDER $\_j$.

      b. [[What]$_i$ HE'S UP TO $\_i$]$_j$ I can't even imagine $\_j$

1.2 Grammatical constraints

Although UDCs are not clause-bounded, they are nonetheless subject to certain constraints, as Ross (1967) first pointed out. For example, whereas extracting a comitative is possible, as in (20a,b), extracting a conjunct is not, as shown by the oddness of (20c,d).

(20) a. It was Hayley [who]$_i$ I saw Roger with $\_i$ yesterday.
          (= *I saw Roger with Hayley yesterday.*)

      b. It was Hayley [who]$_i$ I saw $\_i$ with Roger yesterday.
          (= *I saw Hayley with Roger yesterday.*)

      c. *It was Hayley [who]$_i$ I saw Roger and $\_i$ yesterday.
          (= *I saw Roger and Hayley yesterday.*)

      d. *It was Hayley [who]$_i$ I saw $\_i$ and Roger yesterday.
          (= *I saw Hayley and Roger yesterday.*)

The examples in (20a,b) are near-synonymous, and their non-UDC counterparts shown in parentheses are licit, which indicates that the oddness is caused by extraction itself. Ross dubbed as **islands** the various syntactic environments that block filler-gap dependencies. The ban on such extractions is not specific to a given UDC type. On the contrary, it applies to any kind of UDC, as seen in interrogatives like (21) and declaratives like (22).

(21) a. [Who]$_i$ did you see Roger with _$_i$ yesterday?
          (cf. *Did you see Roger with Hayley yesterday?*)

      b. *[Who]$_i$ did you see Roger and _$_i$ yesterday?
          (cf. *Did you see Roger and Hayley yesterday?*)

      c. [Who]$_i$ did you see _$_i$ with Roger yesterday?
          (cf. *Did you see Hayley with Roger yesterday?*)

      d. *[Who]$_i$ did you see _$_i$ and Roger yesterday?
          (cf. *Did you see Hayley and Roger yesterday?*)

(22) a. Hayley$_i$ is easy to compare Roger with _$_i$.
          (cf. *It is easy to compare Roger with Hayley.*)

      b. *Hayley$_i$ is easy to compare Roger and _$_i$.
          (cf. *It is easy to compare Roger and Hayley.*)

      c. Hayley$_i$ is easy to compare _$_i$ with Roger.
          (cf. *It is easy to compare Hayley with Roger.*)

      d. *Hayley$_i$ is easy to compare _$_i$ and Roger.
          (cf. *It is easy to compare Hayley and Roger.*)

It is therefore unlikely that such island phenomena receive a semantic or pragmatic explanation. It is also very difficult to see how the oddness of (22b,d) could possibly be due to processing difficulty, since their comitative counterparts in (22a,c) are perfectly licit. There are several other syntactic environments that have similarly been claimed to block extraction. The non-exhaustive list in (23) is drawn from Phillips (2013a).

(23) a. *[What]$_i$ did [the Senate approve _$_i$] and [the House reject the bill]?
          (Extraction from a single conjunct)

      b. *[Who]$_i$ did Robin believe [Simon's news about _$_i$]?
          (Extraction from an object with a definite specifier)

      c. *[What]$_i$ did Wallace meet a woman [who hates _$_i$]?
          (Extraction from a relative clause)

      d. *[What]$_i$ did [that Ellen remembered _$_i$] surprise her children?
          (Extraction from a clausal subject)

      e. *[Who]$_i$ does John want to say a prayer [before we interview _$_i$]?
          (Extraction from an adjunct clause)
          (Phillips, 2013a)

Although it is generally held that island constraints are cross-constructionally active, we show in §4.3 that most of the island constraints illustrated in (23) are specific to certain types of UDCs. Another complication is that extraction constraints are not equally strong, even within the same UDC type. For example, the constraint banning extraction of conjuncts, illustrated in (20c,d), (21b,d), and (22b,d), has no exceptions that we know of, and such violations are systematically judged unacceptable by native speakers. But the island types in (23) are of a very different nature, since their acceptability can range from unacceptable to acceptable. For example, the illicit gap in (23a) becomes licit if the second conjunct is also gapped (Ross, 1967):

(24)   [What]$_i$ did [the Senate approve $\_i$] and [the House reject $\_i$]?

In contrast, no amelioration arises in (20c,d), (21b,d), and (22b,d) if a second conjunct is also extracted (e.g. *Who did you see $\_$ and $\_$ yesterday?). A different kind of exception concerns extractions from clausal adjuncts like (23e), which are widely held to be categorically impossible since Huang (1982). Although experimental sentence acceptability studies like Sprouse et al. (2012) usually find that extractions from clausal adjuncts like (25) have very low acceptability, the generality of such results has arguably been overstated.

(25)   a. *[What]$_i$ do you worry [if the boss leaves $\_i$ in the car]?
       b. *[What]$_i$ do you cough [if the tourists photograph $\_i$ in the exhibition]?
           (Sprouse et al., 2012)

Compare the oddness of (25) with the more plausible and acceptable counterparts in (26). In Chapter 6 we show that extractions from clausal adjuncts (among other island violations) range from acceptable to unacceptable, and everything in between.

(26)   a. [What]$_i$ would Mia be impressed [if John cleaned $\_i$]?
       b. [Who]$_i$ would Sue be really happy [if she could speak to $\_i$]?
       c. [Who]$_i$ did Tom get mad [because Phil forgot to thank $\_i$]?

In our experience, constructing acceptable island violations is often like a tightrope act: one needs to minimize all potential sources of difficulty, ambiguity, and awkwardness in order for the UDC to describe a coherent proposition and have a chance of being processed with sufficient ease. The plausibility of the proposition itself, regardless of the UDC, arguably plays a role in such island effects. The non-extracted counterpart of (25a) is pragmatically awkward because a scenario where an employee is worried because their boss left something in the car is a rather unusual situation (though in principle possible); In contrast, a scenario where someone is very impressed by the actions of someone else is a far more prototypical and plausible situation, requiring no special contextualization. Such differences may compound and have an effect on how easily the sentence is processed, and therefore affect its acceptability.

In fact, some island violations become more acceptable (and are read faster) once comprehenders are exposed to multiple exemplars thereof (Snyder, 2000; Francom, 2009; Hiramatsu, 2000; Clausen, 2011; Chaves and Dery, 2014; Hofmeister, 2015; Goodall, 2011;

Snyder, 2017; Do and Kaiser, 2017; Chaves and Dery, 2019).[4] The amelioration effect caused by repeated exposure is often referred to as **satiation**, in analogy to the phenomenon of semantic satiation, whereby repetition causes a word or phrase to temporarily lose meaning for the listener.[5] But whereas semantic satiation is a general reactive inhibition phenomenon, the increase of acceptability during sentence processing seems to be selective and facilitatory in nature. For example, certain island violations robustly ameliorate with repetition, whereas others simply do not. In ideal conditions, the amelioration can be quite extreme, and the island effect can vanish entirely. We direct the reader to Chapter 6 for experimental evidence and more detailed discussion. The amelioration effect seems to be contingent on the particular sentence/proposition, and therefore it is unlikely for it to be an inhibitory effect. Furthermore, the effect can persist up to at least four weeks (Snyder, 2017, forthcoming). We suspect that this amelioration phenomenon is a form of habituation (i.e. learning), and that participants are simply adapting to the unusualness of the sentence. We therefore avoid the term satiation in describing increases in acceptability or decreases in reading/reaction time, and assume that any cognitively plausible theory of islands must explain why some island violations improve with increased exposure, whereas others do not.

There is independent motivation that repeated exposure to syntactic patterns leads to some form of adaptation, such as Wells et al. (2009), Fine et al. (2013), Fine and Jaeger (2016), Malone and Mauner (2018), Bridgwater et al. (2019), and Prasad and Linzen (2020). In particular, Malone and Mauner (2020) provide evidence of a decrease in garden-path effects over time due to repeated exposition to garden-path sentences, as originally found by Fine et al. (2013).[6] In other words, the adaptation observed in island environments is arguably but a special case of a broader statistical phenomenon in which experience prompts speakers to adjust to the input.

1.3 Grammatical theories

Speakers acquire vast amounts of knowledge in order to produce and understand language proficiently. This knowledge includes the meaning, form, and use of words, but also information about how expressions combine to yield richer structures. Grammatical theory aims to characterize this linguistic knowledge, and shed light on how it is acquired and used.

UDCs have had a major impact on the development of linguistic theories. In the dominant Chomskyan paradigm (Chomsky, 1957, 1975, 1977, 1989, 1995, 1998), phrases are inserted in situ in the syntactic tree and can subsequently be displaced to a higher ex situ position via an operation traditionally referred to as **movement**, formulated in terms of a **merge** operation. According to the Minimalist Program (MP) initiated by Chomsky (1995), UDCs are accounted for as illustrated in Figure 1.1.

---

[4] Sprouse (2009) claims that such amelioration effects are due to a design flaw whereby there is an uneven distribution of acceptable and unacceptable items, a hypothesis tested and refuted by Chaves and Dery (2014) and Snyder (2017).

[5] See http://www.csi.uottawa.ca/tanka/files/judg_fatigue.

[6] According to Malone and Mauner, the null syntactic adaptation results reported in Stack et al. (2018) are due to insufficient exposure to the relevant stimuli.

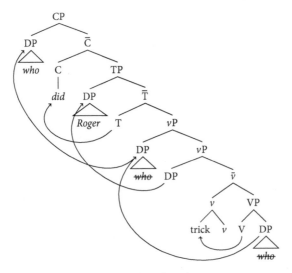

Figure 1.1 A movement-based analysis

The interrogative expression *who* is inserted in the tree as the object of *trick*, and receives accusative case as well as a patient thematic role. Next, it is successively moved to the top of the tree, to the only node that can license its interrogative use. As this example illustrates, movement is a pervasive operation in the MP, and not limited to UDCs. For some authors like Berwick and Chomsky (2016), Bolhuis et al. (2014), and Berwick et al. (2013) movement is psychologically real and the result of a single genetic mutation that endowed one individual with the language faculty.

A given phrase is moved only if some of its morphosyntactic constraints cannot be otherwise satisfied. Moved categories are generally assumed to leave an empty category (e.g. a **trace**) or a 'silent' **copy** of the *wh*-phrase at the original structural position. The existence of trace/copy at the gap site remains controversial, both linguistically (Postal and Pullum, 1982; Sag and Fodor, 1995; Bouma et al., 2001) and experimentally (Gibson and Hickok, 1993; Pickering and Barry, 1991; Traxler and Pickering, 1996; Grodzinsky, 2000; Kay, 2000; Featherston, 2001; Phillips and Wagers, 2007).

For Chomsky (1995, 2001, 2005), extraction constraints are syntactic in nature, and due to computational efficiency of the language faculty. In other words, island phenomena are ultimately due to the **Strong Minimalist Thesis**, which holds that the computational design of the language faculty is optimally efficient, in detriment of communicative function:

> The conclusion, then, is that if language is optimally designed, it will provide structures appropriate for semantic-pragmatic interpretation but that yield difficulties for perception (hence communication). . . . In general, so it appears, structurally ambiguous, garden path, and island structures result from free functioning of the simplest rules, yielding difficulties for perception. Where there are conflicts between communicative and computational efficiency, it seems that the latter prevails.
>
> (Chomsky, 2013, 41)

Because island-violating sentences are ungrammatical and absent from the speech that children hear, the claim has also been made that something internal to the child must contribute this knowledge about which extractions are licit and which are not. Hence, islands are part of the classic **Poverty of the Stimulus** argument (Pinker and Bloom, 1990).

Among the constraints that have been argued to give rise to island phenomena include **Relativized Minimality** (Rizzi, 1990), the **Minimal Link Condition** (Chomsky, 1995), and the **Phase Impenetrability Condition** (Chomsky, 2001), all of which have the effect of imposing limits on the length of each movement step as a way to reduce the computational burden (i.e. memory resource load) and optimize the efficiency of the mapping of syntactic information onto semantics and phonology. Thus, the syntactic machinery that the human brain is biologically endowed with simply cannot, by virtue of its optimal architecture, construct certain UDCs. We refer to this approach as an **architectural view** of island phenomena. The growing consensus, however, is that such constraints cannot explain island phenomena; see Den Dikken (2009), Abels (2012), and Boeckx (2008, ch. 3).

The earliest analytic alternative to the Chomskyan paradigm is Gazdar (1981), where information about filler-gap dependencies is registered inside syntactic nodes. Analogously to how part of speech and information and case incrementally percolate in local syntactic dependencies, the information about filler phrases is likewise passed along local mother-daughter nodes in order to match the properties of the ex situ phrase with those of the in situ location. Gazdar achieved this by simply augmenting standard Context-Free Grammar (CFG) with the notation α/β to specify that the syntactic category α is missing the phrase β, as illustrated in Figure 1.2.

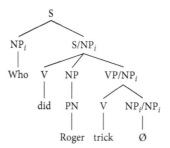

Figure 1.2 A CFG percolation analysis

The information about the existence of an ex situ NP_i is propagated in the tree structure by otherwise conventional CFG rules like '$VP/NP_i \rightarrow V\ NP/NP_i$', which involve nodes annotated with information about an ex situ phrase. At the bottom of the dependency there is a trace NP with the same index i.[7] It is up to the CFG rules to directly govern the propagation of UDCs, rather than some general filler-gap mechanism.

Gazdar's 'slash' percolation approach was later adopted by more sophisticated constraint-based frameworks such as Generalized Phrase-Structure Grammar (Gazdar et al., 1985), Head-driven Phrase-Structure Grammar (Pollard and Sag, 1987, 1994; Ginzburg and Sag, 2000; Levine and Hukari, 2006), Simpler Syntax (Culicover and Jackendoff, 2005), and some varieties of Dependency Grammar (Osborne et al., 2012). As we shall see in Chapter 5, percolation approaches are consistent with various models of incremental sentence processing and particularly well suited to handle a wide range of

---

[7] Although Gazdar's account assumed traces, it can just as well be formulated without them. The same is true for all non-movement theories of UDCs; they can be traceless or not. See, for example, Bouma et al. (2001), Sag (2010), and Levine and Hukari (2006).

filler-gap dependency types, including multiple-gap UDCs that movement-based accounts have struggled with to this day. Finally, Gazdar's approach was noncommittal about how island effects arise, allowing different islands to result from either grammatical or extra-grammatical factors.

Gazdar's account was dismissed by Chomsky (1981, 91) on the grounds that such non-movement-based approaches are 'virtually indistinguishable' from movement theories, and Chomsky (1995, 403) similarly asserted that such theories are 'transformational theories, whether one chooses to call them that or not'. No explicit comparison was offered to back up this claim, however. Still, this misconception has persisted to this day. For example, in Hornstein (2009, 6, n. 11) and Hornstein (2019, 191, n. 5) it is reiterated without demonstration that these theories are essentially notational variants of each other, and therefore there is no point in engaging with non-movement approaches. One of the purposes of this volume is precisely to compare the empirical and theoretical merits of movement and non-movement accounts of UDCs as well as how these approaches stack up with behavioral evidence.

A UDC account that is intimately related to Gazdar's and shares many of the properties of percolation-based approaches is adopted by certain varieties of Categorial Grammar, such as Combinatorial Categorial Grammar (CCG); see Steedman (1985, 2001), and Baldridge (2002). In CCG, lexical and phrasal categories are seen as functions that take other categories as arguments, and various function application rules combine such categories accordingly. Thus, '$X \backslash Y$' is a function called backward function application ($<$) that takes a leftward Y argument and yields X. Analogously, 'X/Y' is a function called forward function application ($>$) that yields X in the presence of a rightward Y argument. Several other rules allow functions to compose with other functions, as in Figure 1.3.

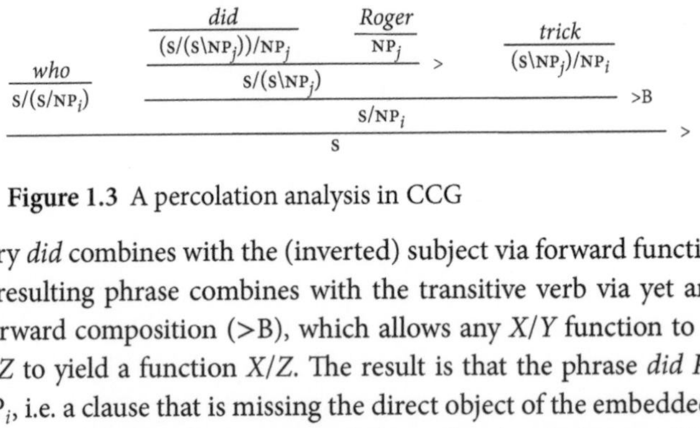

Figure 1.3 A percolation analysis in CCG

The auxiliary *did* combines with the (inverted) subject via forward function application ($>$), and the resulting phrase combines with the transitive verb via yet another type of rule, called forward composition ($>$B), which allows any X/Y function to compose with a function Y/Z to yield a function X/Z. The result is that the phrase *did Roger trick* is a function S/NP_i, i.e. a clause that is missing the direct object of the embedded verb. Finally, the *wh*-phrase syntactically selects a gapped clause that is missing one NP, and yields a gapless clause. Thus, the UDC is captured with the same mechanism that is responsible for local dependencies, and propagates the information about the ex situ phrase through the syntactic representation. According to Steedman (2002, 59–66), various island constraints are syntactic in nature and fall out as consequences of CCG's combinatorial rules. As in the Chomskyan paradigm, CCG's account of islands is too strict, as we shall see.

Lexical-Functional Grammar (Kaplan and Bresnan, 1982; Zaenen, 1983; Kaplan and Maxwell, 1988) and Role and Reference Grammar (Foley and Van Valin, 1984; Van Valin and LaPolla, 1997; Van Valin, 2005) adopt a different approach to UDCs in which filler phrases are linked to their gap sites via a recursive search for an unbounded variable.

In LFG, this recursive search is dubbed **Functional Uncertainty** and defined over Functional structure (i.e. the level of representation concerning syntactic predicate-argument structure and functional relations like subject and object) as a path between a discourse function of the filler phrase and some grammatical function of the gap. A UDC is licensed if something in that path can be identified with the index of the filler, as in Figure 1.4.

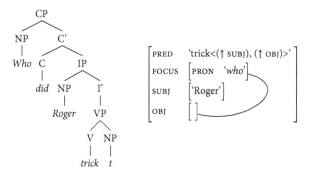

Figure 1.4 A Functional Uncertainty analysis in LFG

In this case, the path is trivial, FOCUS = OBJ, but in general it can be of any size, and is characterized via regular expressions like FOCUS = COMP* OBJ. This allows any sequence of complement nodes to be traversed. There are two competing views about how Functional Uncertainty should be defined. In the (top-down) 'Outside-in' approach, the Functional Uncertainty equation is defined as stating that the dependency starts at the filler phrase and searches for the gap site, deep in the F-structure (Kaplan and Zaenen, 1989; Dalrymple et al., 1995; Asudeh, 2011). In the (bottom-up) 'Inside-out' approach, the dependency starts at the gap site (the trace), and a corresponding filler phrase is searched higher in the F-structure (Bresnan, 1995, 2001). The latter approach is difficult to reconcile with cumulative filler-gap dependencies, and with the behavioral evidence about incremental gap-filling.

The structures inside the extraction pathway have no information about the existence of the UDC, and hence nothing in LFG's account predicts the existence of extraction pathway phenomena. Unlike other approaches, LFG must stipulate that a special feature is present in every F-structure, for the sole reason of distinguishing the domains that contain filler-gap dependencies from those that do not (Zaenen, 1983; Asudeh, 2012; Dalrymple, 2001).[8]

Finally, island phenomena are usually modeled in LFG along the same lines as the Chomskyan paradigm, by assuming that only certain complement paths can be traversed, rather than subject or adjunct paths, for example (Alsina, 2008; Falk, 2011). In some versions of Dependency Grammar (Hudson, 2007; Osborne et al., 2012), a mechanism analogous to Functional Uncertainty allows a fronted phrase to be linked across multiple dependents until its proper governing head is found. Standard Chomskyan assumptions are made about island phenomena. LFG's approach contrasts with RRG's in that fillers are instead linked to gaps in semantic structure, there is no appeal to traces, and island constraints are generally relegated to the realm of pragmatics (Van Valin, 2005, §7.6).

---

[8] Extraction pathway marking is similarly unexpected in Type-Logical Grammar (Moortgat, 1988; Morrill, 1994) since nothing records the presence of a filler-gap dependency in the derivation. See Kubota and Levine (2020, §7) for an approach in which a numerical index is added to syntactic categories, for this very purpose.

1.4 Real-time processing

Ideally, grammatical theory should be consistent with the behavioral facts concerning online sentence processing in general. Although comprehension and production are fundamentally different processes, there is growing experimental evidence that production and comprehension tap into a common source of linguistic knowledge, of the kind that linguistic theory seeks to understand (Pickering and Garrod, 2013; Momma and Phillips, 2018). In particular, production and comprehension recruit strongly overlapping neural circuits in the posterior middle temporal gyrus (pMTG). According to Matchin and Hickok (2019), for instance, the pMTG decodes sequences of auditory phonological representations in the posterior superior temporal gyrus into hierarchical structures, which it then links to conceptual networks (an entity knowledge hub in the anterior temporal lobe, and an event knowledge hub in the angular gyrus). In production, the pMTG converts conceptual information into hierarchical structures, and subsequently transforms them into sequences of morphemes, with the aid of the pars triangularis of the inferior frontal gyrus (i.e. the anterior part of Broca's area).

Recent neurolinguistic research also suggests that the processing of syntax, semantics, and of filler-gap dependencies in particular, appears to be heavily distributed across multiple brain areas in the left and temporal regions (Wartenburger et al., 2003; Matchin, 2014; Rogalsky et al., 2015; Leiken et al., 2015; Balewski et al., 2016; Pylkkänen, 2019).

However grammars are implemented, linguistic input is processed very rapidly and incrementally, using both top-down and bottom-up probabilistic information to predict upcoming structures, in addition to contextual and world knowledge information. This is most consistent with a hybrid top-down and bottom-up parsing model, like the Left-Corner algorithm (Aho and Ullman, 1972). The processing of UDCs poses, of course, a particularly challenging computational problem that naturally lends itself to such a top-down and bottom-up probabilistic approach: locating the gap is not easy because it has no overt manifestation and because there usually are a priori multiple candidate syntactic positions where a gap may reside. At the same time, the filler phrase must be kept in working memory while the linguistic material between the filler and the gap is processed, and it can remain in working memory even after a gap is identified, given that the correct gap position may be later in the sentence, and that often there is more than one gap linked to the same filler.

There is much evidence from a variety of behavioral phenomena that comprehenders are under (top-down) pressure to link the filler to a gap as soon as possible (Fodor, 1978; Crain and Fodor, 1985; Stowe, 1986; Frazier, 1987; Frazier and d'Arcais, 1989; Frazier and Clifton, 1989; Nicol and Swinney, 1989; Tanenhaus et al., 1989; Garnsey et al., 1989; Stowe et al., 1991; Nicol and Pickering, 1993; Pickering, 1994; Nicol et al., 1994; Kaan et al., 2000; Pickering and Traxler, 2003; Aoshima et al., 2004; Phillips, 2006; Omaki and Lidz, 2015; Wagers et al., 2015; Keshev and Meltzer-Asscher, 2020), and that the filler-gap dependency is resolved once the gap subcategorizer is found, not the gap site itself (Pickering and Barry, 1991; Pickering, 1993; Pickering et al., 1994; Boland et al., 1995; Traxler and Pickering, 1996). For example, Ferreira and Henderson (1991) and Bailey and Ferreira (2003) show that garden-path sentences like (27a) are even harder to process when the disambiguator word *joins* and the head of the ambiguous phrase *poodle* are separated lexically, as in (27b).

The longer the parser has been committed to the wrong analysis of the ambiguous phrase, the harder it is to reanalyze it. Once again, the local ambiguity only exists if there is no pause at the critical phrasal boundary to cue the gap site.

(27) a. When the gardener bathes his poodle joins him.
      (i.e. [*When*]*ᵢ the gardener bathes _ᵢ his poodle joins him.*)

   b. When the gardener bathes his poodle with the soft fur joins him.
      (i.e. [*When*]*ᵢ the gardener bathes _ᵢ his poodle with the soft fur joins him.*)

This **digging-in** effect indicates that the language processor is strongly committed to the postulated gap site, which in turn suggests that gap postulation is guided by knowledge of co-occurrence frequencies between fillers and syntactic information. Using a corpus-based probabilistic model, van Schijndel et al. (2014) similarly show that gap-filling is sensitive to the frequencies of the syntactic configurations involved, and Michel (2014) provides further corroborating Event-Related Potential (ERP) data showing that real-time predictability is of central importance for the online processing of filler-gap dependencies. Any grammatical UDC theory that aims to be psycholinguistically plausible must be at least in principle consistent with the incremental, probabilistic, and distributed nature of UDC processing.

As expected, Staub (2007) found that when reading a sentence containing an obligatorily intransitive verb, readers did not show any evidence of linking the filler to the verb. In this case, the bottom-up information trumps the top-down expectation of object extraction. However, when reading sentences containing an unergative—which crucially have a very slight chance of obtaining a transitive interpretation—there was evidence of linking the filler to the verb. This finding suggests that any possibility of transitive interpretation, even if minute, can cause readers to adopt implausible analyses, indicating that the frequency of a direct object interpretation can overwhelm the lexically specific bias of a verb. See van Schijndel et al. (2014) for further evidence that extraction dependencies are resolved attending to both top-down and bottom-up information, and see Ness and Meltzer-Asscher (2019) for evidence that only verbs selecting an argument with features like those maintained in the filler's representation trigger an attempt to resolve the filler-gap dependency. Ideally, our theory of grammar of choice should allow for a top-down and bottom-up incremental and probabilistic conception of how filler-gap dependencies are formed.

Finally, the processing of UDCs strains cognitive resources during online sentence processing, so that the longer the UDC, the harder it is to process (Wanner and Maratsos, 1978; Frazier, 1987; Pickering and Barry, 1991; Kluender and Kutas, 1993b,a; Warren and Gibson, 2002; Sussman and Sedivy, 2003; Chen et al., 2005; Warren and Gibson, 2005) and the less acceptable it is (Alexopoulou and Keller, 2007; Hofmeister and Norcliffe, 2013). In particular, Kind and Kutas (1995), Müeller et al. (1997), Fiebach et al. (2002), and Phillips et al. (2005) show that holding an incomplete filler-gap in memory can elicit a sustained anterior negativity ERP. When it does occur, this negativity persists throughout the UDC, until the point at which the filler-gap dependency is resolved.[9] Moreover, when the filler-gap dependency is resolved, a P600 response is elicited (Kaan et al., 2000), the timing of which is delayed in proportion to the length of the UDC (Phillips et al., 2005). The last finding is consistent with an increased difficulty interpretation in that the information about the filler phrase will have decayed in memory and therefore takes longer to reactivate, prior to its integration into the linguistic representation.

1.5 Overview

In this book we are primarily concerned with five overarching questions, each of which is the focus of its respective chapter, listed below in order of appearance.

1. *What is the possible range of filler-gap dependency types? In particular, what patterns arise when there are multiple gaps?*

   In **Chapter 2** we provide a mostly descriptive and theory-neutral survey of the wide range of empirical data associated with UDCs. The primary purpose of this chapter is to set the stage for larger theoretical discussions which unfold in the chapters that follow. We argue that there are many different types of filler-gap dependencies, and that they can compound and combine with each other in various ways. We identify three major types: singleton (in which a gap is linked to at most one filler), convergent (whereby multiple gaps are co-referential and linked to at most one filler; common in coordination but allowed in a wide range of other structures), and cumulative (where multiple gaps are linked to at most one filler, but are not co-referential; predominantly in coordinate structures, but not always so). Multiple overlapping singleton dependencies can be crossed or nested, and in addition a gap can reside in the filler phrase to another filler-gap dependency. Strikingly, all of these types can compound with each other. We therefore conclude that filler-gap dependencies are extremely flexible, posing problems for certain UDC accounts.

2. *Is there a common constraint at work in most or all island phenomena? If so, why is it the way it is? Are these underlying constraints syntactic, semantic, pragmatic, cognitive, or a combination thereof?*

   Chapter 3 focuses on constraints on extraction, i.e. island phenomena. Our review raises non-trivial questions regarding the nature and motivation of the mechanisms responsible for them. We argue that there is no unifying factor that explains all types of island phenomenon, although there is a general pragmatic constraint at work in all UDCs. Rather, there are clusters of different island phenomena; some are mostly due to semantic and/or syntactic factors, others to pragmatic factors, others to processing factors. In certain cases, a combination of the above is responsible for apparent idiosyncratic empirical and experimental findings reported in the literature.

3. *What are the advantages or disadvantages of movement-based versus non-movement-based approaches?*

---

[9] See also Fadlon et al. (2019) for evidence of retention of a filler representation in the production of sentences with UDCs, until the relevant embedded position.

We engage in a detailed overview of two antithetical approaches to modeling UDCs. The focus of **Chapter 4** is on accounts that regard all UDCs as the result of movement operations, and reject the existence of constructions in the grammar, whereas the focus of **Chapter 5** is on constructional and constraint-based models that reject the existence of movement operations and instead capture UDCs via a feature inspired by Gazdar's work, like any other type of linguistic information.

We argue that constructional and constraint-based models of UDCs are not only empirically superior, but more consistent with human incremental sentence processing. Although there is a single mechanism behind the computation of filler-gap dependencies, it is a principal component of a number of declarative constructional rules in the grammar. Thus, although the computation of UDCs is distributed rather than modular, it involves the same basic operation for the computation of filler-gap dependencies.

4. *How can a theory of grammar account for the fact that some (but not other) island violations have gradient acceptability, are prone to frequency effects, and are sensitive to contextual information?*

Chapter 6 describes experimental data suggesting that a rather large family of island phenomena are due to a general pragmatic constraint, linked to the amount of syntactic and conceptual experience that comprehenders have with linguistic input. Ultimately, the island effects are contingent on the probability of the scene that the proposition is about. We argue that exemplar-based constructional models are readily consistent with the findings, since the results indicate that such island effects can be ameliorated by repeated exposure and are very sensitive to the particular proposition expressed by the utterance.

5. *How can unbounded dependency constructions be learned by speakers? Does the evidence favor nativist approaches or domain-general experience-based approaches?*

We turn our attention to the acquisition of UDCs in **Chapter 7**. We conclude that all the extant evidence about the emergence of grammar, UDCs, and island effects is most consistent with a constructivist exemplar-based developmental trajectory.

2
Extraction types

It is impossible for us to do justice to the full range of UDC phenomena or to all of the literature published in the last half-century. Our goal is to offer a survey of the empirical issues and basic theoretical claims. As we shall see throughout the remainder of this book, many key issues are interconnected, and certain patterns emerge only when one takes into account a broader picture of the phenomena.

We begin by providing a brief and descriptive introduction to UDCs and to the range of filler-gap dependency patterns they allow. These are two very different topics. The former concerns the repertoire of syntactic constructions in which extraction takes place, and their grammatical idiosyncrasies, whereas the latter concerns the types of interaction between fillers and gaps. As we shall see, both present empirical and theoretical challenges alike. On several occasions, we explicitly deviate from the mainstream view with respect to either empirical observation or theoretical interpretation. We next discuss the nature of filler-gap dependencies more closely, and argue that their range is far more flexible than previously held.

2.1 Overview of UDCs

There are three major classes of UDC: **interrogative**, **declarative**, and **subordinate**. Within each class there are invariably many other subclasses, with peculiar prosodic, syntactic, semantic, and/or pragmatic constraints. The latter are particularly relevant, since they will play a major role in the remainder of this work. In light of this, we must introduce some terminology. In what follows we draw from Lambrecht (1994).

Something is pragmatically **presupposed** when it expresses information that the speaker takes for granted, is uncontroversial, or is not at issue, i.e. information in the utterance that the speaker assumes is either familiar, salient, or inferable in context by the addressee. Conversely, something is pragmatically **asserted** if it is not presupposed. Thus, the pragmatic assertion is the proposition expressed by a sentence which the comprehender is expected to know or take for granted as a result of its being uttered.

A phrase is **Topical** if its referent bears an anaphoric contrastive relation with other referents in relation to the asserted content, and **Focal** if it corresponds to the new information in the asserted content. We illustrate these concepts in (1). Note that only (1a) has a Topic, and only (1c) lacks a presupposition.[1]

---

[1] Pitch-accented expressions are in small caps. See Lambrecht (1994) and Gregory and Michaelis (2001) for more on the information-structural correlates of such accents.

Unbounded Dependency Constructions: Theoretical and Experimental Perspectives. Rui P. Chaves and Michael T. Putnam, Oxford University Press (2020). © Rui P. Chaves and Michael T. Putnam.
DOI: 10.1093/oso/9780198784999.001.0001

(1)   a. A: What happened to your car?
          B: It / My car BROKE DOWN.
          Presupposition: *The speaker's car is a Topic for comment x*
          Assertion: *x = broke down*
          Focus: *broke down*

      b. A: Your motorcycle broke down?
          B: No, MY CAR broke down.
          Presupposition: *The speaker's x broke down*
          Assertion: *x = car*
          Focus: *car*

      c. A: Hey, what's wrong?
          B: MY CAR broke down.
          Presupposition: –
          Assertion: *The speaker's car broke down*
          Focus: *The speaker's car broke down*

Focus is **narrow** when it is restricted to the phrase bearing pitch accent. This is the case in (1b), for instance. Focus can also be broader than the pitch-accented phrase, of course, and encompass a larger phrase or even the entire utterance, as in (1c). Here, the Focus 'spreads' in syntactic structure and covers a larger constituent than otherwise explicitly marked by prosody. As will become clear below, different types of UDC assign different pragmatic functions to the filler phrase. If all UDCs share a common pragmatic function, that function is independent from the notions of Topic or Focus.

Kuno (1976), Krifka (1992), and Jacobs (2001) argue that there is an additional pragmatic dimension in which the utterance is divided into the referent that the sentence is about and the properties that the sentence ascribes to that referent (the **Comment**). Kuno originally called the former 'Topic', but to avoid confusion we follow convention and use the term **aboutness**. These and related pragmatic notions will be important for the analysis of several island constraints in Chapter 3.

2.1.1 Interrogative

Perhaps among the most well-studied types of UDCs are **interrogatives**, of which there are two major kinds: **direct questions** and **indirect questions**, illustrated in (2a,b), respectively. The former interrogative triggers Subject-Auxiliary Inversion but the latter does not.

(2)   a. [Who]$_i$ do you think Fido bit __$_i$?
      b. I wonder [who]$_i$ you think Fido bit __$_i$.

The questions in (2) presuppose the open proposition *Fido bit person x*, and give rise to a set of possible alternative instantiations for the Focal referent *x*, one of which is presupposed to be a true and most informative answer. By producing an information request, the speaker is asserting or at least presupposing that an answer exists and that the hearer might know it. Of course, what counts as the most informative answer is context-dependent. As Ginzburg

(1995) points out, (3) can be resolved by an answer like *Europe* in some contexts, but not in others, where finer-grained information is necessary.

(3)   [Where]$_i$ do you live $\_i$?

Lambrecht (1994) notes that the referent of the interrogative *wh*-phrase need not be new in the discourse. For example, in (4) the referent of *the bar* is by no means 'new' in the discourse. Rather, it is the role of *the bar* in the proposition *you ended up going to x last night* which is new information.

(4)   A: Last night you wanted to go to either the coffee shop around the corner or the bar across the street. [Where]$_i$ did you end up going $\_i$?
       B: I went to the bar.

Although interrogatives like (5) do not appear to involve a UDC, since nothing intervenes between the *wh*-phrase and its subcategorizer, we nonetheless assume that there is a UDC.

(5)   [Who]$_i \_i$ laughed?

As Levine and Hukari (2006, ch. 2) and many others note, such interrogatives likely involve extraction (referred to as **string-vacuous** extraction), for three independent reasons.[2] First, as Sadock (1972), Brame (1978), and Fillmore (1985) noted, expletive expressions like *the heck, the hell, the fuck, in heaven's name*, etc. cannot attach to in situ interrogative expressions, however interpreted, as shown in (6); see also Ginzburg and Sag (2000, 229, 314).

(6)   a.   [Who the Hell]$_i$ did you say $\_i$ ordered what?
       b.   *[Who]$_i$ did you say $\_i$ ordered what the Hell?
            (cf. *Who did you say ordered what?*)
       c.   [What the Hell]$_i$ does the 'M' stand for $\_i$?
       d.   *The 'M' stands for what the Hell?
            (cf. *The 'M' stands for what?*)

It therefore follows that the subject phrase in (7) must be extracted, and that string-vacuous UDCs are possible.

(7)   a.   [Who the Hell]$_i \_i$ laughed?
       b.   [Who the Hell]$_i \_i$ are you?

Second, in interrogative coordinations like (8) the answer must satisfy the constraints imposed by both conjuncts. However, the first conjunct must be a clause with a subject gap, and the second conjunct is a gapless clause, since VPs cannot ordinarily coordinate with clauses. It so happens that in this case the coordination is asymmetric, and one of the conjuncts need not be gapped. See Kehler (2002, ch. 5) for a more detailed discussion of asymmetric coordination, as well as §3.2.5.

---

[2] The arguments given by George (1980) and Chomsky (1986a) against string-vacuous extraction (the **Vacuous Movement Hypothesis**) are empirically problematic: (i) the supposed gap parallelism of the coordinate UDCs (see §3.2.5 for counterexamples), (ii) the supposedly syntactic nature of *wh*-island effects (see §3.2.9), and (iii) the putatively illicit subject-parasitic gaps involving finite relative clauses (see §3.2.6).

(8)   [Who]$_i$ [[__$_i$ can come home drunk] and [their spouse not get mad]]?
      (Laura Michaelis, pers. comm. 2019)

Finally, extraction pathway languages such as Kikuyu and Icelandic (see §1.1) exhibit the same morphosyntactic effects in such examples as in non-string vacuous UDCs (Clements, 1984; Zaenen, 1983; Hukari and Levine, 1995), providing explicit cross-linguistic evidence that such subject filler phrases that appear to be in situ are in fact ex situ. String-vacuous extraction in non-interrogative UDCs is discussed in §2.1.2 and §2.1.3.

The *wh*-phrase tends to be extracted in English direct questions, and to remain in situ in rhetorical and reprise questions like (9a, b), respectively. Whereas rhetorical in situ questions can involve flat prosodic contour at the *wh*-phrase, reprise questions usually receive a rising prosodic contour, as indicated by the '↑' symbols.

(9)   a. First question of the quiz: the Magna Carta was signed WHEN?

      b. A: John speaks Dothraki.
          B: He speaks WHAT↑?

As Ginzburg and Sag (2000) argue, reprise questions are kinds of information requests, only more metalinguistic. Similarly, rhetorical questions are questions (only with unsurprising answers); see Rohde (2006) and Caponigro and Sprouse (2007), among others.

Although reprise and rhetorical questions tend to be in situ, this is not necessarily so. It is perfectly possible to arrive at exactly the same interpretations of (9) if the *wh*-phrases are instead extracted. Conversely, extraction is optional in direct questions (Bolinger, 1972, 1978; Bartels, 1999; Ginzburg and Sag, 2000; Pires and Taylor, 2009), although this is often claimed to be otherwise. Consider the examples in (10). The major difference between the extracted and non-extracted counterparts is that the latter are more common in speech than in writing.

(10) a. So, you're expecting WHO↓ at your party next weekend?

      b. You opened WHICH WINDOWS↓ last night? It got really drafty...

Pires and Taylor (2009) identify several types of in situ direct questions. The first is illustrated in (11), and concerns questions which request more specific information about something mentioned immediately prior. Bolinger (1972, 142) dubs these hybrids 'reminder questions', since they somehow evoke a previous question.

(11) a. A: ... As always, I'm only going to be here for a few weeks.
          B: You're going abroad again ↑WHEN↓?
          (Bartels, 1999)

      b. A: Well, Alex is leaving, finally...
          B': Alex will be leaving ↑WHEN↓ exactly?
          (Ginzburg and Sag, 2000, 281)

      c. A: I made desserts.
          B: You make what KIND of desserts↓?
          (Pires and Taylor, 2009, 203)

   d. A: Let's sing a song as we go.
       B: Ok. Let's sing ↑WHAT then↓?

   e. A: I warned you but you're too stubborn to listen...
       B: You warned me about WHAT↓?

As Ginzburg and Sag (2000, 281) point out, if questions like (11b) were reprise questions, it would be possible to paraphrase them as *When did you say Alex will be leaving?* But this is not what the question in (11b) means. A related type of in situ question is (12), which presupposes that an amount of money is routinely requested.

(12)   [Mother:] So, you want how much today?
       (Pires and Taylor, 2009, 204)

A distinct type of in situ interrogative concerns follow-up questions like (13).

(13)   a. B (Attorney): Tell me what happened on January 1st at 4 p.m.
           A (Defendant): I was driving along Andrews Avenue.
           B: And you were driving in ↑WHICH DIRECTION↓?
           (Pires and Taylor, 2009, 203)

       b. A: Gabe, her boyfriend, was helping her, till they had an argument about him missing her birthday for some camping trip.
           B: And you know about this argument ↑HOW↓?
           (Biezma, 2019)

Other in situ questions seem to be in most respects like their ex situ counterparts, such as those in (14).

(14)   a. This is not an easy job ... You've been here for ↑HOW LONG↓?

       b. A: We're going out tomorrow, right?
           B: I guess so. We're going to do WHAT↓ exactly?

       c. A: We're going to buy a house.
           B: Uh huh. And you're going to pay for it ↑HOW↓?

In corpora the most frequent use of English in situ content questions involves VP fragments like (15a), though clausal examples of in situ direct interrogatives also occur, as in (15b).

(15)   a. A: He was going to get himself tested.
           B: Were you worried?
           A: Worried about WHAT?
           [COCA 1993 SPOK]

       b. A: So you can put something inside of this and it'll stay cold FOR HOW LONG?
           B: Six months.
           [COCA 2009 SPOK]

In sum, the only interrogative constructions that truly require extraction are those that involve indirect questions. The pair in (16) illustrates this point. To our knowledge, such a constraint has no exceptions.

(16) a. I wonder who Sam called.
  b. *I wonder Sam called who.

The fact that extraction is not required in order to express such information requests indicates that interrogative meaning is not contingent on extraction. Rather, extraction is optional, and therefore must not contribute something extra to the interrogative force associated with the *wh*-phrase.[3] This is perhaps clearer in Romance languages, for example, which contrast with English in that there is no bias against ex situ *wh*-phrases in direct interrogatives; see Aoun et al. (1981) and Lai-Shen Cheng and Rooryck (2000) for French and Ambar and Veloso (2001) and Pires and Taylor (2009, 202) for Portuguese. For example, the counterparts in (17) and (18) are equally licit. With rising intonation, the in situ questions are reprise questions, but with descending intonation, they are direct interrogatives. In general, the in situ strategy is more common in spoken than in written discourse.

(17) a. O que$_i$ é que o   Pedro comprou __$_i$?
    the what is that the Pedro bought
    'What did Pedro buy?'

  b. O   Pedro comprou o   quê?
    the Pedro bought the what
    'What did Pedro buy?'   (European Portuguese)

(18) a. O   que$_i$ é que tu   achas que o   Pedro comprou __$_i$?
    the what is that you think that the Pedro bought
    'What do you think Pedro bought?'

  b. Tu achas que o   Pedro comprou o   quê?
    you think that the Pedro bought the what
    'What do you think Pedro bought?'   (European Portuguese)

In East Asian languages we have the opposite situation to that in English. The default is in situ interrogatives, but their UDC counterparts are possible, although rare, unexpected, and typically restricted to a colloquial speech register. Consider the minimal pairs in (20) from (Mandarin) Chinese. For a recent and detailed overview of ex situ direct questions in Chinese, see Pan (2014), which shows that the extracted *wh*-phrase can be a Topic or Focus.

(19) a. Zhāngsān mǎi-le   shénme?
    Zhangsan buy-Perf what
    'What has Zhangsan bought?'

---

[3] See §3.4.3 for arguments that in situ interrogatives do not involve 'invisible' (covert) extraction operations of the same kind as those that are observed in canonical UDCs.

b. Shénme Zhāngsān mǎi-le ___$_i$?
   what Zhangsan buy-Perf
   'What has Zhangsan bought?'
   (Wu, 1999, 82)   (Chinese)

(20) a. Nǐ juéde tā huì xǐuān shénme dōngxi?
      you think she will like what thing
      'What do you think that she would like?'

   b. Shénme$_i$ dōngxi nǐ juéde tā huì xǐhuān ___$_i$?
      what thing you think she will like
      'What do you think that she would like?'
      (Yanwei Jin, pers. comm.)   (Chinese)

See Dryer (2012) for a typological overview of cross-linguistic preferences for in situ or ex situ interrogatives, revealing that 60% of the hundreds of languages sampled exhibit a preference for in situ interrogatives. We return to the topic of in situ interrogatives throughout Chapter 3.

There are also various interrogative-like UDCs which have very peculiar idiomatic properties. For example, (21a) expresses a 'why' question rather than a 'what' question (Kay and Fillmore, 1999), and (21b) expresses a sarcastic question (Michaelis and Feng, 2015).

(21) a. [What]$_i$ am I doing ___$_i$ reading this book?

   b. [What]$_i$ are you ___$_i$, a monk?

2.1.2 Declarative

2.1.2.1 Topicalization
One kind of declarative UDC is **topicalization**, illustrated in the examples in (22). The fronted expression must be accented and receive a Topic interpretation relative to the pre-supposed open proposition. Second, there must be another accented phrase corresponding to the Focus. See Prince (1981, 1984, 1998), Ward and Prince (1991), Lambrecht (1994), and Gregory and Michaelis (2001) for more about this and related types of declarative fronting.[4]

(22) a. A: Would you ever consider buying a Tesla?
      B: I'm all for being environmentally responsible, but [a car THAT EXPENSIVE]$_i$ I would NEVER buy ___$_i$.

   b. A: Was my plan brought up at all during the meeting?
      B: [THAT PROPOSAL]$_i$ we discussed ___$_i$ AT LENGTH.

Other than requiring the topic to be interpreted contrastively, Topicalization is semantically and pragmatically equivalent to its in situ counterpart. Thus, (22) and (23) can

---

[4] A (superficially) similar construction is **Left Dislocation**, shown in (i) and (ii). It differs from Topicalization in that it lacks a filler-gap dependency and the matrix clause describes discourse-new information. See Prince (1984) and Gregory and Michaelis (2001).

i. DONALD, I will talk to that idiot$_i$ tomorrow.
ii. SOME WOMEN$_i$, their$_i$ whole lives are focused on men.

express the same meanings, in the same contexts. Again, we have a UDC type which is in some sense optional, in that basically the same message can be conveyed without extraction.

(23) a. I'm all for being environmentally responsible, but I would NEVER buy [a car THAT EXPENSIVE].

   b. We discussed THAT PROPOSAL, AT LENGTH.

Another form of optionality usually allowed by English involves extractions with prepositional phrases, stylistic considerations aside. Speakers may strand the preposition, as in (24a), or string it along, as in (24b).

(24) a. [Which city]$_i$ are you flying to _$_i$?

   b. [To which city]$_i$ are you flying _$_i$?

Ross (1967) dubbed extractions like (24) as **pied-piping**, to suggest that the *wh*-word NP lures the rest of the phrase along with it, and away from the canonical position. In English, the longer the UDC, the more likely pied-piping becomes (Gries, 2002), which suggests that working memory resource limitations are in play.

2.1.2.2 Focus Movement

A related declarative UDC is **Focus Movement**. Here the fronted phrase is pitch-accented and bears a Focus relation to the presupposed open proposition. Accordingly, the rest of the clause can be deaccented, as in (25).

(25) a. They are neat-looking nuts, aren't they? [MACADAMIA NUTS]$_i$ I think they're called _$_i$.

   b. I still remember when this building burned down. What a terrible sight. [TWENTY YEARS ago]$_i$ that was _$_i$ ...

Although *nuts* is under discussion in the second clause of (25a), the exact kind of nut is new. Thus, the fronted phrase *Macadamia nuts* can be in a focus relation to the presupposed open proposition *I think they are called x*, of which *they* is topical.

As in most other UDCs surveyed so far, such extractions are optional, given that essentially the same message can be conveyed without a UDC, as (26) illustrates.[5]

(26) a. They are neat-looking nuts, aren't they? I think they're called MACADAMIA NUTS.

   b. I still remember when this building burned down. What a terrible sight. That was TWENTY years ago...

Another type of declarative UDC can be seen in (27). These degree exclamatives express assertions, in spite of their appearance.

---

[5] String-vacuous UDCs may also be possible in Focus Movement, as (i) suggests, a point originally made by Paul Kay (pers. comm.) at http://listserv.linguistlist.org/pipermail/hpsg-l/2003-July/001254.html.

i. A: I've brought cinnamon rolls for Sandy, Kim, and Pat.
   B: KIM likes DOUGHNUTS. She does NOT like cinnamon rolls.

(27) a. [The fool]$_i$ that I have been __$_i$.
 b. [What an idiot]$_i$ your neighbor turned out to be __$_i$.
 c. [Such an idiot]$_i$ your neighbor turned out to be __$_i$.

Among other idiosyncrasies, the filler phrases of these exclamatives are required to express degree. When that is not possible, oddness ensues, as (28) illustrates.

(28) a. * [What a book]$_i$ nobody read __$_i$.
 b. * [Which house]$_i$ you live in __$_i$.
 c. * [When]$_i$ you arrived __$_i$.

Note also that whereas the UDC in (27a,b) is obligatory, the one in (27c) is not, given that the same message can be conveyed if *such an idiot* remains in situ. The latter UDC type is sometimes referred to as **Yiddish Movement**, and is only present in some varieties of English.

2.1.3 Subordinate

All the UDCs discussed so far consist of finite main clauses, but a large number of UDC types are restricted to subordinate environments. On major difference between the two is that in many (though not all) subordinate UDCs the extraction is not optional, as there is no in situ paraphrase counterpart.

2.1.3.1 Relatives
There are many types of **relative** clauses (McCawley, 1981; Sag, 1997; Huddleston and Pullum, 2002b). Often, a relative pronoun is extracted, and co-referential with an antecedent that the relative clause modifies. For example, in the restrictive adnominal relatives in (29), enclosed by square brackets, the extracted *wh*-phrase *who* is co-indexed with the nominal head *lawyer*.

(29) a. The lawyer$_i$ [who]$_i$ [Robin said Mia hired __$_i$] is very good.
 b. The lawyer$_i$ [who]$_i$ [Robin said __$_i$ represented Mia] is very good.

Even though the modified head antecedent and the filler-phrase are co-referential, they need not share the same morphosyntactic features. For example, in (30) the head is a first-person nominative pronoun but the filler phrase and its gap are third-person accusative.

(30) So it is me$_i$ [who]$_i$ __$_i$ is going to suffer.
  [COCA]

Restrictive relatives express a presupposition of which the *wh*-phrase is the topic, and are used to provide additional information that narrows down the reference of the modified head. The **Lie test** (Erteschik-Shir and Lappin, 1979, 50) is assumed to reflect the fact that these relatives express information that is taken for granted, since only the matrix can be negated. Thus, if the hearer wishes to challenge (29) by replying *That's a lie*, this would be understood as negating the assertion that the lawyer is very good, rather than negating the predication inside the relative.

In (29a) the filler phrase is an object but it is nonetheless co-referential with the subject of the matrix clause, showing that the filler phrase and the adjoined head are pragmatically independent. Although the filler phrase is the Topic of the presupposition expressed by the relative, the pragmatic function of the referent denoted by the filler phrase relative to the main clause is determined by the function of the adjoined head. Thus, it is perfectly possible for the modified nominal to describe a new referent, even though the co-indexed relative *wh*-pronoun is interpreted as the (local) topic in the relative UDC. For example, in (31) the object of *hired* is discourse-new and yet co-indexed with the (local) topic of the relative.

(31)   I hired a lawyer$_i$ [who]$_i$ I think __$_i$ is very good.

Like their string-vacuous interrogative and declarative counterparts already discussed, we assume there is a UDC in subject relatives like (32), even though *who* appears to be in situ.[6]

(32)   The person$_i$ [who]$_i$__$_i$ hired me was Sam.

We make this assumption for several reasons. First, data like (33) suggest that the clause *I met with* __ is being coordinated with the clause __ *hired me*, given that VP and S cannot ordinarily coordinate (e.g. **I met with Alex and hired me*). See Goodall (1987), Levine et al. (2001), and Levine and Hukari (2006, 69) for more evidence and discussion.

(33)   a. The person$_i$ [who]$_i$ [[I met with __$_i$] and [__$_i$ ultimately hired me]] was Sam.
       b. The person$_i$ [who]$_i$ [[__$_i$ hired me] and [I was tasked with assisting __$_i$]] was Sam.

Second, extraction pathway languages overtly mark the presence of such relative subject UDCs the same way their object UDC counterparts are marked (Clements et al., 1983; Zaenen, 1983; Hukari and Levine, 1995).

Relatives sometimes do not involve any filler phrase, like (34), where the gap is simply co-indexed with the head that the relative clause characterizes. The filler phrase is optional in such UDCs, presumably because there is no risk of mistaking the relative clause for a main clause.

(34)   a. I got the book$_i$ ([which]$_i$) you said Fred wanted to read __$_i$.
       b. Every student$_i$ ([who]$_i$) Alex decided to speak with __$_i$ was a physics major.

In subject relatives, however, either a wh-phrase or a complementizer must appear, as seen in (35). The obligatoriness of the complementizer *that* is a bit surprising, because complementizers in subordinate clauses are usually optional, but in this case its absence would cause speakers to confuse the relative clause with a main clause. Thus, the obligatoriness is likely due to grammaticalization (Hawkins, 2004).[7]

---

[6] The *who the hell/heck* test of (6) cannot apply here because *the hell/heck* only attaches to interrogative *wh* pronouns, not to *wh* relative pronouns.

[7] In some varieties of English—including Middle English and Belfast English (Henry, 1995, 107), as well as some varieties of spoken British English (Radford, 1988, 500) and spoken American English (Zwicky, 2002)—the wh-phrase can co-occur with the complementizer, as in (i) and (ii).

(35)   The lawyer$_i$ (that/[who]$_i$) _ impressed me most was Orwell.

In **free relatives** like (36) a filler phrase combines with a gapped relative clause that does not adjoin to any nominal head. Such constructions are unique among UDCs in that the filler *wh*-phrase appears to also be the head of the entire construction. For example, the phrase *what you told me* in (36a) refers to the *i* entity denoted by *what*, not to the open proposition *you told me i*.

(36)   a. I like [[what]$_i$ [you told me _$_i$]]$_{NP_i}$.

      b. I'll sing [[in whatever town]$_i$ [you want me to sing _$_i$]]$_{PP_i}$

Note that in some relatives, like (36a), an assertion is conveyed, rather than presupposed content. Other relatives that express an assertion rather than the presupposed content are **existential relatives** or **presentational relatives**, seen in (37) (Menn, 1974; McCawley, 1981; Lambrecht, 1988; Fox and Thompson, 1990; Duffield and Michaelis, 2011). Hence, (37a) does not assert *There are many Americans*. Rather, it asserts *Many Americans like soccer*. As we will see in §3, this pragmatic aspect of such relatives likely plays a fundamental role in explaining otherwise mysterious constraints on extraction.

(37)   a. There are many Americans$_i$ [who]$_i$ _$_i$ like soccer.

      b. I have many friends$_i$ [who]$_i$ my siblings enjoy hanging out with _$_i$.

Other relative clauses that express assertions are **transparent free relatives** (Wilder, 1998), shown in (38). Hence, (38a) asserts *I have a beer gut*, and (38b) asserts *His survival is a miracle*.

(38)   a. I have [what]$_i$ you could call _$_i$ a 'beer gut'.

      b. His survival is [what]$_i$ many would describe _$_i$ as a miracle.

      c. [What]$_i$ _$_i$ appeared to be a jet airliner had landed on the freeway.

2.1.3.2 Clefts

Very similar to UDC relatives are **Clefts**, shown in (39). These UDCs involve particular intonation, and impose distinct pragmatic constraints (Collins, 1991; Calude, 2008). For example, the phrase that functions as the antecedent for the relative bears a pitch accent, and receives an exhaustiveness presupposition. Thus, (39a) presupposes that the referent of *a boy* exists, asserts that Fido tried to bite him, and conveys the exhaustive inference that no one other than him (in the relevant context) was bitten by Fido.

(39)   a. It was A BOY$_i$ [who]$_i$ Fido tried to bite _$_i$.

      b. It was JOHN$_i$ [who]$_i$ I think _$_i$ was bitten by Fido.

---

  i. Most of my colleagues were amazed [how quickly]$_i$ that I recovered _$_i$.
     (advertisement for Temple University Hospital, WRTI, November 24, 1999)

  ii. Regardless of [which version of the FEC bill]$_i$ that _$_i$ is passed, (...)
     (authority being interviewed on NPR's 'All things considered', August 31, 1994)

Such clefts involve an expletive subject, *it* or *there*, and focus the entity that is being identified by the relative. Clefts are therefore used to mark utterances that give a complete answer to what the speaker takes to be the *current question* (Velleman et al., 2012). Hence, exchanges like (40) are felicitous, in spite of the fact that two individuals laughed, not just one.

(40) a. A: It was DAVID [who]$_i$ laughed $\_i$.
          B: Yes, and Brady laughed too.
          (Velleman et al., 2012)

In (41) are copular clefts, referred to as **pseudo-clefts**. These constructions are similar to free relatives in that the filler phrase functions as the syntactic and semantic head of the entire subordinate clause.

(41) a. [[Who]$_i$ I think Fido tried to bite $\_i$] was JOHN$_i$.
      b. [All]$_i$ I want to eat $\_i$ is A DOUGHNUT$_i$.

Thus, although the subject of *was* in (41a) is the clause *Who I think Fido tried to bite*, the referent that the verb *was* takes as its argument is not the event denoted by that clause, but, rather, the entity denoted by the filler phrase *who*.

2.1.3.3 Comparatives

Various kinds of comparative UDCs exist, each with rather complex syntactic and semantic peculiarities; see Huddleston (2002) for an overview. Some kinds induce their own special variety of filler-less UDCs, as in (42a), and others impose very specific constraints on the (degree) filler, like (42b).

(42) a. You made more mistakes$_i$ than I think Robin made $\_i$
      b. I understand more, [the more]$_i$ I read $\_i$.

The comparative correlative construction in (42b) is also interesting in that it allows both daughters to have their own UDC if the clause order is reversed (Abeillé and Borsley, 2008; Borsley, 2011):

(43) [The more]$_i$ I read $\_i$, [the more]$_j$ I understand $\_j$.

Other types of comparative UDC are simply combinations of comparatives with standard UDC varieties, as the interrogatives in (44) illustrate.

(44) a. [Who] do you think Alex is as good as $\_i$?
      b. [Who]$_i$ did you say Robin was taller than $\_i$?

2.1.3.4 Dangling modifiers

A very different type of fronting occurs in dangling modifier clauses involving complementizers like *although, though, even though*, or *as*, and typically involve a linking verb, as in (45) and (46). We refer to these as **though-fronting** and **as-fronting** respectively.

(45)   a. [Difficult]$_i$ though the puzzle was __$_i$, Robin managed to solve it.
       b. [Happy]$_i$ though she may appear to be __$_i$, Mia is very worried.

(46)   a. [As hard]$_i$ as he tried __$_i$, John couldn't finish the book.
       b. [As talented]$_i$ as Sam is __$_i$, she didn't win the competition.

It is clear these are different kinds of constructions because the examples in (45) have licit in situ counterparts (e.g. *Though the puzzle was difficult, . . .*) whereas those in (46) do not (e.g. **As he tried as hard, . . .*). These can precede the matrix clause, as in (45), or follow it, or appear inside it, parenthetically.

2.1.3.5 Missing object constructions

In **missing object constructions** (MOC) there is no filler phrase, and the gap is instead co-indexed with a subject or object antecedent; see Postal and Ross (1971) and Nanni (1978, 1980) for an exposition. One class of MOC is typically allowed by adjectives expressing some kind of resistance degree such as *easy, fun, cheap, trivial, difficult, tough, rare, expensive, impossible, worthwhile, a pain*, etc. as in (47).[8]

(47)   a. Kim$_i$ is easy to please __$_i$.
       b. That problem$_i$ is tough for anyone to solve __$_i$.

In these examples, the subject phrase is interpreted as if it were the complement of an embedded infinitival phrase. In other words, although the main predicate of the sentence has a subject, it assigns no semantic role to it. The subject is strictly predicated by the embedded (gapped) verbal structure. Thus, in constructions where the subject can be elided, there is nothing overtly linked to the gap:[9]

(48)   a. Being easy to please __ has its advantages.
       b. Don't be so hard to please __.

This type of MOC is special among others in that it allows alternation between uses where the infinitival phrase is non-gapped, and either appears as a subject, as it does in (47a,b), or is *it*-extraposed, as in (47c,d). The extraposed form is the most frequently occurring of the two.

(49)   a. To please Kim is easy.
       b. For anyone to solve that problem is tough.
       c. It is easy to please Kim.
       d. It is tough for anyone to solve that problem.

Since the gap is not linked to any filler phrase, and merely co-indexed with the subject, the identity between the subject and the gap is weaker than in other UDCs. As (50) makes clear, an accusative gap can be co-indexed with a nominative subject.

---

[8] This class is not exclusively composed of resistance adjectives, as illustrated by adjectives like *unsafe* and verbs like *cost* and *take*.

[9] Calcagno (1999) and Levine and Hukari (2006, 373) argue that the gap can be nominative, with examples like (i) and (ii), but the informants we consulted find such MOCs to be marginally acceptable at best.

i. ?*TOM MITCHELL wasn't very hard to imagine __ would die in poverty.
ii. ?*THAT RING is hard to imagine __ could be worth more than $500.

(50)   [I$_i$]$_{NOM}$ am easy to please [$\_\_i$]$_{ACC}$

Following Mair (1990, 57–72), we assume that MOCs are a kind of Topic construction where an extracted phrase is a kind of (local) Topic to the assertion expressed by the infinitival structure.

A related type of MOC is one where the adjective is derived from certain verbs that select an experiencer object, like *amuse, entertain, please, bore*, etc., as (51) illustrates. Again, these constructions have alternates where the infinitival is gapless and in subject position, or is *it*-extraposed.

(51)   a.   Mia's reaction$_i$ was amusing to see $\_\_i$.
       b.   The game$_i$ was a little boring to watch $\_\_i$.

A different type of MOC is licensed by some degree adjectives like *pretty, gorgeous*, and *ugly*, in which a subjective property is projected from the predicated referent. These MOCs do not allow the infinitival to be a subject, and consequently, do not allow the *it*-extraposed alternate either:

(52)   a.   This painting$_i$ is pretty to look at $\_\_i$.
       b.   *To look at this painting is pretty.
       c.   *It is pretty to look at this painting.

Here, the infinitival expresses the means by which the unexpressed experiencer construes the subjective judgment about the predication. As such, it is tempting to regard this kind of infinitival phrase as an adjunct. A related type of MOC is licensed by certain verbs that have a patient argument, such as *buy, bring, open, clean*, etc., as illustrated in (53). In this case, the infinitival phrase expresses purpose, and cannot be realized as a subject. Again, the infinitival phrase appears to be an adjunct.

(53)   a.   I bought this$_i$ [(for you) to play with $\_\_i$].
       b.   I stole this ring$_i$ [(for you) to sell $\_\_i$].

MOCs involving purpose phrases are special in that they link the gap to the patient of the main predication, even if the latter is realized as a subject, as in (54a,b), or even extracted, as in (54c).

(54)   a.   This game$_i$ was [given to you to play with $\_\_i$ during the flight].
       b.   The patient$_i$ was stripped naked [for the doctors to examine $\_\_i$].
       c.   This is the book$_i$ that I brought $\_\_i$ with me [for us to read $\_\_i$ during the flight].

Yet another type of MOC is licensed by comparatives like those seen in (55), in which case the infinitival expresses the cause for the degree being above a given threshold.

(55)   a.   This soup$_i$ is too hot (for me) to eat $\_\_i$.
       b.   This box$_i$ is too heavy (for me) to lift $\_\_i$.

Different types of MOC can compound on each other, as illustrated in (56). Here we use the symbol '–' to indicate an intonation phrase boundary.

(56) a. This toy$_i$ was difficult for me to bring __$_i$ – for you to play with __$_i$ during the flight.

b. This calculus problem$_i$ is too difficult for the freshmen students to solve __$_i$ – for us to include __$_i$ on the final exam.

It is nonetheless very clear that MOCs are UDCs. First, such extractions can cross infinitival clausal boundaries, as in (57).

(57) a. [This radio]$_i$ would be easy to ask Robin [to try [to fix __$_i$]].

b. [This book]$_i$ will not be easy to convince kids [to try [to read __$_i$]].

MOCs can also cross finite clause boundaries, as shown in (58), although such constructions are rare and not easy to process. For more discussion about these and related data, see Kaplan and Bresnan (1982), Calcagno (1999), Pollard and Sag (1994, 166), and Levine and Hukari (2006, 373).

(58) a. These errors$_i$ were hard for John to admit [that he had made __$_i$].

b. This book$_i$ will not be easy to convince the kids [that they should read __$_i$].

c. That kind of incident$_i$ would be hard for Trump to deny [he had no prior knowledge of __$_i$].

d. This $500 bribe$_i$ will cost the government $500,000 to prove [that Senator Jones accepted __$_i$].

Second, MOCs exhibit classic extraction constraints, including the Adjunct Constraint, as in (59a), the Subject Constraint, as in (59b), and the Complementizer Constraint, as in (59c); for more on these and other extraction constraints, see §3.2.

(59) a. *Mia$_i$ is difficult to believe that Tom cried because you hit __$_i$.
    (cf. *It would be difficult to believe that Tom cried because you hit Mia*)

b. *Mia$_i$ is difficult believe that the picture of __$_i$ was stolen.
    (cf. *It is difficult to believe that the picture of Mia was stolen*)

c. *Mia$_i$ is difficult to believe that __$_i$ was fired.
    (cf. *It is difficult to believe that Mia was fired*)

Finally, like other UDCs, various gaps can be linked to the same filler, as (60) illustrates. As usual, pauses are necessary at the gap sites.[10]

(60) a. THESE ERRORS$_i$ are usually difficult to find __$_i$ and to correct __$_i$.

b. The patient$_i$ was stripped naked [for the doctors to examine __$_i$ and subsequently diagnose __$_i$].

---

[10] French seems to lack true MOCs, given that such constructions cannot cross clausal boundaries, and do not admit multiple gaps (Canac Marquis, 1996, 36–7).

    c. THAT HYPOTHESIS_i is easy for opponents of __i to poke holes in __i.

    d. Astrophotography_i, for example, would be difficult for anyone to excel at __i without reading a lot about __i.

    e. THIS BOOK_i will take the authors of __i approximately TEN YEARS to write __i.

2.2 Filler-gap dependency types

There are three major types of filler-gap dependencies, quite independent of the UDC type. The first we call **singleton**, in which there is at most one filler phrase linked to a gap. This definition allows for UDCs where there is a gap but no filler, as can occur in non-subject relative UDCs, for example. As we shall see, singleton dependencies can compound and interweave in various complex ways. The other two kinds of filler-gap dependencies discussed are **convergent** (in which case multiple gaps are co-referential), and **cumulative** (in which case multiple gaps are additively combined to form a plurality). Any of the above types of filler-gap dependencies can combine to form more complex dependencies.

2.2.1 Singleton

The range of phrases that can be extracted is quite large, both in form and function. Subjects, objects, and modifiers can be extracted, including clauses, verb phrases, prepositional phrases, and adjectival phrases, among others. Below are various kinds of singleton non-nominal extractions, from subject and object positions.

(61) a. [How happy]_{ADJP} did Mia appear to be _?

    b. [More typical]_{ADJP} I think _ is $1.50 to $2.50 per square foot.

(62) a. [Under the rug]_{PP} I didn't find anything _.

    b. [Under the rug]_{PP} I don't think _ is a good place to hide house keys.

(63) a. [To give up right now]_{VP} it would make no sense _.

    b. [To give up right now]_{VP} I think _ makes no sense.

(64) a. [Sam HATES olives]_S, I later discovered _.

    b. [That this was NOT ILLEGAL]_{CP}, I think _ surprised people the most.

    c. [That Robin had been a spy]_{CP}, I very much doubt _ can be proven at this point.

As Bouma et al. (2001) note, there is also a wide range of adverbial phrases which can be extracted. The examples in (65) illustrate temporal, frequency, locative, manner, and reason adverbial extraction. Some of these examples are ambiguous between a reading where the adverb modifies the matrix verb (short construal) or the embedded clause verb (long construal).

(65) a. [When]$_i$ do you suspect Robin will be home __$_i$?

b. [On Monday]$_i$ I think that Kim went home very late __$_i$.

c. [TOMORROW] I think I might go to the beach __.

d. [How often]$_i$ do you think Sam goes out at night __$_i$?

e. [Where]$_i$ did you say Mia found a fossil __$_i$ last summer?

f. It was [only very RARELY]$_i$ that Sam missed a campus party __$_i$.

g. [How easily]$_i$ do you think Alex completed the exam __$_i$?

h. [How]$_i$ do you think he wants us to stack the boxes __$_i$?

i. [Why]$_i$ do you suppose Robin tried to do that __$_i$?

The distinction between short and long construals in reason interrogatives like (65h,i) is clearer in extraction pathway-marking languages like Irish. In (66a) the complementizer of the embedded clause is *goN*, and therefore the question is interpreted as asking why Ciarán said something. In (66b), however, the complementizer in the embedded clause is *aL*, which means that the gap site is deeper. Hence, the question must be interpreted as asking why Ciarán would be present. See §3.4.3 and Chapman and Kučerová (2016) for more on long and short construals of reason interrogatives.

(66) a. Cén fáth   **aL** dhúirt Ciarán **goN** mbeadh sé i láthair __?
       what reason c   said Ciarán c   would.be he present
       'Why did Ciarán say that he'd be present?'

b. Cén fáth   **aL** dhúirt Ciarán **aL** mbeadh sé i láthair __?
       what reason c   said Ciarán c   would.be he present
       'Why did Ciarán say that he'd be present?'
       (Van Valin, 1998)   (Irish)

Certain other types of adverbial phrase are quite impossible to extract, however. Consider the sample in (67). Crucially, the in situ counterparts of these constructions are licit.

(67) a. *[DEFINITELY] I thought Sam __ skipped school.
       (cf. *I thought Sam definitely skipped school*)

b. *[NEVER] did Kim claim that Sandy __ sang for her.
       (cf. *Did Kim claim that Sandy never sang for her?*)

c. *[ALWAYS] I think Robin __ was a good student.
       (cf. *I think Robin always was a good student*)

d. *[ALMOST] I think Kim __ found the solution.
       (cf. *I think Kim almost found the solution*)
       (Bouma et al., 2001, 48)

For Fillmore (1982), Croft (2001, ch. 7), and various others, a wide range of phrases that would traditionally be regarded as adjuncts are analyzed as non-core arguments (i.e. optional complements). According to Bouma et al. (2001), many English post-verbal adverbs are post-verbal precisely because they are complements, such as those in (65), which in turn explains why they are extractable; see §2.2.1 for more examples. In contrast, the adverbs in (67) normally only appear to the left of VPs, and therefore are not extractable presumably because they are true adjuncts rather than complements.

The traditional reasons for viewing adverbial phrases as adjuncts rather than complements are twofold: their ability to iterate, and their optionality. These criteria are problematic, however. Adverbs that have the same semantic function cannot be iterated, as in (68), just as subject/object phrases cannot be iterated because they have the same grammatical function.[11]

(68)   *Robin laughed all week yesterday just now often.

Second, there are various constructions in which subjects and direct objects are unrealized. For example, imperatives, directives, diary-style sentences, and label statements are all subjectless:

(69)   a. Ø Go home!
       b. Ø Press any key to continue.
       c. Ø Went out last night. Ø Got drunk again.
       d. Ø Contains alcohol.

In particular, there are also instances where otherwise obligatory direct objects become null, as in (70); see Ruppenhofer and Michaelis (2014) for more examples and discussion.

(70)   a. Ø Store Ø away from sunlight.
       b. She knitted Ø her way across the Atlantic.
       c. He devoured Ø his way to victory in this hot dog-eating competition.

Finally, there are constructions where adverbs are obligatory, suggesting that they are sometimes subcategorized like canonical objects.

(71)   a. John scares *(easily).
       b. This book reads *(well).
       c. These substances behave *(similarly).[12]

The argument vs. modifier split is blurred in a number of other ways. Extraction pathway languages such as Irish, Icelandic, Yiddish, French, and others overtly register the extraction of adverbs in the same way as subjects and complements are signaled. See Hukari and Levine (1995), Levine and Hukari (2006, 119–34), and Levine (2017, 263–76) for data and discussion. Case spreading in VPs blurs the distinction between valents and modifiers in languages like Korean (Maling, 1989), Chinese (Li, 1990), Finnish

---

[11] There is to our knowledge only one construction that allows sequences of adverbials of the same kind to iterate, but this construction is special in that it characterizes a trajectory along a path. Such complex adverbial sequences form a constituent, nonetheless:

i. Was it [in 1945, on the 16th of July, at 5:39 a.m.]$_i$ that the first nuclear bomb was detonated __$_i$?
ii. Q: [When]$_i$ was the first nuclear bomb detonated __$_i$?
    A: [In 1945, on the 16th of July, in the morning].

[12] Note that the relevant use of *behave* here is synonymous with *act*, as in *behaved poorly*, rather than the use in which *behave* means *behave well*.

(Maling, 1993), and Polish (Przepiórkowski, 1999). This is illustrated in (72). The case marking on the frequency adverbial—like the case marking on the object NP—must change from accusative to nominative when the sentence is passivized.

(72)   a. Suni-ka cip-ul   pheyinthu-lul twu pen-ul   chilha-yss-ta
Suni$_{NOM}$ house$_{ACC}$ paint$_{ACC}$ 2   times$_{acc}$ brush
'Suni painted a house three times'

   b. Cip-i   Suni-eyuyhay pheyinthu-ka twu pen-i   chilha-y ci-ess-ta
house$_{NOM}$ Suni$_{DAT}$ paint$_{NOM}$ 2   times$_{nom}$ brush
'A house was painted two times by Suni'
(Wechsler and Lee, 1996, 635)   (Korean)

If post-verbal adverbial phrases are complements, then Binding Theory applies as usual, and explains the oddness of Principle C violations like (73), as Levine and Hukari (2006, 84) note. For more discussion about anaphora in adverbial phrases, see Reinhart (1983, 102) and Hukari and Levine (1996).

(73)   *They$_i$ were in a good mood after [the twins]$_i$ had their usual morning argument.
(Levine and Hukari, 2006, 84, n. 20)

Finally, the existence of prepositional passives like (74) and (75) becomes unproblematic if such PPs are optional arguments instead of adjuncts.

(74)   a. My new hat has been sat on.
   b. This bridge has already been flown under twice.
   c. This table is sat at by everybody.
   d. This bed was slept in by George Washington.
      (Ward et al., 2002, 1433,1446)

(75)   There were curative trees, parish meeting trees, celebrity trees. Trees believed to have been planted by Chaucer, sat under by Queen Elizabeth, hidden in by Charles II.
[*The Ash and the Beech*, Richard Mabey]

In other words, it is difficult to carve an absolute divide between arguments and adverbials. Further evidence that the distinction between core arguments and non-core arguments is one of degree comes from behavioral studies such as Bock (1989), Koenig et al. (2003), and Tutunjian and Boland (2008), as well as from co-occurrence patterns (MacDonald et al., 1994; Manning, 2003). We conclude that not all adverbs are created equal. Some are best seen as optional non-core arguments, and others as true adjuncts.

2.2.1.1 Overlapping

Multiple singleton dependencies can overlap in the same utterance, without interacting. In (76), there are multiple gaps linked to different fillers. The presence of multiple UDCs can tax sentence processing, especially in the absence of an ideal prosodic phrasing.

(76)   a. [Which problem]$_j$ don't you know [who]$_i$ to talk to $_$$_i$ about $\_$$_j$?
   b. Robin is someone [who]$_j$ I never know [what]$_i$ to say $_$$_i$ to $\_$$_j$.

    c. [THAT PROBLEM]$_j$ I have no idea [what]$_i$ to do $\_i$ about $\_j$.

    d. That's the representative [who]$_j$ I can't remember [which documents]$_i$ I sent copies of $\_i$ to $\_j$.

Overlapping dependencies can involve co-arguments, as in (77). Here, the filler phrase corresponds to both the subject and the object of the same verb. Such UDCs are hard to process, but are acceptable, especially in the proper context. For example, (77a) is plausible in a situation where a wife receives flowers from a friend and her husband assumes they are from a lover.

(77)   a. These are the flowers$_j$ that I'd like to know [who]$_i$ you think [$\_i$ bought $\_j$ for me].

     b. This is the subtle lie$_i$ that I'm wondering [who you]$_j$ think [$\_i$ told Sue $\_j$].

     c. [Which treatment]$_j$ did you forget [which patient]$_i$ is supposed to [$\_i$ receive $\_j$]?

     d. [Which outfit]$_j$ did you forget [which model]$_i$ wanted to [$\_i$ wear $\_j$]?

Similarly, (78) illustrates overlapping extractions of two objects of the same verb. See Pollard and Sag (1994, 382, n. 42), Levine and Hukari (2006, 74, 96), and Radford (2009, 327) for more data and discussion.

(78)   a. This is a man [to whom]$_i$ LIBERTY$_j$ we would never grant $\_j$ $\_i$.
     (Baltin, 1982, 18)

     b. [On which violins]$_i$ are these sonatas$_j$ difficult to play $\_j$ $\_i$?
     (Hukari and Levine, 1987, 220)

All of the overlapping filler-gap dependencies in (76–78) are **nested**: the first filler is linked to the second gap, and the second filler is linked to the first gap. Had the first filler been linked to the first gap, and the second filler linked to the second gap, the dependency would be **crossed**. Various authors such as Pesetsky (1987, 105), Kitahara (1997), and Richards (2001) claim that it is not possible to cross filler-gap dependencies: if two UDCs overlap, one must contain the other, as per the **Nested Dependency Constraint** (Fodor, 1978) or the **Path Containment Condition** (Pesetsky, 1982, 268). But counterexamples like (79) indicate that non-crossing isn't a necessary condition for the well-formedness of UDCs.

(79)   a. [Which TV show]$_i$ did you wonder [how often]$_j$ I saw $\_i$ $\_j$?
     (Bouma et al., 2001, 53, n. 33)

     b. Ten thousand dollars is a sum of money which$_i$ [to a cause like THAT]$_j$ I would GLADLY give $\_i$ $\_j$.
     (Levine and Hukari, 2006)

     c. He is the kind of guy [who]$_i$ [under no circumstances]$_j$ should you trust $\_i$ $\_j$.
     (adapted from Hooper and Thompson (1973, 472))

     d. A university is the kind of place [at which]$_i$ [that kind of behavior]$_j$ we cannot tolerate $\_i$ $\_j$.

     e. [Patients this old]$_j$ I never know [when]$_i$ to send home $\_j$ $\_i$.

In these examples, the two filler phrases have very different categories and syntactic roles, but this need not be the case. In examples like (80a) both gaps correspond to objects. Examples involving prepositional stranding like (80b) are harder to process, but not insurmountably so once a phonological phrasing that allows pauses at the gap sites is identified.[13]

(80) a. That's the person [who]$_i$ I never know [what]$_j$ to get$\_i\_j$ for Christmas.

   b. That's the co-worker [who]$_i$ I never know [what]$_j$ to talk to$\_i$ about$\_k$ at office parties.

Counterexamples where the extracted phrases are not dependents of the same exact head also exist, as in (81). See Huddleston and Pullum (2002b, 1095), Levine and Hukari (2006, 357), and Chaves (2012b) for more discussion.

(81) a. [Someone THAT STUPID]$_j$, [how much time]$_i$ do we really want to waste$\_i$ arguing with$\_j$?

   b. [How much]$_i$ will these cars$_j$ cost$\_i$ to recall$\_j$?

   c. [Which of the two instruments]$_i$ will this piece$_j$ be easier to play$\_j$ on$\_i$?

   d. You know [what]$_j$ [Rocco and Melissa]$_i$ are like$\_j$ to talk to$\_i$, right?

   e. [A violin THIS WELL CRAFTED]$_i$ even [the most DIFFICULT SONATA]$_j$ will be easy to PLAY$\_j$ on$\_i$.

2.2.1.2 Chaining

Multiple UDCs can also be 'chained' to each other, whereby a filler phrase itself contains a gap that is linked to another gap in a distinct UDC, as in (82), drawn from Chaves (2012b). Here, the sentence-final gap is linked to a filler phrase j which itself contains a second gap i, linked to another filler phrase i. Thus, the two singleton UDCs are chained together, so to speak. The topicalized phrases in (82d–e) must be independent intonational phrases, as indicated by the parenthesis. Sauerland (1999) refers to such dependencies as **surfing**, but we won't adopt the term here.

(82) a. This is the handout [which]$_i$ I can't remember [how many copies of$\_i$]$_j$ we have to print$\_j$.

   b. This is the wine brand [which]$_i$ I can't remember [how many bottles of$\_i$] we decided to order$\_i$.

   c. This is the type of person [who]$_i$ [even the seemingly good advice of$\_i$]$_j$ I would not trust$\_j$.

   d. This is an animal [which]$_i$ – [for us to STUDY$\_i$ up close]$_j$ – we would need MONTHS of planning$\_j$.

---

[13] The main disadvantage of (80b) over (80a) may be that it involves multiple preposition strandings in sequence, which imposes a very unusual prosodic phrasing.

   e. This is a problem [which]$_i$ – [to SOLVE $\_i$ once and for all]$_j$ – I think $\_j$ would be
      EXTREMELY difficult.

In the face of such examples, we reject the widespread claim that such filler-gap dependencies are impossible, e.g. Browning (1989, 481), Takahashi (1994), Sauerland (1999), Boeckx (2003), Stepanov (2007), Rizzi (2007b), Richards (2001, 185), Haegeman et al. (2013), to name only a few. See Sauerland (1999), Levine and Hukari (2006), and §4.3 for more discussion.

    The same chaining pattern can arise in missing object constructions as well, as (83) illustrates. Here the missing object of the preposition *to* contains a gap linked to the fronted relative pronoun *who*.

(83) a. There are certain heroes [who]$_i$ [long stories about $\_i$]$_j$ are always very easy to
       listen to $\_j$.

     b. There are certain heroes [who]$_i$ [long stories about $\_i$]$_j$ are too boring to listen
       to $\_j$.
       (Polly Jacobson (pers. comm.) in Pollard and Sag (1994, 199, n. 35))

2.2.2 Convergent

The same filler phrase can be simultaneously linked to multiple gaps, and by far the most frequent construction in which this phenomenon occurs is coordination, illustrated in (84).

(84) a. [Who]$_i$ will we play with $\_i$, learn from $\_i$, love $\_i$ unthinkingly, and fight with $\_i$
       ferociously, knowing all the while that we can do these things because we are
       linked together by an indissoluble common tie?
       [COCA ACAD 1997]

     b. [Who]$_i$ did you meet $\_i$ at a party and date $\_i$ for a few months?

     c. This is a type of mentality$_i$ that I've encountered $\_i$ often enough but certainly had
       not expected to find $\_i$ here.

But it should be stressed that convergent dependencies are also possible in a wide range of other constructions. For example, in (85a) the filler phrase is co-indexed with the direct object of *inform*, in the matrix clause, and the direct object of *arrest*, in the subordinate clause. A similar pattern is observed in (85b,c). As usual, gaps that are not sentence-final require a pause to cue them.

(85) a. [Who]$_i$ did you inform $\_i$ that the police were about to arrest $\_i$?

     b. [Which company]$_i$ did you forget to notify $\_i$ that we were going to audit $\_i$?

     c. [Which jar]$_i$ was it $\_i$ that she says she put the keys in $\_i$?
       (Huddleston and Pullum, 2002b, 1088)

Each of the gaps in these examples is independently legitimate. For example, the filler phrase can be linked exclusively to a gap in the matrix (86a), to a gap in the embedded clause (86b), or to both at the same time (86c). In these UDCs the pause at the gap site is absolutely crucial for interpreting the sentence as intended. In sum, none of these gaps resides in an island.[14]

(86) a. These are the people [who]$_i$ I'd like to remind you __$_i$ are still single.
 b. These are the people [who]$_i$ I'd like to remind __$_i$ you are still single.
 c. These are the people [who]$_i$ I'd like to remind __$_i$ __$_i$ are still single.

Other non-coordinate constructions which likewise allow multiple gaps to be co-indexed with the same filler phrase are listed in (87). Multiple gaps can appear in the complements of the same verb, as in (87a), in the subject and the complement of the same verb, as in (87b), in the complements of different verbs (87c), across different comparative expressions (87d,e); see Engdahl (1983) for various other examples.

(87) a. [Who]$_i$ did you show pictures of __$_i$ to __$_i$?
 b. [Which student]$_i$ are [the parents of __$_i$] picking up __$_i$ around noon?
 c. [Which engineer]$_i$ did you hire __$_i$ without talking to __$_i$ first?
 d. [Who]$_i$ did the article insult __$_i$ more than it praised __$_i$?
 e. [Which physicist]$_i$ do you consider __$_i$ smarter than most contemporaries of __$_i$?
 f. This is someone [who]$_i$ I believe __$_i$ hates me as much as you believe __$_i$ hates you.
 g. [Who]$_i$ did you say [John's criticism of __$_i$] would make us think [__$_i$ was stupid]?

The attentive reader may have noticed that the convergent dependency in (86c) is **syncretic**: the same filler simultaneously satisfies two very different case constraints. The same phenomenon arises in a wide range of other UDCs, as (88) illustrates; see Engdahl (1983, 93), Levine and Hukari (2006, 94), and Culicover (2001, 36) for more examples.

(88) a. Robin is someone [who] – until you get to know __$_{ACC}$ – I suppose [$_{NOM}$ can seem quite strange].
 (Haegeman, 1984)

 b. [Who] did the judge remind __$_{ACC}$ [__$_{NOM}$ was still under oath]?

 c. There are certain stories that [if you repeat __$_{ACC}$ to the wrong people] __$_{NOM}$ will get you into all kinds of trouble.

 d. Robin is someone [who] even [good friends of __$_{ACC}$] believe __$_{NOM}$ should be closely watched.
 (Levine et al., 2001)

 e. [Which neighbors] did you invite __$_{ACC}$ without thinking __$_{NOM}$ would actually come?
 (Levine, 2004)

---

[14] Engdahl (1982, 11) and others since claim that the second gap in (86c) is dependent (i.e. 'parasitic') on the existence of the other gap. But in such a view, (86a) should be ungrammatical, contrary to fact. See §3.2.7.1 for more discussion.

Syncretic UDCs also arise in coordination, as (89) shows. The status of such examples has been somewhat controversial (Williams, 1978; Gazdar, 1981), because there is a tendency for the structure across conjuncts to be parallel, perhaps because of priming (Dubey et al., 2005). We consider such coordinate UDCs licit nonetheless, though non-canonical.

(89) a. Nancy Reagan was wearing a gown that Galanos designed $\_{ACC}$ and $\_{NOM}$ reputedly cost over \$5,000.
          (Anderson, 1983, 3)

      b. This is the man [who] Robin saw $\_{ACC}$ and thinks $\_{NOM}$ is handsome.
          (Goodall, 1987, 70)

      c. The trick was to give away information that $\_{NOM}$ would tantalize hard-core fans, but casual viewers wouldn't need $\_{ACC}$.
          (Whitman, 2006)

      d. It is no wonder that I am already missing New York, a city that $\_{NOM}$ is extremely easy to fall in love with $\_{ACC}$ and that staying away from $\_{NOM}$ is tremendously challenging.[15]
          (Culicover and Winkler, 2019)

      e. This is the book that I haven't read $\_{ACC}$ yet but $\_{NOM}$ is highly recommended by all my friends.
          (Chaves, 2012b)

2.2.3 Cumulative

Cumulative filler-gap linkages are in a sense a more extreme variant of convergent dependencies in that the former allows multiple filler-gap dependencies to combine to form a plurality; see Munn (1998) and Chaves (2012a). In other words, the same filler phrase denoting a set of entities can be connected to two or more gaps in such a way that the referent linked to each gap is disjoint from the other gaps' referent. This cumulative type of multiple UDC is illustrated in (90). These examples also allow a convergent reading where $i = j$, with the exception of (90a), since the object of *eat* in (90a) must be a solid, and therefore cannot be co-referential with the complement of *drink*.

(90) a. [What]$_{\{i,j\}}$ did Kim eat $\_{i}$ and drink $\_{j}$ at the party?
          (answer: 'Kim ate pizza and drank beer')

      b. A: [Which stocks]$_{\{i,j\}}$ did Sam buy $\_{i}$ and Robin sell $\_{j}$?
          B: Sam bought Sony stocks and Robin sold Facebook stocks.

      c. [Which cities]$_{\{i,j\}}$ did Jack TRAVEL TO $\_{i}$ and Mia decide to LIVE IN $\_{j}$?
          (answer: 'Jack traveled to Bern and Mia decided to live in Rome')

The cumulative interpretation can usually be forced with the aid of the adverb *respectively*, as the examples in (91) illustrate.[16] These are called **Interwoven Dependency Constructions** in Postal (1998) and Zhang (2007).

---

[15] [Farah Nabulsi. 2009, LLM Diary: Finding more than academic fulfillment in the Big Apple, *Financial Times*].
[16] Note, however, that *respectively* is optional and does not require any coordination, as (i–iii) show. See Kay (1989), Gawron and Kehler (2004), Chaves (2012a), and Kubota and Levine (2016a) for more discussion and accounts of *respectively* readings.

(91) a. [What book$_i$ and what magazine$_j$]$_{\{i,j\}}$ did John buy __$_i$ and Bill read __$_j$ (respectively)?

b. [Where]$_{\{i,j\}}$ did Mary vacation __$_i$ and Bill decide to live __$_j$ (respectively)?

Whether cumulative readings arise in non-coordinate UDCs is unclear. For Vicente (2016) and for some of the speakers we consulted, cumulative readings also arise in non-coordinate UDCs like those in (92). But even for the speakers who accept such readings the convergent ($i = j$) interpretation is difficult to override, perhaps because they are unusual and compete with far simpler and more frequent alternative interrogative formulations.

(92) [Context: several employees berated their company on social media during the weekend, and were fired. However, someone at HR failed to inform certain project leaders of some of the firings.]
Q: [Who]$_{\{i,j\}}$ did you forget to inform __$_i$ that we had fired __$_j$?
A: I neglected to inform Dr. Yang about the firing of his senior engineer, and inform Dr. Keller about the firing of her lead programmer.

A related phenomenon arises in some Slavic languages, whereby it is possible to coordinate phrases with different grammatical functions. This was originally noted by Browne (1972), and is illustrated in (93).

(93) a. Kto   i   kogo   peremig?
who$_{NOM}$ and whom$_{ACC}$ won
'Who took over whom?'

b. Kto-to   i   kogo-to   obidel
someone$_{NOM}$ and someone$_{ACC}$ offended
'someone offended somebody'

c. Vsem   i   vse   do lampochki
everyone$_{DAT}$ and everything$_{NOM}$ don't care
'Nobody cares about anything'
(Chaves and Paperno, 2007)   (Russian)

Here, each of the conjoined phrases has a completely different grammatical role, as shown by the disparate case marking. Thus, subjects, objects, and adjuncts can be conjoined and displaced around in the sentence, as a unit. In particular, it is possible to extract such 'hybrid' coordinate structures, as in the topicalization UDC in (94a) and the relative UDCs in (94b,c).

(94) a. Vsem$_i$ i   vsegda$_j$ etot professor rad   pomoch' __$_i$ __$_j$
everyone and always, this professor is-eager to-help
'this professor is always eager to help everyone'

---

i. The three best students received the three best scores (respectively).
ii. These dots correspond to those cities (respectively).
iii. It is essential that an agreement be reached as to the costs that each party will (respectively) bear.

b. Vezde$_i$ i   vse$_j$ kto _$_i$ byl dobrozhelatelen _$_j$ pomogali mne.
everywhere and all who   was benevolent   helped me
'Everyone benevolent was helping me everywhere'

c. Vezde$_i$ i   vsio$_j$ chto _$_j$ mne pokazyvali _$_i$ mne nravilos.
everywhere and everything that   me showed   me pleased
'I liked whatever was shown to me anywhere'
(Chaves and Paperno, 2007)

There is likely a special constructional template at work, given that there are very strong constraints on the conjuncts. For example, proper nouns cannot be coordinated, and conjuncts are preferentially and almost exclusively lexical:

(95) Kto-to   vysokii i   kogo-to   obidel?
someone$_{NOM}$ tall   and someone$_{NOM}$ offended$_{3SG}$
'Someone tall offended someone?'

Similarly, conjuncts with different quantificational force such as 'someone and everything' are not allowed either, unlike what happens in 'regular' coordination (Chaves and Paperno, 2007). Whitman (2004), Zhang (2007), and others claim that this type of hybrid coordination exists in English as well, given examples like (96).

(96) [What]$_i$ and [when]$_j$ does John normally eat _$_i$_$_j$?
(Grosu, 1985, 232)

But we are skeptical that English truly allows hybrid coordinations like *what and when*. For example, English hybrid coordination is for some mysterious reason restricted to interrogative expressions, as illustrated by the deviance of the declarative frontings in (97).

(97) a. *Everyone$_i$ and everything$_j$ would be easy to tell _$_i$ to _$_j$.
(cf. *It would be easy to tell everyone everything*)

b. *[EVERYONE]$_i$ and [ALWAYS]$_j$ I don't think you can please _$_i$ to _$_j$.
(cf. *I don't think you can please everyone, always*)

A simpler explanation is that English does not allow hybrid coordination, and that one of the conjuncts in (96) is elliptical, either as a sluice (e.g. *What does John normally eat, and when?*), or perhaps as a Right-Node Raising construction (e.g. *What ~~does John normally eat~~, and when does John normally eat?*). The ellipsis account correctly predicts the oddness of English hybrid coordinations like those in (98), simply because the ellipsis parse is not possible. See Chaves and Paperno (2007) and Chaves (2014).

(98) a. *Who$_i$ and what$_j$ _$_i$ found _$_j$?
(cf. * *Who ~~found~~ and what found?*)

b. *Who$_i$ and whom$_j$ did you say _$_i$ saw _$_j$?
(cf. * *Who ~~did you say saw~~ and whom did you say saw?*)

Lewis et al. (2012) report that *wh*-coordinations like (99a) are more acceptable than (99b), and propose that the difference stems from the fact that *eat* is optionally transitive, whereas *find* is not, conjecturing that the left conjunct does not form a syntactic dependency with the verb. But a simpler explanation is that the question expressed by (99a) is semantically and pragmatically awkward, as evidenced by the counterparts in brackets below. Further research that controls for the plausibility of the non-*wh*-coordination counterparts is necessary.

(99)   a.   What and when will we eat at the conference?
       (cf. *What will we eat at the conference, and when?*)

       b.   *What and when will we find at the conference?
       (cf. ??*What will we find at the conference, and when?*)

2.3 Filler-gap mismatches

As already discussed in Chapter 1, it is generally the case that filler phrases must be morphosyntactically consistent with the constraints that are imposed on their in situ counterparts. Consider the contrasts in (100).

(100)   a.   The city [to which]$_{\text{TO-PP}}$ Robin went [_]$_{\text{TO-PP}}$ last summer was Paris.
        b.   *The city [which]$_{\text{NP}}$ Robin went [_]$_{\text{TO-PP}}$ last summer was Paris.
        c.   *The city [at which]$_{\text{AT-PP}}$ Robin went [_]$_{\text{TO-PP}}$ last summer was Paris.

Data like (100) suggest that UDCs involve both syntactic and semantic identity constraints. That said, there are some apparent counterexamples. For instance, (101a) is understandably odd because the complement of *is* is missing a determiner, but for some reason the UDC counterpart does not exhibit such a constraint, as illustrated by the acceptability of (101b).

(101)   a.   *Though he is a good linguist, he could not have written this book by himself.

        b.   [(A) good linguist]$_i$ though he is _$_i$, he could not have written this book by himself.
        (Huddleston and Pullum, 2002b)

The optionality of the determiner in (101b) may be due to phonological reduction of the determiner in a sentence-initial position. Such reduction phenomena occur independently of UDCs, as (102) suggests. Here, subject phrases that ordinarily require a determiner are permitted to drop it.

(102)   I ran into Hoshi Sato the other day. Great linguist. Fantastic software engineer too.

Another apparent filler-gap mismatch concerns preposition doubling, as in (103); such mismatches are attested in corpora, and can be deemed relatively acceptable in speeded acceptability experiments but not in untimed acceptability experiments (Radford and Felser, 2011).[17] Interestingly, Nykiel (2010) provides evidence that preposition doubling

---

[17] The symbol '?' indicates intermediate acceptability.

is unlikely to be a length effect. Nonetheless, we speculate that the phenomenon is due to superficial—'good enough'—sentence-processing errors (Ferreira and Patson, 2007).

(103)   a.   ?If insurance dictates that they go to a particular hospital, that's the hospital [to which]$_i$ they must go [to $\_\_{}_i$].

      b.   ?The amount of support they are receiving is more than justified, given the conditions [in which]$_i$ they're [in $\_\_{}_i$].

An even more extreme mismatch is illustrated in (104). Here, the preposition is the wrong one, and yet this type of construction is attested in real discourse. Again, we consider such cases to be due to incomplete or sloppy processing.

(104)   A businessman from Carletonville is complaining that he was almost forced to pay fines [of which]$_{PP}$ he knew nothing about $\_\_{}_{NP}$ to ensure a new Professional Driving Permit.[18]

One final case of apparent filler-gap mismatch involving prepositions is perhaps the most interesting one. In (105a) there is a filler-gap mismatch in the second gap: whereas the filler is a PP headed by *on* (henceforth abbreviated as ON-PP), the second gap is required to be an NP. If the mismatched gap is the first rather than the second, then oddness ensues, as in (105b). Finally, if the two gaps and the filler match morphosyntactically, then, of course, the UDC is licit, as (105c) illustrates.

(105)   a.   It was [ON SUE]$_{ON-PP}$ that I think John relied [$\_$]$_{ON-PP}$ the most but didn't thank $\_\_{}_{NP}$ nearly enough in his speech.

      b.   *It was [ON SUE]$_{ON-PP}$ that I think John thanked [$\_$]$_{NP}$ the most but didn't rely $\_\_{}_{ON-NP}$ nearly enough in his speech.

      c.   It was [SUE]$_{NP}$ that I think John thanked [$\_$]$_{NP}$ the most but didn't rely on $\_\_{}_{NP}$ nearly enough in his speech.

The acceptability of (105a) is perhaps due to memory decay of the filler phrase. Before a suitable gap is found, comprehenders are under pressure to postulate a gap whenever possible, link it to the filler, and discharge it from memory as soon as possible. But once the filler is linked to a gap, and the filler is no longer reactivated by the search for another gap, the filler becomes 'inactive' in the sense of Frazier (1987). As a consequence, its morphosyntactic features are more susceptible to decay from memory, and mismatches like (105a) are tolerable.

We conjecture that (105a) is such that an upcoming VP conjunct is not strongly predicted, and therefore there is no strong expectation of a second gap. Adversative coordinations like (105) are more frequently S coordinations than VP coordinations. This is relevant because convergent-gap UDCs are more common in VP coordination than in S coordination. For example, we find that in the Brown Treebank (Taylor et al., 2003) 80% of *but* occurrences are S coordinations ($n = 897$), 10% are NP coordinations ($n = 114$), and the remaining 10% are VP coordinations ($n = 108$). In contrast, only 33% of *and* occurrences

---

[18] https://carletonvilleherald.com/4647/businessman-warns-about-licensing-issues/.

are S coordinations (*n* = 2299), 40% are VP coordinations (*n* = 2835), and 25% are NP coordinations (*n* = 1744). Our expectation-based memory decay hypothesis for the acceptability of (105a) is consistent with the findings of Wagers and Phillips (2009) and Parker (2017) concerning dual active search in conjunction: the processing of UDCs involving (symmetric) conjunctions causes active search for gaps in both conjuncts, but no such dual active search is triggered when processing structures where the upcoming gap is much less likely, as in asymmetric conjunctions or adjunct structures, even though a second gap would be completely licit. For more on symmetric and asymmetric coordination, see §3.2.5.

Another type of apparent filler-gap mismatch is (106a), where the ex situ complement of the verb *hope* is the NP *what*, although this verb does not usually take NP complements, as the contrast in (107) illustrates. Thus, only (106b) would be expected to be acceptable.

(106) a. [What]$_i$ I'm hoping __$_i$ is that nobody will notice my absence.

  b. [What]$_i$ I'm hoping for __$_i$ is that nobody will notice my absence.
   (Huddleston and Pullum, 2002b, 1087)

(107) a. *I'm hoping [this outcome].
  b. I'm hoping [for this outcome].

A possible explanation for the acceptability of (106a) is that the morphosyntactic category of at least some *wh*-expressions is underspecified, or polymorphic, as in (108) and (109). Thus, there is no mismatch in (106a).

(108) a. A: I was hoping to not pass my driving test.
    B: You were hoping ↑WHAT??

  b. "Yes, yes, I know all that. But I was just hoping."
    Dana glowered at me. 'Hoping WHAT?'
    [COCA 2003 FIC]

  c. A: They want to talk about the economy.
    B: What are they hoping? Are they hoping that Bob Schieffer brings it up and neither of them has to?
    [COCA 2008 SPOK]

(109) a. So what happens now? My stuff goes to WHERE?
    [COCA 1993 SPOK]

  b. So the rest of it goes WHERE?
    [COCA 1996 SPOK]

Independent motivation for this polymorphic view of *wh*-expressions comes from relative pronouns, which typically refer to individuals, but can also refer to states, events, or propositions, as seen in (110).

(110) a. It was sad$_s$ [which]$_s$ Sam appeared to be __$_s$, not angry.
  b. It was to warn$_e$ everyone that I think Alex sent this message __$_e$.

    c. Kim learned$_e$ how to ride a camel, [which]$_e$ is not an easy thing to do __$_e$.
    d. Sam was fired$_e$ yesterday, [which]$_e$ I didn't expect __$_e$ to happen at all.
       (Arnold and Borsley, 2008)

Such a polymorphic account predicts apparent mismatches like (111), where the extracted verbal complement is linked to a relative filler phrase *which*. Note that the verb *can* in (111a) is not compatible with an NP complement of any kind (e.g. **They can't that*).

(111)   a. We'd be in trouble if the lions escaped the cages, [which]$_e$ they can't __$_e$, of course.
      b. It's Sam being more popular than you that I think __ makes no sense.
      c. It's that Sam is more popular than you that I think __ makes no sense.

The mismatch in (112) is more challenging, in part because not all speakers accept such structures. Here the puzzle is that the extracted counterpart is more acceptable than the in situ counterpart. Prepositions do not usually combine with CPs, but the acceptability improves if the CP is extracted. See also Bresnan (1991).

(112)   a. [That he was sick]$_i$ we talked about __$_i$ for days.
       (cf. **We talked about [that he was sick] for days*)
       (Bresnan, 2001, 16–24)

      b. [That they'll give him a second chance]$_i$ I wouldn't gamble on __$_i$.
       (cf. **I wouldn't gamble on [that they'll give him a second chance]*)
       (Huddleston and Pullum, 2002b, 1087)

It is tempting to assume the extracted CPs have been coerced into an NP of some kind, but this requires stipulating that the in situ CP is somehow barred from being coerced into an NP. Another possibility is that the fronted CP does not directly correspond to the gap, and that the linkage is unlike that of a regular UDC (Webelhuth, 2012); see also Higgins (1973, 158–9) and Bouma et al. (2001, 24) for an analysis.

    Another analysis is that the in situ counterparts are grammatical, but comprehenders incorrectly assume that the preposition combines with *that* as a pronoun—the most frequent use of *that*. Gibson (1998) shows that top-down (syntactic) expectations about the occurrence of complementizers are independent from bottom-up (lexical) frequency-based expectations in sentence processing. Thus, his findings suggest that comprehenders postulate the most frequent category for *that* even in syntactic contexts where that category is not grammatical. This is consistent with the fact that (113) is more acceptable, given that the preposition is no longer adjacent to *that*.

(113)   We talked about Mr. Colson and that he had worked at the White House.
       (Sag et al., 1985, 166)

One final account is proposed by Levine and Hukari (2006, 23), whereby the contrasts in (112) are due to the relevant uses of the verbs requiring that their CP complement be ex situ. In other words, when such verbs select a CP complement, the extraction becomes obligatory. Levine and Hukari (2006, 23) base this approach on the fact that certain uses of *assure* appear to require object extraction, as first noted by Kayne (1984, 5) and illustrated in (114).

(114)   a. *I assure you Chris to be the most competent.

      b. ?[Who]$_i$ can you assure me $\_{i}$ to be the most competent?

2.4 Summary

This chapter began with a survey of the various kinds of interrogative, declarative, and subordinate UDCs that exist in English. The resulting picture is one of astonishing richness and complexity. There are three major families of UDCs, which subdivide into smaller families, each with their special syntactic, pragmatic, and phonological similarities, and their idiosyncrasies. Some of these UDCs are optional, in the sense that essentially the same content can be expressed without extraction; others are not. Even within the same family, constructional peculiarities abound. For example, there are at least five types of relative clause. Some express presuppositions, others do not, some can be filler-less, others cannot, some require the complementizer *that*, others do not, and so on. Such idiosyncratic content and structure must be stipulated somewhere in the grammar, regardless of which theory one adopts. In the theory we will explore later in the book, UDC regularities and irregularities can be captured directly, at the level of the phrasal template that captures the relevant subfamily pattern.

Next, we focused on the nature of the linkage between fillers and gaps, and argued that it generally involves a strict form of semantic and morphosyntactic identity, with the exception of case information. Finally, we further showed that UDCs can interweave and create complex dependencies, beyond what is widely accepted in the literature. For example, a given utterance can host multiple overlapping dependencies, crossed or otherwise. Moreover, dependencies can be recursive or chain with each other. In dependencies where multiple gaps are linked to the same filler, gaps can be co-referential (a convergent dependency) or not (a cumulative dependency).

3

Extraction constraints

Since their discovery, island phenomena have generally been claimed to be syntactic in nature (Chomsky, 1973; Huang, 1977; Chomsky, 1986b; Lasnik and Saito, 1992), and have more recently been assumed to ultimately result from computational efficiency constraints that shape the fundamental design of the human language faculty (Chomsky, 1995, 2001, 2005, 2008, 2013). For example, various extraction constraints are claimed to follow from principles like Relativized Minimality (Rizzi, 1990) or the Minimal Link Condition (Chomsky, 1995), which have the effect of imposing limits on the length of each movement step. Another such example is the Phase Impenetrability Condition (Chomsky, 2001), which reduces the computational burden (i.e. memory resource load) via the periodic 'forgetting' of derivational information and in the process limits the distance over which each movement operation can apply. This is in essence a processing account which shifts the explanatory burden to the evolution of the very architecture of language. We therefore dub this the **architectural** view, wherein island-violating UDCs are not constructed by the language processor, presumably because of innate (evolutionary or developmental) universal constraints:

> Let us interpret the Minimal Link Condition (MLC) as requiring that at a given stage in the derivation, a longer link from α to K cannot be formed if there is a shorter legitimate link from β to K . . . It is not that the island violation is deviant; rather, there is no such derivation.'
>
> (Chomsky, 1995, 295)

Fodor (1978, 1983), Berwick and Weinberg (1984), Hawkins (2004), and others argue for a weaker view, in which islands result from the **grammaticalization** of structural patterns, as an adaptation to constraints on learning or parsing. In such a view, island phenomena are emergent with experience rather than due to innate restrictions on the language system. As will become clear, both the architectural and the grammaticalization views are too strong: most islands are not absolute, and even within exactly the same island type the acceptability can sometimes vary wildly across minimally different sentences.

An alternative perspective is one where at least some island phenomena are due to independently motivated pragmatic constraints which cause certain extractions to be infelicitous or incoherent (Erteschik-Shir, 1973, 1977, 1981; Van Valin, 1986; Kuno, 1987; Takami, 1988, 1992; Van Valin, 1994; Goldberg, 2006; Erteschik-Shir, 2007). The existence of some variation in the strength of some island effects can be explained in terms of information-structural biases or degree of contextualization difficulty. As we shall see, most islands (though not all) are consistent with an overarching and independently motivated pragmatic constraint.

Unbounded Dependency Constructions: Theoretical and Experimental Perspectives. Rui P. Chaves and Michael T. Putnam,
Oxford University Press (2020). © Rui P. Chaves and Michael T. Putnam.
DOI: 10.1093/oso/9780198784999.001.0001

For some authors like Deane (1992) and Kluender (1992), island constraints are ultimately due to cognitive and processing constraints, including working memory limitations, memory decay, interference, and/or processing biases; see, for example, Kluender (1992, 1998), Kluender and Kutas (1993b), Hofmeister et al. (2007), and Hofmeister (2011). Sprouse et al. (2012) refer to such accounts as 'reductionist', but the choice of this term is objectionable since any account that explains some phenomena in terms of simpler and more fundamental factors is by definition *reductionist*. More mainstream grammatical theories of islands are in no sense 'holistic', in contrast. Moreover, processing-based advocates have made it clear that grammatical factors (including syntactic, semantic, and pragmatic constraints) are likely to be at play as well; see Kluender (2004, 495), Hofmeister and Sag (2010, 368), Hofmeister, Casasanto, et al. (2013, 49), and Hofmeister et al. (2015).

There has been much controversy surrounding the role of working memory in island effects. In order to determine whether islands could be reduced to the processing costs incurred by length and complexity, Sprouse et al. (2012) and Sprouse et al. (2016) used an experimental design called **super-additivity**, which dissociates the reduction in acceptability induced by the island effect itself from the reduction predicted by the length and complexity of the UDC. Sprouse and colleagues tried to achieve this by crossing the length of the dependency and its complexity to create four conditions, in which case a disproportionate decrease in ratings for the island structure would indicate that the acceptability is influenced by processing length and complexity and also by an additional factor, tied to the island constraint itself. Sprouse et al. (2012) argue that the evidence indicates that there are factors over and above length and complexity, though the nature of such factors could be grammatical or otherwise. But Keshev and Meltzer-Asscher (2019a) more recently provided experimental evidence that the super-additivity phenomenon results from confounding different kinds of processing costs, specifically, interference caused by the simultaneous maintenance of multiple dependencies.

Another problem with Sprouse et al. (2012) concerns how working memory capacity was measured. Sprouse et al. (2012) use n-back and serial recall tasks to argue that individual memory capacity correlates only partially or poorly with island acceptability, but as Hofmeister et al. (2012) point out, there is no reason to believe that n-back and serial recall tasks are strongly correlated to working memory capacity to begin with. More recently Goodall and Michel (2013) found ERP evidence that high-span readers are better able to adjust their gap predictions in certain island environments, though no ERP evidence that online processing cost alone can account for island effects.

In their reply Hofmeister et al. (2012, 396) also note that the literature on experimental island research has not systematically controlled for multiple factors that can impact the processing and comprehension of complex sentences; so if the experimental items are excessively complex, then readers are less likely to give up understanding the utterances and subtler effects will not be measurable. As Schütze (1996, §5.3.3) argues, parsability can influence acceptability. Surprisingly, Phillips (2013b, 402) considers concerns about semantic and pragmatic plausibility to be irrelevant to the debate, and furthermore already to have been refuted by experiments reported in Sprouse (2007b). It is unclear to us which experiments are being alluded to. The only experiment in Sprouse (2007b) that involves discourse felicity is Experiment 1, where examples are 'contextualized', as (1) illustrates.

(1)   You think the speech by the president interrupted the TV show about whales. [Who]$_i$
       do you think the speech by $\_\_\_i$ interrupted the TV show about whales?
       (Sprouse, 2007b, 58)

But this is hardly what linguists would consider contextualization, and says nothing about
the concern raised by Hofmeister et al. (2012, 396) that if most or many items in an
experiment express pragmatically unusual or strange situations, then they are harder to
interpret, less acceptable, and more prone to causing null effects.

   Working memory limitations plausibly play some role in island phenomena, to some
degree, simply because complex sentences generally strain cognitive resources (Wanner
and Maratsos, 1978; Frazier, 1987; Pickering and Barry, 1991; Kluender and Kutas, 1993b,a;
Warren and Gibson, 2002; Sussman and Sedivy, 2003; Chen et al., 2005; Warren and Gibson,
2005). For example, indefinite filler phrases like *what* and *who* hamper the processing and
acceptability of UDCs, as compared with definite filler phrases. Thus, (2a) is somewhat less
acceptable than (2b).[1]

(2)   a. ?[What]$_i$ did you write a paper about the history of $\_\_\_i$?
       b. [Which country]$_i$ did you write a paper about the history of $\_\_\_i$?

There are independently motivated processing reasons for such a contrast. First, indefinite
fillers are plausible with more candidate gap sites simply because they are semantically more
abstract (Kluender and Kutas, 1993b; Van Valin, 1994; Hofmeister et al., 2007; Hofmeister
and Sag, 2010), and therefore there is potentially more processing and less certainty about
the correct filler-gap resolution. For example, in (2a) the word *what* is temporarily a
plausible direct object of *write*, whereas *which country* is not. Second, indefinites have
by definition more abstract semantic content than definites and therefore more rapidly
decay in memory while the rest of the sentence is processed, which makes them harder
to retrieve downstream; see Schwanenflugel (1991), Kounios and Holcomb (1994), Swaab
et al. (2003), among numerous others for various kinds of concreteness effects in language
processing. For example, Hofmeister et al. (2007) show that the underlined phrase that
the cleft modifies in (3a) leads to faster retrieval times at the gap site than its less complex
counterpart in (3b), even though what is extracted is not the underlined NP.

(3)   a. It was an influential communist-leaning dictator$_i$ that Sandy said she liked $\_\_\_i$.
       b. It was a dictator$_i$ that Sandy said she liked $\_\_\_i$.

The major challenge that island phenomena pose to linguistic theory lies in precisely identifying whether a given phenomenon is due to syntax, semantics, pragmatics, processing,
or some combination thereof. Hofmeister, Jaeger, et al. (2013) refer to this problem as
the **source ambiguity problem**: how to identify which grammatical and which processing
factors underlie low acceptability judgments. In our view it is likely that different island
phenomena are due to different combinations of these factors interacting in complex
ways to further complicate the range of permissible UDCs and to make it impossible to
arrive at a simple and general explanation for the phenomena. We refer to theories of

---

[1] See §4.3.2 for a different view of such definiteness phenomena.

island phenomena where different kinds of islands result from different linguistic and/or cognitive factors as **eclectic**. In what follows we discuss the source ambiguity problem in more detail, by underscoring the well-known fact that a myriad of factors can conspire to cause any given sentence (including UDCs) to be difficult to process and low in acceptability.

3.1 The source ambiguity problem

Chomsky and Miller (1963) and Chomsky (1965, 11–15) recognized that speakers do not have direct access to the grammatical system, and can at best only report introspective and subjective percepts about sentence quality. Such sentence acceptability judgments are graded and sometimes shaped by the combination of many different factors, including memory limitations, intonation, and the likelihood of the utterance relative to the situation (Chomsky, 1965, 11, n. 5).

> We may make an intuitive judgment that some linguistic expression is odd or deviant. But we cannot in general know, pretheoretically, whether this deviance is a matter of syntax, semantics, pragmatics, belief, memory limitations, style, etc.
>
> (Chomsky, 1977, 4)

The clearest example of acceptability hypersensitivity to small changes in wording comes from double center-embedding relative-clause sentences like (4). The symbol ' _ ' is omitted so as not to provide any cues to the reader about the gap locations.

(4)   a.   *People people people left left left.
           (Rogers and Pullum, 2011)

      b.   *The rat the cat the dog chased ate died.
           (Chomsky and Miller, 1963)

      c.   The game those boys I met invented resembles chess.
           (Smith, 1989, 56)

      d.   The movie everyone I know raved about was *Inception*.
           (adapted from Jackendoff (1992, 32))

Sentence (4a) is very difficult to understand, but is perfectly grammatical. The verb *leave* can be intransitive (e.g. *People leave*) or transitive (e.g. *People leave people*), and any speaker who has acquired relative clauses has enough information to parse each of the two UDCs. The example in (4b) is less extreme, but still difficult to process. However, (4c) is passable, especially if there is a pause between *invented* and *resembles*, and (4d) is impeccable and easy to process, again provided there is a pause between the matrix subject and its verb phrase. How can these structurally identical sentences differ so much in terms of their processing difficulty and acceptability?[2]

---

[2] Conversely, some ungrammatical center-embedding sentences can at first glance be deemed fairly acceptable. An example of such grammatical illusions is (i), which speakers often find acceptable, at first glance (Frazier, 1985; Gibson and Thomas, 1999). Crucially, however, speakers are generally unable to paraphrase such sentences or

There may be at least two factors at work. First, pronouns are independently known to be easier to process than non-pronominal phrases (Ariel, 2001; Warren and Gibson, 2002, 2005), and so it is not unreasonable to assume that center-embedding constructions become easier to process and more acceptable if the nominals are easier to process (e.g. pronominal), especially if they bear an easily recognizable semantic relationship to the correct verb; cf. Hudson (1996), Kluender (1998), and Gibson (1998). See in particular Frank et al. (2015) for self-paced and modeling evidence that word contingencies can go a long way in explaining cross-linguistic variation in how center-embedding structures are processed.

Second, phonological phrasing plays a crucial role in aiding the processing of relative clauses in general, because it aids gap site identification. In double center-embedded relatives the prosodic phrasing is therefore crucial to successfully process the subsequent parsing of each subordinate clause; see, for example, Quinn et al. (2000), Kitagawa and Fodor (2006), Zahn and Scheepers (2011), and Fodor and Nickels (2011) for experimental evidence. Indeed, prosodic information seems to be crucial in the processing of various other types of complex UDCs. For example, the classic garden-path sentence in (5) at first glance is unintelligible.

(5) The radio that Robin built Sam exploded.

But if a pause is added immediately after *built*, we obtain a parse where *The radio that Robin built* is extracted from the object position. Here, the verb is interpreted transitively, and Sam is the agent:

(6) [The radio$_i$ that Robin built $\_i$]$_j$ Sam exploded $\_j$.

If a pause is instead added immediately after *Sam*, then we obtain a parse where the complex NP *The radio that Robin built Sam* is the subject of the intransitive use of *exploded*:

(7) [The radio$_i$ that Robin built Sam $\_i$] exploded.

In general, gap sites are signaled explicitly in UDCs via a small pause, especially in syntactic environments where no natural prosodic boundary would otherwise exist. For instance, Moore-Cantwell (2013) provides evidence suggesting that speakers 'buy time' during the planning of upcoming low-probability syntactic structures by producing prosodic boundaries with longer duration before low-probability than before high-probability structures, in particular at the gap sites of UDC. We suspect that most, if not all island effects can be severely exacerbated if the correct prosodic structure is not employed, and that local syntactic ambiguities can interfere with the processing of complex UDCs and create low acceptability due to misparsing.

Island phenomena resulting from such factors should similarly range from low to high acceptability, and be very sensitive to the particular words in the structure and their phonological phrasing. One such example is the **Clause Non-Final Incomplete Constituent Constraint** (CNFICC; Kuno, 1973, 130), which prohibits extraction out of phrases in a clause non-final position, as in (8).

---

provide a context in which they would be felicitous, simply because such sentences are missing a verb and are therefore incoherent. See Schütze (1996, 31) and Phillips et al. (2011) for more discussion.

i. ?*The patient the nurse the clinic had hired met Jack.

(8)   a. *[Who]$_i$ did you give to __$_i$ the canary that I brought home yesterday?
      b. *[Who]$_i$ did you offer to __$_i$ the chance to win $1,000?

But as Jackendoff and Culicover (1972), Hukari and Levine (1991), Fodor (1992), and many others note, it is easy to construct counterexamples to the CNFICC. For instance, Haegeman et al. (2013) provide several attested cases like those in (9).

(9)   a. [Who]$_i$ can I talk to __$_i$ about my depression?
      b. [What]$_i$ do astronauts like to take pictures of __$_i$ from space?

The CNFICC is most likely due to misparsing of the sentence, because of the local ambiguity of how the sentence-medial preposition is integrated into the neighboring structures. In other words, CNFICC effects may result from a highly frequent and locally licit (but globally illicit) syntactic resolution where the preposition is not stranded, preempting a far less frequent syntactic resolution where the preposition is stranded sentence-medially. Thus, small differences in wording and the absence of the ideal phonological phrasing cues can make it difficult for comprehenders to opt for the correct parse. It is also known that the more committed the parser becomes to a particular syntactic parse, the harder it is for it to reanalyze the string (Ferreira and Henderson, 1991, 1993; Tabor and Hutchins, 2004), a phenomenon known as **digging-in**. Consequently, it may be particularly difficult to recover the correct parse of (8) because the final clause is longer, enabling the parser to become more committed to a filler-gap linkage that is locally licit but globally illicit.

Another example of a UDC constraint that is similarly brittle and sensitive to the particular wording is that the recipient argument of the ditransitive seems to resist extraction (Erteschik-Shir, 1979):

(10)   a. ??[Who]$_i$ did Sam give __$_i$ the book?
       b. ??The person [who]$_i$ Sam gave __$_i$ the book is me.

But by making the theme more complex and heavy, the recipient can become somewhat more readily extractable, as in (11a). The presence of a long theme phrase is important because it motivates the use of the double object ditransitive (Wasow, 2002). In (11b) we see an extraction from the recipient of the ditransitive, suggesting that the recipient is not a syntactic island.

(11)   a. [Who]$_i$ did he give __$_i$ credit for the success of the program?
          (adapted from Goldberg 2013)

       b. [Which company]$_i$ did they give the CEO of __$_i$ a hard time?
          (Thomas Wasow, pers. comm.)

Goldberg (2006, 137–42) argues that recipients are difficult to extract because they are by default secondary topics, and therefore unlikely foci. If a referent is part of the presupposed content, then it cannot be regarded as the focus.

Let us consider one more example of how ephemeral island effects can be. According to Lasnik and Saito's (1992) account, it is not possible for co-arguments to be extracted, as in (12). The constraint that bars such UDCs is deemed to be a fundamental and universal architectural constraint, in the *Barriers* framework of Chomsky (1986a).

(12) a. * [What]$_i$ [who]$_j$ _$_j$ saw _$_i$?
(Lasnik and Saito, 1992, 14)

     b. * [Who]$_i$ [what]$_j$ _$_i$ saw _$_j$.
(Lasnik and Saito, 1992, 17)

     c. *I wonder [who]$_i$ [this book]$_j$ _$_i$ likes _$_j$.
(Lasnik and Saito, 1992, 96)

But such UDCs are very sensitive to the particular wording of the sentence. For example, Pollard and Sag (1994) provide a (slightly) better example, shown in (13).

(13) ?[THESE RARE OLD BOOKS]$_i$, I wonder [who]$_j$ John thinks [_$_j$ stole _$_i$].
(Pollard and Sag, 1994, 382, n .42)

We can make this type of extraction much more acceptable by constructing a sentence that overall describes a more plausible situation and does not involve a one-word intonational phrase. Compare with (14), repeated from §2.2.1.1.

(14) [Context: a wife reacts to her husband hinting that some flowers she got from a friend may be from a lover]
These are the flowers$_j$ that I'd like to know [who]$_i$ you think _$_i$ bought _$_j$ for me.

There is no syntactic ban against extracting co-arguments. Rather, any oddness most likely comes from semantic, pragmatic, and/or prosodic reasons. It is somewhat unusual for a sentence to be composed of a single verb, both prosodically and syntactically, but if the embedded clause is heavier, the problem is reduced. Constructing acceptable complex UDCs is sometimes akin to a tightrope act, as many factors can hamper the processing and interpretation of a sentence.

    Other constraints on extraction are absolute, such as the impossibility of preposition stranding in the vast majority of the world's languages that have prepositions. According to Emonds and Faarlund (2014, 84–96), preposition stranding is limited to Scandinavian and North Germanic languages (including Danish, Dutch, English, Frisian, Norwegian, and Swedish), Berber, Hungarian, and the Mesoamerican language Zoque. Thus, whereas the English counterpart of (15) is acceptable, its counterpart is illicit in all Romance languages, for example. If extracted, the NP must be pied-piped along with the preposition.

(15) a. *[Que cidade]$_i$ é que a Ana foi para _$_i$?
      which city is that the Ana went to
      'Which city did Ana go to?'

     b. [Para que cidade]$_i$ é que a Ana foi _$_i$?
      to which city is that the Ana went
      'To which city did Ana go?'   (European Portuguese)

Prepositions seem to be leaners in many languages, in the terminology of Zwicky (1986), requiring them to prosodify with the NP they select. Perhaps preposition stranding is not possible in most languages because of phonological constraints that lead to grammaticalization. Such a hypothesis is consistent with the fact that not all English prepositions are equally likely to be stranded (Gries, 2002).

Other constraints on extraction are almost certainly due to syntactic constraints. Consider, for example, Slavic languages, which prevent extraction from indicative clauses, as (16a) illustrates. Extraction from such constructions is marginal for many speakers and becomes much worse with more contentful verbs like *deny* or *assume*. See Bailyn (1992), Fodor (1992, 109–80) and Stepanov and Georgopoulos (1995) for more discussion.

(16) a. *[Kavo]$_i$ gavorit Ivan [chto Marija   ljubit __$_i$]?
          who-ACC says   Ivan that   Mary-NOM loves
          'Who does Ivan say that Mary loves?'   (Russian)

    b. *[Kogo]$_i$ myślisz   [że Janek widziałł __$_i$]?
          who   (you) think that John   saw
          'Who do you think that John saw?'   (Polish)

No such constraint is in effect when extracting from Russian subjunctive clauses, or if the complementizer *chto* is omitted. It is rather unclear why the constraint illustrated in (16) exists in the first place, but it seems to be a stipulation that some Slavic languages impose on UDCs.

Other constraints on extraction are more likely to be due to independently motivated pragmatic factors. For example, any theory of grammar must incorporate the basic fact that interrogatives presuppose that the filler phrase describes a unique referent that makes the open proposition true. This can sometimes lead to pragmatically implausible interrogative UDCs. For example, (17a) is illicit because it presupposes that the hearer was born in all states but one. No such problem occurs in (17b) because it is possible for someone to be interested in all states except one. The difference between the two UDCs is, of course, that *born* is a 'one-time' predicate (i.e. a property that can be true of at most one object), but *interest* is not (Szabolcsi and Zwarts, 1993).

(17) a. *[Which state]$_i$ weren't you born in __?

    b. [Which state]$_i$ weren't you interested in __?

It is clear that the oddness of (17a) has little to do with syntax or with processing difficulty. Rather, such UDCs are odd simply because the propositions that they convey are infelicitous, and any theory that captures uniqueness presuppositions and interrogative semantics will predict the oddness of (17a), regardless of the choice of syntactic framework. Another example of illicit extractions caused by independently motivated pragmatic constraints is (18). The extracted phrase is required to bear a Topic relation to the open proposition, but *a necklace* is discourse-new, and therefore not licit.

(18) A: Good morning, how may I help you today?
    B: *[A NECKLACE]$_i$ I would like to buy __$_i$.

Given that UDCs impose particular pragmatic constraints on the extracted phrase, it follows that semantically vacuous (expletive) pronouns cannot be extracted, as (19) illustrates. Again, such a constraint is completely independent from the syntactic theory of choice. No syntactic stipulations are necessary to explain such phenomena.

(19) a. *It was [it] that I found _ odd that Roger tricked Hayley.
        (cf. *I found it odd that Roger tricked Hayley*)

     b. *It was [THERE] that I thought _ wouldn't be a Christmas bonus.
        (cf. *I thought there wouldn't be a Christmas bonus*)

Another island phenomenon that strikes us as possibly semantic in nature is the so-called **Crossover** effect (Postal, 1971), which hampers extraction over a co-referential element, as in (20).

(20) a. *[Who]$_i$ did he$_i$ think that we liked _$_i$?
     b. ?[Who]$_i$ did his$_i$ mother think that we liked _$_i$?

However, note that the filler phrase must be Focal in an information request (by definition, new information), which entails that it cannot be co-indexed with a discourse-old (known) referent in that information request. We suspect that the pragmatic role of the filler phrase must in general not be inconsistent with that of any referent co-indexed with it, in the same utterance. Crossover effects weaken when the referent is a possessor, as in (20b), perhaps because such pronouns are not as biased to be interpreted as discourse-old, and vanish in (21) because the possessive pronoun in the accented noun phrase is interpreted as discourse-new. Be that as it may, a purely syntactic account is unlikely, in light of these contrasts.

(21) a. There's a lawyer in this firm [who]$_i$ even his$_i$ CLIENTS despise _$_i$.
     b. Heck, there's a lawyer in this firm [who]$_i$ even HE$_i$ despises _$_i$!

Given the range of factors that can cause low acceptability of sentences in general, the problem surrounding diagnosing island phenomena is clear: how to determine whether a given extraction constraint is due to syntax, semantics, pragmatics, processing, or some combination thereof? In what follows we attempt to shed some light on this question.

3.2 Island phenomena

In what follows we survey various island effects and their exceptions. Drawing from a wide range of previous work by numerous authors, we argue that the evidence is strongly suggestive of an eclectic account wherein different islands are due to different combinations of factors:

- **Grammatical factors**

  - CONTEXTUALIZATION DIFFICULTY
    General Gricean constraints require all utterances to be felicitous discourse moves in the given context, but the more implausible the required context, the less acceptable the proposition is, regardless of whether it is a UDC or not. Thus, if the proposition that a UDC describes requires very

specific and unusual contexts, it is deemed pragmatically odd; see Kroch (1998), Ginzburg and Sag (2000, 248), Hofmeister, Jaeger, et al. (2013), and Abrusán (2014). As discussed in Chapter 2, UDCs impose specific pragmatic constraints, different from those imposed by their non-extraction counterparts. Subjective prior probabilities assigned to events affect sentence interpretation.

- RELEVANCE PRESUPPOSITION VIOLATION
  The extracted referent of a UDC must be relevant for the main action that the proposition conveys (Kuno, 1976; Erteschik-Shir and Lappin, 1979; Reinhart, 1981; Kuno, 1987; Deane, 1991). UDCs involve a non-canonical and marked structure in which the speaker draws attention to a particular event participant x, but if this participant plays no role in the main event that the sentence is about, and instead plays a role in content that is not at issue, then the extraction of x violates Grice's (1975) Maxims of Quantity ('Be brief') and Manner ('Avoid Prolixity'): the hearer's attention is being directed to a referent that has no significant bearing on the goal of the utterance (Van Valin, 2005, 288). As Tonhauser et al. (2018) show experimentally, the notion of at-issueness is gradient, and dependent on a number of factors, including the prior probability of the event described by the expression that conveys the content. Thus, speakers are more committed to content conveyed by expressions that describe more a priori likely events.

- SEMANTIC-PRAGMATIC CONFLICTS
  Sometimes the particular UDC type and the semantics of the extracted phrase itself impose conflicting semantic and pragmatic constraints (Kroch, 1998; Abrusán, 2011; Goldberg, 2006; Oshima, 2007; Abrusán, 2014). Such islands are only active in the types of UDC that can give rise to such pragmatic conflicts, and therefore are not cross-constructionally active.

- PHONOLOGY-SYNTAX CONFLICTS
  Phonological phrasing is sensitive to units of meaning (Selkirk, 1984), and has been experimentally demonstrated to be crucial for disambiguating sentence processing (Price et al., 1991; Watson and Gibson, 2004). If the correct intonation is not adopted for a given parse, then it will be harder to arrive at the correct interpretation of an utterance (Fodor, 2002a,b). As discussed, pauses are crucial for the cuing of gap sites, and failing to produce an ideal prosodic phrasing can severely hamper comprehension.

- SYNTAX
  Some expressions are impossible to extract because of their grammatical function. In other words, they are invisible to the mechanism that constructs filler-gap dependencies. The acceptability of such UDCs is without exception systematically low, as it is immune to frequency or contextualization effects. The *Conjunct Constraint* (§3.2.5), and the *Left Branch Constraint* (§3.2.12) are in this class, since their unacceptability is robust (e.g. exceptionless, and impervious to contextualization or frequency effects); see Sag et al. (2009) and Hofmeister and Sag (2010, 368).

- **Processing factors**

  - VIOLATED EXPECTATIONS

    In general, more cognitive effort is required to process input that is less
    expected (Hale, 2001; Levy, 2008; Demberg and Keller, 2008; Roark et al., 2009;
    Smith and Levy, 2008), so that the more likely the sentence, the more acceptable
    it tends to be (Keller, 2003; Lau et al., 2015). Thus, very unusual UDCs are at a
    disadvantage, especially if they involve local syntactic or semantic ambiguities
    that mislead processing and cause digging-in effects; see Boston (2012) and
    Dąbrowska (2008) for relevant experiments, and in particular see Michel (2014,
    ch. 7) for ERP evidence showing the importance of real-time prediction for the
    online processing of islands. This is consistent with the fact that certain island
    effects can sometimes weaken, provided that comprehenders are exposed to
    enough exemplars (Snyder, 2000, 2017, forthcoming; Francom, 2009; Hira-
    matsu, 2000; Clausen, 2011; Chaves and Dery, 2014, 2019; Hofmeister, 2015;
    Goodall, 2011).

  - WORKING MEMORY LIMITATIONS

    The processing of UDCs is known to strain cognitive processing resources
    (Wanner and Maratsos, 1978; Frazier, 1987; Pickering and Barry, 1991; Klu-
    ender and Kutas, 1993b,a; Warren and Gibson, 2002; Sussman and Sedivy,
    2003; Chen et al., 2005; Warren and Gibson, 2005; Kind and Kutas, 1995;
    Müeller et al., 1997; Fiebach et al., 2002; Phillips et al., 2005; Fadlon et al.,
    2019). Comprehenders must maintain a filler phrase in working memory while
    all other material between the filler and the gap is processed, and the more
    material that appears in the domain of a UDC, the more difficult it is to
    retrieve the filler phrase, integrate it into the proposition, and interpret the
    entire utterance. As Michel (2014) shows, high-span readers are better able to
    adjust their predictions for a gap online than low-span readers, though there
    is no evidence of a large online processing cost that would by itself account for
    island effects.

Grammatical factors affect sentence acceptability more robustly than performance factors;
a garden-path effect can often be reduced with a judicious prosodic phrasing, but a
semantic or pragmatic contradiction is not so easily countered, especially in the presence of
other sources of difficulty. As we will see below, different island types are interconnected in
complex ways, not only structurally, semantically, and pragmatically, but also historically.

3.2.1 NP Constraint

Chomsky (1964) noted the first and one of the weakest island effects in the literature,
illustrated in (22). Following Horn (1972), we refer to this as the **NP Constraint**, as
it pertains to the reduced acceptability caused by extraction of an NP from an object
NP, sometimes also referred to as **subextraction**. Square brackets are used below and
throughout this chapter to indicate the island environment more explicitly.

(22)   a.   *[Who]$_i$ did you lose [a book about __$_i$]?
          (cf. *You lost a book about who?*)

       b.   *[What]$_i$ did you open [a book about __$_i$]?
          (cf. *You opened a book about what?*)

       c.   *[What]$_i$ did you discard [a book about __$_i$]?
          (cf. *You discarded a book about what?*)

Since these interrogatives are less acceptable than their extracted counterparts, it must be the extraction that causes oddness; see §2.1.1 for more on in situ English questions, and §3.4.3 for the lack of in situ island effects.[3]

Chomsky (1964) and Ross (1967) were quick to point out that the NP Constraint is rather weak, and prone to counterexamples. For example, the NP Constraint violations in (23) are more acceptable than those in (22). See Sprouse (2007b, 63–8) for experimental confirmation that NP Constraint violations are highly variable.

(23)   a.   [What]$_i$ did you read [a book about __$_i$]?
       b.   [Who]$_i$ did you buy [a book about __$_i$]?
       c.   [Who]$_i$ did you forget [the name of __$_i$]?
       d.   [What]$_i$ is John not telling [the truth about __$_i$]?

Syntactic accounts like Chomsky (1964), Bach and Horn (1976), and Bosque and Gallego (2014) contended that any counterexamples to the NP Constraint were illusions: whenever extraction is licit, the PP is not actually inside the preceding NP, and therefore no actual NP Constraint violation exists. This is illustrated in Figure 3.1.

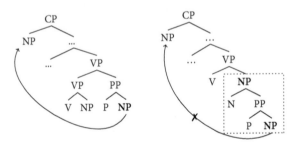

Figure 3.1 An account of (apparent) NP Constraint violations

But this analysis creates more problems than it solves (Godard, 1992, 1988; Davies and Dubinsky, 2003). For example, given that (24a) is acceptable, it would follow that the NP does not combine with the PP. If that were true, it would follow that the former should be pronominalizable. This is contrary to fact, as the oddness of (24b) shows.

(24)   a.   [What]$_i$ did you read [a book about __$_i$]?
       b.   *Did you read it about chemistry?

---

[3] There are UDCs which are odd simply because the underlying utterance is bad to begin with. For example, (i) is odd, but so its unextracted counterpart. Compare with the more acceptable datum in (ii). We try to avoid this kind of confound in the present volume.

i. *[Which topic]$_i$ do you like a book about __$_i$?
   (cf. ??*Do you like a book about* THIS *topic?*)

ii. [Which topic]$_i$ would you like a book about __$_i$?
    (cf. *Would you like a book about* THIS *topic?*)

Such an account also sheds no light on the fact that different verbs lead to weaker or stronger subextraction violations, as illustrated by the contrast between (22) and (23). In these examples, the NP and the PP are held constant.

Davies and Dubinsky (2003) argue that for subextraction to be licit the complement nominal must denote an abstract concept rather than a concrete object. Thus, subextraction out of representational NPs like 'picture' and 'book' is only licit if these nominals are interpreted in the informational sense, not the physical object sense. This is incorrect, as it predicts that (25) is illicit. In these examples the verb clearly requires a physical object sense.

(25) a. [Which politician]$_i$ did you burn [the picture of __$_i$] on national TV?

      b. [What]$_i$ did you say you found [a cool book about __$_i$] in the attic?

Other accounts are more semantic in nature. Bolinger (1972), Cattell (1979), and Kuno (1987) argued that subextraction requires that the head noun of the object phrase denotes an attribute of the extracted PP-embedded nominal. Thus, *Who have you forgotten the name of?* is acceptable because 'name' is an attribute of 'person'. But this attribute constraint is too strong. For example, there is no sense in which 'book' is an attribute of its content in (24a). Indeed, Chaves and King (2020) note many attested counterexamples like (26), which show that a much wider range of semantic relations is allowed in subextraction.[4]

(26) a. ... extended the Internet tax moratorium, which I was [a fan of __].
         [COCA SPOK 2010]

      b. ... it also helps me practice my patience, which I don't have [a lot of __].
          [COCA SPOK 1997]

      c. ... possibility of contaminated oxygen being in the plane. What would that have been [the result of __]?
          [COCA SPOK 1997]

      d. ... Cuomo is a leading rival because of who he is [the son of __].
          [COCA SPOK 2018]

Deeper NP Constraint violations, in which the extracted NP is doubly embedded, appear to be more robust, as (27) illustrates, but a closer look reveals a far more complicated empirical state of affairs.

(27) a. *Who did you hear [stories about [pictures of __]]?
         (Chomsky, 1973)

      b. *Who did you write [articles about [pictures of __]]?
         (Bach and Horn, 1976, 274)

      c. *??Who did you take [a photograph of [a statue of __]]?
         (Fodor, 1983, 190)

      d. *Who did you see [enemies of [friends of __]]?
         (Bošković, 2017)

---

[4] These data also show that NP Constraint violations extend well beyond representational NPs contrary to what is often assumed; see Davies and Dubinsky (2003).

As noted as early as Ross (1967) and Chomsky (1973), there are licit UDCs like (28), where subextraction crosses two NP nodes.

(28)   a.   [Who]$_i$ did you write [a book about [the impeachment of $_{\_i}$]]?

   b.   [Which recent president]$_i$ did the House of Representatives lack [enough votes for [the impeachment of $_{\_i}$]]?

   c.   [Which newspaper]$_i$ did you say that the editor exercises [strict control over [the publication of $_{\_i}$]]?

   d.   [Which committee]$_i$ were you offered [an appointment to [the chairmanship of $_{\_i}$]]?
       (Deane, 1992)

To be sure, such deep subextractions are extremely rare in real language usage, but not unattested:

(29)   [Which segment]$_i$ do you think it is [time for [another edition of $_{\_i}$]]?
       [*The Tonight Show Starring Jimmy Fallon*; 2014]

Chomsky (1986a) offers a partial account of these facts that is essentially a semantic one: subextraction is allowed if the extracted nominal is a semantic argument of the head NP.[5] Chomsky's formulation was meant to prevent extractions from adjunct PPs like (30), among others.

(30)   a.   *[Which title]$_i$ did you read a book with $_{\_i}$?
           (cf. *You read a book with* ↑WHICH TITLE↓?)

   b.   *[Which book]$_i$ do you have a photo inside $_{\_i}$?
           (cf. *You have a photo inside* ↑WHICH BOOK↓?)

Although it is not by any means easy to find good counterexamples where the PP is an adjunct, it is not impossible. Observe the contrast between (30) and the relative acceptability of (31), informally validated by native speakers.

(31)   a.   [Which options]$_i$ are you looking for [a car with $_{\_i}$]?

   b.   [Which dog]$_i$ did Greg throw [the toys of $_{\_i}$] in the garbage?

   c.   [Which author]$_i$ did you write about [a book by $_{\_i}$]?

In our estimation, one of the best characterizations of the phenomena comes from Kuno (1987, 23), which proposes that all UDCs are subject to a general constraint requiring that the open proposition must be in some sense *about* the extracted phrase; see Kuno (1976), Reinhart (1981), Krifka (1992), and Jacobs (2001) for further discussion. To illustrate Kuno's **aboutness** constraint at work, consider the contrast in (32).

---

[5] The constraint is expressed as **L-marking**: a category is L-marked *iff* it is θ-marked by a lexical head. This is in turn ultimately defined in purely syntactic terms as agreement and c-command (a node X c-commands node Y if a sister of X dominates Y).

(32)   a.   [Who]$_i$ did you write a book about __$_i$?
       b.   *[Who]$_i$ did you lose a book about __$_i$?

The acceptability difference between (32a) and (32b) is due to the fact that the content of a book is more important for the (volitional) act of writing a book than for the (non-volitional) act of losing a book, all else being equal. Readers attend to a text in order to access its information, and therefore the content of the text is crucial for the action of reading. In contrast, the properties of what is lost have no relevance for the action of losing something. Kuno (1987, 121) notes that even non-extracted examples like (33) already exhibit an acceptability contrast precisely when the extracted nominal is irrelevant for the situation type described by the main predication.

(33)   a.   Speaking of Napoleon, I just read a book about him.
       b.   ?Speaking of Napoleon, I just lost a book about him.
       c.   Speaking of fur, Sam was looking for a dog with SHORT FUR.
       d.   ?Speaking of fur, Sam was running from a dog with SHORT FUR.

Kuno's notion of 'pragmatic aboutness' is akin to the notion of **dominance** proposed by Erteschik-Shir and Lappin (1979, 672), defined as the content that the speaker intends to direct the attention of the hearer to in the utterance. Only extractions from dominant content are felicitous. This kind of approach has surfaced multiple times. Takami (1988) makes a similar characterization in terms of what is more **important** (i.e. new, or not predictable), and Na and Huck (1992) in terms of **primacy** of a clause (a clause is primary/important if it can be omitted without seriously distorting the message expressed, and otherwise secondary). Deane (1991) offers a similar proposal in terms of **salience**. More recently, Goldberg (2006, 135) articulates a related account in terms of **background**, whereby extractability is hampered from phrases that are backgrounded (i.e. neither Topical nor in the Focus domain). In our view, all of these accounts are perhaps best recast in terms of the independently motivated discourse pragmatic notion of **relevance** from Lambrecht (1994):

> A referent is contextually relevant to the degree that it can be taken to be a center of current interest with respect to which a proposition is interpreted as constituting relevant information.
>
> (Lambrecht, 1994, 53)

From this definition it follows that if a referent x is of little relevance for the state of affairs that the sentence conveys, then it is not pragmatically licit to draw attention to x by extracting it via a marked and specialized construction. As Van Valin (2005, 288) points out, such a discourse move constitutes a Gricean violation: the hearer's attention is being directed to a referent that has no significant bearing on the goal of the utterance. In other words, such extractions are pragmatically anomalous because of a conflict: the extracted referent x is taken as being discourse-prominent (in that it is singled out for extraction) but at the same time x does not participate in the main action that the utterance describes.

This kind of account explains Kuno's observation that contextualization can sometimes improve such extractions. Consider (34a,b), which are odd out of the blue, but appropriate in the context of a book-burning rally and of a book-illustration meeting, respectively.

(34)   a. ?[Who]$_i$ did you burn a book about __$_i$?

   b. ?[Who]$_i$ did you illustrate a book about __$_i$?

According to Deane (1992) what determines whether a referent is relevant or not to the main action conveyed by the proposition is whether the extracted referent is a participant of the background **frame** that is evoked by the main predication. Essentially the same conclusion is reached by Lambrecht and Michaelis (1998), who argue that an expression is relevant for the utterance if it is a predictable argument (broadly construed) of its main predication. For experimental evidence that the more relevant the NP-embedded referent is, the easier it is to extract, see Chaves and King (2020), discussed in more detail and expanded upon in Chapter 6.

3.2.2 Specified Subject Constraint

Chomsky (1973, 239) claimed that examples like (35) exhibit a 'three-way gradation of acceptability', which came to be referred to as the **Specified Subject Constraint** (Chomsky, 1973; Bach and Horn, 1976; Fiengo and Higginbotham, 1981). The judgments in (35) are consistent with a acceptability experiment reported in Cowart (1997, 15–18).

(35)   a. [Which actor]$_i$ did you take [a picture of __$_i$]?

   b. ?[Which actor]$_i$ did you take [the picture of __$_i$]?

   c. *[Which actor]$_i$ did you take [that picture of __$_i$]?

   d. *[Which actor]$_i$ did you take [Bob's picture of __$_i$]?

The graded acceptability is supposedly linked to the definiteness of the NP from which extraction takes place. But this is not likely, as there are many attested counterexamples, such as those in (36).

(36)   a. That's another question$_i$ that we don't really have [the answer to __$_i$].
        [COCA SPOK 2011]

   b. ... and then ask her [which one]$_i$ she likes the sound of __$_i$?
        [COCA FIC 2011]

   c. Just in case there turned out to be somebody$_i$ you couldn't stand [the sight of __$_i$]?
        [COCA FIC 2008]

   d. ... surrounded at the borders of the screen by the tool icons of a creative photo-retouching program$_i$ that Gurney was just starting to get [the hang of __$_i$].
        [COCA FIC 2010]

   e. ... possibility of contaminated oxygen being in the plane. [What]$_i$ would that have been [the result of __$_i$]?
        [COCA SPOK 1997]

   f. ... Cuomo is a leading rival because of [who]$_i$ he is [the son of __$_i$].
        [COCA SPOK 2018]

g. ...and thought that I might find a ribbon appropriate for the violence$_i$ that abortion providers, clinics, and patients have been [the target of __$_i$].
[COCA MAG 2000]

The (mild) oddness of (35b) may be simply due to difficulty in establishing a context where the definite reference *the picture* is appropriate. This would have to be a context where the entity depicted by the picture is not known to the speaker (because it is the focus of the question), but the reference of the picture is (precisely because it is described with the definite determiner). It is not easy to have a specific photo of person *x* without knowing the value of *x* (Culicover and Jackendoff, 1999, 336). In other words, (35b) may be odd simply because it expresses a pragmatically strange proposition, and therefore is difficult to contextualize. If the proposition describes a situation where the definite reference is more plausible, then the acceptability improves:

(37) a. [Which ex-boyfriend]$_i$ did you rip [the/your pictures of __$_i$]?

b. [Which ex-boyfriend]$_i$ did you rip [your sister's picture of __$_i$]?

We suspect the unacceptability of (35c) is because the determiner *that* is deictic. This forces the nominal to have a specific and given reference, which in the case of (35c) clashes with the fact that interrogatives require the reference of the interrogative pronoun to be new rather than given, in order to establish an alternative set of answers (one of which is the true answer). If the referent of the picture is already known to the speakers, then how can the depicted entity not be known? These two semantic-pragmatic constraints can't be satisfied simultaneously.[6] Compare with the counterexample in (38), which requires a context where a particular (famous) baseball game is salient in the common ground, but one of the involved teams is not. This means that the Specified Subject Condition is not cross-constructionally active, since it is restricted to certain UDC types.

(38) [Context: hearer is a big fan of the Phillies]
[Who]$_i$ were the Phillies hoping for that victory over __$_i$?

As it would be expected, no oddness arises in non-interrogative counterparts of (35c) like (39) either. This is simply because there is no clash between given and new referents in relative UDCs.

(39) The person who$_i$ you took [a/the/this/that picture of __$_i$] passed away.
(adapted from Grosu (1973, 89))

Clearly, definiteness does not block extraction. If definite NPs were truly a syntactic barrier for UDCs, then universally quantified NPs like (40) should be illicit, since such determiners have definite (universal) reference.

(40) [Which school]$_i$ does Dana say she hates [every inch of __$_i$]?

---

[6] Note also that the in situ counterpart *You took that picture of* WHO? is similarly illicit, which suggests that the oddness has to do with the semantics and pragmatics of the interrogatives rather than anything to do with extraction; see §3.4.3 for more discussion.

Further evidence against syntactic accounts was noted by Bolinger (1972), Pustejovsky (1985, 48), Kuno (1987, 13), and Grosu (1973, 89), who pointed out licit extractions like (41), which are direct counterexamples to (35d). See Yoshida (2003) for more discussion.

(41)   a.   [Which theorem]$_i$ did you read [Kripke's proof of __$_i$]?
       b.   [Whose book]$_i$ did you read [Bill's comments on __$_i$]?
       c.   [Which solo]$_i$ did you like [Mary's rendition of __$_i$]?

Tollan and Heller (2016) show that the acceptability of subextractions from definite NPs is quite high, and that comprehenders actively postulate gaps inside definite complement NPs. Dillon and Hornstein (2013) provide sentence-acceptability evidence showing that subextraction from definite NPs is less acceptable than semantically equivalent controls, but the overall acceptability of the former is still quite high. Note that Dillon and Hornstein (2013) did not control for the plausibility of the expressed propositions, and therefore it is not clear how robust their findings are.

Given all the available empirical facts, we consider that the Specified Subject Constraint results from low pragmatic plausibility of the expressed proposition and from contextualization difficulty.

3.2.3   Complex NP Constraint

The **Complex NP Constraint** (CNPC; Ross, 1967) prevents extraction from NP-embedded complement clauses like those in (42) and from NP-embedded relatives like (43). We refer to the former as NP-complement CNPC instances and to the latter as NP-relative CNPC instances.

(42)   a.   *[Who]$_i$ did John believe [the claim that Mary saw __$_i$]?
            (cf. *John believed the claim that Mary saw Robin?*)
       b.   *It is THAT KID [who]$_i$ John believes [the claim that Mary saw __$_i$].
            (cf. *John believes the claim that Mary saw that kid*)

(43)   a.   *[Which kid]$_i$ should we report [the teacher who punished __$_i$]?
            (cf. *We should report the teacher who punished ↑WHICH KID↓, then?*)
       b.   *It is THE CELLO$_i$ that I know [a girl who plays __$_i$].
            (cf. *I know a girl who plays THE CELLO*)

The attested in situ example (44a) from Ginzburg and Sag (2000) is acceptable, contrasting sharply with the oddness of its UDC counterpart in (44b), which in turn suggests that the CNPC effect is due to the extraction itself.

(44)   a.   [Context: Talk show host Michael Krasny addresses a guest who has not said anything yet, about the interim chief of the US Attorney's office]
            This is a position that is HOW IMPORTANT in your judgment, Rory?
            [Forum KQED—July 29, 1998]
       b.   *[How important]$_i$ is this a position that is __$_i$ in your judgment, Rory?

But counterexamples to the CNPC have long been noticed (Erteschik-Shir and Lappin, 1979; Kuno, 1987; Deane, 1991; Kluender, 1998; Culicover, 1999). Let us first focus on NP-complement CNPC cases such as (45). The acceptability seems to be aided by the presence of indefinite expressions, not only in terms of the nominal phrases, but also of the verbal phrases. Main verbs such as *hear* and *know* are almost devoid of semantics, and therefore make it more likely for the main action to be conveyed by the subordinate clause:

(45)   a. [Which kid]$_i$ did you hear [a rumor that my dog bit __$_i$]?

      b. [Which terrorist]$_i$ did you hear [rumors [that the CIA assassinated __$_i$]]?

Thus, even though the NPs heading the complement phrases in (46) are definite, the matrix verbs in the expressions *spread the rumor, make the claim, get the impression* are almost devoid of meaning, and form very frequent collocations with the immediately following nominal.

(46)   a. [Which company]$_i$ did John spread [the rumor [that he had started __$_i$]]?

      b. [Who]$_i$ did you make [the claim [that he had been looking at __$_i$]]?

      c. [What]$_i$ did you get [the impression [that the problem really was __$_i$]]?

NP-relative CNPC counterexamples also exist, like (47). Again, the intervening nominal is indefinite, the main verbs *say* and *know* are almost devoid of semantics, and the embedded clause has a generic rather than a specific interpretation.

(47)   [Which instrument]$_i$ did you say you know [someone who plays __$_i$]?

Extractions seem to be possible to the extent that the action expressed by the main clause is itself presupposed, so that the relative clause can more easily be deemed as at-issue to the interlocutors. An example is given in (48), inspired by Kluender (1998).

(48)   A: We need to hire a guide who can understand some of the local languages. Otherwise, we risk not being able to resupply before reaching the expedition site.

      B: Ok. And [which languages exactly]$_i$ do we need to hire someone who can understand __$_i$?

The strongest counterexamples to the CNPC come from presentational relatives, as in (49). See Kush et al. (2013) for experimental confirmation of their acceptability. Recall from §2.1.3 that these relatives are special in that they convey assertions rather than presuppositions. Thus, (49) is paraphrasable as *There are people who like this kind of weather.*

(49)   a. This is the kind of weather$_i$ that there are [many people who like __$_i$].
        (Erteschik-Shir and Lappin, 1979)

      b. Violence is something$_i$ that there are [many Americans who condone __$_i$].
        (McCawley, 1981, 108)

      c. There were several old rock songs$_i$ that she and I were [the only two who knew __$_i$].
        (Chung and McCloskey, 1983)

  d. John is the sort of guy_i that I don't know [a lot of people who think well of __i]. (Culicover, 1999, 230)

  e. [Which diamond ring]_i did you say there was [nobody in the world who could buy __i]? (Pollard and Sag, 1994, 206)

The existence of all the aforementioned CNPC violations is exactly as expected in Kuno's (1987) account, as Van Valin (1998) and Goldberg (2006, ch. 7, 2013) note. It is possible to extract from a relative clause to the extent that the relative clause expresses the main action in the utterance. Extraction from a standard restrictive relative clause is difficult (though not impossible) because the information expressed by the relative clause is usually presupposed and therefore a referent embedded in a standard relative cannot be deemed to be what the assertion is about, and extracted. But since presentational relatives express the asserted content, it is much easier to extract from them.

It was Erteschik-Shir (1977, ch. 2) who first noted that in CNPC exceptions the matrix predicate is in general less informative than the embedded clause. For example, if the matrix predicate is an existential 'there is' with an indefinite object, or 'I know', 'I said', or 'I have', then it is easier to construe the embedded clause as conveying the main action. These factors are supposed to be particularly robust in Swedish, Danish, and Norwegian (Allwood, 1976; Engdahl, 1980; Andersson, 1982; Engdahl, 1982):

(50)   a. Suppe_i kender jeg mange der kan lide __i.
          soup   know   I   many   who could like
          '[SOUP]_i I know many people who like __i.'
          (Erteschik-Shir, 1973, 67)   (Danish)

      b. Johan_i känner jag ingen   som tycker om __i.
          Johan   know   I   no one   that   likes
          '[JOHAN]_i, I do not know anyone who likes __i'
          (Engdahl, 1980, 95)   (Swedish)

      c. Her er en bok_i som jeg ikke har   møtt noen   som har lest __i.
          here is a   book that I   not   have met   anybody that has   read
          'Here is a book [which]_i I haven't met anyone who has read __i'
          (Taraldsen, 1982, 205)   (Norwegian)

Note however that the relatives in all of the examples in (50) express assertions rather than presuppositions. In other words, the difference between English and these languages may not be as sharp as usually held.

We conclude that CNPC effects are for the most part pragmatic in nature. This explains why presentational relatives are immune to such extraction constraints, and why semantically more abstract matrix verbs facilitate extraction, especially when suitably contextualized and when there is less uncertainty about the correct gap site. Such a conclusion is consistent with the findings of Snyder (2000, 2017), Hofmeister and Sag (2010, 402–4), and Goodall (2011), whereby repeated exposition to CNPC island violations causes their acceptability to improve significantly. See also Do and Kaiser (2017) for evidence that CNPC violations can be primed.

3.2.4 Bridge verb phenomena

Ross (1967) and Erteschik-Shir (1973) noted that manner-of-speaking verbs and factive verbs hamper extraction, as (51) illustrates. We refer to the oddness of (51b) as a **Manner Island** and that of (51c) as a **Factive Island**. The term **bridge verb** is reserved for verbs that allow extraction pathways across clauses, as in (51a).

(51)   a.   [Who]$_i$ did Sam say/think that Sam likes __$_i$?
           (cf. *Sam said/thought that Sam likes* WHO?)

       b.   ?[Who]$_i$ did Sam mumble/whisper that Sam likes __$_i$?
           (cf. *Sam mumbled/whispered that Sam likes* WHO?)

       c.   ?[Who]$_i$ did Sam know/understand that Sam likes __$_i$?
           (cf. *Sam knew/understood that Sam likes* WHO?

In the scale of extractability, temporal, manner, and reason phrases are the hardest to extract from non-bridge verb clauses, as (52) illustrates, perhaps because there is in general a strong bias for adverbial phrases to be interpreted as modifying the higher verb, even with bridge verbs.[7]

(52)   a.   *[When]$_i$ does Max know/whisper [that Alice first kissed Sam __$_i$]?
           (cf. *Does Max know/whisper* [*that Alice first kissed Sam last year*]?)

       b.   *[Where]$_i$ does Max know [that Alice kissed Sam __$_i$]?
           (cf. *Does Max know/whisper* [*that Alice kissed Sam on the lips*]?)

       c.   *[How]$_i$ does Max know/whisper [that Alice kissed Sam __$_i$]?
           (cf. *Does Max know* [*that Alice kissed Sam passionately*]?)

Bridge verbs permit such adverbial extractions more easily, as in (53). The intended parse is one where the adverb characterizes the embedded verb, not the matrix verb.[8]

(53)   a.   Q: [When]$_i$ do you suppose [that Alice first kissed Sam __$_i$]?
           A: Last year.

       b.   Q: [Where]$_i$ does Max say [that Alice kissed Sam __$_i$]?
           A: On the lips.

       c.   Q: [How]$_i$ does Max think [that Alice kissed Sam __$_i$]?
           A: Passionately.

Note that sometimes such bridge constructions are ambiguous, as (54a,b) illustrate. In the former, extraction crosses a clausal boundary, but not in the latter, where 'that' introduces a prosodically independent relative clause. Only the former parse may induce island effects with manner and factive verbs. We try to avoid this confound in this volume.

---

[7] Some of the examples in (52) are, of course, licit if the filler is interpreted as a modifier of the matrix verb *know/whisper* (short construal). The point here is that the filler cannot be understood as the modifier of the embedded verb *kissed* (long construal).

[8] Liu et al. (2019) claim that factive and manner islands are not in effect in clefts. This is clearly not true for adverbial extraction, e.g. *It was yesterday that Max says/*whispers/*knows that Alice kissed Sam__*.

(54)   a. [[Who]$_i$ did you say [that Fred heard __]]?
           (= *Who is x such that you said that Fred heard x?*)

   b. [[Who]$_i$ did you say __$_i$] [that Fred heard __$_i$]?
       (= *Who is x such that you said x and Fred heard x?*)

Kothari (2008) and Liu et al. (2019) show that there is no sharp categorical difference between the acceptability of extraction from the clausal complements of Factive and Manner verbs and the acceptability of extraction from the clausal complements of bridge verbs.

3.2.4.1 Manner-of-speaking islands

Erteschik-Shir (2006a) argues for a pragmatic account of manner islands. She notes that if it is contextually known that a speaker has a lisp, then an extraction like (55) becomes somewhat more acceptable.

(55)   ?[What]$_i$ did Mike Tyson lisp he'd do __$_i$?

This follows from the fact that *lisp* is not as informative in (55) as it would be if the speaker is not known to lisp (Erteschik-Shir, 1973). Thus, the embedded clause is more likely to be presupposed rather than being part of the assertion. In other words, (55) is odd because it is not easy to contextualize. It requires a very peculiar situation type, but in a suitable context, the oddness is attenuated. Along similar lines, Deane (1991, 37) and Van Valin (1998) argue that manner verbs such as *whisper*, *mumble*, and so on cause island effects because they are semantically very informative, and therefore the subordinate clause cannot be construed as the focus of the question.

   This means that manner islands can be ameliorated by setting up a context where the main verb is already presupposed, making it easier for the embedded clause to express the main action, as in (56). The fact that contextualization can circumvent such islands provides further evidence that they are pragmatic in nature, not syntactic.

(56)   A: I didn't whisper that the house was green..!
       B: Ok, [what]$_i$ did you whisper that the house WAS __$_i$,then?

In sum, this is what Kuno's (1987) aboutness account would predict: the more semantically rich the main verb is, the more likely it is to express the main action in the utterance, and therefore the subordinate clause is harder to extract from. Independent experimental support for this view comes from Kothari (2008), which provides sentence acceptability and self-paced reading evidence that semantic priming can eliminate differences between bridge and manner constructions. For example, the context in (57) was found to ameliorate the island violation.

(57)   Context: The freshman mumbled that he had drunk seven shots of vodka that night.
       [What]$_i$ did the freshman mumble that he had drunk __$_i$?

Ambridge and Goldberg (2008) provide experimental evidence for a correlation between acceptability judgments of factive and manner island violations and the degree to which the matrix verb can be construed to express the main action of the clause or not, according to the Lie Test of Erteschik-Shir and Lappin (1979); see §2.1.3.1. Finally, Liu et al. (2019) also show in their Experiment 3 that the island effect is weaker in clefts than in interrogatives, and posit that this reflects the fact that the former express asserted content (more likely to correspond to the main action), and the latter express presupposed/backgrounded content (less likely to correspond to the main action).

3.2.4.2 Factive islands

We now turn our attention to an apparently similar phenomenon triggered by factive verbs, which blocks the extraction of adverbials like *how* and *why*. The examples in (58) and (59) illustrate an island effect usually referred to as the Factive Island Constraint.

(58) a. [Who]$_i$ do you regret that John invited __$_i$?

  b. *[How]$_i$ do you regret that John behaved __$_i$?

(59) a. [Who]$_i$ did you realize that John invited __$_i$?
  b. *[How]$_i$ do you realize that John behaved __$_i$?
  c. *[Why]$_i$ do you realize that John insulted Pat __$_i$]?

Szabolcsi and Zwarts (1993, 269–72) and Oshima (2007) show that the extraction of non-adverbial phrases *who* and *what* is generally insensitive to the presence of a factive verb, all else being equal. Contrasts like the one in (60) are simply due to the fact that the complement clause denotes a one-time predicate.

(60) a. [Who]$_i$ does Sam know that Alex got a Christmas card for __$_i$ yesterday?
  b. *[Who]$_i$ does Sam know that Alice got married to __$_i$ on June 1st?

The verb *know* triggers a factive presupposition, and *wh*-interrogatives presuppose that there is at least one true answer. Therefore, what (60a) asks is essentially: 'Of the *x*'s such that it is in the common ground that Alex got a Christmas card for *x* yesterday, which *x* is such that Sam knows Alex got a Christmas card for *x* yesterday?' This is a felicitous discourse move.

  Interrogatives with a one-time predicate, on the other hand, can have only one true answer. For example, *Who left first?* can only have one true answer among a candidate set of possible answers. The question in (60b) thus means 'Of the *x*'s such that it is in the common ground that Alex got married to *x* on June 1st, which *x* is such that Sam knows Alex married *x* on June 1st?' Usually the same person will not marry multiple people on the same day, and since *know* presupposes the truth of its complement clause, it follows that the speaker would already know who Alex married before asking the question. Hence, the contrast in (60) is tied to the uniqueness requirement among a set of alternatives imposed on the filler phrase, one-time predicates, and the presuppositions triggered by factive verbs. Oshima (2007) observes that the same explanation extends to *why* and *how* factive island effects like (58) and (59): if a proposition is required to have only one reason or manner in a given context, it follows that such questions are infelicitous. See Abrusán (2011) and Schwarz and Simonenko (2018) for related accounts. and see Tonhauser et al. (2018) for experimental evidence consistent with this view.

Before concluding, we note that both Kothari (2008) and Liu et al. (2019) argue that the frequency of CP complements of manner and factive verbs plays a role in the magnitude of their island effects. In particular, Kothari (2008) suggests that the acceptability contrasts may simply reflect language users' expectations about the typical usage patterns of a verb. This is plausible, given that 96% of adult's UDCs involve the main verb *think* or *say* (Dąbrowska, 2004, 197), and manner-of-speaking verbs are predominantly used without a clausal complement. But in our view verb-frame frequency alone cannot explain the acceptability of manner and factive islands because there are verbs that have very low clause-complement frame frequency (as low as that of many manner verbs and generally lower than that of most factive verbs), but which are nonetheless bridge verbs, such as *muse*, *plead*, *perceive*, *respond*, *establish*, and *answer*. If instead one considers the proportion of the clausal complement verb frame, then the exceptions are verbs like *respond*, *answer*, *repeat*, and *write*, which are more biased against the clausal complement verb frame than various manner verbs and than most factive verbs, but are bridge verbs nonetheless. See Richter and Chaves (2020) for more data, experiments, and discussion.

3.2.5 Coordinate Structure Constraint

The **Coordinate Structure Constraint** was first observed by Ross (1967) and it basically prohibits the extraction coordinate structures. Following Grosu (1973), we refer to the constraint banning extraction *of* a conjunct as the **Conjunct Constraint**, and to the constraint banning extraction *from* conjuncts as the **Element Constraint**. As we shall see, these two constraints are most likely due to completely different factors.

The Conjunct Constraint is illustrated in (61), and is special in that it has no known robust counterexamples.[9]

(61) a. *[Hayley] who I saw Roger and _ yesterday.
          (= *I saw Roger and Hayley yesterday*)

      b. *It was [Hayley] who I saw _ and Roger yesterday.
          (= *I saw Hayley and Roger yesterday*)

      c. *[Who]$_i$ did you see Roger and _ yesterday?
          (= *You saw Roger and* WHO *yesterday?*)

      d. *[Who]$_i$ did you see _$_i$ and Roger yesterday?
          (= *You saw* WHO *and Roger yesterday?*)

As in various other islands, the in situ interrogative counterparts of (61c,d) are licit and express essentially the same propositions. No such island effect arises in the comitative counterparts seen in (62), even though their meaning is almost the same. The Conjunct Constraint is very robust and to our knowledge there are no exceptions.[10] The evidence suggests that the Conjunct Constraint is absolute and syntactic in nature.

---

[9] Apparent rightward movement counterexamples are discussed in Chaves (2012b, n. 2).

[10] Levine (2017, 317–18) proposes that conjuncts are required to contain at least one stressed syllable. Given that traces are phonologically silent, nothing is there to bear stress, and the Conjunct Constraint follows as a consequence. It is not clear why such a constraint would exist, and why it would only target conjuncts.

(62) a. It was Hayley [who]$_i$ I saw Roger with __$_i$ yesterday.
 b. It was Hayley [who]$_i$ I saw __$_i$ with Roger yesterday.
 c. [Who]$_i$ did you see Roger with __$_i$ yesterday?
 d. [Who]$_i$ did you see __$_i$ with Roger yesterday?

The restriction preventing the extraction from elements embedded in conjuncts is the Element Constraint, as illustrated in (63).

(63) a. *[Which game]$_i$ did you say Kim dislikes __$_i$ and Sam absolutely hates Scrabble?
  (cf. *Did you say Kim dislikes—and Sam absolutely hates—Scrabble?*)

 b. *[Which game]$_i$ did you say Kim dislikes Scrabble and Sam absolutely hates __$_i$?
  (cf. *Did you say Kim dislikes Scrabble and Sam absolutely hates chess?*)

 c. *This is the castle$_i$ that I think Sandy photographed __$_i$ and Chris wrote about the lake.

 d. *This is the castle$_i$ that I think Sandy photographed the lake and Chris wrote about __$_i$

As expected, the Element Constraint is not active in other constructions, including comparatives, as the data in (64) illustrate.[11]

(64) a. [Which board game]$_i$ did you say David enjoys __$_i$ more than he enjoys playing videogames?

 b. [Which game]$_i$ did you say that the sooner we start playing __$_i$, the quicker we can go home?

 c. [What kind of TV shows]$_i$ do men watch __$_i$ as often as women watch soap operas?

The Element Constraint has two types of exception. The first is referred to as the **Across-The-Board (ATB) Exception**, which states that the Element Constraint is inactive if extraction targets all coordinate phrases, as (65) illustrates.[12]

(65) a. This is the castle$_i$ that I think Sandy photographed __$_i$ and Chris wrote about __$_i$.

 b. [Which game]$_i$ did you say Kim dislikes __$_i$ and Sam absolutely hates __$_i$?

 c. This is the show$_i$ that I've always wanted to see __$_i$ but could never afford tickets for __$_i$.

 d. This is something$_i$ that most cognitive scientists think about __$_i$ but never consider the implications of __$_i$.

Note that the ATB exception is not valid for the Conjunct Constraint, as (66) shows, suggesting that the Element Constraint and the Conjunct Constraint are due to different factors (Bouma et al., 2001).

---

[11] Comparatives have been argued to be coordinate-like in nature (McCawley, 1964; Hankamer, 1973; Napoli, 1983; Moltmann, 1992), and therefore to obey the CSC (Corver, 1990; Hendriks, 1995). But as (64) shows, comparatives are not UDC islands.

[12] See Parker (2017) for online experimental evidence that comprehenders make detailed predictions about the location of the second gap during active dependency formation in such coordinate ATB extraction structures.

(66) a. *[Which of her books] did you find both [[a review of $_i$] and [$_i$]]?

   b. *[Which of her books] did you find [[$_i$] and [a review of $_i$]]?

   c. *[Which rock legend] would it be ridiculous to compare [[$_i$] and [$_i$]]?
      (cf. *Would it be ridiculous to compare Bono with himself?*)

Note also that it is unlikely that these are Principle C Binding Theory violations because there are reasons to doubt Principle C is robustly active in coordinate structures, *contra* Goodall (1987), Munn (1993), and others:

(67) a. We invited [Betsy$_i$'s mother and her$_i$] to the ceremony.
         (Sag, 2000)

   b. We invited [Jack$_i$'s friends and him$_i$] both.
      (Bouma et al., 2001, 43, n. 19)

   c. I wish to inform [him$_i$ and all of Dr. Phil$_i$'s viewers] that real counseling sessions take place behind closed doors, not on TV.
      (Chaves, 2007, 43)

The second type of exception to the Element Constraint concerns coordinations which are interpreted **asymmetrically** (Goldsmith, 1985; Lakoff, 1986; Levin and Prince, 1986). Basically, in asymmetric coordination the order of the conjuncts has a major impact on the meaning of the utterance. For example, (68a) does not mean the same as the reversed counterpart (68b).[13]

(68) a. Robin jumped on a horse and rode into the sunset.
   b. Robin rode into the sunset and jumped on a horse.

Compare (68) with the pair of equivalent sentences in (69), in which the order of the conjuncts is irrelevant.

(69) a. Robin likes beer and Sue likes wine.
   b. Sue likes wine and Robin likes beer.

The participants in the propositions conveyed in (69a) have pairwise equal (or parallel) status across the two conjuncts. Thus, Robin's role in the first conjunct is contrasted with Sue's role in the second conjunct; the action of drinking is in some sense contrasted with the action of eating, and so on. Hence, we obtain contrasts like (70), because the verbal arguments are not pragmatically interpreted in the same way across the two conjuncts.[14]

(70) *SUE ate a burger and Robin drank A BEER.

---

[13] As a consequence, asymmetric coordination allows clauses of different semantic types to be conjoined, as in (i), where an imperative is coordinated with a declarative.

i. Drink this and you'll fall asleep instantly.

[14] Levine (2001a) and Kehler (2002, ch. 5) show that there is good empirical evidence that asymmetric coordinations are, in all other regards (including their syntax), exactly like coordination structures, and cannot be taken to be anything other than coordinate.

The fact that the conjuncts in (69) are in this sense on an equal pragmatic footing makes it possible to refer to both actions collectively by adding modifiers like *simultaneously*. That possibility is not afforded to coordination like (68), where one conjunct expresses a preparatory action and the other expresses the main action. For a formalization of this and various other coherence relations, see Asher and Lascarides (2003).

Lakoff (1986), Deane (1991, 23), Na and Huck (1992), and others note that Element Constraint violations correlate with several kinds of asymmetric 'scenarios' that coordination can express, whereby some conjuncts express actions more central to the proposition and others express more incidental actions. In (71), the gapped conjuncts express main actions, whereas the non-gapped conjuncts express preparatory, scene-setting, or incidental actions. Because of their pragmatically peripheral status, the latter conjuncts are exempt from being gapped. See Huddleston and Pullum (2002b, 1094) for attested data.

(71)   a. [Who]$_i$ did Sam pick up the phone and call __$_i$?

    b. [Who]$_i$ did Fred lose his balance and fall on __$_i$?

    c. There are some letters$_i$ that I must go downstairs and check __$_i$ over.

In (71) the preparatory conjuncts precede the main conjuncts, but in other kinds of 'scenes' the pattern is reversed, as it is in (72). The first conjunct merely expresses a preparatory action, and therefore an interrogative expression in the second conjunct can outscope the entire coordination.[15]

(72)   a. What was the maximum amount$_i$ that I can contribute __$_i$ and still get a tax deduction?

    b. [How much]$_i$ can you drink __$_i$ and still stay sober?

    c. [How many forests]$_i$ can they destroy __$_i$ and not arouse public antipathy?

Similarly, a single interrogative can remain in situ in asymmetric coordinations, as (73) illustrates.

(73)   A: [So you can put something inside of this] and [it'll stay cold for ↑HOW LONG↓]?

    B: Six months.
        [COCA 2009 SPOK]

Asymmetric extractions are predominantly found in VP coordination, but Culicover and Jackendoff (1997, 1999), Johannessen (1998, 233), and Kehler (2002, 128) note that clausal asymmetric extraction is possible, as in (74).[16]

---

[15] See Kubota and Levine (2020, 309) for examples with coordinations other than *and*.

[16] The same is true for clausal comparatives like those in (i) and (ii), which share properties with coordination structures.

i. [Which theory]$_i$ does he say that the more you study philosophy, the more you'll like __$_i$?
   (Culicover and Jackendoff, 1999)

ii. This is the company$_i$ that they said [__$_i$ hired more consultants] than [PARC hired programmers].
    (Chaves, 2012b)

(74)   [Which theory]$_i$ do you walk into his office and he immediately starts ranting about $\_i$?
       (Culicover and Jackendoff, 1999)

Kehler (2002, ch. 5) and Kubota and Lee (2015) show in more detail how the Element Constraint and all of its exceptions are explained as pragmatic constraints, drawing from Kuno and Lakoff's insights. In symmetric coordination, the referents that are predicated in the coordinated phrases must play parallel roles. As discussed in §2.1, the fronted element in a UDC generally has a special pragmatic role (e.g. Topic or Focus, depending on the UDC type). So, it is not possible to pragmatically interpret one participant as Focus, say, without doing the same vis-à-vis its counterpart in the other conjunct. To do so would violate the parallelism requirement. But when the coordination is not interpreted symmetrically, there is no such parallelism constraint, and extraction targets the conjunct that expresses the main action, and optionally any other conjuncts, as in (75).

(75)   [What]$_i$ did Harry buy $\__i$, come home, and devour $\__i$ in thirty seconds?
       (Ross, 1967)

Since asymmetric coordination is exempt from the ATB proviso, it allows overlapping UDCs that are not convergent. In the examples in (76), each conjunct contains a gap that is linked to a different filler. The prosodic cues are absolutely crucial given the complexity of such an example.

(76)   a.   [A bird THIS RARE]$_i$ – [how many years]$_j$ could someone spend $\__j$ and never actually see $\__i$?

       b.   [A problem THIS HARD]$_i$ – [how many years]$_j$ could someone spend $\__j$ in the field and not even come close to solving $\__i$?
            (Chaves, 2012b)

Let us take stock. Whereas the Element Constraint and its ATB and asymmetric exceptions all follow naturally from Kuno's aboutness constraint, depending on whether the conjuncts are interpreted symmetrically or not, the Conjunct Constraint is exceptionless and therefore more likely to be of a very different nature. We conclude that the former is due to the Relevance constraint that all UDCs are subject to, and the latter is due to constraints that are more syntactic in nature. See §5.2.4 for more discussion.

3.2.6 Subject Constraint

Whereas subextractions from object NPs are relatively acceptable (§3.2.1), subextractions from subject NPs like (77) are not. This effect has been known as the **Subject Constraint** since Chomsky (1977, 106), and regarded as one of the strongest island constraints in English; see Kayne (1981, 114), Huang (1982, 497), Nunes and Uriagereka (2000, 21), Jackendoff (2002, 48), Lasnik and Park (2003), among others.

(77)   a.   *[Which man]$_i$ was [the friend of $\__i$] fired?
            (cf. *The friend of that man was fired?*)

b. *[Who]$_i$ did [close friends of $\_i$] laugh?
   (cf. *Close friends of yours laughed?*)

c. *It was that man who [the friend of $\_i$] was fired.
   (cf. *The friend of this man was fired*)

d. *It was Sam who [close friends of $\_i$] laughed.
   (cf. *Close friends of Sam laughed*)

The asymmetry between subject and object subextraction is not entirely surprising. Subject phrases are typically reserved for topic continuity rather than for introducing new referents (Kuno, 1972; Lambrecht, 1994; Chafe, 1994). Thus, subject phrases are more likely to be pronominal or elliptical than objects. According to Michaelis and Francis (2007), of approximately 31,000 subjects of declarative sentences in the Switchboard corpus (Marcus et al., 1993), only 9% are lexical NPs, while 91% are pronouns. In contrast, of approximately 7,500 objects of transitive verbs, 34% are pronominal. It follows that extraction from subject phrases should be difficult because there is a conflict between the discourse function of the extracted element and the discourse function of the subject phrase itself. For example, in (77) the extracted phrase is required to be new information (as Focus), but at the same time it is embedded in a subject phrase required to be the Topic (i.e. part of the presupposition) (Van Valin, 1986; Takami, 1988; Erteschik-Shir, 2006b; Goldberg, 2006).

This means that Subject Island effects should vanish if the particular construction does not require the Subject to be the Topic. This is exactly what happens in restrictive relative clauses. Although the pragmatic function of the extracted phrase in a restrictive relative is of a local Topic, the function of its referent in the higher clause is independent. If the relative attaches to an NP that is interpreted as Focus, then the relativized (local Topic) referent is Focus relative to the matrix, for example; see §2.1.3.1 for more discussion and examples. The function of the relativized element is whatever is the function of the head it modifies. Abeillé et al. (2018) and Abeillé et al. (2020) point out that the UDC type where it should be easiest to find weakened Subject Island effects would be relative clauses, because there is less of a conflict between the pragmatic function of the filler and the pragmatic status of the subject phrase. This prediction is supported by corpus data and acceptability judgments. For example, in the attested data in (78) a PP is extracted from relative clauses; see Santorini (2007) for various other naturally occurring examples.[17]

(78) a. They have eight children [of whom] [five $\_i$] are still living at home.
      (Huddleston and Pullum, 2002b, 1093)

      b. ... a letter [of which] [every line $\_i$] was an insult ...[18]
      (Santorini, 2007)

---

[17] The in situ counterparts are attested as well, as (i) and (ii) illustrate.

i. He leaned back in his seat, and refrained from pushing buttons some combination of which might execute the self-destruct maneuver.
[COCA 1999 FIC]

ii. Maletskos was one of several scientists involved in the Fernald experiment, the results of which proved that certain cereals can block the absorption of calcium ...
[COCA 1994 SPOK]

[18] [Jane Austen. 1981. *The Complete Novels*. New York: Gramercy, 84.]

c. Already Agassiz had become interested in the rich stores of the extinct fishes of Europe, especially those of Glarus in Switzerland and of Monte Bolca near Verona, [of which]$_i$, at that time, [only a few __$_i$] had been critically studied.
(Santorini, 2007)

d. ...ran a documentary featuring a young Auckland family [of which]$_i$ [the father __$_i$] earned $70,000 a year ....
[NOW]

e. It is believed the suspects left the scene with three bags containing new cellphones [of which] [the value __$_i$] was unknown.
[NOW]

Abeillé et al. (2018) and Abeillé et al. (2020) provide experimental evidence showing that this kind of Subject Island violation is acceptable in English and in French. Similar results have been found for Italian (Rizzi, 1982; Sprouse et al., 2016) and Spanish (Goodall, 2011). More recently, Culicover and Winkler (2019) found numerous attestations of extraction from relative subjects without pied-piping, as in (79).

(79)   a. There are some things [which]$_i$ [fighting against __$_i$] is not worth the effort. Concentrating on things which can create significant positive change is much more fruitful.
[https://news.ycombinator.com/item?id=13946026, January 7, 2020]

b. I'm looking for someone who I click with. You know, the type of person [who]$_i$ [spending time with __$_i$] is effortless.
[https://3-instant.okcupid.com/profile/mpredds, January 7, 2020]

c. Survived by her children, Mae (Terry), Dale (Andelyn), Joanne (Gary), Cathy (Jordan), George, Betty (Tim), Danny (Angela); a proud grandmother of 14 grandchildren and 16 great-grandchildren, [who]$_i$ [spending time with __$_i$] was one of her finest joys;
[http://www.mahonefuneral.ca/obituaries/111846, January 7, 2020]

This means that Subject Islands are not cross-constructionally active, contrary to widespread assumption. Several authors had already questioned the claim that Subject Islands were exceptionless, as the sample in (80) illustrates.[19] All of these examples involve relative clauses, as expected.

(80)   a. It's the kind of policy statement$_i$ that [jokes about __$_i$] are a dime a dozen.
(Levine et al., 2001, 204)

---

[19] In fact, Ross (1967) never claimed that subject NPs were impervious to extraction. On the contrary, he argued that PP extractions from subject NPs like (i) are passable (his judgments). More recently, even Chomsky (2008) claims that examples like (ii) and (iii) are acceptable as well, according to his judgments.

i. [Of which cars]$_i$ were [the hoods __$_i$] damaged by the explosion?
(Ross, 1967, 4.2542)

ii. [Of which car]$_i$ was [the driver __$_i$] awarded a prize?
(Chomsky, 2008, 147)

iii. [Of which books]$_i$ did [the authors __$_i$] receive the prize?
(Chomsky, 2008, 160, n. 39)

b. There are certain topics$_i$ that [jokes about ___$_i$] are completely unacceptable.
(Levine and Sag, 2003, 252, n. 6)

c. That is the lock [to which]$_i$ [the key ___$_i$] has been lost.

d. A house [of which]$_i$ only [the front ___$_i$] has been painted will be on your left at the second light; you make a right turn there.
(Levine and Hukari, 2006, 291)

This includes adverbial fillers extracted out of gerundial subjects like (81).

(81)   a. The 'Hunan' restaurant is a place [where]$_i$ [having dinner ___$_i$] promises to be most enjoyable.

b. The pre-midnight hours are the time [when]$_i$ [sleeping soundly ___$_i$] is most beneficial to one's health.
(Grosu, 1981, 72)

Let us now return to Subject Island effects in interrogatives. If extraction from subjects is harder than extraction from objects because these argument roles come with very different pragmatic biases, then it should in principle be possible to counteract such biases. For example, *Who was the friend of fired?* should be more acceptable in a context where the open proposition *the friend of x was fired* is already presupposed and known to the interlocutors, but the value of *x* in that proposition is somehow still unknown to the speaker. That is, a context in which the subject-embedded referent is more easily understood as having a different pragmatic function than that of the nominal head that it depends on. Kluender (2004) makes the following observation:[20]

> Subject Island effects seem to be weaker when the *wh*-phrase maintains a pragmatic association not only with the gap, but also with the main clause predicate, such that the filler-gap dependency into the subject position is construed as of some relevance to the main assertion of the sentence.
>
> (Kluender, 2004, 495)

In other words, if the referent denoted by the extracted phrase is irrelevant for the situation expressed by the predication, then there is no reason to draw the hearer's attention to it by extracting it. If the referent is irrelevant for the main predication, then assigning it a distinguished pragmatic role arguably constitutes a Gricean violation. This is essentially Kuno's aboutness constraint at work: if there is no obvious link between a subject-embedded referent and the main predication, then how can the assertion be about that subject-embedded referent? It follows that if the referent denoted by the extracted phrase can be made relevant for the situation described by the predication, then the Subject Island effect should be weaker, as in (82).

(82)   [What]$_i$ did [the attempt to find ___$_i$] end in failure?
(Hofmeister and Sag, 2010, 370)

[20] According to Haig (1996) and Shimojo (2002), such a relevance constraint is responsible for several island effects in Japanese, including Subject Islands. See Shimojo (2020) for a more detailed overview of the Japanese facts and evidence against syntactic accounts.

In this example, the matrix predication *end in failure* is rather abstract and therefore the subject-embedded predication *attempt to find x* is more likely to be part of the main action that the proposition describes. Second, whether or not the attempt to find *x* ends in failure crucially hinges on the identity of *x*; the search failed precisely because of the nature of what was sought.

Acceptable examples like (82) have been noted before, such as (83); see also Kluender (1998, 268), Sauerland and Elbourne (2002, 304), and Jiménez–Fernández (2009, 111). Here, the extracted nominals are specific and cohere particularly well with the subject head nominal (i.e. impeachment vs. president/judge, punishment vs. crime, cure vs. disease, resolution vs. problem), such that the extracted nominal is highly predictive of the corresponding noun controlling the gap.

(83) a. [Which President]$_i$ would [the impeachment of __$_i$] not shock most people?
  b. [Which President]$_i$ would [the impeachment of __$_i$] not cause much outrage?
  c. [Which crime]$_i$ will [the punishment for __$_i$] never be carried out?
  d. [Which disease]$_i$ will [the cure for __$_i$] never be discovered?
  e. [Which problem]$_i$ would [the resolution of __$_i$] surprise you the most?
  f. [Which disease]$_i$ did [the vaccine for __$_i$] suddenly stop working?
  g. [Which airline]$_i$ is [the crew of __$_i$] currently on strike?
  (Chaves, 2013)

Whether or not an impeachment causes shock or outrage crucially depends on what the accused official has done. Thus, the referent of *President* is crucial for the scenario evoked by a political action causing a psychological reaction. This may again be a framing effect: the verb and the subject together elicit a particular scenario where the object of the subject nominal plays a critical role. Consultation with informants reveals that most have no difficulty understanding and paraphrasing most of the items in (83) even without repeated exposure to such UDCs. As usual, a small pause at the gap site is needed to preempt the parse in which the stranded preposition combines with the following word.

Although the examples above involve definite subjects, this is by no means necessary. Consider for example the indefinite extractions in (84).

(84) a. [Which problem]$_i$ will [a solution to __$_i$] never be found?
  b. [Which disease]$_i$ will [a cure for __$_i$] never be discovered?
  c. [Which politician]$_i$ did [opponents of __$_i$] organize a protest?
  d. [Which law firm]$_i$ did [partners of __$_i$] receive the most awards?
  e. [Which building]$_i$ did [tenants of __$_i$] decide to start an illegal business?
  (Chaves and Dery, 2014)

According to Abeillé et al. (2020), interrogative Subject Island violations are only possible if such sentences are 'all focus', providing only new information. We are skeptical of this view, given that the subject phrase can clearly be part of discourse-old information, as in

(85), which should be impossible according to Abeillé et al. (2020). Rather, we speculate that what is special about such examples is that they more readily allow a referent that is embedded in a Topic subject to be the Focus by virtue of the proposition expressed and the fact that the extracted nominal is highly predictive of the noun that selects the gapped PP.

(85) For quite some time now, medical science has been seeking a cure for the flu and for tuberculosis. Recent breakthroughs in genetic engineering suggest that it may be possible to cure one of these diseases in the very near future, but not the other. In your opinion, [which disease] will [a cure for _] most likely be found in the near future?

Many of the counterexamples reported above involve passive or unaccusative verb phrases. Kravtchenko et al. (2009) found that the subjects of such verb phrases are more transparent to extraction than subjects with unergative predicates. This is not unexpected. A subject that is an agent initiates or controls the event and is therefore by default the most relevant participant for the assertion. However, if the subject is a patient, for example, then it is easier for a phrase other than the subject to be construed as relevant. All this is as expected in Kuno's account. If this view is correct, then complex NPs with embedded PPs should be more frequent as direct objects than as subjects. This is because it should be easier for the former PP-embedded referents to be relevant enough to be worth mentioning than for the latter, from a purely Gricean perspective. Indeed, Chaves and Dery (2019) show that direct objects with embedded PPs occur about twice as often as subjects with embedded PPs in large English corpora.

The idea that Subject Island violations are contingent on the proposition expressed by the utterance—and in particular, on how important the extracted referent is for the main predication—is consistent with the fact that the acceptability of Subject Island violations sometimes increases with repeated exposure (Francom, 2009; Hiramatsu, 2000; Clausen, 2011; Chaves and Dery, 2014), and sometimes does not (Sprouse, 2009; Goodall, 2011; Crawford, 2011; Do and Kaiser, 2017). For evidence that comprehenders can, in ideal conditions, be induced to postulate gaps inside such subject phrases in self-paced reading, see Chaves and Dery (2019). Different experiments have probably arrived at different results because they used different experimental items, of different complexity, conveying very different propositions. Consider for example the sample of experimental items in (86).

(86) a. *[Who]$_i$ do you think [the email from _$_i$] is on the computer?
          (Sprouse, 2007a)

      b. *[Who]$_i$ does [the guide believe a crowd of _$_i$] arrived late?
          (Crawford, 2011)

      c. *[What]$_i$ does [that you bought _$_i$] anger the other students?
          (Sprouse, 2009)

Aside from the fact that *the email is on the computer* in (86a) is awkward and ambiguous, (86a) is only felicitous in a very particular context: a specific email is under discussion, but its author is unknown. The hearer is left wondering why this particular email is being referenced. In other words, if the interlocutors know that a particular email *y* is in the mailbox, then the author of *y* is of no obvious consequence to whether *y* is in the mailbox or not. Compare (86) with a more acceptable version in (87). A pause at the gap site is crucial.

(87)   ?[Who]$_i$ do you think [an email from __$_i$] is missing from your inbox?

Here, the email referent is less specific, and the required context is less exotic: people receive many emails and sometimes emails are accidentally deleted. Moreover, expressing concern over losing something important is common enough, and the utterance is therefore more easily justified. Finally, since the email referent is less specific, it is easier for its author to be unknown, and not part of the presupposed content.

The occurrence of two *from* prepositions in (87) is distracting, and therefore the example is suboptimal. A much better UDC can be constructed by rewording the sentence slightly:

(88)   [Who]$_i$ do you think [an email from __$_i$] is missing an attachment?

The items in (86b,c) suffer from similar problems, we believe. Guides usually interact with organized groups of people, not with crowds. Moreover, it is unclear why the identity of the crowd members is of relevance to the fact that the crowd was late. The contexts in which such an utterance would be felicitous are extremely unusual, as there is no typical situation involving guides, crowds, and being late. Similar objections can be raised about (86c), as there is no prototypical situation that comes to mind that involves buying things and angering students. To be clear, we are not claiming these propositions are infelicitous. Rather, our claim is that they are awkwardly expressed, and describe atypical situations in which the extracted referent has little relevance for the main action described by the utterance.

3.2.6.1 Parasitic subject-embedded gaps
Subject Island violations tend to become more acceptable if there is a second gap outside the island environment, as illustrated in (89)–(91). The subject-embedded gap in the island environment is said to be **parasitic** on the gap outside the island (Engdahl, 1983; Kayne, 1983).

(89)   a.   *[Who]$_i$ did [your pictures of __$_i$] amuse Mia the most?
       b.   [Who]$_i$ did [your pictures of __$_i$] amuse __$_j$ the most?

(90)   a.   *That was the rebel leader [who]$_i$ [rivals of __$_i$] assassinated the British consul.
       b.   That was the rebel leader [who]$_i$ [rivals of __$_i$] assassinated __$_j$.
            (Levine and Sag, 2003)

(91)   a.   *[What]$_i$ did [the attempt to repair __$_i$] ultimately damage the car?
       b.   [What]$_i$ did [the attempt to repair __$_i$] ultimately damage __$_j$?
            (Phillips, 2006)

The latter acceptability contrasts have been experimentally validated by Phillips (2006). Moreover, Culicover and Winkler (2019) find various attestations of such convergent extractions:[21]

(92)   a.   In fact, there are a couple of Bajas sitting in my back yard right now [which]$_i$ [the owner of __$_i$] is talking about selling __$_j$.

---

[21] Park and Sprouse (2017) assume that only subject-embedded infinitival phrases like (91) allow parasitic gaps, but this is not the case; see Engdahl (1983) and §2.2.2.

[www.thesamba.com/vw/forum/archive/index.php/o-t-t-607965–start-0–index. html, January 7, 2020]

b. ... there is stock on the property [which]$_i$ [the owner of $\_i$] is liable for $\_i$ if they get onto the road and cause damage then nobody cares whether a gate is open or closed.
[https://forums.whirlpool.net.au/archive/2473729, January 7, 2020]

The contrasts in (89)–(91) are predicted by Kuno's aboutness constraint. If Subject Island effects are indeed contingent on how likely the subject-embedded referent is to be interpreted as the Focus, then the contextualization should aid in improving such extractions. Indeed, (91a) becomes more acceptable if it is contextually established that x is a component of the car. It makes sense that attempting to fix x can cause damage to x, which would explain why (91b) is acceptable, even out of the blue. The two sentences in (91) express very different propositions and have different pragmatic requirements, and therefore there is no a priori reason to expect that (91a) and (91b) should receive identical acceptability judgments. The contexts in which (91a) is felicitous are stricter than those of (91b) because the pragmatic status of subjects is different from that of objects. This point is underscored by the experimental results of Chaves and Dery (2014), which suggest that the acceptability contrast between extraction from objects and extraction from subjects can vanish, in ideal conditions. Chaves and Dery compared acceptability and the online processing of near-synonymous sentence pairs like (93), which express essentially the same proposition. Any extractability differences must come from the extraction itself.

(93) a. [Which stock]$_i$ does the value of the dollar often parallel [the price of $\_i$]?
      b. [Which stock]$_i$ does [the value of $\_i$] often parallel the price of the dollar?

Unlike previous experimental studies on islands, Chaves and Dery (2014) normed the declarative counterparts of all items so that each pair of sentences expressed equally highly felicitous propositions to begin with.

Although subject subextraction examples like (93b) were initially judged much worse than the object subextraction counterparts like (93a), by the end of the experiment the former became as acceptable as the latter. Such dramatic acceptability increase did not occur in the ungrammatical controls, and is also reflected in reduced reading times around the gap site on a subsequent experiment in Chaves and Dery (2014). The results suggest that—all else being equal—Subject Island effects can weaken once comprehenders have the opportunity to adjust to the unusual gap position and associated pragmatic consequences. The asymmetry between subject and object subextraction is not categorical, and can be countered in ideal conditions. See §6.2.1 for a replication of this experiment. Such results indicate that working memory limitations cannot play a major role in these islands (Chaves, 2013), a conclusion which is consistent with fMRI evidence from Matchin et al. (2018) suggesting that Subject Island effects activate networks involved in conceptual-semantic processing, rather than those involved in working memory.

The widespread assumption that non-island gaps 'rescue' the island gaps from being ungrammatical is predicated on the claim that the latter are co-indexed to the former. But this flies in the face of the many licit non-parasitic counterexamples discussed so far.

Second, in cases like (94) the subject-internal gap is not co-referenced with the object gap, and therefore it is unclear in what sense the 'real gap' is rescuing the 'parasitic' one.[22]

(94)   a. There are certain heroes$_i$ that [long stories about __$_i$]$_j$ are always very easy to listen to __$_j$.

   b. There are certain heroes$_i$ that [long stories about __$_i$]$_j$ are too boring to listen to __$_j$. (Polly Jacobson (pers. comm.) in Pollard and Sag (1994, 199, n. 35))

   c. [People that sensitive]$_i$, I never know [which topics]$_j$ jokes about __$_j$ are likely to offend __$_i$. (Pollard and Sag, 1994, 199)

Third, Levine and Sag (2003), Levine and Hukari (2006, 256), and Culicover (2013, 161) note examples like (95), which involve not one but two Subject Island violations. Such UDCs should be completely ungrammatical, contrary to fact. The conclusion that Subject Island effects are contingent on the proposition and its pragmatics seems unavoidable.

(95)   This is a man [who]$_i$ [friends of __$_i$] think that [enemies of __$_i$] are everywhere.

Levine et al. (2001) and Levine and Hukari (2006, 292) conclude—correctly, in our view— that there is no grammatical distinction between 'parasitic' and 'real' gaps. In §3.2.7.1 we discuss analogous evidence against the notion of parasitic gaps in Adjunct Island violations.

3.2.6.2 Sentential subject constraint

Although Ross (1967) proposed no constraint to block extraction from NP subjects, he did propose the **Sentential Subject Constraint** in order to block the extraction from clausal subjects. As illustrated in (96a) and (97a), extracting from clausal subjects is illicit, but no such extraction constraint is present in paraphrases where the complementizer phrase (CP) subject has been *it*-extraposed, as in (96b) and (97b).

(96)   a. *[Which book]$_i$ did [that Robin bought __$_i$] surprise you?
      (cf. *That Robin bought this book surprised you?*)

   b. [What]$_i$ did it surprise everyone [that Robin bought __$_i$].

(97)   a. *[Who]$_i$ was [that the principal would fire __$_i$] unexpected?
      (cf. *That the principal would fire Fred was unexpected?*)

   b. [Who]$_i$ did the reporters expect [that the principal would fire __$_i$]?

It is natural that propositional subjects yield stronger Subject Island environments. First, clausal subjects are dispreferred, and tend to be extraposed. Miller (2001) shows that in large corpora like the BNC sentential subjects must be discourse-old or inferable, and that they are extraposed if discourse-new. Second, clausal subjects lead to increased processing difficulty right at the beginning of the utterance, straining memory resources needed to process the remainder of the utterance (Kluender, 2004).

---

[22] See also Levine and Sag (2003) for empirical arguments against Kearney-style reconstruction phenomena (Chomsky, 1986b).

Finally, clausal subjects express a completely different situation from that which is expressed by the main predication. Hence, the same pragmatic conflicts that arise in Subject Island violations involving NP subjects also arise in Subject Island violations involving clausal subjects. No such pragmatic conflicts arise in relative clauses, which in turn predicts that extraction from verbal subjects in relative clauses should be rather acceptable. In (98) we see attested extractions from infinitival VP subjects, in which the subject is implicitly understood. See Chaves (2012b, 471) and Culicover and Winkler (2019) for various other naturally occurring examples.

(98) a. The eight dancers and their caller, Laurie Schmidt, make up the Farmall Promenade of nearby Nemaha, a town$_i$ that [to describe $\_i$ as tiny] would be to overstate its size.
       (Huddleston and Pullum, 2002b, 1094, n. 27)

      b. In his bedroom, [which]$_i$ [to describe $\_i$ as small] would be a gross understatement, he has an audio studio setup.
       (Chaves, 2012b, 471)

      c. Leaving the room, she is quick to offer you some Arabic coffee and dates [which]$_i$ [to refuse $\_i$] would be insane because both are delicious, and an opportunity to relax and eat is welcome when working twelve hours.
       [www.thesandyshamrock.com/being-an-rt-in-saudi-arabia/, May 22, 2020]

      d. The moment itself was something [which]$_i$ [to deny $\_i$] would be a blasphemy.[23]
       (Culicover and Winkler, 2019)

In (99) we list extractions from infinitival clausal subjects. The bracketed subject phrases must be pronounced as independent phonological phrases, almost as if they were parenthetical.

(99) a. This is something [which]$_i$ [for you to try to understand $\_i$] would be futile.
       (Kuno and Takami, 1993, 49)

      b. I just met Terry's eager-beaver research assistant [who]$_i$ [for us to talk to $\_i$ about any subject other than linguistics] would be absolutely pointless.
       (Levine and Hukari, 2006, 265)

      c. There are people in this world$_i$ that [for me to describe $\_i$ as despicable] would be an understatement.
       (Chaves, 2012b, 471)

To our knowledge all the convergent extractions from subject-embedded tensed relative clauses that have been noted in the literature involve relative clauses that similarly express assertions, as in (100). See Chaves and Dery (2019) for experimental evidence that such constructions can be deemed highly acceptable (Experiment 3) and that comprehenders do actively postulate gaps inside such subject-embedded tensed relatives (Experiment 4).

---

[23] [Whitaker Chambers, 2014 *Witness*]

(100) a. She is the kind of person$_i$ that [everyone who meets _$_i$] ends up falling in love
with _$_i$.
(Kayne, 1983)

b. John is someone [who]$_i$ [everyone who meets _$_i$] ends up disliking _$_i$.
(adapted from Culicover (1999, 179))

c. This is the book$_i$ that [everyone who reads _$_i$] raves about _$_i$.
(Kathol, 2001, 321)

In sum, the Subject Constraint is most likely tied to essentially the same pragmatic
factors that seem to be at work in NP Complement and CNPC island effects. The more
circumstantial the subject-embedded referent is for the main predication, the harder it
is to extract, i.e. the less relevant the subject-embedded referent is for the proposition,
the less extractable it is. The main difference between subject-embedded referents and
object-embedded referents is that they are subject to completely different pragmatic
biases. Subject-embedded gaps in main clauses are therefore rare, and very unexpected.
In contrast, extracting from objects is much more frequent, as objects are usually at-issue.

3.2.7 Adjunct Constraint

Cattell (1979), Huang (1982), Lasnik and Saito (1992), and others noted that adjuncts
often block extraction, a restriction known as the **Adjunct Constraint**. We illustrate this
phenomenon with the examples in (101). As in other islands, the in situ counterparts are
not subject to island effects.

(101) a. *[Who]$_i$ did Susan watch TV [while talking to _$_i$ on the phone]?
(cf. Did Susan watch TV while talking to Kim on the phone?)

b. *[Which meal]$_i$ did Robin read a magazine [during _$_i$]?
(cf. *Robin read a magazine during* WHICH MEAL?)

But the oddness of (101) is expected within Kuno's framework: the event described by the
adjunct is disjoint from the event described by the main verb, and therefore it is rather
unclear why the identity of an interlocutor is of any relevance for the action of watching
TV, or why a particular meal is of any relevance for the action of reading a magazine, out
of the blue. Adverbials expressing information that bears no relation to what is at issue are
not part of the main action (Takami, 1988; Van Valin, 1994; Erteschik-Shir, 2006b, 2007;
Goldberg, 2013).

Truswell (2011) proposes that Adjunct Island violations are allowed when the main
predicate and the modifier characterize the same event. So, the examples in (101) are odd
because the events expressed by the predicate and the modifier are (aspectually) unrelated.
Analogously, (102a) is licit because the PP specifies the time of the matrix event (and
therefore, there is a single event in the clause), whereas in (102b) the PP introduces a
different time, merely abutting the time of the matrix verb.

(102) a. [What day]$_i$ did he leave [on _$_i$]?
b. *[What time]$_i$ did you talk to him [until _$_i$]?

Kohrt et al. (2018a, b) found sentence acceptability evidence that the acceptability of Adjunct Island violations is contingent on semantic factors, but the results did not align particularly well with Truswell's (2011) predictions. Although Truswell's account is on the right track, it is too restrictive. First, in comparatives like (103a) there is no sense in which the event described by the main VP is the same as the one described by the comparative. The point of such comparatives is precisely to compare the frequency of two completely different events. Similarly, in (103b) there is no sense in which the event of changing an address is the same as the reason for changing an address.

(103)   a. [Which people]$_i$ can Robin run [nearly as fast as __$_i$]?
            (Hukari and Levine, 1995)

        b. Shawn is the type of ex-boyfriend$_i$ (that) you have to change your address [over __$_i$].

Second, Truswell (2011, 175) predicts that tensed clausal adjuncts cannot be extracted from, precisely because the event described by the matrix verb cannot be the same as the adjunct's. But as Truswell admits, this is problematic, given (104); see §3.2.7.2 for more examples and discussion.

(104)   This is the watch$_i$ that I got upset when I lost __$_i$.
        (attributed to Ivan A. Sag (pers. comm.) by Truswell (2011, 175, n. 1))

If semantics plays a key role in Adjunct Islands, then there should be strong acceptability variability. Indeed, phrasal Adjunct Islands are renowned to have robust and well-known counterexamples, as illustrated in (105). See Chomsky (1982), Engdahl (1983), Kayne (1983), Cinque (1990), and Truswell (2011) for more examples and discussion.

(105)   a. [Who]$_i$ did you go to Girona [in order to meet __$_i$]?
            (Hegarty, 1990)

        b. [Which room]$_i$ does Robin teach his class [in __$_i$]?
            (Pollard and Sag, 1994, 191)

        c. [Who]$_i$ did Robin claim that Sandy sang a song [for __$_i$]?

        d. [What]$_i$ do you think Robin computed the answer [with __$_i$]?
            (Bouma et al., 2001, 45)

        e. [How long] were you waiting out here for __$_i$?

        f. [Which temperature]$_i$ should I wash my jeans [at __$_i$]?
            (Chaves, 2013)

        g. [Which movies]$_i$ does Sean Bean die [in __$_i$]?

        h. All that was left was me and the cloak$_i$ I slept under __$_i$.
            [COCA 1999 FIC]

3.2.7.1 Parasitic Adjunct-embedded gaps

As in Subject Islands, sentences with Adjunct Island violations sometimes involve convergent UDCs with a second gap outside the island:

(106) a. Some are computer printouts, [which]$_i$ Dion discards $\_i$ without reading $\_i$.
            [COCA 1996 NEWS]

       b. ... with a name other than its original, making that file$_i$ difficult to locate $\_i$ after downloading $\_i$.
            [COCA 2001 MAG]

Such convergent UDCs can even involve tensed adverbial clauses:

(107) a. [Which colleague]$_i$ did John slander $\_i$ [because he despises $\_i$]?

       b. This is the kind of food$_i$ you must cook $\_i$ [before you eat $\_i$].
            (Engdahl, 1982, 9–11)

Since Engdahl (1982) it is widely assumed in the literature that adjunct-embedded gaps are only licit if 'parasitic' on a second gap. The paradigm is illustrated in (108).[24]

(108) a. Which student did the teacher accuse $\_i$ of being lazy while arguing with $\_i$ in class?

       b. *Which student did the teacher accuse Sam of being lazy while arguing with $\_i$ in class?

As in the case of Subject Islands, the paradigm in (108) is somewhat deceptive. The two sentences do not mean the same thing and do not come with the same pragmatic requirements. Thus, it is not entirely unexpected that one sentence is more acceptable than the other. For example, the proposition expressed by (108a) is certainly coherent: accusing x of wrong-doing can certainly be done via a heated argument with x. This is a rather prototypical combination of actions, and is trivial to contextualize. This is not the case with (108b), which is coherent but does not express a prototypical combination of actions: it is unclear what Sam's laziness has to do with the teacher arguing with some other student? Surely a suitable context can be constructed, but it is not trivial to do so. In other words, the main difference between (108a,b) may simply be due to two factors: (i) Contextualization difficulty (the former sentence expresses a mundane, yet complex situation; the other expresses a rather unusual one) and (ii) Kuno's aboutness constraint (if there is no obvious link between accusing Sam of laziness and arguing with a student, then there is no way for said student to be relevant to the action of accusing Sam of laziness).

The claim that parasitic gaps are responsible for licensing regular gaps in islands raises more problems than it solves. First, it flies in the face of counterexamples like (105),

---

[24] Cinque (1990) and others propose that all parasitic gaps are 'silent' resumptive pronouns. But as Steedman (1996, 98, n. 41), Levine et al. (2001), Levine (2001a), and Levine and Hukari (2006, 256, 273) show with examples like (i), such gaps can be non-nominal. See §3.3 for more on resumption.

i. [How harshly]$_{\text{AdvP}}$ do you think we can treat them$\_$ without in turn being treated $\_$ ourselves?

where there is only one gap, as well as counterexamples like (109), where all gaps reside in adverbial phrases.

(109)   [Which AC unit]$_i$ did you drive Alex crazy [complaining about $\_\_i$] yesterday [after buying $\_\_i$ from Craigslist]?

The UDC in (109) should be completely illicit, but instead it is passable. In fact, it is possible to compound a Subject Island and an Adjunct Island violation in the same UDC, as Levine and Sag (2003) and Levine and Hukari (2006, 256) note with (110). The fact that (110a,b) are less acceptable than (110c) is unexpected for a purely syntactic account, given that, in the latter, both gaps reside inside islands.

(110)   a.   *[What kinds of books]$_i$ do authors of $\_\_i$ argue about royalties after writing malicious pamphlets?

        b.   ?[What kinds of books]$_i$ do authors of malicious pamphlets argue about royalties after writing $\_\_i$?

        c.   [What kinds of books] do the authors of $\_\_i$ argue about royalties after writing $\_\_i$?

Again, the evidence is consistent with a semantic-pragmatic explanation. First, note that small changes to (110b) suffice to render it more acceptable:

(111)   [What kinds of books]$_i$ did they argue about royalties after writing $\_\_i$?

We suspect that (110a) is somewhat odd because writing malicious pamphlets would not usually lead to book authors arguing about book royalties. The two events do not cohere particularly well, as they do not describe a typical situation in the real world. When the verb phrase and the adverbial phrase describe a more canonical state of affairs, it is easier for the adverbial to express at-issue information rather than circumstantial information.

There are many claims in the literature about constraints that parasitic gaps supposedly adhere to, many of which are known to be empirically dubious, as Haegeman (1984), Horvath (1992), and Levine et al. (2001) discuss. For example, nothing prevents a gap in subject position from c-commanding another (Culicover and Postal, 2001, 42–6):

(112)   a.   [Which papers]$_i$ $\_\_i$ got published without the editor having read $\_\_i$?

        b.   [Who]$_i$ do you expect $\_\_i$ to withdraw his candidacy before the Committee has a chance to interview $\_\_i$?
             (Horvath, 1992)

        c.   [Who]$_i$ $\_\_i$ filed an HR complaint after $\_\_i$ being reprimanded?

        d.   [Which file]$_i$ $\_\_i$ got deleted after $\_\_i$ being downloaded from the server?

        e.   [Which documents]$_i$ $\_\_i$ got accidentally destroyed before anyone could review $\_\_i$?

Similarly, nothing requires that the adverbial-embedded 'parasitic' gap must follow the 'real' gap, as (113) illustrates, with clausal adjuncts. See §2.2.2.

(113) a. Robin is someone [who]$_i$ – until you get to know $_i$ – I suppose $_i$ can seem quite
strange.
(Haegeman, 1984)

  b. There were pictures of herself$_i$ [which]$_i$ once Mary$_i$ finally decided she$_i$ approved
of $_i$, John put $_i$ into circulation.
(Levine and Hukari, 2006, 49)

We conclude that the extant data about convergent UDCs involving adjuncts are more likely
to be governed by semantic-pragmatic factors than by strictly syntactic constraints. This is
consistent with the experimental evidence found by Kohrt et al. (2018a, b) and Kohrt et al.
(2020), showing that comprehenders attempt to fill gaps in English adjuncts according to
the semantic connectivity of the phrases involved. In particular, Kohrt et al. (2020) report
evidence that the gap is not predicted, and only postulated after the syntax and semantics
of the adjunct phrase is computed. We suspect the same is true for tensed clausal adjuncts,
which we now turn to.

3.2.7.2 Tensed adjunct island violations

Since Ross (1967), tensed adverbial clauses have been almost universally regarded as one
of the strongest environments prohibiting extraction. Consider, for example, (114). Such a
view is experimentally supported (Sprouse, 2007b; Sprouse et al., 2012, 2013, 2016).

(114) a. *[Who]$_i$ did John come back before I had a chance to talk to $_i$?
(Huang, 1982, 491)

  b. *[Who]$_i$ did Mary cry after John hit $_i$?
(Huang, 1982, 503)

But the empirical facts are not as clear-cut as traditionally assumed, as in the case of Subject
Islands. Over the years, various authors have noted that some of these extractions are
relatively acceptable, such as Grosu (1981, 88), Deane (1991, 29), Kluender (1998, 267),
Levine and Hukari (2006, 287), Goldberg (2006, 144), Taylor (2007), Truswell (2011, 175,
n. 1), Chaves (2013), and Jin (2015). Indeed, a closer look at experimental items from past
English experiments like those in (115) from Sprouse et al. (2012) suggests that the low
acceptability of tensed adjunct island violations is—at least in part—due to the plausibility
of the experimental items. More specifically, due to the fact that the matrix predication
and the adjunct's predication cohere very poorly, and therefore describe rather unusual
situations. For example, people don't routinely faint when something is forgotten on stage,
as in (115a), or typically sneeze if dog owners leave something open at night, as in (115c).
These sentences do not describe particularly plausible situations.[25]

(115) a. *[What]$_i$ do you faint if the actors forget $_i$ on stage?
  b. *[What]$_i$ do you sneeze if the dog owner leaves open $_i$ at night?
  c. *[What]$_i$ do you cough if the tourists photograph $_i$ in the exhibit?

---

[25] Similar concerns about the naturalness of experimental items used in island experiments are expressed by
Hofmeister and Sag (2010), Chaves and Dery (2014), Juzek and Häussler (2017), and Chaves and Dery (2019).

    d. *[What]$_i$ do you laugh if the heiress buys _$_i$ at the auction?
       (Sprouse et al., 2012)

Now compare with the more acceptable examples in (116), all of which express prototypical states of affairs, i.e. becoming upset after losing something, understanding a topic better after reading a book about it, and so on.

(116) a. [Which toy]$_i$ did Timmy get really upset when he lost _$_i$?

      b. [Which book]$_i$ will Sue understand linguistics better if she reads _$_i$?

      c. [Who]$_i$ would Robin be really happy if she could speak to _$_i$?

      d. [What]$_i$ would Mia be impressed if Robin cleaned _$_i$?

      e. [What]$_i$ did Tom get mad because Phil forgot to say _$_i$?

In the propositions in (116) the matrix verb expresses a psychological state and the embedded clause expresses key information about that state, rather than circumstantial information. Hence, it may be easier for the subordinate clause to express information that is relevant to the main action. Müller (2017) provides sentence acceptability evidence from Swedish suggesting that extraction from tensed adjuncts is contingent on the degree of semantic-pragmatic cohesion between the matrix clause and the subordinate. Similar results are reported for Norwegian by Bondevik (2018). We believe the same is essentially true for English Adjunct Constraint effects. Further evidence for this comes from the fact that the most acceptable Tensed Adjunct Island violations involve relative clauses which express assertions rather than backgrounded information, as illustrated in (117). For example, Sprouse et al. (2016) found no evidence of an Adjunct Island effect in relative clauses like (117b).

(117) a. I got to do things$_i$ in the film that, if you did _$_i$ on the street they'd send you away.
       [Dwaine Epstein. 2013 *Lee Marvin: Point Blank*, Schaffner Press, 98]

      b. I called the client [who]$_i$ the secretary worries if the lawyer insults _$_i$.
       (Sprouse et al., 2016)

      c. This is the watch$_i$ that I got upset when I lost _$_i$.
       (attributed to Ivan A. Sag (pers. comm.) by Truswell (2011, 175, n. 1))

All this evidence is consistent with Kuno's aboutness condition on UDCs. If the main action is construed as being a complex one, consisting of both the matrix predication and the embedded adverbial predication, then extraction from the adverbial expression is easier because the extracted entity is relevant to the main action. But if the adverbial expresses circumstantial (not at-issue) information and in addition the main action and the adjunct together describe an unusual situation, as in (118), then extreme oddness ensues. People don't usually laugh before the act of reading, and thus it is most unclear why the reference to a book matters for the laughing event.

(118) *[Which book]$_i$ did you laugh [before reading _$_i$]?
      (Sprouse and Hornstein, 2013, 13)

This is analogous to what happens in bridge verb constructions: if the matrix verb corresponds to a semantically impoverished event description such as 'say' or 'think', then it is easier for the subordinate clause to be what the entire utterance is about, as noted by Erteschik-Shir (1977, ch. 2, 1973), and Van Valin (1998). As we will show in §6.2.5, Adjunct Island violations are graded, and range from completely unacceptable to highly acceptable, depending on the type of semantic connection between the matrix and the subordinate clause.

3.2.8 Negative islands

We now arrive at a type of island that is not related to Kuno's aboutness constraint, but which is most likely semantic-pragmatic in nature, nonetheless. Ross (1984) observed that negative words like *not, no, never,* and *nobody* impose constraints on interrogative extractions, as illustrated in (119) and (120), involving degree questions and manner questions, respectively.

(119)   a.   [How fast]$_i$ did John drive __$_i$?
        b.   *[How fast]$_i$ didn't John drive __$_i$?
        c.   *[How fast]$_i$ don't you think John drove __$_i$?

(120)   a.   [How]$_i$ did Robin behave __$_i$?
        b.   *[How]$_i$ didn't Robin behave __$_i$?
        c.   *[How]$_i$ don't you think Robin behaved __$_i$?

It is widely assumed (Huang, 1982; Kroch, 1998; Rizzi, 1990; Cinque, 1990; Szabolcsi and Zwarts, 1993) that Negative Islands arise only in questions ranging over manners and degrees, and not in questions ranging over individuals, as illustrated by (121). These and various other facts strongly suggest a semantic-pragmatic account. See Kuno and Takami (1997, 559, n. 5), Szabolcsi and Zwarts (1993, 266), Szabolcsi (2006), Kroch (1998), Abrusán (2007, ch. 4, 2014) for criticism of syntactic accounts.

(121)   a.   [Who]$_i$ didn't you invite __$_i$ to the party?
        b.   [Who]$_i$ didn't you show this letter to __$_i$?
        c.   [Which song]$_i$ doesn't Robin like __$_i$?

For example, Kuno and Takami (1997) and Kroch (1998) note that Negative Islands become more acceptable in contexts where the possible answers are contextually restricted to a specific set, as illustrated in (122).

(122)   a.   A: The IRS is after me because I couldn't pay all of my taxes on time.
             B: [How much]$_i$ did you fail to pay __$_i$?
             (Kuno and Takami, 1997)

   b. [How much]$_i$ didn't you pay __$_i$ that you were supposed to?

   c. [How]$_i$ did you not play chess __$_i$? A: Blindfolded. B: Drunk. C: In a bathing suit.
       (Kroch, 1998)

Similarly, (123) is licit because going to the gym is typically restricted to particular days and times, and therefore it is not an open-ended question.

(123)   A: [When]$_i$ don't you go to the gym __$_i$?
        B: Tuesdays and Thursdays.

The same phenomenon is observed in manner interrogatives, as in (124). Such a UDC is licit in a context where there is a particular way in which John was expected to fix the car.

(124)   [How]$_i$ did John NOT fix the car __$_i$?
        (Szabolcsi and Zwarts, 1993)

Kuno and Takami (1997) and Szabolcsi and Zwarts (1993) also note that Negative Islands can be circumvented by certain modals, a phenomenon referred to as **modal obviation**. More specifically, Fox and Hackl (2006) observe that this phenomenon is restricted to environments where an existential modal is under the scope of negation, as in (125), or a universal modal outscopes negation, as in (126). The existence of such contrasts also speaks against processing-based accounts like Gieselman et al. (2011).

(125)   a. [How]$_i$ was John not allowed to behave __$_i$?
        b. *[How]$_i$ was John allowed not to behave __$_i$?
        c. [How many circles]$_i$ are you not allowed to draw __$_i$?
        d. *[How many circles]$_i$ are you allowed not to draw __$_i$?

(126)   a. [How fast]$_i$ is John required not to drive __$_i$?
        b. *[How fast]$_i$ is John not required to drive __$_i$?

   The most successful approaches to Negative Islands assume that the phenomena are semantic/pragmatic (Rullmann, 1995; Szabolcsi and Zwarts, 1993; Fox and Hackl, 2006; Abrusán, 2011). Although such accounts differ in the technical details, the emergent consensus seems to be that the oddness arises because such questions are ill-formed because of independently motivated general constraints on the semantics of interrogatives. Questions presuppose that there is a unique true answer among a set of alternatives, but in negated degree and manner questions, there cannot be such an answer. On the contrary, there is an infinite set of true answers. For example, suppose John drives a car at 35 mph. There is no unique speed at which John did not drive a car, since there is no discrete and unique amount of speed immediately above 35 mph. Rather, John didn't drive at any of the speeds above 35 mph, and therefore the only possible answer is a functional answer with an interval rather than a single number, e.g. *John didn't drive at any speed above 35 mph.* We believe this kind of account is on the right track. Note that it correctly predicts that Negative Islands are inoperative in UDCs which do not require the filler phrase to be in such a privileged position, like the declarative UDCs in (127).

(127)   a. [THAT FAST]$_i$ NOBODY would drive __$_i$.
            (cf. *How fast would nobody drive __?)

     b. [THAT FAST]$_i$ NOBODY drove __$_i$.
            (cf. *How fast did nobody drive __?)

We conclude that Negative Islands are not cross-constructionally active, and are most likely due to a semantic-pragmatic contradiction specific to UDCs that impose a uniqueness constraint on the filler.

3.2.9 Wh-islands

An extracted phrase can hamper the extraction of another phrase to a higher position. One such example is the **Wh-Complement Constraint**, illustrated in (128). This island is rather weak, and often is described as merely inducing degradation rather than unacceptability.

(128)   a. *How much did Bill wonder whether to pay __$_i$ for the book?
            (cf. *Did Bill wonder whether to pay $42?*)

     b. *[What]$_i$ did you wonder [whether John saw __$_i$]?
            (cf. *Did you wonder whether John saw the shooting star?*)

     c. *[Which book]$_i$ did the teacher ask you [whether Tom read __$_i$]?
            (cf. *Did the teacher ask you whether Tom read the book?*)

     d. *[Which problem]$_i$ did you wonder [how John solved __$_i$]?
            (cf. *Did you wonder how John solved the problem?*)

But counterexamples exist, like those in the attested sentences in (129). In both of these examples the relative clause expresses the assertion rather than presupposed content.

(129)   a. Seth, you had something$_i$ happen on your last film that I don't know [how anyone could be prepared for __$_i$].
            [www.latimes.com/entertainment/envelope/la-en-online-supporting-actors-panel-20151222-story.html, December 20, 2019]

     b. So that's Quick Look, a huge time saver and a feature$_i$ that you will wonder [how you could have ever lived without __$_i$].
            (Santorini, 2007)

For Kroch (1998) the reduced acceptability of interrogatives like (128) is due to these examples expressing implausible presuppositions. For example, (128a) presupposes the existence of a specific amount that Bill has in mind as a purchasing price and that he was wondering whether to pay that exact amount for it. This is not a particularly probable state of affairs. Compare with the more acceptable examples in (130). For instance, (130a) presupposes that there is an amount i such that the judges are arguing whether it should be the case that i points are deducted. One can immediately evoke contexts where such a question is likely to be asked.

(130) a. [How many points]$_i$ are the judges arguing about [whether to deduct _$_i$]?
            (Kroch, 1998)

       b. [Which shoes]$_i$ are you wondering [whether you should buy _$_i$]?

       c. [Who]$_i$ is John wondering [whether or not he should fire _$_i$]?
            (Chaves, 2012b)

       d. [Which glass of wine]$_i$ do you wonder [whether I poisoned _$_i$]?
            (Cresti, 1995, 81)

Licit extractions from infinitival clauses like (131) have been noted right from the onset, by Ross himself, and various others since. Again, in these cases the implicit subject of the embedded clause is the same as the subject of the higher clause, and the two events cohere rather well.

(131) a. He told me about a book which$_i$ I can't figure out [whether to buy _$_i$ or not].
            (Ross, 1967)

       b. [What]$_i$ did you wonder [whether to read _$_i$]?
            (Kluender, 1998)

       c. [Which topic]$_i$ did John ask [whether to talk about _$_i$]?
            (Szabolcsi, 2006)

       d. [Which shoes]$_i$ are you wondering [whether to buy _$_i$]?
            (Truswell, 2011, 14)

For Kroch (1998), Pollard and Sag (1994, 181), and others, Wh-Complement Constraint violations are syntactically licit, though sometimes pragmatically anomalous. See Abrusán (2014, ch. 4) for a detailed account whereby such island effects arise when the informative true answer requires very special and unnatural contexts, rendering them pragmatically odd.

Wh-Complement island effects also weaken with repeated exposure (Snyder, 2000; Hiramatsu, 2000; Francom, 2009; Crawford, 2011; Hofmeister, 2011), and according to Snyder (2017, forthcoming) the acceptability increase lasts for at least four weeks. This suggests that speakers can get better at processing such structures with repeated exposure, which should not happen, according to Chomsky (1995, 295) and Sprouse (2007a, 123), if such constructions were truly impossible to construct in the first place.

Finally, Michel (2014) provides ERP data suggesting that comprehenders postulate and fill gaps embedded in wh-islands just as readily as they do for control sentences. The difference concerns gap predictability inside the island environments: gaps are less predicted in an island domain, and when evidence for a gap is encountered there, an N400 response is elicited. This effect is significant in high working-memory-span readers only, and does not influence the ability to associate the filler and the gap. All of these sources of behavioral evidence suggest that subtle constraints are at work, and are consistent with Kroch's hypothesis that the unusualness of the expressed proposition (and therefore the low probability of the gap) plays a role in the decreased acceptability of such UDCs.

A related phenomenon is **Superiority** (Chomsky, 1973), classic instances of which are illustrated in (132). In sentences with multiple *wh*-phrases, the most deeply embedded one supposedly cannot be extracted 'over' the other. For some experimental validation of such contrasts in English, see Clifton et al. (2006), Fedorenko and Gibson (2010), and Häussler et al. (2015).

(132) a. [Who]$_i$ _$_i$ read what?
  b. *[What]$_j$ did [who]$_i$ _$_i$ read _$_j$?
  c. I can't remember [who]$_i$ _$_i$ carried what.
  d. *I can't remember [what]$_j$ [who]$_i$ _$_i$ carried _$_j$.

But judgments are murky, and a number of counterexamples have been noted (Bolinger, 1978; Kayne, 1984; Fiengo, 1980), such as those in (133); see also Clifton et al. (2006) and Hofmeister, Jaeger, et al. (2013) for attested counterexamples.

(133) a. [What]$_j$ will [which patient]$_i$ _$_i$ get _$_j$?
        (Pesetsky, 1987)

  b. [Which book]$_j$ did [which student]$_i$ _$_i$ read _$_j$?
        (Pesetsky, 2000)

  c. [What]$_j$ did [who]$_i$ _$_i$ see _$_j$ where?

  d. [Where]$_j$ did [who]$_i$ _$_i$ see what _$_j$?
        (Fiengo, 2007, 126)

In all such examples one wh-phrase is extracted over another. Erteschik-Shir (1973), Kluender (1998), and others note that counterexamples like (134) are not hard to find. All of these involve relative clauses which express assertions, and contain bridge verbs (i.e. verbs that have very weak and bleached semantics, which are unlikely to express the main action). Kroch (1998), Ginzburg and Sag (2000, 248), and Levine and Hukari (2006, 270) point out that Superiority effects and their counterexamples may simply result (at least in part) from the plausibility of background assumptions associated with the proposition.

(134) a. John is someone [who]$_i$ I never know [what]$_j$ to say _$_j$ to _$_i$.

  b. That's the article$_i$ that I was wondering [who]$_j$ _$_j$ was supposed to present _$_i$ in class tomorrow.
        (Levine, 2017, 308)

  c. [THIS BOOK]$_i$ she knows [who]$_j$ _$_j$ has written _$_i$.
        (Erteschik-Shir, 2006b)

Clifton et al. (2006) report that adding a third wh-phrase to a clause with a Superiority violation (e.g. I'd like to know where who hid it when) actually causes their acceptability to increase relative to the shorter version (e.g. I'd like to know where who hid it) for half the informants; cf. Fedorenko and Gibson (2010).

Pesetsky (1987), Cinque (1990), Rizzi (1990), and Pesetsky (2000, 16) propose that wh-elements which are connected with previous discourse are D(iscourse)-Linked, and, as such, are not extracted from any base position. Hence, they directly appear in the fronted position, are linked to their subcategorizers via a completely different mechanism, and therefore do not yield island effects. However, there is no experimental evidence that contextualization can lead to a D-Linking effect of a bare *wh*-phrase (Sprouse, 2007b; Villata et al., 2016), and as we shall see in §4.3.2, the notion of D-Linking raises more problems than it solves.

Hofmeister et al. (2007) and Sag et al. (2009) provide some experimental evidence suggesting that the distance between fillers and gaps—and the relative degree of activation in memory—very likely play a role in the processing difficulty and relative acceptability of English Wh-Complement and Superiority islands. Such results are consistent with the processing-cost models independently proposed by Gibson (2000) and Lewis et al. (2006). Working within a computational modeling perspective, Boston (2012) compares online reading-time data with a computational model that takes into consideration the cost of activating filler phrases in memory and the cost of interference caused by referents that are found while processing a UDC according to Gibson's (2000) model. Her results suggest that difficulty in processing Wh-Complement islands is associated with both activation and interference, whereas difficulty in processing Superiority violations appears to mainly be a result of interference difficulty.

Much more research is needed in order to pinpoint the combination of factors that give rise to English Wh-island effects and Superiority, but what seems clear is that purely syntactic accounts are unlikely to explain the full range of facts, given their gradience, sensitivity to context, and correlation with established models of sentence-processing difficulty.

3.2.10 Complementizer Constraint

Complementizer clauses hamper the extraction of subject phrases (Perlmutter, 1968, 1971). This is known as the **Complementizer Constraint**, among various other names, and is illustrated in (135) and (136). Mysteriously, violations with *that* are rather mild, but violations with *if* are extremely odd.

(135)   a.   What do you think $\_{-i}$ broke the window?
        b.   *What do you think that $\_{-i}$ broke the window?
             (cf. *Do you think that the ball broke the window?*)
        c.   What do you think (that) the ball broke $\_{-i}$?

(136)   a.   *[Which machine]$_i$ do you want to know [if $\_{-i}$ malfunctioned]?
             (cf. *Do you want to know if this machine malfunctioned?*)
        b.   [Which machine]$_i$ do you want to know [if I can fix $\_{-i}$]?
             (cf. *Do you want to know if I can fix this machine?*)

If the complementizer is omitted, then no island effect arises, as in (137b).

(137)   a.   *[Who]$_i$ did Sue claim [that $\_{-i}$ didn't read the book]?
             (cf. *Did Sue claim that these students didn't read the book?*)
        b.   [Who]$_i$ did Sue claim $\_{-i}$ didn't read the book?
        c.   [Who]$_i$ did Sue claim (that) the book was not read by $\_{-i}$?

The Complementizer Constraint is observed in many languages, but there is also much cross-linguistic variation. For example, Icelandic and Norwegian display **anti-Complementizer Constraint** effects (Taraldsen, 1978; Keer, 1999): it is the absence of the complementizer that is illicit when subject extraction takes place.

Rizzi (1990) argues that the Complementizer Constraint is universal, but that it can be sidestepped in languages that allow the subject to be clause-final. But counterexamples to this hypothesis abound. Some varieties of American English (Pesetsky, 1982) lack Complementizer Constraint effects. In fact, in Old English there simply was no such island constraint (Allen, 1980). Conversely, Lakhota does not exhibit Complementizer Constraint effects, even though the verb can never be clause-final (Van Valin, 1987). Moreover, Van der Auwera (1984), Gilligan (1987, 131–3,148–9), and Croft (2003, 82), identify several languages which have subject inversion but exhibit no Complementizer Constraint effects, including Basque, Papiamentu, varieties of Dutch, West Flemish, and Finland Swedish. We refer the reader to Pesetsky (2019) for a recent survey.

Besides the acceptability contrast caused by *that* and *if* violations, one of the main problems for syntactic accounts of Complementizer Constraint effects is that the constraint vanishes once extra material is added immediately after the complementizer, as Bresnan (1977, 194, n. 6), Culicover (1993), and others note. This **adverbial amelioration** effect is illustrated in (138).

(138) a. [Which students]$_i$ did you claim that as far as you could tell __$_i$ had read the book cover to cover?

   b. [Who]$_i$ do you think that after years and years of cheating death __$_i$ finally died?

   c. Robin met the man [who]$_i$ Leslie said that for all intents and purposes __$_i$ was the mayor of the city.

   d. [Which problem]$_i$ do you often wonder if at some point in the future __$_i$ will turn out to be unsolvable?

Kandybowicz (2006) proposes an independently motivated phonological account, whereby complementizers and subject gaps cannot be adjacent in the same prosodic (intonational) domain.[26] The basic idea ultimately stems from the observation that gaps are typically adjacent to stress peaks in phonology (Aoun et al., 1987; Culicover, 1993). In subordinate clauses with subject gaps, the complementizer combines with an Intonational Phrase, a phrasal boundary the left edge of which consists of a gap, a prosodic configuration that is not allowed, according to Kandybowicz (2006). Complementizers are leaners, in the sense of Zwicky (1986), meaning that they must prosodify with the Intonational Phrase introduced by the subordinate clause. But if there is a subject gap, then there is a prosodic boundary that prevents the complementizer from leaning. The break at a gap site and the lack of phonological reduction of the complementizer are both phonetic reflections of the existence of this prosodic boundary.

---

[26] For a related conclusion for German, see Salzmann et al. (2013), and for more on how prosody interacts with and potentially constrains extraction, see Dobashi (2010, 2014), Richards (2010, 2016), Erlewine (2016), and Mathieu (2016).

This explains why Complementizer Constraint violations weaken if the complementizer and the following verb can cliticize and contract, as the contrast in (139) illustrates.

(139) a. *Who did you allege that quit the company?

  b. ?Who did you allege th'td FINALLY quit the company last week?

There is a break between two Intonational Phrases in (139a), i.e. [*who did you allege*] [*that quit the company*]. Since the complementizer occurs after a pause, it is likely lengthened. In (139b), on the other hand, the complementizer cliticizes with the auxiliary verb into a portmanteau [ðɨɾɨd], and does so in a larger Phonological Phrase.

Kandybowicz (2006) argues that there are no Complementizer Constraint effects in subject relatives like *I saw the person that_ quit the company* because the prosodic phrasing of relative clauses is different from that of clausal complements. The latter is ultimately a consequence of the way in which the syntax of adjunct and complement clauses is reflected in phonology. The relative 'that' complementizer can much more easily prosodify with the following verb, as evidenced by the /æ/ → /ə/ vowel reduction that is typical of relatives, but uncommon in complement clauses. But the prosodic structure of complement clauses with subject gaps doesn't allow this reduction to take place. In Kandybowicz's account, the adverbial amelioration effect falls out as a prediction: the inserted adverbial phrase is prosodically independent from the surrounding phrases, and therefore the complementizer can lean on the adverbial phrase, while the gap site is cued by a break or pause. See Levine (2017, 315–19) for more discussion, and Ritchart et al.'s (2016) attempt to measure some of Kandybowicz's (2006) predictions.

According to Kandybowicz (2006, 2009), prosody also circumvents extraction asymmetries in Nupe, a Benue-Congo language poken in south-central Nigeria. Nupe displays Complementizer Constraint effects in (140a), but the omission of the complementizer does not cause amelioration (140b).

(140) a. *Zě$_i$ Gana gàn [gànán _$_i$ du   nakàn] o?
      who Gana say COMP   cook meat   FOC
      'Who did Gana say cooked the meat?'

  b. *Zě$_i$ Gana gàn [_$_i$ du   nakàn] o?
      who Gana say   cook meat   FOC
      'Who did Gana say cooked the meat?'
      (Kandybowicz, 2009, 329–30)   (Nupe)

However, the reduction of the multisyllabic complementizer to a monosyllabic form *án* improves the acceptability of subject extraction, as in (141).

(141) a. *Etsu$_i$ Musa gàn [gànán _$_i$ nì   enyà] o.
      chief Musa say COMP   beat drum FOC
      'Musa said that THE CHIEF beat a drum.'

  b. Etsu$_i$ Musa gàn [**án**   _$_i$ nì   enyà] o.
      chief Musa say COMP   bat drum FOC
      'Musa said that THE CHIEF beat a drum.'   (Nupe)

Kandybowicz (2009) also notes that if other material appears between the complementizer and the subject gap, then the prosodic constraint is not violated and the Complementizer Constraint effect is absent:

(142) a. Zě$_i$ Gana gàn [gànán **pányí** lě ___$_i$ du nakàn] o?
      who Gana say COMP long ago formerly cook meat FOC
      'Who did Gana say that long ago cooked meat?'

    b. Zě$_i$ Gana gàn [gànán ___$_i$ è/à/*∅ du nakàn] o?
      who Gana say COMP PRS/FUT/PST cook meat FOC
      'Who did Gana say is cooking/will cook the meat?' (Nupe)

Kandybowicz (2009) takes these patterns as evidence that complementizers and subject gaps cannot be adjacent in the same prosodic (intonational) domain in Nupe. We tentatively conclude that the Complementizer Constraint is due to conflicting prosodic phrasing requirements.

3.2.11 Frozen Structure Constraint

Ross (1967) and Wexler and Culicover (1980) noted that extraposition causes a phrase to become an extraction island. For example, the sentence-final PP in (143a,c) can be extracted, but if the NP is extraposed to the right of the PP, then the latter becomes an island, as in (143b,d). This constraint is generally known as **Freezing**, and, in particular, the instances where extraction takes place from an extracted phrase are sometimes referred to as Surfing (Sauerland, 1999).[27]

(143) a. I know the person [who]$_i$ you gave a book [to ___$_i$].
    b. *I know the person [who]$_i$ you gave [to ___$_i$]$_j$ a book ___$_j$.
    c. [Who]$_i$ do you think that John gave a book [to ___$_i$]?
    d. * [Who]$_i$ do you think that [to ___$_i$]$_j$ John gave a book ___$_j$?

To be sure, direct object extrapositions are, of course, attested, as in (144), as are direct object subextractions like those in (145). However, what is not attested is cases where both direct object extraposition and object subextraction occur in the same structure. These would constitute Freezing violations.

(144) a. Webb approved the sale ___$_i$ to Iraq [of military transport helicopters]$_i$ ...
      [COCA 1995 MAG]

    b. And what was the value ___$_i$ to Michelangelo [of being part of that]$_i$?
      [COCA 2008 SPOK]

    c. Just two weeks ago, Britain stopped a shipment ___$_i$ to Iraq [of devices that could be used to trigger nuclear weapons]$_i$.
      [COCA 1990 SPOK]

---

[27] See Corver (1990) for an overview of rightward Freezing effects, as well as Strunk and Snider (2013), Culicover and Winkler (2018), and Chaves (2018) for evidence that rightward movement island effects are graded and malleable rather than categorical.

(145)   a. ... this was something$_i$ James didn't seem to have [a problem with __$_i$].
        [COCA 2007 FIC]

        b. [OTHERS]$_i$ we're going to have to find [some housing for __$_i$].
        [COCA 1994 SPOK]

        c. There was one last question$_i$ my editor was dying to know [the answer to __$_i$].
        [COCA 2004 NEWS]

Syntactic accounts of UDCs typically assume that extraction is not possible from displaced phrases (Lasnik and Saito, 1992; Takahashi, 1994; Chomsky, 2001; Rizzi, 2007a), but, as discussed in Sauerland (1999) and §2.2.1.2, this assumption is empirically incorrect.[28]

There are several reasons why the acceptability of constructions with both extraposition and extraction should be penalized. Huck and Na (1990) and Bolinger (1992) note that in Freezing violations there are *two* phrases that are interpreted as Foci: the extracted phrase and the extraposed phrase. This naturally imposes stronger constraints on the context than utterances with a single Focus do. Moreover, the stranded preposition in (143b, d) is almost completely devoid of meaning. As Huck and Na (1990) note, stressing a semantically defective preposition is prosodically odd, as there is nothing to be contrasted. Because the preposition is devoid of meaning, all the semantics of the PP is contributed by the NP inside it, which in turn means that the referent that the NP describes would have two different pragmatic roles simultaneously, one obtained via extraction and the other by extraposition. Huck and Na (1990) note that this problem can be weakened if the preposition is semantically richer and less likely to take animate NPs as complements. In such cases the island effect becomes more acceptable, as (146) suggests.

(146)   a. This is a bridge [which]$_i$ I think I would never park UNDERNEATH __$_i$.

        b. This is a bridge [which]$_i$ I think [UNDERNEATH __$_i$]$_j$ I would never park __$_j$.
        (Chaves, 2018)

Fodor (1978, 457) notes that because a preposition is stranded in the middle of the sentence in (143b, d), this very likely gives rise to a competing temporary parse in which it combines with the adjacent NP as its complement, giving rise to a misparse. The existence of this local ambiguity can disrupt the parsing, especially given that it occurs in the critical portion of the sentence that contains multiple extraction dependencies in close succession (Hofmeister et al., 2015, 477). The existence of a locally licit but globally illicit parse can lead to a 'digging-in' effect (Ferreira and Henderson, 1991, 1993; Tabor and Hutchins, 2004), analogous to the garden-path/digging-in processing explanations for Kuno's Clause Non-Final Incomplete Constituent Constraint discussed in §3.1. Indeed, there is a weaker type of Freezing violation, shown in (147), where there is no sentence-medial preposition stranding. Here, the direct object is extraposed and extracted from. As Chaves (2018) experimentally shows, this type of Freezing violation is milder than its P-stranding variety in (143).

---

[28] Under the **VP-Internal Subject** Hypothesis (Koopman and Sportiche, 1991), exceptions to the Subject Island Constraint like those discussed in §3.2.6 would also constitute counter-evidence for the Freezing Constraint. See §4.3.1 for more discussion.

(147)   a. *[Who]$_i$ did you give __$_j$ to Robin [a picture of __$_i$]$_j$?
           (Wexler and Culicover, 1980)

       b. *[What]$_i$ did you give __$_j$ to John [a book about __$_i$]$_j$?
           (Lasnik and Saito, 1992, 103)

Hofmeister et al. (2015) and Culicover and Winkler (2018) experimentally show that
Freezing effects have graded acceptability, ranging from unacceptable to acceptable. In
particular, their acceptability can increase with repeated exposure (Chaves, 2018). We
conclude that it is very unlikely that Freezing effects are due to a syntactic ban on extraction
from moved phrases. Rather, this phenomenon is probably due to a mix of syntactic,
pragmatic, phonological, and processing biases (Fodor, 1978; Huck and Na, 1990; Bolinger,
1992; Hofmeister et al., 2015; Culicover and Winkler, 2018; Chaves, 2018).

3.2.12 Left Branch Condition

Along with the Conjunct Constraint, the only other island effect that we are aware of that
has no exceptions in English is the **Left Branch Condition** (LBC), illustrated in (148). Here,
what is extracted is the specifier phrase. For a UDC to be possible in these cases, the nominal
must be moved along with the specifier, via pied-piping, e.g. *Whose friend did you meet __?*
Alternatively, the *wh*-phrase can remain in situ and no island effect arises. As usual, if the
prosodic contour is not rising, no reprise or echo reading arises.

(148)   a. *[Whose]$_i$ did you meet [__$_i$ friend]?
           (cf. *You met* WHOSE FRIEND?)

       b. *[Which]$_i$ did you buy [__$_i$ book]?
           (cf. *You bought* WHICH BOOK?)

       c. *It was her$_i$ that I saw [__$_i$ car].
           (cf. *I saw her car*)

       d. *[ROBIN's]$_i$ I bought [__$_i$ book].
           (cf. *I bought Robin's book*)

Contrary to many of the previous island phenomena, Left Branch Constraint violations do
not become more acceptable with increased frequency (Snyder, 2000, 2017; Sprouse, 2009;
Goodall, 2011).

   Languages that apparently allow LBC violations, like most Slavic languages, don't have
determiners (Uriagereka, 1988, 113). These exceptions may therefore not involve true LBC
violations, since the extracted phrase need not form a constituent with the putative nominal
remnant. More likely, the extracted phrase is simply in apposition to the nominal head.
There are also languages that obey the LBC but have a special construction in which
such extractions seem possible; see Corver (2014) for a detailed overview. For example,
extractions like (149a) are illicit in French because of the LBC, but expressions like *combien*
appear to sidestep this constraint.

(149) a. *Quels$_i$ avez-vous acheté _$_i$ livres?
       how-many have-you bought   books
       'How many books have you bought'

     b. Combien$_i$ a-t-il   vendu _$_i$ de livres?
       how-many has-he sold   of books
       'How many books did he sell?'

     c. Combien$_i$ crois-tu   qu'il   a   _$_i$ de livres?
       how-many think-you that-he has   of books
       'How many books do you think he has?'   (French)

There are empirical reasons to believe that there is no LBC violation in (149b,c). The *de livres* phrase has been argued to be a kind of post-verbal NP in French, and it has been claimed that *combien* behaves more like a nominal than a canonical quantifier (Kayne, 1981; Abeillé et al., 2004). For example, the former can appear without the latter in the presence of other licensors, including the preposition *sans* ('without') or negation, e.g. *Paul n'a pas lu [de livres]* ('Paul did not read any books'). If *combien* and the *de*-phrase are autonomous, then no LBC violation occurs in (149b, c). We return to the LBC in §5.2.4.

Before concluding, we note certain UDCs that are not quite LBC violations, but which instead involve extraposition. In (150) an NP is split into two phrases, one that is fronted and a PP that is not.

(150)   a. [How many books]$_i$ do you have _$_i$ about astronomy?
       b. [How many pictures]$_i$ do you have _$_i$ of Marilyn Monroe?
       c. [How many attempts]$_i$ did you make _$_i$ to repair the computer?

But as (151) shows, the PP can appear outside the VP that the extracted NP would otherwise belong to, suggesting that the PP is extraposed from the extracted phrase. Displacement from a displaced phrase is sometimes called **Remnant Movement**; see also chaining dependencies like those in §2.2.1.2.

(151)   a. [How many books _$_j$]$_i$ did you buy _$_i$ yesterday [about astronomy]$_j$?
       (cf. 'Did you [[buy [many books about astronomy]] yesterday]?')

       b. [How many videos _$_j$]$_i$ are there _$_i$ on the web [of Mitt Romney getting booed]$_j$?
       (cf. '[Many videos of Mitt Romney getting booed] are on the web')

We now turn our attention to phenomena that do not involve overt filler-gap linkages but which nevertheless have been argued to exhibit island effects, and therefore to involve the same syntactic mechanism as that responsible for UDCs.

3.3 Resumptive UDCs

In certain conditions, a pronoun is realized at the bottom of a UDC instead of a gap. Such long-distance dependencies are known as **resumptive**. Drawing from Asudeh (2004, ch. 8), we identify several kinds of resumption. The first kind is grammatically licensed, and in all respects like a standard UDC. The second kind is also grammatically licensed, but is used to avoid grammatical constraints such as certain islands. Finally, the third kind is not grammatically licensed, and instead is used in an attempt to cope with UDCs that are difficult to process.[29]

3.3.1 Grammatical resumption

Although English usually disallows pronouns at the bottom of a filler-gap dependency, there are cases where such resumptive UDCs are licit, as in (152–154). Note that in these examples the gaps and resumptive pronouns are in free variation, and there are no island violations whatsoever.

(152)   a. [Which girl]$_i$ did you say that you think of her$_i$ whenever it rains?

      b. [Which girl]$_i$ did you say that you think of __$_i$ whenever it rains?

(153)   a. This is a movie [which]$_i$ the older I get, the more I enjoy it$_i$.

      b. This is a movie [which]$_i$ the older I get, the more I enjoy __$_i$.

(154)   a. [Which boy]$_i$ did you say that—if it thunders—he$_i$ wets the bed?

      b. [Which boy]$_i$ did you say that—if it thunders—__$_i$ wets the bed?

McKee and McDaniel (2001) (Experiment 3) provide evidence that speakers readily accept resumption types like (155b); see also Ackerman et al. (2018) for more experimental evidence, and Loss and Wicklund (2020) for results suggesting that resumptives tend to be more acceptable in appositive relatives than in other relatives. If this is correct, then pragmatics plays a role in resumptive use, as argued by Cann et al. (2005).

(155)   a. This is the girl [who]$_i$—whenever it rains—she$_i$ cries.

      b. This is the girl [who]$_i$—whenever it rains—__$_i$ cries.

Although it is unclear why some resumptives are acceptable and others aren't, it is cross-linguistically common for resumption to be construction-dependent. For example, in Hebrew some UDCs require gaps, some require resumptives, and some allow both gaps and resumptives in free variation (Doron, 1982; Borer, 1984; Sells, 1984; Shlonsky, 1992).

    English arguably also exhibits such a mix of resumption types. Some are like standard extraction, as illustrated by the non-island examples in (152–154), and other uses are less so, such as the Left Branch constraint violations in (156). In the latter examples, the resumptive removes the island effect.

(156)   a. This is the girl [who]$_i$ her$_i$ dog cries all night when it storms.

      b. [Which boy]$_i$ did you say his$_i$ father had won the lottery?

---

[29] The latter resumptives are also referred to as **intrusive** pronouns (Sells, 1984, 17).

c. [Which famous actress]$_i$ did you say that you went to school with her$_i$ father?

d. This is the boy [who]$_i$ I think his$_i$ father recently won the lottery...

In some languages, resumption involves the same kind of extraction mechanism as those in regular UDCs. In Swedish (Engdahl, 1982; Sells, 1984), Igbo (Goldsmith, 1981), and Vata (Koopman and Sportiche, 1986), both gap and resumptive UDCs exhibit the same island effects. Moreover, island constraints that in other languages can only be satisfied with a gap can also be satisfied with a resumptive. For example, Swedish and Hebrew exhibit the same ATB exception to the CSC that English does, but either a gap or a pronoun can be used for that purpose (Zaenen et al., 1981; Borer, 1984; Sells, 1984).

Resumptive UDCs can have an overt syntactic effect, just like that of standard extraction. Palauan (Georgopoulos, 1991), Welsh (Borsley, 2010), Hausa (Crysmann, 2012), and Irish (McCloskey, 1979) are extraction pathway-marking languages where the extraction pathway marking is triggered in exactly the same way by resumptives and by gaps. Consider the case of Irish, as an illustration. In addition to the complementizer *goN* that combines with non-gapped clauses, and the complementizer *aL* that combines with gapped clauses, there is a third complementizer *aN* that is reserved for resumptive dependencies. As McCloskey (1979, 2002) notes, a single non-local dependency pathway can partially be marked with the *aL* and with the *aN* gap markers, as illustrated in (157).

(157) rud **aN** raibh coinne   aige **aL** choimhlíonfadh _ an aimsir
       thing that was   expectation him that fulfill-COND   the time
       'something that he expected time would confirm'

The lower clause contains a gap, and this dependency is accordingly marked by the *aL* complementizer, but the dependency in the matrix clause is marked by the resumptive complementizer *aN*. In (158), we observe the opposite pattern, with the embedded clause exhibiting the resumptive dependency and the matrix exhibiting a dislocation dependency, respectively. Both combine to yield a single dependency crossing both clauses.

(158) aon duine **aL** cheap   sé **aN** raibh ruainne tobac   aige
       any person that thought he that was   scrap   tobacco at.him
       'anyone that he thought had a scrap of tobacco'

3.3.2 Constraint-avoidance resumption

There is independent evidence that pronouns are used by speakers to sidestep grammatical violations, for example, to avoid the realization of discourse-new referents in positions that disfavor discourse-new entities, like the subject position (Prince, 1990, 1997):

(159) It's supposed to be such a great deal. The guy$_i$, when he came over and asked if I wanted a route, he$_i$ made it sound so great. Seven dollars a week for hardly any work. And then you find out the guy told you a bunch of lies.
       (Prince, 1997, 121)

Similarly, resumptive pronouns tend to appear in certain island environments, as illustrated by the Left Branch Constraint violations in (156). Other examples are Wh-Complement

Constraint violations like (160) and Tensed Adjunct Constraint violations like (161). What these resumption uses have in common is that they are predominantly found in speech (Prince, 1990; Cann et al., 2005; Ferreira and Swets, 2005). See Radford (2019, ch. 2) for a wealth of attested examples, all from colloquial spoken British English.

(160) a. A: You bought Anttila?
          B: No, this is Alice Freed's copy.
          A: My copy$_j$ of Anttila I don't know [who]$_i$ _$_i$ has it$_j$.
          (Prince, 1997, 133)

       b. There are always guests who$_i$ I'm curious about [what]$_j$ they$_i$ are going to say _$_j$.
          (Prince, 1990, 482)

       c. I had some other point [which]$_i$ I can't remember [what]$_j$ it$_i$ is _$_j$.
          (Cann et al., 2005)

       d. That's the kind of house$_j$ that there's no point in finding out [how much]$_i$ it$_j$ costs _$_i$.

(161) a. Apparently there are such things as bees in the area [which]$_i$ [if you get stung by them$_i$] you die.
          (Prince, 1990, 483)

       b. This is one of those movies$_i$ that I will always watch [when it$_i$'s on].

Ross (1967) Kroch (1981), Prince (1990), and Erteschik-Shir (1992) argue that one of the uses of resumptives is to avoid violating island constraints. This may be true in some examples, but most likely not true in general. McDaniel and Cowart (1999), Morgan and Wagers (2008, 867) and Keffala (2013) find evidence that subject-resumptive pronouns are more acceptable than subject gaps in certain island violations like (162), from McDaniel and Cowart (1999). No such amelioration occurs with object resumptives, as (163) illustrates.

(162) a. *That's the girl$_i$ that I wonder when _$_i$ met you.
       b. That's the girl$_i$ that I wonder when she$_i$ met you.

(163) a. *That's the girl$_i$ that I wonder when you met _$_i$.
       b. *That's the girl$_i$ that I wonder when you met her$_i$.

The example in (162b) is fairly acceptable, again suggesting that this type of island-avoiding resumption may in fact be grammatical. Further evidence in favor of this view comes from the experiment in Ackerman et al. (2018), which suggests that some resumptives can—in ideal conditions—circumvent island effects, challenging all prior null results. Consider the sample of resumptive UDCs in (164), from Ackerman et al.'s (2018) study.

(164) a. [Which woman]$_i$ did Carlos report that the newscaster who exposed her$_i$ threatened the detective's case?

       b. [Which woman]$_i$ did Carlos report that, when the newscaster exposed her$_i$, the criminal threatened the detective's case?

c. [Which woman]$_i$ did Carlos question how the newscaster exposed her$_i$?
(Ackerman et al., 2018)

Such items are clearly related to those in McKee and McDaniel (2001), discussed in §3.3.1. Although much more work is needed, there is some reason to believe that some types of resumption are grammatical in English, for some grammatical functions and in certain constructions, as in other languages.

3.3.3 Processing resumption

Although resumption can cause some amelioration, some studies find it does not usually cancel the island effect entirely (Ferreira and Swets, 2005; Alexopoulou and Keller, 2007; Heestand et al., 2011; Han et al., 2012; Chacón, 2019b), at least for the islands tested and for the items used. Morgan and Wagers (2018) show that the lower acceptability of a given structure with a gap is positively correlated with the frequency of resumptives in that same structure. Island violation structures increase the tendency to use a resumptive, which is suggestive of a processing strategy deployed during unplanned speech production in an attempt to avoid an island violation.

Resumptives also seem to be less egregious in difficult-to-process contexts (Erteschik-Shir, 1992; Asudeh, 2012). This is experimentally confirmed by Alexopoulou and Keller (2007), Heestand et al. (2011), Hofmeister and Norcliffe (2013), and Chacón (2019b). In particular, Hofmeister and Norcliffe (2013) report self-paced reading evidence which suggests that resumption facilitates the processing of complex UDCs. This is consistent with the findings of Morgan and Wagers (2018), which indicate that resumption is more frequent in doubly embedded object relatives than in simple object relatives, despite the fact that the former constructions are not islands and therefore such gaps are fully grammatical.

More recently, Chacón (2019a) provides experimental evidence which suggests that as the representation of a filler phrase fades from working memory, owing to sentence length or to increased strain on working memory, comprehenders become less sensitive to ungrammatical continuations of the sentence, and have more difficulty in incorporating the filler into the semantic representation.

We suspect that different researchers have arrived at conflicting results about English resumption not only because of different methodologies and items, but also because there are different types of resumptive use. Some forms of resumption seem to be truly licit (regardless of the presence of an island environment), whereas others are more likely due to processing difficulty and are not fully sanctioned by the grammar.

3.4 Islands in other dependencies?

We now turn to three long-distance phenomena which have traditionally been claimed to involve the same extraction operation that is responsible for UDCs, even though no overt extraction takes place. As we shall see, there is no clear empirical evidence that such long-distance dependencies involve the same syntactic mechanism that gives rise to filler-gap dependencies.

3.4.1 Ellipsis

Ross (1969) noted that ellipsis seems to render island constraints inactive, as in the **sluice** constructions in (165). See Lasnik (2000) and Merchant (2001) for more examples and discussion.

(165) a. That he'll hire someone is possible, but I won't divulge [who].
          [Sentential Subject Constraint violation]

     b. Bo talked to the people who discovered something, but we don't know [what].
          [Complex NP Constraint violation]

     c. He wants a detailed list, but I don't know [how detailed].
          [Left Branch Constraint violation]

Merchant (2001, 2004) and Fox and Lasnik (2003) argue that extraction is followed by phonological deletion in sluice constructions. A simpler and more parsimonious account is one which assumes that *wh*-phrase remnants like (165) do not involve any UDC. Rather, they are directly assigned an interpretation based on the surrounding discourse context (Tanenhaus and Carlson, 1990; Hardt, 1999; Ginzburg and Sag, 2000; Culicover and Jackendoff, 2005; Jacobson, 2008; Sag and Nykiel, 2011; Kertz, 2013; Martin and McElree, 2008, 2009, 2011; Miller and Pullum, 2013). In such accounts, ellipsis resolution is a context-dependent anaphoric mechanism that does not require complex structure at the ellipsis site. Rather, the missing content is recovered from the common ground, via the Question Under Discussion (Roberts, 1996, 2012). This direct interpretation approach is independently motivated by the fact that fragments can have the same distribution and interpretation as clauses, if properly contextualized:

(166) a. A: Does Mia know BRENDAN?
          B: No, [Frank] (knows Brendan).

     b. A: What do you think Robin wants?
          B: (Robin wants) [Drugs], probably.

     c. A: What did Sam give you on your birthday?
          B: (Sam gave me) [Flowers], which was nice.

     d. B: Who owns a dog?
          B: [Kim] (owns a dog), and it's a dachshund.
          (Arnold and Borsley, 2008, 328)

The direct interpretation account correctly predicts that the antecedent for the elided phrase need not correspond to overt discourse, as in (167), based on Hankamer and Sag (1976), and Sag and Hankamer (1984).

(167) a. [Context: one more person enters an elevator]
          Which floor?

     b. [Context: volunteers step forward to aid in a task]
          Who else? Nobody else?

Finally, the direct interpretation account explains why such remnant constructions are immune to island constraints: since there is no UDC, there can be no island effect. In other words, ellipsis does not amnesty island violations. Rather, there is no extraction to begin with, and therefore no island violation occurs. As Ginzburg and Sag (2000, 314) point out, this explains why sluiced *wh*-phrases generally resist modification by *what the heck* and *what the hell*, as in (168). This suggests that the sluiced *wh*-phrase is not extracted. As discussed in §2.1.1, such expletives can only modify extracted *wh*-phrases.

(168)   a.   A: A friend of mine came in.
             B: Who (*the hell)?
        b.   A: A friend of mine must have stepped in while I was out.
             B: I wonder who (*the heck).

We refer the reader to Kubota and Levine (2020, ch. 8) for in-depth discussion and detailed criticism of ellipsis accounts that assume covert syntactic structure.

Fragment answers are similarly not sensitive to islands, in spite of claims to the contrary by Merchant (2004). The relevant examples are (169).[30]

(169)   a.   A: Did you leave the party because ABBY was rude to you?
             B: No, MOLLY. She was the one who was rude.
             [Adjunct Constraint violation]
        b.   A: Did you meet the person who ABBY is dating?
             B: No, MOLLY.
             [Complex NP Constraint violation]
        c.   A: Did you want ONE scoop of ice cream?
             B: No, TWO.
             [Left Branch violation]
        d.   A: Did you flirt with me AND ABBY?
             B: No, MOLLY.
             [Coordinate Structure Constraint violation]

Sluices where the antecedent is an implicit object, as in (170a), are called **sprout type sluicing**, and are likewise supposed to exhibit island effects according to Merchant (2001). Consider for example the Adjunct Constraint violation in (170b).

(170)   a.   John was smoking, but I don't know what.
        b.   *John got upset because Sam was smoking, but he didn't tell me what.

But Romero (1998) and others since note that the oddness of (170b) can be explained by the fact that the implicit argument takes narrow scope in the first conjunct but the *wh*-phrase must take wide scope in the second conjunct. This is a problem because symmetric coordinations usually induce scopal parallelism between conjuncts. See Yoshida et al. (2013) for acceptability and self-paced reading evidence that is consistent with Romero's analysis.

---

[30] Claims about island sensitivity in Gapping constructions are similarly empirically problematic, as Culicover and Jackendoff (2005, 273), Repp (2009, 11), Kubota and Levine (2016b, 120), and Park (2019, 101) show.

However, there are island-insensitive sprouting constructions (Culicover and Jackendoff 2005, 258, Kim and Kuno 2013). For example, in (171) the act of playing poker entails the existence of at least two players, so the statement that the identity of the adversary is unknown is pragmatically licit.

(171)   I believe the reports that the victim was playing poker on the night of the murder, although we don't know with whom.
[CNPC]

Similarly, the act of playing the piano entails the existence of some tune, so in (172) it is plausible that the speaker would know what is the denotation of the missing complement, which then provides the motivation to use an adversative as a way to express that the expectation is violated. See Culicover and Jackendoff (2005:258) and Kim and Kuno (2013) for other examples, involving clausal subjects and relative clauses.

(172)   Alex arrived when Ben was playing the piano, but I don't recall which tune.
[Clausal Adjunct Island]

In contrast, the violated expectation that motivates the use of the adversative in (173) would be that the speaker should know what was eaten. But knowing that Sam arrived before Ben ate does not lead to the expectation that the speaker would know the food that was eaten. This information is not relevant, i.e. in the speaker's awareness, to use Kim and Kuno's (2013) terminology. The meal itself is of little importance to the described situation, and therefore its mention is pragmatically odd. Sprouting island phenomena seem to be pragmatic in nature.

(173)   *Sam arrived before Ben ate, but I can't recall what / which meal.

3.4.2 Quantifier scope

Another type of dependency that has sometimes been argued to involve an invisible syntactic extraction operation is quantifier scope. Sentences like (174) have two possible interpretations. Either the existential quantifier has scope over the universal or the universal has wide scope over the existential. The latter somehow requires a syntactically embedded scopal operator to obtain wide scope.

(174)   Every arrow hit a target.

... It ended up loaded with arrows.
Reading 1: 'A particular target was hit by every arrow'
$\exists y(target(y) \land \forall x(arrow \rightarrow hit(x, y)))$

... The closest targets were hit more than the others.
Reading 2: 'Every arrow hit a (potentially) different target'
$\forall x(arrow(x) \rightarrow \exists y(target(y) \land hit(x, y)))$

May (1985), Ruys (1993), Fox (2000), Sabbagh (2007), Bachrach and Katzir (2008), and various others claim that quantifier scope ambiguities result from essentially the same operation that is responsible for filler-gap dependencies, except that in the case of quantifier scope the extraction is 'covert' and has no impact on surface realization. Such a **covert movement** operation is what allows a syntactically embedded quantifier to be interpreted as if it were in a syntactically higher position, and obtain wide scope. Indeed, many authors have claimed that quantifier scope exhibits island effects (May, 1985; Ruys, 1993; Fox, 2000; Winter, 2001; Sabbagh, 2007; Bachrach and Katzir, 2008). This claim is problematic for two reasons. First, whereas comprehenders attempt to resolve filler-gap dependencies as soon as possible (Frazier, 1987; Fodor, 1978; Stowe, 1986; Frazier and d'Arcais, 1989; Boland et al., 1995), scope ambiguities have been shown to sometimes remain unresolved until the end of the utterance (Frazier and Rayner, 1982; Dwivedi et al., 2008; Dwivedi, 2013). This suggests that quantifier scope ambiguities are of a very different nature from UDCs.

Second, Steedman (2001, 79), Culicover and Jackendoff (2005, 141), Copestake et al. (2005, 303, 304), Chaves (2007), Yatabe (2007), and Keshet (2008) note that 'missing' quantifier scopings are often due to interpretive biases of the chosen examples rather than to a grammatical constraint. For example, even though the phrases *each of the castles* and *every language* are embedded in relative clauses in (175a,b), they can have wide scope over the indefinite *someone* outside the relatives. This would constitute a CNPC violation if it were active in semantic scope.

(175) a. We were able to find someone who was an expert on each of the castles we planned to visit.
        (Copestake et al., 2005, 304)

      b. John was able to find someone who is willing to learn every language that we intend to study.
        (Chaves, 2014)

Similarly, the NP Constraint and the Subject Island Constraint are not in effect in examples like (176). The embedded universal quantifier phrase *every company* can obtain wide scope over the entire sentence, including the indefinite object.

(176) A representative of every company tried a product sample.

Scope island effects are also absent in Complementizer Constraint violations. In (177), the *each/a student* phrase in the embedded clause can outscope the subject phrase of the matrix clause.

(177) a. Some teacher claimed that each student had cheated.
      b. Every teacher claimed that a student had cheated.

If quantifier scope were subject to island constraints, then environments that categorically ban extraction should also ban wide scope. But this is not borne out. In (178) the universal quantifier can outscope the indefinite subject, constituting a Left Branch constraint violation.

(178) Someone took a picture of each student's bicycle.
(Copestake et al., 2005, 303)

Coordination structures are another classic syntactic island environment that similarly imposes no island effects on quantifier scope. For example, in (179a) the existential subject *an official representative* can be outscoped by the universal quantifiers in the conjuncts, which is exactly the reading that is supposed to be impossible according to the CSC. The same is true for the existential *some student* in (179b).

(179) a. The White House is very careful about this. An official representative [[will personally read each document] and [reply to every letter]].

   b. We had to do this ourselves. By the end of the year, some student [[had proof-read every document] and [corrected each theorem]].
(Chaves, 2007)

Furthermore, it is possible for quantifiers to interact across conjuncts. Consider the examples in (180), which allow one of the conjuncts to outscope the other. See Carpenter (1997, 325) for more discussion of these and related data. There are simply no scope island effects in coordination.

(180) a. Your task will be to document the social interaction between each female and an adult male.

   b. Let us suppose that the goal is to promote a closer relationship between every customer and a new product.

   c. In order to blackmail the entire Linguistics department, a model and each professor were photographed together at the party.
(Chaves, 2007)

We conclude that island phenomena do not provide empirical support in favor of the existence of covert movement. Rather, scope ambiguities are most likely purely semantic in nature, and computed very differently from UDCs. To be clear, we do not deny that there are constraints on quantifier scope. Rather, we see no parallel between UDC constraints and quantifier scope constraints. A variety of alternative accounts of scopal phenomena exist which do not rely on a covert version of the operation responsible for UDCs such as Steedman (2001, 76–83), Cooper (1983), Reyle (1993), Copestake et al. (2005), and Richter and Sailer (2004).

3.4.3 Interrogative scope

Something analogous to quantifier scope occurs in the interpretation of questions with in situ interrogatives. The sentence in (181a) expresses the Yes/No question *do you know the answer to the question: which person x did Mia see?* Conversely, (181b) expresses a content question: *which person x do you know that Mia saw?* It is clear that the relative position of the *wh*-phrase determines the scope of the interrogative semantics: if the fronted *wh*-phrase stays within the embedded clause rather than in the matrix clause, then the sentence expresses a Yes/No question rather than a content question.

(181) a. Do you know who Mia saw_?   (Yes/No question)

      b. Who do you know Mia saw_?   (Content question)

But when the *wh*-phrase is not fronted at all, as in (182), then how can the sentence end up expressing a content question? It somehow needs to outscope the entire proposition, just as in (181).

(182) a. You're expecting ↑WHO↓ at your party next weekend?

      b. You opened ↑WHICH WINDOWS↓ last night? It got really drafty.

      c. You saw ↑HOW MANY PATIENTS↓ today? Fifty? A hundred?

The same phenomenon arises in multiple interrogatives, as in (183), as noted by Baker (2001). The matrix-fronted *who* phrase causes the utterance to be a content question. The *where* phrases fronted in the embedded clause are not part of the question. However, the in situ phrase *what* may or not be part of the question. Again, we have a long-distance dependency that does not appear to involve extraction.[31]

(183) Q: Who remembers where we bought what?

      A_1: Alice remembers where we bought the vase.

      A_2: Alice remembers where we bought what.

Further evidence that wide scope is involved in interrogative meaning comes from languages that have a particle which overtly marks the scope of the interrogative, referred to as a **Q(uestion)-particle** (Kuroda, 1965; Hagstrom, 1998; Kishimoto, 2005; Cable, 2010; Tsoulas and Yeo, 2017).

Some theories of interrogatives like Baker (1970) and Cheng (1991) reject the idea that in situ interrogatives with wide scope involve any form of invisible extraction. Rather, the phenomenon is viewed as being due to a completely different type of mechanism, involving a binding operation at a distance. Others like Van Valin and LaPolla (1997) model it via illocutionary operators, and Ginzburg and Sag (2000) and Sag (2010) model interrogative scope via a storage feature WH. If interrogative scope is not due to invisible extraction operations, then it follows that it should not exhibit island effects. This prediction is correct. For example, sentences like (184) would be predicted to be impossible, as covert Left Branch violations; see §3.2.12 for more examples.

(184) a. A: Mueller is looking into exactly this issue right now.

         B: And he is investigating this under WHOSE↓ authority?

      b. A: This just isn't right!

         B: . . . It isn't right by ↑WHOSE↓ standards?

---

[31] A related type of dependency that seems to be unbounded as well is pied-piping, as (i) and (ii) illustrate. Here, a deeply embedded interrogative phrase must gain wide scope over the entire clause. See, however, Van Eynde (2004) for arguments that pied-piping is merely an edge-feature phenomenon.

  i. [[[Whose cousin]'s friend]'s dog]$_i$ is she going to buy_$_i$?

  ii. [How much smarter than Paul]$_i$ do you think she really is _$_i$?

c. He moved his pen down a line. 'Roddy and Neil are whose sons?'
'Different people's, Glenda said.
'I see. And she's taking whose place?'
[COCA 1997 FIC]

Other examples of island violations via a multiple *wh* interrogative construction are shown in (185). Such data led Huang (1982) to conclude that only overt movement is subject to island constraints in languages like English, assuming that interrogative scope is due to a 'covert' movement operation. As we have argued, however, the notion of 'covert' extraction is dubious.

(185)   a. Who wonders whether John brought what?
        b. Who thinks the joke about what is funny?
        c. Who leaves if John does what?

Huang (1982) also claimed that in situ interrogative languages like Chinese exhibit island effects with adjunct in situ interrogative phrases, which would mean that covert extraction does in fact exist (Watanabe, 1992; Lasnik and Saito, 1984, 1992). But as Cheng (2009), Jin (2016), and others argue, the facts of Chinese interrogative island effects have been misrepresented. Consider the grammatical examples in (186). Whereas the English ex situ counterparts are illicit CNPC violations, no oddness arises in the Chinese in situ counterparts.

(186)   a. Ni   kanjian [yao-le   shei] de gou?
           You see   bite-PRF who REL dog
           *'Who$_i$ did you see the dog that [bit __$_i$]?'

        b. Ni   xuyao [na'er neng mai-dao] de   shu?
           You need where can buy-RES REL book
           *'Where$_i$ do you need the book(s) that [one can get at __$_i$]?'

As Jin (2016) notes, acceptable in situ interrogatives in Chinese include temporal, manner, and reason *wh*-phrases, as the sample in (187) from Jin (2016, 25) illustrates. The same holds for Japanese (Nishigauchi, 1990, 99).

(187)   a. Ni   xihuan [ta shenmeshihou xie] de   shu?
           You like   he when   write REL book
           *'When$_i$ do you need the book(s) that [he wrote __$_i$]?'

        b. Ni zhi ken   mai [ta zenme zuo   chulai] de   jianbing?
           You only be.willing buy he how   make   out   REL crepes
           *'How$_i$ would you only buy the crepes that [he made __$_i$]?'

        c. A: Shangdian de   heiban   shang xie-zhe   mei-zhong nailao
              Store   REL blackboard   TOP   write.IMPF   each.CLF cheese

              chushi shi zenme zuo de.
              cook   FOC how   make PRT.

'On the blackboard of the store reads the instruction of how the cook made each type of cheese.'

B: Guke   jueding mai [chushi zenme zuo] de nailao?
Customer decide buy cook how   make REL cheese

'Did the customer decide to buy the (type of) cheese [that the cooks made how]?'

d. Ni xiang mai [ta yinwei   shenme mai] de shu?
You want.to buy he because.of what   sell REL book

*'What is the reason$_i$ such that you want to buy the book [that he sold for _$_i$]?'

(Chinese)

If properly contextualized, even *how much* extractions are licit, as in (188).

(188) A: Wo gangcai zai shudian   kan-dao ji-ben   xiang mai
I   now   LOC bookstore see-RES one-CLF want.to buy

de shu. Wo cha-le   yixia mei-ben shu mai duoshaoqian.
REL book. I   check-PRF once each-CLF book sell how.much.

'I saw several books that I want to buy at the bookstore. I checked for each book, how much it costs.'

B: Ni hui mai [mai duoshaoqian] de shu?
You will buy sell how.much   REL book

'Will you buy the book(s) [that was sold for how much]?'
(Jin, 2016, 26)

Chinese, Japanese, and Korean in situ interrogatives are illicit in complex NP environments only for particular varieties of manner and reason interrogatives (Huang, 1982; Nishigauchi, 1990; Lasnik and Saito, 1992; Watanabe, 1992; Fujii and Takita, 2007; Cheng, 2009; Jin, 2016). Namely, oddness only arises in clauses with *weishenme* ('why'), and *ma* (a yes/no marker). For example, compare the illicit *weishenme* reason interrogative in (189a) with the licit *yinwei* reason interrogative in (189b). The relevant interpretations are the ones where *why/for what reason* modifies the embedded verb *buy*, not the matrix verb *want*.[32]

(189) a. *Ni xiang mai [ta weishenme mai] de shu?
You want.to buy he why   sell REL book
'Why$_i$ do you want to buy the book [that he sold _$_i$]?'

b. Ni xiang mai [ta yinwei   mai] de shu?
You want.to buy he because.of what sell REL book
'What is the reason$_i$ such that you want to buy the book [that he sold _$_i$]?'
(Jin, 2016, 14)

Since there is no parallel between supposed in situ CNPC violations in Chinese and ex situ CNPC violations in English, this casts doubts on the claim that in situ *wh*-phrase

---

[32] For more about long construals in *why* questions, see Chapman and Kučerová (2016).

interrogatives involve a 'covert' filler-gap dependency subject to the same constraints of 'overt' filler-gap dependencies.

Heycock (2006) and Jin (2016) offer a plausible explanation for the oddness that arises in *weishenme*-clauses and *ma*-clauses: the adverb is generally banned from occurring in embedded clauses even if the environment is not an island-inducing one, as seen in (190). In other words, the oddness induced by such interrogatives has nothing to do with islands. Rather, expressions like *weishenme* directly scope over the clause they syntactically combine with. Thus, if embedded, only the indirect interrogative interpretation is unavailable, if any (Jin, 2016).

(190) a. *Ni   xiangxin ta weishenme cizhi?
          You believe   he why   resign
          'You believe that [he resigned why]?'

       b. *Ni jide   [Lisi weishenme qu Meiguo]?
          You remember Lisi why   go America
          'Do you recall [Lisi going to America why]?'

       c. Ni   xiangxin ta yinwei   shenme cizhi?
          You believe   he because.of what   resign
          'Do you believe that [he resigned for what reason]?'

       d. Ni jide   [Lisi yinwei shenme qu   Meiguo]?
          You remember Lisi why   go   America
          'Do you recall [Lisi going to America for what reason]?'

As a consequence, *weishenme*-clauses, the *ma* Q-particle—and certain adverbs that denote a speaker's epistemic attitude towards a propositional content—are main (finite) clause propositional modifiers (Jin, 2016), semantically and pragmatically.

The observation that *why* has a main-clause construal is not restricted to Chinese, given the classic observation that such adverbs cannot cross a clausal boundary of any kind (Reinhart, 1998). Take, for instance, the contrast in the German examples in (191), caused by the use of *weil* and *denn*. The two sentences cannot mean the same thing, since *denn* cannot be clause-embedded and yet obtain matrix scope. The only felicitous interpretation for (191b) is one where the reason adverb only has scope over the embedded clause, not the matrix.

(191) a. Tom ist nicht zu spät gekommen weil   er den Bus verpasst hat.
          Tom is not   too late come   because he the bus missed has
          'Tom wasn't late because he missed the bus (but rather, because he still had work to do).'

       b. *Tom ist nicht zu spät gekommen denn   er hat den Bus verpasst
          Tom is not   too late come   because he has the bus missed
          'Tom wasn't late because he missed the bus (but rather, because he still had work to do).'
          (Pasch et al., 2003)   (German)

A similar constraint banning *why* from crossing clausal boundaries is illustrated for English in the examples in (192).

(192) a. *[Why]$_i$ did you realize [Robin read that book $\_i$]?
(= 'You realized [Robin read that book for WHAT REASON]?'

b. [Why]$_i$ did Robin read that book $\_i$?

c. *[Why]$_i$ did you discover [Robin read that book $\_i$]?
(= 'You discovered [Robin read that book for WHAT REASON]?')

In other words, *why* cannot be extracted across a clausal boundary. The only (apparent) exceptions to (192) involve highly frequent and 'light' indirect discourse structures like *think, feel,* and *suppose,* when interpreted as idiomatic or suppletive expressions. Consider the examples in (193). As Cattell (1978, 61) noted, such examples are ambiguous between a short and a long construal of the reason adverb.

(193) a. [Why]$_i$ do you think Robin tried to do that $\_i$?

b. [Why]$_i$ do you suppose Robin tried to do that $\_i$?

c. [Why]$_i$ do you say Robin tried to do that $\_i$?

The relevant sense for *say* in (193c) is one that means almost the same as *think*. In these sentences, the indirect discourse verb makes little, if any, semantic contribution. The main verb of the matrix is interpreted almost as if it were parenthetical, in which case the embedded clause expresses the main action (Erteschik-Shir, 1973; Van Valin, 1998). If *why* is required to modify the proposition denoted by the clause that it syntactically combines with (Jin, 2016), and if discourse verbs like *think, suppose,* and *say* have interpretations in which they are semantically bleached (Lakoff, 1969; Thompson, 2002; Verhagen, 2006), then it follows that in cases like (193) the event introduced by *try* is the main event, and therefore the event that *why* predicates. In other words, such discourse verbs appear to allow long-range extraction of *why* precisely because the verb is almost devoid of meaning. Semantically and pragmatically, it is almost as if the clauses in (193) are monoclausal.

A similar long/short construal phenomenon of *why* arises in Chinese, as illustrated in (194). Jin (2016, 48) argues that, as in (192), there is no embedding in this clause, given that the matrix verb structure has an idiomatic/suppletive interpretation, which makes it function more like a parenthetical. As such, the licit *weishenme*-extraction from an (apparent) embedded clause is not inconsistent with the facts in (190), and is independently motivated by (193).

(194) a. Ni   juede/renwei [ta weishenme cizhi]?
You feel/think   he why   resign
'Do you feel/think [that he resigned why]?'

b. ??Ni   xihuan [ta weishenme cizhi]?
You like   he why   resign
'Do you like that [he resigned why]?'

The requirement that *why* combine only with finite main clauses does not prevent it from appearing in situ, of course, as in (195). Rather, the scope of *why* is restricted to the clause it combines with.

(195) a. A: Bo left because she was exasperated.
           B: Right; and Sandy left WHY?
           (Ginzburg and Sag, 2000, 245, n. 17)

       b. So, if he were going to commit suicide, that would hurt your case WHY?
           [COCA SPOK 1996]

       c. A: We have a lot of people that want to come work for us, but who I don't believe
           would make it in the long run.
           B: They wouldn't make it WHY?

       d. One of the main reasons students have poor grades, according to your study,
           is that they don't read their textbooks. During your research you realized that
           [students don't read textbooks WHY]?

An even more extreme case than *why* is *how come*, which cannot be embedded in any
construction, main or otherwise, as (196) illustrates. Thus, whereas *why* is restricted to
modifying main (finite) clauses, *how come* is restricted to modifying matrix clauses and to
being clause-initial.

(196) a. I know why / *how come.
       b. I discovered [why]$_i$/*[how come]$_i$ Jill is not here __$_i$.

The main difference between *why* and *how come* is that the former involves a clause-
bounded extraction and the latter involves no extraction at all. Since there is no UDC in
the latter, inversion is not allowed (Zwicky and Zwicky, 1973) and *what the hell* expletives
are blocked, as shown in (194); see Brame (1978) and Fillmore (1985).

(197) a. Why did Sue leave?
       b. *How come did Sue leave?

(198) a. How come (*the hell) Sue left?
       b. *Why Sue left?

In sum, the case of Chinese and other in situ languages is not so different from that of
English. Island effects typically vanish with in situ interrogatives, and yet the interrogative
operator obtains wide scope. Certain adverbials, such as *why*, are matrix propositional
modifiers and therefore cannot be embedded. The same is true of English, except that
English is biased towards ex situ interrogatives. As already noted in §2.1.1, extraction is
completely optional in Romance, and has no effect on interpretation. Thus, in (199), the
wh-phrase can remain in situ or be fronted, and still be interpreted as the same information
request, with falling intonation.

(199) a. Nós vamos a   que   praia?
           we   go   to which beach
           'Which beach are we going to?'

       b. A que   praia vamos nós?
           to which beach go   we
           'Which beach are we going to?'   (European Portuguese)

Crucially, the ex situ counterparts are island-sensitive but the in situ counterparts are not, as (200) illustrates, from Pires and Taylor (2009).

(200) a. A   Sofia corou   quando o   Carlos   insultou quem?
the Sofia blushed when   the Carlos   insulted who
'Sofia blushed when Carlos insulted ↑WHO↓?'

b. Então queres   uma casa   que tenha quantos   quartos?
so   you-want a   house that has   how-many bedrooms?
'So you want a house with ↑HOW MANY bedrooms↓?'

c. Estás a falar da   areia de que   praia?
are   to speak of-the sand of which beach
'Are you talking about the sand of ↑WHICH beach↓?'

Pires and Taylor (2009) conclude that in situ interrogatives in Portuguese do not involve any kind of movement, and that a different mechanism is responsible for interrogative scope. As far as we can tell, the same is true for all other languages discussed in the present chapter, including English.

To be clear, we do not reject the existence of constraints on interrogative scope, nor do we reject the idea that some of these constraints bear a connection to island phenomena. Our claim is that the mechanism that enables interrogative scope is fundamentally different from that which enables quantifier scope and UDCs. Consider, for example, the case of CNPC effects in Lakhota. As Van Valin (1994) notes, expressions like *táku* can be interpreted as indefinite pronouns or as in situ interrogative *wh*-phrases. Crucially, within a definite restrictive relative clause (or adverbial clauses) only the former interpretation is allowed, as (201) illustrates. Thus, only the Yes/No interpretation allowed by the indefinite reading for *táku* is possible.

(201) Wičhása ki šų́ka wą táku   yaxtáke
man   the dog a *what/something bite
'*What did the man see the dog which bit _?'
'Did the man see the dog which bit something?'
(Van Valin, 1994, 249)   (Lakhota)

Van Valin (1994) and Van Valin and LaPolla (1997, 621) argue that these facts follow from Lakhota-specific structural restrictions on the scope of the illocutionary force operator, which effectively prevent Focus *wh*-expressions from residing restrictive relatives and clausal adjuncts. Such a constraint can be formulated in a number of ways, including in terms of Ginzburg and Sag's (2000) WH feature, by requiring that restrictive relatives bear an empty set specification [WH {}]. Regardless of how this is best formalized, it in effect means that English CNPC effects and the Lakhota phenomena in (201) are—in part—due to the same Gricean Relevance constraint: restrictive relatives are not at issue, and therefore not part of the main action expressed by the proposition. Thus, a Gricean Relevance constraint is violated if such backgrounded clauses are required to predicate the Focus of the interrogative, extracted or otherwise.

3.5 Summary

We have argued that there are several different kinds of island constraints, due to different combinations of independently motivated factors, and that most islands are not cross-constructionally active. That is, most island phenomena are restricted to certain kinds of UDCs.

Many islands are primarily caused by drawing the hearer's attention to a referent that is not at issue and is of little consequence to what the utterance conveys (Kuno, 1976; Erteschik-Shir and Lappin, 1979; Kuno, 1987; Takami, 1988; Na and Huck, 1992; Deane, 1991; Goldberg, 2006). If the referent is merely circumstantial for the main action, drawing attention to it via a non-canonical construction constitutes a Gricean Maxim violation (Van Valin, 2005, 288). More specifically, the NP Constraint, the Complex NP Constraint, the Factive/Manner Islands, the Element Constraint, the Subject Constraint, and the Adjunct Constraint are chiefly due to the referent of the extracted phrase not being pragmatically relevant for the main action. Such an account emerges naturally from the observation that not all propositions express equally likely states of affairs and that different constructions come with different biases with respect to how information structure is packaged, and consequently, to which referents it is pragmatically licit to single out by extraction.

Some of these 'Relevance Islands' can be exacerbated by a variety of other factors, such as contextualization difficulty (i.e. if the expressed proposition expresses an unlikely or unusual state of affairs to begin with), violated expectations (when the postulation of a gap competes with locally more likely alternative parses that do not lead to licit interpretations), and/or phonological phrasings that fail to cue the correct sentence structure and, in particular, the location of the gap. Thus, some island violations are quite mild and others are very strong, even within the same type of island. Finally, these Relevance Islands have robust exceptions precisely in UDC types that happen to not convey presupposed content, such as presentational relatives. This means that these islands are not cross-constructionally active, but, rather, restricted to particular UDC types.

For example, the main difference between subextraction from objects and subextraction from subjects in a main clause is that objects are usually part of the asserted content, whereas subjects are not (Chaves, 2013; Chaves and Dery, 2019). Such a bias does not exist in relative clauses, and therefore extraction from subject NPs is easier *within* relative clauses (Abeillé et al., 2018, Abeillé et al., 2020). Subject Island effects usually vanish in so-called 'parasitic' extractions precisely because the extracted referent is then directly predicated by the main action, and therefore its relevance to the situation that the utterance describes.

Analogously, extraction from relative clauses is, for the most part, contingent on whether the relative expresses an assertion, as is the case of presentational relatives; see Goldberg (2006, 146) and Goldberg (2013). Many other island effects are similarly explained. The main difference between acceptable and non-acceptable extractions from coordinate structures has to do with whether the conjuncts are on equal ground pragmatically, or whether one conjunct expresses the main action and the other does not (Kehler, 2002, ch. 5). More broadly, extraction from an embedded clause (adverbial, relative, or otherwise) is permitted to the degree to which that clause can be interpreted as being part of the main action conveyed by the proposition; see Tonhauser et al. (2018) for experimental evidence that what is at issue is gradient, and dependent on a number of factors, including the prior probability of the event described by the expression that conveys the content.

Hence, if the matrix verb is semantically very abstract and unlikely to express the main action of the utterance, then extraction from a subordinate environment is facilitated (Erteschik-Shir, 1977; Van Valin, 1998; Deane, 1992; Erteschik-Shir, 2006a; Goldberg, 2006). This explains why it is hard (but not impossible) to extract from restrictive relatives, or from adjunct clauses. The more semantically abstract and backgrounded the matrix clause is, the easier it is for subordinate structures to be interpreted as being at issue. Thus, none of these islands is cross-constructionally active.

Other island effects do not involve UDCs that violate the Relevance constraint, and instead arise from independent factors. For example, Negative Islands are limited to negated degree and manner interrogatives, and can be explained without appeal to theory-dependent syntactic stipulation: such questions are ill-formed because they are open-ended and cannot have a single answer (Abrusán, 2011; Abrusán and Spector, 2011). This also explains why the addition of existential adverbials makes the island effect disappear. A similar answer naturally presents itself for Factive Islands (Oshima, 2007; Abrusán, 2014).

In contrast, the Complementizer Constraint is arguably due to conflicting phonological phrasing requirements caused by language-specific phrasing rules (Kandybowicz, 2006, 2009; Levine, 2017, 315–19). Other islands are more likely to result from a combination of phonological phrasing constraints, processing preferences, and the plausibility of the expressed proposition, as in the case of the CNFICC, crossover effects, Wh-Complement Constraint, Superiority, and Freezing. Finally, some islands are very robust and truly exceptionless, as in the case of the Left Branch Constraint and the Conjunct Constraint. We take these to be syntactic in nature, which would explain why they do not ameliorate with contextualization, prosodic phrasing, rewording, or increased frequency.

4

Movement-based approaches

4.1 Introduction

Carnap ([1934]1968) drew a distinction between 'formation rules', which combined sentences via logical operators, and 'transformation rules', which enabled one sentence to be inferred from another. The latter kind of rule is related to the transformational rules proposed by Zelig Harris in unpublished lecture notes in the early 1940s (Harris, 1951), and in subsequent work (Harris, 1957), as a way of analyzing relations between sentences. For example, in Harris's system, passive sentences were related to active sentences via a co-occurrence rule that linked 'N_1 V N_2' and 'N_2 is V -*en by* N_1', capturing the fact that passives and actives shared the same truth-conditional information.[1] Harwood (1955) and Chomsky (1956) reconceptualized Harris's rules as CFG rewrite rules like (1), drawing from immediate constituency analysis (Wells, 1948), in work formally related to Emil Post's conception of proofs and computations as string rewriting (Post, 1943, 1947).

(1) Sentence → NP VP

Later, Chomsky (1957, 1965, 1975) proposed a theory of grammar consisting of (i) a lexicon, (ii) CFG phrase-structure rules responsible for forming complex constituents from smaller linguistic units, and (iii) Context-Dependent 'transformational' rules that convert certain sentence types into other, related types of sentence. For example, consider the string in (2) from Chomsky (1975, 434). This rule allowed sentences like *Did you see him yesterday?* to be transformed into *wh⌢him did you see?* by positioning the substring $Y_2 = him$ before the substrings $Y_1 = did you see$ and $Y_3 = yesterday$. A morphological rule would replace *wh⌢him* with *whom*.

(2) $Y_1 - Y_2 - Y_3 → wh⌢Y_2 - Y_1 - Y_3$

Another rule would model interrogative UDCs, another rule would model relative-clause UDCs, and so on. Thus, UDCs were initially modeled by construction-specific rules. As in Harris's system, transformations allowed grammars to explain why different sentences can have similar meaning, which became a major source of empirical motivation for such rules (Chomsky, 1957, 1965; Katz and Postal, 1964). But as phrase-structure grammars struggled to cope with discontinuity phenomena (Chomsky, 1975, 190), transformations became increasingly more central to the theory of grammar and so construction-specific rules were progressively abandoned. Starting with Chomsky (1977), the notion of transformation was superseded by a far more general and abstract **movement** operation, ultimately

---

[1] The connection between Carnap's and Harris's conceptions of transformation is recognized by Bar-Hillel (1954), Harwood (1955, 409), and Chomsky (1955, 37, n.4).

Unbounded Dependency Constructions: Theoretical and Experimental Perspectives. Rui P. Chaves and Michael T. Putnam,
Oxford University Press (2020). © Rui P. Chaves and Michael T. Putnam.
DOI: 10.1093/oso/9780198784999.001.0001

formulated as **Move-α** (Chomsky, 1986a). This was argued to be responsible for all types of displacement phenomena, and viewed as a fundamental component of human language. Although the theory still contained a phrase-structure component called **X′-Theory**, it was very abstract and not responsible for UDCs.

Chomsky's notion of movement led to controversy for at least two reasons. First, the phenomena that had originally been used to motivate transformations could be modeled better without them, as argued by Bresnan (1978), Gazdar (1981), Koster (1987), Brody (1995), and various others. Second, the arguments purportedly showing that movement creates a trace (or copy) were shown to be empirically problematic; in particular, there currently is no independent empirical motivation for the existence of traces from 'wanna-contraction' (Postal and Pullum, 1982; Kaplan and Zaenen, 1989; Pullum, 1997), from auxiliary contraction (Pullum and Zwicky, 1997), from 'floated' quantifiers (Fodor and Sag, 1982; Sag, 2000), from strong crossover phenomena (Postal, 2004), or from weak crossover (Dalrymple et al., 2008).

In Chomsky (1989, 1995, 1998) the movement generalization was taken further: phrase-structure rules of any kind were rejected altogether in favor of a single general operation called MERGE, sometimes also referred to as EXTERNAL MERGE:

> the notion of grammatical construction is eliminated, and with it, the construction-particular rules. Constructions such as verb phrase, relative clause, and passive remain only as taxonomic artifacts, collections of phenomena explained through the interaction of the principles of UG, with the values of the parameters fixed.
>
> (Chomsky, 1995, 4)

Thus, in the Minimalist Program (Chomsky 1993, 1995; henceforth MP) all syntactic structure in all languages is assumed to be the result of iterative applications of MERGE, and UDCs are the result of (INTERNAL) MERGE, sometimes referred to as MOVE. For Chomsky, this is the ideal stance:

> The optimal computational procedure consists, then, of the operation Merge and operations to construct the displacement property: transformational operations or some counterpart. The second of the two parallel endeavors sought to reduce the transformational component to the simplest form; though unlike phrase-structure rules, it seems to be ineliminable.
>
> (Chomsky, 2000b, 13)

> Recourse to any device to account for the displacement phenomena also is mistaken, unless it is independently motivated (as is internal Merge). If this is correct, then the radically simplified form of transformational grammar that has become familiar ('Move α' and its variants) is a kind of conceptual necessity, given the undeniable existence of the displacement phenomena.
>
> (Chomsky, 2004, 8–9, n. 29)

For Berwick and Chomsky (2016), Bolhuis et al. (2014), and Berwick et al. (2013) MERGE is the result of a single genetic mutation. But the view that all displacement is due to a single general operation faces empirical and conceptual problems once a broader range of empirical and behavioral facts is taken into consideration.

4.2 MERGE **and** MOVE

The MP assumes that the syntactic component of a grammar plays a central role, as it operates independently of the semantic and phonological components. In other words, syntax is **autonomous**. This means that there must be a syntactic level of phrase structure which is in some sense equivalent to semantic interpretation. Thus, truth-conditional sentences like (3) must in some sense have the same core phrasal structure.

(3)   a. Sam helped Robin.
      b. It was Robin who Sam helped.
      c. It was Sam who Robin was helped by.

Although there is a great deal of heterodoxy within the MP, a grammar usually consists of two things: a lexicon and a computational system, the latter of which is also referred to as **Narrow Syntax**. Whereas the lexicon contains lexical entries composed of sets of features, the computational system comprises the operations MERGE and MOVE, as well as various derivational principles. The features contained in lexical entries can either be **interpretable**, in which case they express semantic information, or **uninterpretable**, in which case they are needed exclusively for the computation of syntactic structure. Through the course of a derivation, features that are uninterpretable must be **checked** in particular syntactic positions.

There are two additional systems which interpret the structures that are generated. One is **Logical Form** (LF), which accounts for semantic interpretation, whereas the other is **Phonological Form** (PF), which accounts for speech articulation. Most versions of the MP assume that these interfaces are external to Narrow Syntax. A common assumption within the MP is that there is a one-to-one relation between syntactic position and semantic interpretation, as in Rizzi (1997), Cinque (1999), and much subsequent work. Figure 4.1 illustrates the kind of nodes that are relevant for fronted phrases. The clause is located inside the Tense Phrase (TP), sometimes also referred to as the Inflectional Phrase (IP).

The node **Force** specifies illocutionary force (e.g. asserting, inquiring, and exclaiming acts), **Topic** hosts fronted topics, the node **Focus** hosts *wh*-phrases in interrogatives, and so on. The Kleene '*' signals that one or more projections of the relevant type can occur in that position. This kind of approach is called **cartography**; see Shlonsky (2010, 2015), Rizzi (2013, 2015), and Ramchand and Svenonius (2014).

The cartographic approach is controversial, however. First, it does not align well with the idea that grammars are optimal (minimal), as there is a massive proliferation of categories and nodes which are supposed to be part of the human biological language endowment; see Boeckx (2014b) and Chomsky et al. (2019, 19) for some criticsm. Second, as Borsley (2006) notes, positing the existence of functional projections with a certain set of properties and a specific interpretation is not very different from employing a phrase-structure-rule approach to the same effect. Third, cartographic approaches are inconsistent with the extreme range of variation across the languages of the world (Croft, 2003; Newmeyer, 2004, 2006).[2] Finally, it is also unclear how such hyper-abstract scaffolding offers any advantage

---

[2] Wiltschko (2014) acknowledges the latter problem and proposes that what is universal across languages is a more abstract scaffolding of categories—the **universal spine**—which can be instantiated in multiple

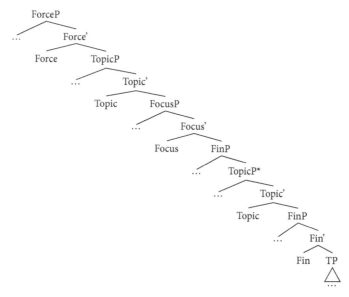

Figure 4.1 An extended/split COMP (CP) projection

to learners as compared with shallower phrase-structural models of grammar that more directly reflect the actual input that the learner is exposed to (Sakas and Fodor, 2001; Clark and Lappin, 2011).

The MERGE operation builds syntactic structure by combining two items (lexical or otherwise) into a larger phrase, whereas MOVE displaces syntactic nodes from one position in the tree to another position. MERGE is a function that takes two distinct syntactic objects α and β and outputs a set K such that $K = \{H(K), \{\alpha, \beta\}\}$. The value of $H(K)$ is either α or β, depending on which of the two objects is the head (i.e. which of the two selects the other). Hence, MERGE(α, β) creates an unordered set K labeled by the head of the phrase. We illustrate this schematically in Figure 4.2, where δ is the head, either α or β.

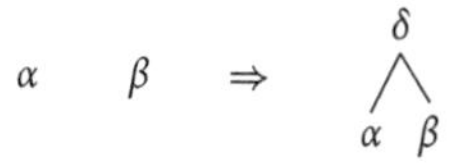

$$\alpha \quad \beta \quad \Rightarrow \quad \overset{\delta}{\underset{\alpha \ \beta}{\wedge}}$$

Figure 4.2 Constituents α and β merge to form constituent δ

This concept looks simple enough, but formalizing it within the broader context of the MP is not trivial. The only explicit attempt to formalize MERGE that we are aware of is Collins and Stabler (2016), though the authors note that their model is preliminary and differs from the mainstream. Importantly, Collins and Stabler discover that it is not possible to define MERGE in isolation, independently from the definition of lexical item, lexical item token, syntactic object, and derivation stages, among various other non-trivial notions. However

---

language-specific cartographic configurations. It is difficult to see how this theory can be in principle falsified, or how it could evolve as part of the language endowment.

defined, the intuition underlying MERGE is that it combines two elements, and the features of the head are passed on to the projected mother node.[3]

According to Berwick and Chomsky (2016), the language faculty involves a workspace that has access to the lexicon and contains any linguistic object that is constructed. To carry a computation forward, two elements α and β are selected from the workspace and combined via MERGE. The basic mechanism underlying merge operations is feature check-ing, as previously discussed. For example, a determiner like *the* bears an uninterpretable part-of-speech [D] feature and an uninterpretable [uN] feature. The latter can be checked (i.e. uN) if the determiner is merged with a nominal like *frog*, which bears an interpretable part-of-speech [N] feature. Since D selects N (as per the need to check the [uN] feature), then it is the determiners' features that are present in the mother node. In this work we follow the convention of using the symbols 'DP', 'VP', 'PP', and so on for nodes that are labeled 'D', 'V', 'P' and no longer contain any uninterpretable features. Analogously, a verb like *kiss* bearing an interpretable part-of-speech [V] feature and an uninterpretable feature [uD] can be merged with a DP, as in Figure 4.3.[4] Various other features are present as well, such as case features and thematic role features, but these are omitted here for ease of exposition.

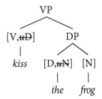

Figure 4.3 Feature-driven MERGE

For Chomsky (2001), Berwick and Chomsky (2016), and others, MERGE and MOVE boil down to the same operation: if α and β are distinct elements in the workspace, then their combination is an instance of EXTERNAL MERGE, as in Figure 4.2. But if β is part of α, then this is a case of an INTERNAL MERGE. More formally, MOVE($\{\alpha, \beta\}, \beta$) = $\{\{\alpha, t_i\}, \beta_i\}$. In this approach, a trace t_i is co-indexed with the ex situ phrase and remains at the extraction site. For Chomsky (1993) and Nunes (2004), however, MOVE is the combination of three operations: COPY + MERGE + FORMCHAIN + CHAINREDUCTION. In a nutshell, a node is first copied, and then merged into the phrase structure, forming a chain between the copy node and the original one. Finally, only the highest copy in the tree is pronounced.[5] Thus,

---

[3] Modification structures have been problematic for the MP because modifiers like adverbs and adjectives are not the heads of the phrases they project. Chomsky (2001) proposes that a more complex form of MERGE, called PAIRMERGE, is required specifically for adjoined structures: PAIRMERGE(α, β) = $\langle \alpha, \beta \rangle$ indicates that β is adjoined to α, which requires an additional operation SIMPL. Fox and Nissenbaum (2004) and Putnam and Stroik (2009) criticize this move, and Langendoen (2003) proposes yet another kind of operation, LISTMERGE, which is a list constructor rather than set-theoretic.

[4] For an alternative to feature-driven MERGE, see Chomsky (2008, 2013), Boeckx (2014a), and Cecchetto and Donati (2015), where the category of the phrase built by MERGE is determined by the feature which asymmetrically triggers MERGE.

[5] Additional assumptions are necessary in order to cope with filler-less UDCs, such as object relatives (e.g. *the person I called___ helped me*), comparatives (e.g. *You made more mistakes than Robin made___*), missing object constructions (e.g. *Being difficult to reach___ has its advantages*), *Not*-fragments (e.g. *No, not that I can think of___*), and a few others, like UDCs in Romance languages where a pronominal filler is realized as a 'climbing' affix rather than a phrase.

instead of a trace, the gap site corresponds to a silent (deleted) copy of the extracted item. This operation is illustrated in Figure 4.4.

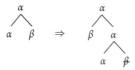

Figure 4.4 Movement as COPY and DELETE

Movement takes place in order for a feature to be checked, in certain structural positions. Consider for example Figure 4.5. The sentence is headed by a projection, here headed by a complementizer C, that possesses an interpretable feature [Q] indicating that this sentence type is interrogative. If the complementizer C also has a uninterpretable *wh*-feature [*u*wh], that requires a lexical item introduced lower in the tree structure to MOVE into the specifier position of the head bearing this feature, referred to as [Spec,CP]. This is what causes the fronting of *who*. The T node corresponds to the auxiliary verb, which is fronted before the subject in English interrogatives because of the need to check its own Q feature.

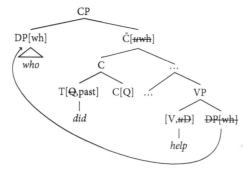

Figure 4.5 Feature-driven *wh*-movement (schematic)

Crucially, movement is responsible for many other phenomena beyond UDCs. For example, a four-word sentence like *Who did Meg help?* requires at least four movement operations to obtain the derivation shown in Figure 4.6. Movement triggered by the need to check case and agreement features is called **A-movement**, and movement caused by features related to UDCs, such as [wh]-features, is called **A'-movement**.

The verb *help* moves to *v*, which in turn licenses the insertion of the subject phrase and gives rise to a causative interpretation. The subject *Meg* then moves up to the specifier position of TP (i.e. [Spec,TP]) in order to check (nominative) case and agreement features via the auxiliary *did* on T. In that position under *v*P, the DP is interpreted as an Agent.[6] The *wh*-item has its (accusative) case feature valued by *v* in its base position. In order to satisfy

---

[6] According to Sportiche (1988) and others, the movement of the subject can sometimes leave a predeterminer behind, as in [*The boys*] were [all ~~the boys~~] *on the same team*. In such an analysis, the stranding of *All* is obligatory in examples like (i) and (ii).

i. They/We were all at the same party.
    (cf. with *All they/we were at the same party*)

ii. Robin, Sam, and Kim were all in the same class.
    (cf. with *All Robin, Sam, and Kim were in the same class.*)

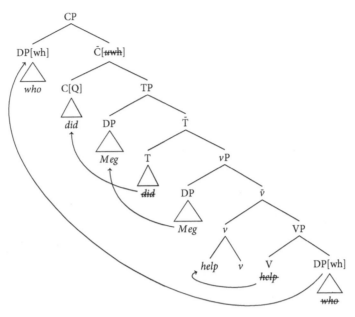

Figure 4.6 Derivation of *Who did Meg help?* (preliminary)

the (strong) uninterpretable *wh*-feature on C, [*u*wh], *who* moves to [Spec,CP], which is an instance of A′-movement.

Nothing in the approach discussed so far prevents movement from merging nodes that are not root nodes. Thus, it is possible for a phrase to move lower down into its tree. To ban these cases, Chomsky (2008, 138) proposes the **No Tampering Condition** (NTC):[7]

(4) No Tampering Condition: Merging α and β leaves the two structures unchanged.

A consequence of the NTC is that movement must leave a copy rather than a trace behind, since replacing the fronted element with a trace would constitute tampering.

The NTC and other such constraints like the **Merge Before Move Constraint** (Chomsky, 1995, 2000a, 2005; Hornstein, 2000) force structures to be constructed in a bottom-up fashion, starting from the deepest part of the syntactic tree. This is very different from how human beings process sentences. Comprehenders do not have to wait for the complete utterance to start processing the input, and actively make probabilistic top-down and bottom-up predictions about upcoming linguistic information; see §1.4 as well as §4.4 for more discussion.

The checking of the feature [*u*wh] determines where a *wh*-item can be phonologically produced and where it is semantically interpreted. The operation known as Spell-Out transfers syntactic structures to LF and PF, at particular points in the course of the phrasal derivation, known as **phases**. According to Chomsky (2000b, 2004) and others, finite CPs and *v*Ps are phases.[8] Crucially, once a phrase is targeted by Spell-Out, its subconstituents

---

[7] The NTC needs to be taken with a grain of salt, however, since MERGE causes features to be valued and subsequently deleted.

[8] Although this is a widely accepted view, there are also alternative proposals that argue for the phasehood of DP (Matushansky, 2005) and TP in some instances (Richards, 2011). There have also been a number of proposals

can no longer be accessed by any other syntactic operations, including MOVE. Thus, the **Phase Impenetrability Condition** (PIC) (Chomsky, 2000a, 2001, 2004) states that only elements at the edge of a phase are accessible for additional operations:

(5)   PHASE IMPENETRABILITY CONDITION: In phase α with head H, the domain of H is not accessible to operations outside α, only H and its edge are accessible to such operations.

(Chomsky, 2000a, 108)

Thus, displacement proceeds in a series of short movement operations known as **the Strict Cycle** (Chomsky, 1973). The notion of short movement is called **Minimal Link Condition** (MLC) and is formalized in Chomsky (1995, 296–311) via the notion of **Attract**:

(6)   a.   MINIMAL LINK CONDITION: a target node K attracts a phrase α if and only if there is no node β such that β is closer to K than α and K attracts β.

      b.   ATTRACT: K attracts a phrase with feature F if it is the closest that can enter into a feature-checking relation with K.

Chomsky's rationale for the existence of multiple iterations of SPELL-OUT is, in part, that it optimizes the efficiency of the mapping between syntax and the external systems by reducing the computational burden (i.e. memory resource load) via the periodic 'forgetting' of derivational information. Multiple SPELL-OUT and derivation by phases is consistent with the Strong Minimalist Thesis, which assumes optimal efficient design for the satisfaction of interface conditions. However, multiple SPELL-OUT also poses a problem, since a *wh*-phrase must be able to move out of a phase before that phase is sent to SPELL-OUT. Take, for example, the structure in Figure 4.6. As the tree is built bottom-up, the first phase *v*P causes the $\bar{v}$ node to be sent to the interfaces via SPELL-OUT, in effect preventing $\bar{v}$ from being targeted by any other syntactic operations. But *who* must have been moved out of $\bar{v}$ before SPELL-OUT, or else it cannot move to the required higher positions.

In order to allow *wh*-phrases to escape phases, Chomsky (1998) proposes that a phase node can optionally project another mother node of the same kind, with an empty specifier position that can host a moved phrase. More specifically, Chomsky assumes that each core phase-head category (*v* and C) has an **Extended Projection Principle** (EPP) feature that allows such nodes to create a vacant specifier branch. Thus, in Figure 4.6 the DP *who* is not able to move out of the *v*P phase. In Chomsky's approach, however, the *v*P is allowed to project another *v*P, resulting in multiple specifiers of *v*P, so that *who* can move to the edge of the higher *v*P before SPELL-OUT applies to $\bar{v}$. This is illustrated in Figure 4.7.

The edges of phases thus function as 'escape hatches' in allowing A′-dependencies that span across clauses, by moving *wh*-phrases cyclically from the edge of one phase to the next. For example, in (7) there must be five such phase projections just for the purpose of allowing the *wh*-phrase to move upward.[9]

(7)   What did you [~~what~~ think [~~what~~ that Bob [~~what~~ thought [~~what~~ Mary ate ~~what~~]]]]?

in the literature that suggest the edge of every XP constitutes a (potential) phase (Takahashi, 1994; Stroik, 2009; Müller, 2011).

   [9] Hence, phases are not very different from Chomsky's (1986b) concept of *Barriers*, as Boeckx and Grohmann (2007) and others note.

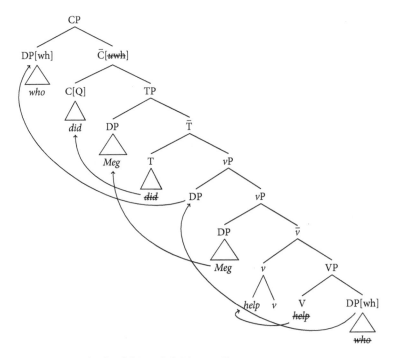

Figure 4.7 Derivation of *Who did Meg help?* (revised)

Three important questions present themselves at this juncture. First, the stipulated multiple *v*P projections become indistinguishable from adjunction, which, unlike other types of movement, is not commonly motivated by the need to check any formal features. Second, Boeckx and Grohmann (2013, 61–73) show in detail that the escape hatch introduced by Chomsky ultimately entails that nothing should be an island, contrary to fact; Boeckx and Grohmann (2013, 61–73) also show that attempts to solve this problem, like Müller (2010), are technically problematic. Lastly, it is unclear what feature is supposed to actually drive the movement of the *wh*-phrase to the empty position at *v*P, since accusative case is handled in situ, as Felser (2004) notes. This is a fundamental problem which we discuss in more detail in §4.2.1.

In sum, the idea that phases function as escape hatches in order to preserve phases as derivation units raises more problems than it solves. It is, therefore, rather unclear how exactly UDCs are modeled in the MP at all. See Collins and Stabler (2016) for more on puzzles raised by MOVE, namely how to ensure that each constituent is transferred to the interfaces just once, and how this interacts with phase impenetrability effects.

4.2.1 The Strict Cycle

Although there is debate within the MP about the exact nature of movement operations and about how they interact with SPELL-OUT, there is good empirical evidence that UDCs involve a sequence of local dependencies rather than a single long-distance one. Take, for example, (8), where *wh*-phrases appear in intermediate positions between the filler and the gap.

(8)   **Wen**   glaubt Hans [$_{CP}$ (**wen**) Jakob _ gesehen hat]?
      who$_{ACC}$ thinks Hans   who$_{ACC}$ Jakob   seen   has
      'Who does Hans think that Jakob saw?'
      (McDaniel, 1989)   (German)

Although interpreted only once, the *wh*-element *wen* 'whom' can optionally appear at the left edge of the matrix clause. Additional evidence for some version of the Strict Cycle is, of course, provided by extraction pathway phenomena, already discussed in §1.1, whereby specific phonological or morphosyntactic phenomena appear exclusively in the structures intervening between the filler phrase and the gap. For ease of exposition, we return to the case of Irish complementizer alternations (McCloskey, 1979, 2002). Recall that the complementizer *goN* can only appear outside UDCs, whereas *aL* can only appear inside UDCs, as in (9).

(9)   an fear   **aL** dúirt sé **aL** shíl   _ **goN** mbeadh sé ann.
      [the man]$_j$ c said he c thought _$_j$ c   would-be he there
      'the man that he said thought he would be there'   (Irish)

McCloskey (1979, 2002) and Assmann et al. (2010) propose a movement-based account in which the complementizer *aL* bears an EPP feature, which creates a structural position for the movement of the *wh*-phrase. The *goN* complementizer lacks this EPP feature, and therefore does not offer an escape hatch for any *wh*-phrase to escape its clause, given that the complementizer node is already filled by the complementizer itself.

   In general, movement-based analyses for UDCs are faced with the question of what drives the cyclic movement in the first place. If *wh*-movement is feature-driven, then what motivates the intermediate movement steps required by the Strict Cycle hypothesis? This is known as **the Triggering Problem** (Felser, 2004, 547):[10]

(10) THE TRIGGERING PROBLEM: On the assumption that agreement (and hence, move-
      ment) is triggered by matching but uninterpretable features of the probe, what trig-
      gers movement of a wh-expression to the specifier of intermediate non-interrogative
      heads?

McCloskey (2002) proposes that the features involved in these intermediate movement steps are formal (uninterpretable) features (*q, top, foc, r*, etc.) that correspond with sub-stantial (interpretable) features (*Q, Top, Foc, R*, etc.) to motivate intermediate movement steps; see also Rizzi (2007b). In other words, additional machinery that has no independent motivation is needed to force movement to continue cyclically across clauses, which goes against the spirit of minimality and computational economy.

   The obvious way around the Triggering Problem is to replace movement operations with something else entirely. For example, Abels (2012) proposes a radically different account of cyclicity by assuming that movement is implemented as a form of feature sharing. For example, an unvalued feature [uF↓] signifies that there must be a bearer of the feature

---

[10] This difficulty is acknowledged but not resolved by Collins and Stabler (2016, 75).

F somewhere lower in the syntactic structure, and [uF↑] corresponds to an unvalued feature that requires an upward syntactic relation with a bearer of [F]. Finally, [uF↓↑] is an unvalued feature that requires both an upward and a downward syntactic relation with a bearer of [F]. All of these arrowed features are **probes**, i.e. elements that seek out corresponding features within other nodes in the tree and share their value. A related account is Den Dikken (2018), in which extended AGREE relations between phases replace movement. Indeed, for den Dikken there is no movement operation at all. In conclusion, the strongest source of evidence for local movement operations turns out to be problematic for movement accounts, giving rise to the Triggering Problem. Whereas some authors stipulate uninterpretable features in order to ensure movement, others abandon movement operations entirely.

4.2.2 Multiple-gap UDCs

Although UDCs are among the primary empirical motivations for movement approaches, some of the strongest challenges to movement-based accounts come precisely from UDCs. First and foremost, there is no standard way in the MP to model convergent UDC constructions like (11); see §2.2.2 for more discussion. In such UDCs, multiple gaps are linked to exactly the same filler, which is impossible to obtain via MERGE as standardly defined.

(11)   a. [Who]$_i$ does Jack like __$_i$ and Mary hate__$_i$?

     b. [Who]$_i$ did you say was easy to accommodate __$_i$ and entertain __$_i$?

     c. [Which defendant]$_i$ did you inform __$_i$ that the jury had acquitted __$_i$?

In an attempt to cope with such convergent UDCs, Nunes (1995, 2001, 2004) proposes that the *wh*-phrase is first copied from one subtree to the other before the two subtrees are combined into a single unified structure. Later in the derivation, these *wh*-phrases are then copied to the front of the sentence, forming a complex chain between the copies, as the account of (11a) in Figure 4.8 shows. This type of movement is called **Sideward Movement**. In this example, *who*$_1$ is first copied from the second conjunct to the first conjunct, before the two conjuncts are coordinated. Then, each copy independently moves up. Two chains are formed: one between the highest copy of *who* and the *who* in the first conjunct, and another between the highest copy of *who* and the copy in the second conjunct. Only the copy at the top of the chain is phonetically realized at SPELL-OUT.

But Sideward Movement raises more problems than it solves. For example, in syncretic convergent UDCs like (12) the same extracted phrase would have to simultaneously bear two different cases, nominative and accusative.[11]

(12)   a. [Which witness] did the judge remind __$_{ACC}$__$_{NOM}$ was still under oath?

     b. [Which professor] did you say__$_{NOM}$ was not very easy to please__$_{ACC}$?

---

[11] Moreover, as discussed in §2.2.2, both gaps in examples like (12a,b) are syntactically legitimate in ideal conditions, as neither is parasitic on the other. Thus, a 'parasitic gap' account of such cases is not without challenges.

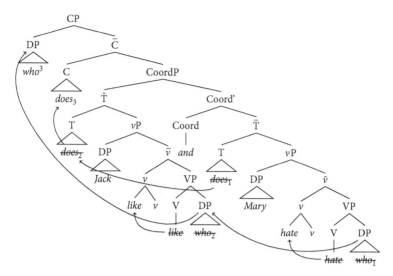

Figure 4.8 Sideward Merge in ATB movement

> c. Nancy Reagan was wearing a gown that [Galanos designed __ACC] and reputedly [__NOM cost over $5,000].
> (Anderson, 1983, 3)
>
> d. We went to see a movie which [the critics praised __ACC] but [__NOM was too violent for my taste].
> (Goodall, 1987, 75),
>
> e. A car THAT BIG, I suspect [__NOM would have poor gas mileage] and [that it would be difficult for me to handle __ACC].

Nunes (2004, 176, n. 12) suggests that this problem can be solved by case underspecification, but this is problematic because the copies of the *wh*-phrases would no longer count as non-distinct, and therefore would not form chains, and consequently all copies would be phonetically realized. The difficulty lies in defining chain formation in Sideward Movement in such a way as to allow case underspecification while at the same time not over- or undergenerating UDCs.

Furthermore, there are other UDC types that directly challenge any copying account like Sideward Movement. Consider the cumulative UDCs in (13). As discussed in §2.2.3, in these cases the *wh*-phrase does not correspond to any of the extracted phrases, but rather, to the sum of the extracted phrases. There simply is no sense in which the two gaps are copies of each other, since they are not co-indexed.

> (13) a. [Where]$_{\{i,j\}}$ did Mary vacation __$_i$ and Bill decide to live __$_j$?
> (answer: 'Mary vacationed in Bern and Bill decided to live in Rome')
>
> b. [Who]$_{\{i,j\}}$ did you forget to inform __$_i$ that we had fired __$_j$?
> (answer: 'I neglected to inform Dr. Yang of the firing of his senior engineer')

Munn (1998, 1999) proposes to account for cumulative UDCs like (13a) by using special doubly indexed functional traces, as illustrated in (14). The subscript *i* represents a function *f* associated with the trace, such that when applied to *Mary* it yields the place she vacationed, and when applied to *Bill* it yields the place he decided to live.

(14) [Where]$_i$ did Mary$_x$ vacation $\_\_^x_i$ and Bill$_y$ decide to live $\_\_^y_i$?
      (= *Which f such that Mary vacationed in f(Mary) and Bill decided to live in f(Bill)?*)

But as Gawron and Kehler (2003) note, Munn predicts that questions with a conjoined VP such as (15) cannot have cumulative interpretations because in such cases only a single binder is available for the two traces (i.e. *f(Bill)*). See Gawron and Kehler (2003) for other problems with Munn (1999).

(15) [What]$_{i+j}$ did Bill eat $\_\_i$ and drink $\_\_j$?
      (answer: 'He ate a hamburger and drank a coke')

An alternative approach to convergent UDCs is to abandon the idea that syntactic constituency is best described in terms of trees, and instead allow nodes to have multiple mothers (Williams, 1978; Goodall, 1987), as illustrated in Figure 4.9. Such a multidominance approach is sometimes referred to as **Parallel Merge**, or as **Parallel Move**.

Figure 4.9 Parallel Merge as a hybrid of MOVE and MERGE

Citko (2005) and de Vries (2009) propose a multidominance account of convergent UDCs, as depicted in Figure 4.10. Two coordinate VPs share the same DP complement daughter, and then the latter is extracted to the top of the sentence via a standard movement operation. Unfortunately, syncretic convergent UDCs like (12) and cumulative UDCs like (13) are as problematic for multidominance accounts as they are for Sideward Movement because the putative in situ *wh*-phrases refer to different entities, and therefore can neither be copies of each other nor be shared across structures.

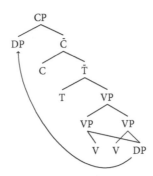

Figure 4.10 Schematic depiction of multidominance syntax

Citko (2011, 56) argues that Parallel Move explains why ATB extraction is exempt from the Coordinate Structure Constraint. The rationale is that since there is only one *wh*-phrase, then in a sense there is no multiple extraction, and therefore no need for an ATB exception to the CSC. This is problematic because not all ATB extraction is legitimate, as seen in

(16). Unlike the Element Constraint, the Conjunct Constraint has no ATB exceptions; see §3.2.5. Further assumptions are therefore necessary in order to prohibit Parallel Move from generating these particular convergent UDCs. Incidentally, it is not obvious how Sideward Movement can capture these facts either, without non-trivial stipulations.

(16) a. *I wonder [who]$_i$ you saw [_$_i$ and _$_i$].

   b. *[Which of her books]$_i$ did you find both [[a review of _$_i$] and _$_i$]?

Citko (2011, 57) also argues that Parallel Move correctly predicts that multiple ATB movement is impossible, as illustrated by the oddness of (17).

(17) a. *[Who]$_j$ [what]$_{i}$ _$_j$ find _$_i$?

   b. *[What]$_j$ [what]$_i$ did John lose _$_j$ and Bill find _$_i$?
      (Citko, 2011, 57)

Without going into the technical details of why Parallel Move prevents such extractions, we simply note that Citko's (2011) data in (17) are not representative of the full range of facts. As Levine and Hukari (2006, 74, 357) and Chaves (2012b) note, such multiple UDCs are possible. The sample in (18) illustrates this. See also §3.2 for more examples.[12]

(18) a. This is a man [to whom]$_i$ liberty$_j$ we would never grant _$_j$ _$_i$.

   b. Ten thousand dollars is a sum of money which$_i$ [to a cause like THAT]$_j$ I would GLADLY give _$_i$ _$_j$.

   c. [On which violins]$_i$ are [these sonatas]$_j$ difficult to play _$_j$ _$_i$?

   d. [These rare old books]$_i$, I wonder [who]$_j$ John thinks [_$_j$ stole _$_i$].

   e. [A bird this unique]$_i$ [how many years]$_j$ could someone spend _$_j$ and never actually see _$_i$?

   f. [A problem THIS HARD]$_i$ [how many years]$_j$ could someone spend _$_j$ in the field and not even come close to solving _$_i$?

The MOVE operation faces a surprising number of theoretical and empirical challenges when modeling UDCs. The problems posed by convergent and cumulative dependencies, for example, seem to require complex stipulations that raise more problems than they solve. MOCs pose particular problems of their own, to which we now turn.

---

[12] Citko (2011, 91) also claims that coordination requires conjuncts to match in tense, voice, and aspect, and that this is a virtue of her account. On the contrary, such claims are empirically false, as shown by (i)–(iii). See Larson (2012) and Chaves (2014) for further criticism of multidominance accounts in general.

  i. Tom went to NY yesterday and he will stay there until March.
 ii. One convict escaped to South America, and the other was last seen in Canada.
iii. Our tenants are very good, and the neighbors have been predominantly good too.

4.2.3 Improper Movement

As discussed in Chapter 2, in missing object constructions (MOCs) the syntactic subject semantically corresponds to a gap embedded in an infinitival phrase or clause. Chomsky (1977) first proposed that MOCs should be treated on par with other UDCs, which is correct, in our view. However, to achieve this result, Chomsky stipulated that the filler-gap dependency involves a special (null) *wh*-operator Op that allows the linkage between the extracted phrase and the subject:

(19)   John$_i$ is tough [$_{CP}$ Op$_i$ [$_{TP}$ PRO$_i$ to please $\_\__i$]].

But it is not obvious how a phrase can move from the object position in an embedded clause to being the subject of a different clause. The latter would be a canonical instance of A-movement, driven by the need to receive nominative case. However, that same phrase already checked its case feature as the object of the embedded verb. This type of illicit movement from an A′-position to an A-position is called **Improper Movement**. Several accounts (Rezac, 2006; Hicks, 2009; Hartman, 2011; Keine and Poole, 2017) have been advanced to explain why MOCs exhibit a hybrid A/A′–movement nature. Hicks's (2009) analysis is used to illustrate the gist of such accounts.

Consider Figure 4.11. Not all movement operations are shown, for exposition purposes. The extracted phrase is not *Robin*, but rather a more complex determiner phrase headed by a null interrogative operator Op. It starts as the complement of the verb *please*, where the case feature of the D-head is checked through an AGREE-relation with *v*. Next, the complex

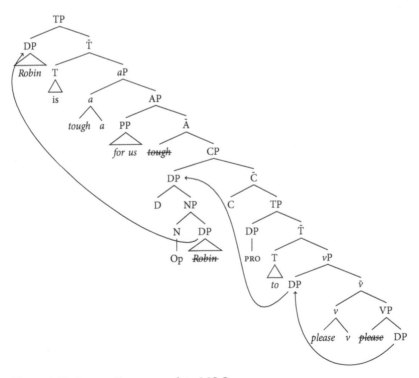

Figure 4.11 A smuggling approach to MOCs

DP moves out of the VP for two reasons: first, because *Robin* still needs to check its own case feature, and, second, to conform to the PIC, thus avoiding having the lowest phase (*v*P) contain any uninterpretable features prior to SPELL-OUT. The next movement step is necessitated by the need for the *wh*-operator (Op) to check its uninterpretable Q-feature at C. Thus, the complement clause of *tough* is an interrogative CP, and the DP that contains the interrogative Op is fronted accordingly. This instance of movement to [Spec,CP] is to the edge of another phase (CP), thus ensuring that the complex DP remains visible in the next phase. The final movement step involves the subextraction of the DP *Robin*, which is driven by the remaining uninterpretable case feature on this DP and the EPP feature on the matrix T. The embedded DP *Robin* is thus **smuggled** to [Spec,CP] followed by A-movement via subextraction; see also Collins (2005). In accounts like Rezac (2006) and Keine and Poole (2017), the last movement operation does not take place, as the subject is inserted directly in the tree and the subject *Robin* is semantically bound to the DP moved from the object position.

In sum, the existence of MOCs is unexpected within a movement-based paradigm, and requires the introduction of theory-dependent silent operators for which there is no clear empirical justification. For example, the account we have discussed above entails various other stipulations, including that the Op-head selected by the D-head must be null, and special constraints to prevent Op from combining with a DP that is itself a DP containing another null Op. It is also unclear how the smuggling account is supposed to handle MOCs that involve adjuncts, as in (20); see §2.1.3.5. This is relevant because adverbial phrases are generally regarded as adjuncts in the MP, and therefore constitute syntactic environments from which no extraction is supposed to take place, according to MP theorizing.

(20) a. I bought this$_i$ [(for you) to play with __$_i$].
      b. The patient$_i$ was stripped naked [for the doctors to examine __$_i$].
      c. This is the book$_i$ that I brought __$_i$ with me [for us to read __$_i$ during the flight].

That difficulties are raised by MOCs within the MP is all the more ironic because MOCs are one of the empirical reasons given by Chomsky (1995, 188) in support of the MP over its movement-based predecessors.

4.3 Island constraints

Accounts of island constraints within the MP have in common the assumption that constraints on movement are syntactic in nature and cross-constructionally active. Both assumptions are empirically problematic, as we noted in §3.2. It is not possible for us to provide a comprehensive survey of MP accounts, and therefore we shall limit our attention to a representative sample. See Müller (2011) and Boeckx (2012) for more detailed overviews.

Attempts to constrain movement operations have always been a hallmark of generative research, starting with Chomsky's (1964) **A-over-A Principle**. Subsequent attempts to generalize extraction constraints, such as **Subjacency** (Chomsky, 1973), **Empty Category Principle** (ECP) (Chomsky, 1981; Lasnik and Saito, 1992), and **Relativized Minimality** (Rizzi, 1990) imposed local constraints on the well-formedness of movement chains and the positions in which traces/copies could appear (i.e. government). The advent of the MP and its call to eliminate local derivational constraints (like Subjacency), as well as local representational constraints, known as **filters** (like the ECP), gave rise to transderivational (translocal) constraints, which rely on predetermined evaluation metrics such as locality (Müller, 2011, ch. 2). Within the MP, island effects result from elementary operations like MERGE and AGREE (Sabel, 2002; Rackowski and Richards, 2005), from cyclic spell-out (Uriagereka, 1999; Nunes and Uriagereka, 2000; Nunes, 2004), or from phase effects (Takahashi, 1994; Kitahara, 1995; Boeckx, 2003; Rizzi, 2007b; Gallego and Uriagereka, 2007; Stepanov, 2007). In what follows we take a closer look at two kinds of islands from the MP perspective.

4.3.1 CED effects

Since Huang (1982) the term Condition on Extraction Domains (CED) has collectively referred to Subject Islands and Adjunct Islands, and reflects the idea that subjects and adjuncts share certain properties which are critical for explaining such island effects. As we shall see, extant accounts of the CED are excessively strong, and have reduced empirical coverage. First, extraction from subjects and adjuncts is predicted to be impossible in the MP, and therefore there is no explanation for the wide range of exceptions discussed in §3.2.6 and §3.2.7. What's more, there is no working MP account of convergent or cumulative UDCs in general, let alone those that involve extraction from subject phrases and/or adverbial phrases, as in (21).

(21) a. This is the kind of person [who]$_i$ even [friends of $\_\_i$] think that [enemies of $\_\_i$] are everywhere.
    (double subject-internal gap UDC)
   b. This is the AC unit [which]$_i$ I drove Alex crazy [complaining about $\_\_i$] yesterday [after buying $\_\_i$ from Craigslist].
    (double adjunct-internal gap UDC)
   c. [What kinds of books]$_i$ do [the authors of $\_\_i$] argue about royalties [after writing $\_\_i$]?
    (subject- and adjunct-internal gap UDC)

Let us begin our overview with Takahashi (1994), who argues that CED effects are due to the conditions of **Shortest Move** (the requirement that the displaced element must reach its target site by a series of short successive movement steps to the maximal projections along its path) and **Chain Uniformity** (the displaced element and its in situ copy constitute a chain, and uniform chains cannot contain other chains). Consider, for example, the analysis in Figure 4.12, taken from Takahashi (1994).

The DP *a picture of who* moves out of its *v*P, and in the process the DP and its original copy form a chain. Next, the DP *who* must move as well, but in order to adhere to Shortest Move the DP *who* has to move to the closest phrase by adjoining to *a picture of who*, as shown in Figure 4.12. A complex chain is formed because the first chain now overlaps the second chain, constituting a violation of Chain Uniformity. Thus, the DP never has the chance to move to its final position, over the auxiliary *does*.

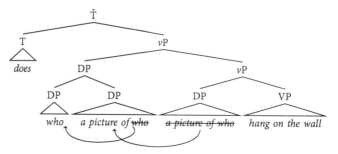

Figure 4.12 Subject Island *Who does a picture of hang on the wall?*

Such an account is at odds with the fact that extraction from nominal subjects is possible, as noted as far back as Ross (1967); see §3.2.6 for a wide range of examples. Takahashi's complex chains approach is also problematic on independent grounds. As we have already noted in §2.2.1.2, complex chains like (22) are quite possible.

(22)   This is the handout [which]$_i$ I can't remember [how many copies of $\_i$]$_j$ we have to print $\_j$.

As for Adjunct Islands, Takahashi (1994) assumes that adjunction is a covert form of coordination, and stipulates that adjunction to a coordination position is not allowed. Thus, in (23) the clause *Did Mary cry* is coordinated with *after Peter hit who*, and therefore the *wh*-phrase *who* cannot satisfy Shortest Move without violating Chain Uniformity: the shortest move involves an adjunction to a coordinate structure, which is disallowed.

(23)   *[Who]$_i$ did Mary cry [after Peter hit $\_i$]?

The assumption that modification is a form of coordination is empirically unmotivated, as it flies in the face of the fact that coordinate structures exhibit very different properties from modification structures; see, for example, Postal (1993), McCawley (1998, ch. 9), and Levine (2001a). Furthermore, there is ample evidence that extraction from adjuncts is often licit: see §3.2.7.

Nunes and Uriagereka (2000) propose a derivational structure-building approach to CED effects in which subjects and adjuncts are assumed to be built in parallel with the structures with which they combine. For example, the phrases *a picture of who* and *hang on the wall* are built independently in the derivational space, and, once merged together, the former becomes opaque for extraction via the constraint in (24).

(24)   If a phrase marker X was assembled in parallel with a phrase marker Y, and then X and Y were Merged, whereupon Y projects, no extraction is ever possible from X.

(Nunes and Uriagereka, 2000)

According to (24), the extraction of *who* in Figure 4.12 is banned because it constitutes an extraction from the non-head daughter. The same rationale applies to block extraction from modifiers. Nunes and Uriagereka's (2000) account is not only stipulative and excessively strong in banning extraction from subjects and adverbials; it is also technically problematic. As Müller (2011) notes, (24) is incompatible with the idea that phases are the relevant domain for cyclic spell-out. In sum, Nunes and Uriagereka's (2000) account is at least as problematic as Takahashi (1994).

Sabel (2002) proposes to account for various island effects via the constraint in (25). This rule states that non-head phrases become opaque to movement when they are merged with non-lexical head nodes.

(25)   BARRIER: a category *A* may not be extracted from a subtree *T2* (maximal projection) of *T1* if *T2* was merged at some stage of the derivation with a complex category.

This notion of barrierhood prevents extraction from modifiers because the adjunct becomes a barrier when it merges with the VP, since the VP is phrasal rather than lexical. Similarly, extractions from subject phrases are ruled out because subjects are by definition merged with a complex category, the head of the VP. Like all other accounts surveyed so far, the ban on subject- and adjunct-internal gaps is too strict. Moreover, it has technical problems, as Müller (2011, 79) notes. Sabel's analysis is incompatible with the concept of phase, because checking whether an extraction is licit or not requires the scanning of large portions of syntactic structure.

Rackowski and Richards (2005) propose another version of barrier which instead involves the operation AGREE, but which is no less stipulative and no less empirically problematic. In a nutshell, *wh*-expressions move from one phase head to the next only if these phase heads have already first undergone AGREE with the CP containing the *wh*-phrase. The ban on extraction from CPs containing subjects and adjuncts follows from neither entering into an AGREE-relation with *v*. But Müller (2011, 82) points out that this would require that adjunct CPs must also always be outside of the c-command domain of the probe *v*, and it is not clear how cyclic movement takes place for elements that are in an embedded [Spec,CP] position. Consider once again the German *wh*-copying data in (26).

(26)   a. Was*i* meinst du [*CP* wen*i*   wir __*i* einladen sollen?]
           what think you   whom we   invite   should
           'Who(m) do you think we should invite?'

        b. Wen*i* meinst du [*CP* wen*i*   wir __*i* einladen sollen?]
           whom think you   whom we   invite   should
           'Who(m) do you think we should invite?'
           (Müller, 2011, 28)   (German)

As discussed by McDaniel (1989) and others, *was* 'what' in (26a) is a scope marker, whereas the *wen* 'whom' in (26b) is a copy of the *wh*-phrase in the embedded clause. The copy of *wen* in the embedded clause is in the same position that subjects would appear in subject islands. Müller (2011, 28) notes that such data undermine Rockowski and Richards' AGREE-based barrierhood.

Chomsky (2008) assumes that elements at the edge of a phase are opaque for subextraction, which he refers to as the **Edge Condition**. Subject Island contrasts like (27) arise under the assumption that the subjects of transitive verbs are located in different nodes than derived subjects (i.e. subjects of passives and unaccusatives). Chomsky assumes that transitive subjects originate within *v*P and that derived subjects originate within VP. Thus, the former is at the edge of a phase and subextraction is disallowed. But in the latter case the subject is an internal argument, and therefore the Edge Condition does not apply.

(27)   a. *[Of which car]$_i$ did [the driver __$_i$]$_j$ [$_{vP}$ __$_j$ cause a scandal]?

     b. [Of which car]$_i$ was [the driver __$_i$]$_j$ [$_{vP}$ awarded __$_j$ a prize]?
       (Chomsky, 2008, 147)

This account is based on the idea that a specifier of v and C is rendered internally frozen, so that their subparts cannot be extracted. Passive subjects are inserted at a lower position of the verbal structure, at which point subextraction can take place before the larger phrase moves to a phase edge and becomes frozen. Chomsky's proposal is a departure from the widely accepted VP-Internal Subject Hypothesis (Koopman and Sportiche, 1991), whereby *all* subject phrases are derived. Regardless, Chomsky's account is too permissive, as it incorrectly predicts that extractions like (28a) are acceptable, since they involve extraction from a derived subject (Haegeman et al., 2013; Polinsky et al., 2013).

(28)   a. *[Of which man]$_i$ was [the friend __$_i$] fired?

     b. *[Of what]$_i$ was [the owner __$_i$] arrested?

Second, Chomsky (2008, 160, n. 39) acknowledges that the account incorrectly predicts that extractions from non-derived subjects like (29) are ungrammatical. All of these examples involve a transitive verb.

(29)   a. [Of which books]$_i$ did [the authors __$_i$] receive the prize?

     b. [Of which car]$_i$ is [the driver __$_i$] likely to cause a scandal?
       (Chomsky, 2008)

     c. [Which doctors]$_i$ have [patients of __$_i$] filed malpractice suits in the last year?

     d. [Which President]$_i$ would [the impeachment of __$_i$] not cause much outrage?

     e. [Which problem]$_i$ would [the resolution of __$_i$] surprise you the most?
       (Chaves, 2013)

Finally, Haegeman et al. (2013) propose that eight different constraints are at play in Subject Islands. Some of these are stipulative, such as 'extraction is only possible from the head of a chain' and 'the edge of a phase is opaque for extraction'. Others are empirically dubious, such as 'specific nominals are opaque domains for extraction', which would mean that subextraction from a definite NP is illicit. See the counterexamples in (29) and the attested data in §3.2.2. Another problematic constraint is 'a moved constituent is frozen for extraction', which means that extracted phrases cannot contain gaps. This is also contrary to fact, as discussed in §2.2.1.2.

   In sum, the MP currently lacks a coherent and empirically adequate account of CED phenomena. We agree with Boeckx and Grohmann (2007), Müller (2011), Abels (2012), and Den Dikken (2018, §2.3.4) in concluding that the notion of phase sheds no light on island phenomena.

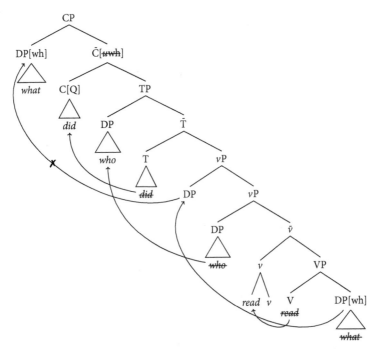

Figure 4.13 Superiority violation: *What did who read?*

4.3.2 Wh-islands

We now turn to Superiority effects, already discussed in §3.2.9 and illustrated in (30). In the MP, such acceptability contrasts follow from Rizzi's Relativized Minimality and Chomsky's Minimal Link Condition.

(30) a. Did you forget [[who]$_i$ Sam had given the present to __$_i$]?
      b. [What]$_i$ did you forget [Sam had given __$_i$ to Mia]?
      c. *[What]$_i$ did you forget [[who]$_j$ Sam had given __$_i$ to __$_j$]?

In a nutshell, a CP must attract the closest *wh*-phrase, but if that position is already occupied by another *wh*-phrase, then the former cannot move to the closest CP node. Figure 4.13 illustrates how the Superiority violation in (30b) is captured. The explanation for Wh-Condition violations like (31) is analogous: *what* cannot move to the specifier position of the embedded clause's CP node because it is already occupied by the complementizer *whether*.

(31) a. *[What]$_i$ does the teacher wonder [whether George read __$_i$]?
      b. *[Which book]$_i$ did you wonder [whether Robin bought __$_i$]?

But as noted in §3.2.9, there are many apparent counterexamples, such as (32) and (33). The existence of such cases casts doubt on accounts which rely on shortest configurational distance, like Rizzi's and Chomsky's accounts, whereby a *wh*-element lower in the structure is not allowed to move over another *wh*-element in its movement path.

(32) a. What$_i$ will which patient get __$_i$?
          (Pesetsky, 1987)

      b. [Which book]$_i$ did which student read __$_i$?
          (Pesetsky, 2000)

(33) a. [What]$_i$ did you wonder whether to read __$_i$?
          (Kluender, 1998)

          [Which topic]$_i$ did John ask whether to talk about __$_i$?
          (Szabolcsi, 2006)

Another major problem with such accounts has to do with crossing dependencies. Kitahara (1997) notes that crossing extraction dependencies are ruled out as a consequence of Cyclic Movement and Shortest Move, but as we discussed in §2.2.1.1, crossing extraction dependencies does not always result in illicit UDCs:

(34) a. [Which TV show]$_i$ did you wonder [how often]$_j$ I saw __$_i$ __$_j$?
      b. That's the person [who]$_i$ I never know [what]$_j$ to get __$_i$ __$_j$ for Christmas.
      c. [How much]$_i$ will these cars$_j$ cost __$_i$ to recall __$_j$?

This counter-evidence is problematic not only for any account that assumes crossing dependencies are necessarily illicit, but also for any account that adopts the Shortest Move condition. Either the Shortest Move, Minimal Link Condition, and Relativized Minimality are too strong or the above counterexamples are illusions. Pesetsky (1987), Cinque (1990), and Pesetsky (2000, 16) adopt the latter view, and propose that *wh*-elements which are connected with previous discourse are 'D(iscourse)-Linked', and not extracted from a base position. This includes *who* and *what*, according to Pesetsky (2000, 16). The D-Linked *wh*-phrases are more like pronouns and therefore get their interpretation not via movement, but via a different device called **unselective binding**, analogous to how the scope of indefinites is computed in Heim (1982). In short, such apparently extracted *wh*-phrases are not extracted at all, and that's why they don't yield island effects. Rizzi (1990) advanced a similar proposal, whereby referential phrases can receive a referential index, which semantically binds a trace. According to this proposal, semantic binding need not be subject to the locality conditions of short, local chains in the syntax. As a result, D-Linked, 'fully elaborated' *wh*-phrases can remain in situ, avoiding violating Relativized Minimality and the Minimal Link Condition.[13]

However, D-Linking is problematic in a number of ways. First, a clear semantic definition of D-Linking has proven to be elusive (Erteschik-Shir, 1997, 2006b, 2007; Cresti, 1995; Rullmann, 1995; Abrusán, 2011; Abrusán, 2014; Abrusán and Spector, 2011). In what concerns islands, there is currently no non-circular definition of D-Linking, as Ginzburg and Sag (2000, 247–50), Chung (1994, 33, 39), and Levine and Hukari (2006, 242, 268–71) note. Second, D-Linking is empirically dubious. Acceptable counterexamples like (32) are given out of the blue, and therefore cannot evoke any preexisting set of

---

[13] Cresti (1995) stipulates that an extra specifier position can appear as a landing site for individual-denoting phrases, in order to avoid having to resort to the notion of D-Linking.

referents, as D-Linking would require. Or, at least, it is not clear how the set of referents is more salient than others in any meaningful way. Even more problematic are sentences like (35), which simply cannot be uttered with a particular denotation in mind for the filler phrase. The acceptability of such data is completely unexpected in a D-Linking account.

(35)   At this point, I can't remember [which girl]$_i$ [which boy]$_j$ _$_j$ kissed _$_i$.

Finally, there is no experimental evidence that contextualization can lead to a D-Linking effect of a bare *wh*-phrase (Sprouse, 2007b; Villata et al., 2016). In sum, D-Linking raises more problems than it solves.

Abrusán (2014, 85) claims that D-Linking effects are not a unitary phenomenon. Rather, they are due to several unrelated phenomena, such as selection of non-contradictory alternatives, exhaustivity, and scope:

> the grammar is simpler than generally agreed in the syntactic literature, as there is no need to postulate syntactic rules of UG such as Relativized Minimality (Rizzi, 1990) or the Minimal Link Condition (Chomsky, 1995) to explain the deviance of weak islands. The compositional semantics of questions supplies everything we need for the explanation of weak islands, without invoking any further special rules.'
>
> (Abrusán, 2014, 3)

4.4 Psychological plausibility

Although MOVE plays a pivotal role in human language according to the MP, it remains unclear what exactly it is supposed to be. Is it merely a convenient mathematical abstraction, disconnected from how language is processed in the brain, or does it play an active role during language processing? In other words, how psychologically real is movement? Chomsky and Miller (1963) expressed the following view when discussing the psychological reality of transformations, the precursors to MOVE.

> The psychological plausibility of a transformational model of the language user would be strengthened, of course, if it could be shown that our performance on tasks requiring an appreciation of the structure of transformed sentences is some function of the nature, number and complexity of the grammatical transformations involved.
>
> (Chomsky and Miller, 1963, 481)

Later, Chomsky (1965) famously drew a distinction between linguistic knowledge (**competence**) and the psychological mechanisms responsible for linguistic behavior (**performance**). Whereas the former consists of the linguistic information (phonology, morphology, syntax, etc.) that a speaker must know in order to use and understand their language, the latter pertains to the unconscious mental processes involved in using that internalized linguistic knowledge to produce and comprehend utterances in real time. Hence, whereas lexical knowledge and inflectional rules are part of competence, hesitations, omissions, stuttering, malapropisms, misparses, and the like fall under the purview of performance. To draw an analogy from the game of chess, competence involves knowing the game board, all the different pieces, and how they are set and move, as well as the objective of the game, openings, and tactics. Performance, however, consists of actual time-constrained gameplay, with all its blunders and brilliance. Under such a view, it is reasonable to assume that only unacceptable sentences whose oddness cannot be explained by any independently motivated extragrammatical (i.e. performance) factors of behavior are ungrammatical (Bever, 1974).

Although Chomsky (1965) made it clear that the theory is meant to model competence, not performance, he also argued that models of competence and models of performance should be integrated:

> it is worthwhile to reiterate that a generative grammar is not a model for a speaker or a hearer. It attempts to characterize in the most neutral possible terms the knowledge of the language that provides the basis for actual use of language by a speaker-hearer... No doubt, a reasonable model of language use will incorporate, as a basic component, the generative grammar that expresses the speaker-hearer's knowledge of the language.
>
> (Chomsky, 1965, 9)

Chomsky (1986b, 49) offered the following analogy from biology: the heart may be simply and elegantly described as a pump, with disregard for how it actually works, but it does not follow that such a description is superior to one which involves the actual anatomy and physiology of that organ. Therefore, if grammar G_1 is simpler and more elegant than grammar G_2, but G_2 is more plausible as a psychologically real description of the speaker-hearer's knowledge of their language, then it is obvious that G_1 should not be preferred to G_2. Hence, the goal of the theoretical grammarian is not a merely descriptive one; rather, the goal is to discover what the language faculty really is, and how it actually works, and why it is the way it is.

Many other authors similarly make the assumption that human language processing operates according to the linguistic information contained by the competence grammar (Chomsky and Miller, 1963; Chomsky, 1965; Bresnan, 1978; Kaplan and Bresnan, 1982; Sag, 1992; Steedman, 2001; Van Valin, 2006; Phillips, 2006; Sag and Wasow, 2011, 2015; Phillips and Lewis, 2013). All things being equal, the rules and categories in the competence grammar should reflect upon how speakers use language in real time (at least to some degree). Although the above authors do not share exactly the same set of assumptions, the following quotation captures some of that common ground:

> We assume that an explanatory model of human language performance will incorporate a theoretically justified representation of the native speaker's linguistic knowledge (*a grammar*) as a component separate both from the computational mechanisms that operate on it (*a processor*) and from other nongrammatical processing parameters that might influence the processor's behavior. To a certain extent the various components that we postulate can be studied independently, guided where appropriate by the well-established methods and evaluation standards of linguistics, computer science, and experimental psychology. However, the requirement that the various components ultimately must fit together in a consistent and coherent model imposes even stronger constraints on their structure and operation.
>
> (Kaplan and Bresnan, 1982)

Although production and comprehension are very different processes, there is some experimental evidence that comprehension and production share the same linguistic system (Pickering and Garrod, 2013; Momma and Phillips, 2018; Matchin and Hickok, 2019). Thus, any parsimonious theory of language should ultimately not only be consistent with the observable empirical facts about language structure, but also be consistent with the basic behavioral evidence about how it is represented and processed, as discussed in §1.4.

It is clear that the MP aspires to be psychologically plausible. Recall that one of the stated rationales for Multiple Spell-Out is to precisely unburden working memory (Chomsky, 2000a, 106) and that both the Phase Impenetrability Condition (Chomsky, 2001) and the Edge Condition (Chomsky, 2008, 148) are similarly justified on the grounds that they reduce the working memory burden. Moreover, the MP is regarded by some as being squarely consistent with research on evolutionary psychology. Movement, for example, is claimed to be the result of a single genetic mutation (Berwick et al., 2013; Bolhuis et al., 2014; Berwick and Chomsky, 2016). For more on this **biolinguistics** enterprise, see Boeckx and Grohmann (2013) and Chomsky (2016, 173). See also Jackendoff (2002, 2017), Martins and Boeckx (2019), and Chapter 7 for criticism.

Over the years, many studies have attempted to detect movement operations during language processing. For example, early work by Nicol and Swinney (1989), Gibson and Hickok (1993), Nicol and Pickering (1993), and others found that the filler phrase was activated when at the corresponding gap position. However, Sag and Fodor (1995) noted that this finding is compatible with any account of UDCs in which the filler phrase is semantically linked to the corresponding in situ argument role. All of the extant theories of UDCs, movement-based or otherwise, have such a property, and therefore the aforementioned evidence is merely consistent with movement rather than evidence of it.

Experimenters then turned to psycholinguistic evidence for traces in order to test the predictions of a movement operation. Pickering and Barry (1991), Pickering (1993), Pickering et al. (1994), Boland et al. (1995), and Traxler and Pickering (1996) argued against the existence of traces and movement by demonstrating that, during the processing of UDCs, comprehenders do not wait until the purported gap location is found. In their classic experiment, Traxler and Pickering (1996) monitored the eye movements of participants who read sentences like those in (36), in which the gap site is located after the direct object, rather than verb-adjacent. Crucially, comprehenders took longer reading the verb *shot* in (36a) than in (36b), which suggests that the filler-gap dependency is resolved at the verb, not at the gap site.

(36)   a. That's the garage [with which]$_i$ the heartless killer shot the man $\_\_i$ yesterday afternoon.

    b. That's the pistol [with which]$_i$ the heartless killer shot the man $\_\_i$ yesterday afternoon.

Gorrell (1993) and Gibson and Hickok (1993) countered that Traxler and Pickering's evidence is equally compatible with an account where the sentence processor posits a trace as soon as it has sufficient information to do so, although the syntactic position at which such trace will enter the tree structure is farther downstream in the sentence. In other words, it is possible that there is a dissociation between the time at which the trace is postulated and the position at which it is placed. Thus, either there is a disconnect between movement operations and language processing or the mechanism that resolves filler-gap dependencies does not involve anything like MOVE. Since then, the existence of a linguistic entity (a trace or a copy) at the gap site remains controversial linguistically (Postal and Pullum, 1982; Sag and Fodor, 1995; Bouma et al., 2001) and experimentally (Pickering and Barry, 1991; Gibson and Hickok, 1993; Traxler and Pickering, 1996; Grodzinsky, 2000; Kay, 2000; Featherston, 2001; Phillips and Wagers, 2007).

The fact remains that the behavioral evidence surrounding filler-gap dependencies, detected by Pickering and Barry (1991), Pickering (1993), Pickering et al. (1994), Boland et al. (1995), and Traxler and Pickering (1996), is at best exactly the behavioral facts that follow immediately from a non-movement analysis of extraction where the filler phrase is linked to the argument structure of the respective subcategorizer. See also Branigan and Pickering (2017) for more recent discussion.

The lack of direct evidence for movement also extends to neurolinguistic research focusing on the processing of UDCs. Although all extant psycholinguistic and neurolinguistic models of sentence processing agree that the left frontal and temporal lobes are responsible for such syntactic representations, there is no consensus on the division of labor, among its constituent brain regions, or on where UDCs are processed (Friederici, 2009; Bornkessel-Schlesewsky and Schlesewsky, 2013). On the whole, neuropsychological evidence supports a distributed view of syntactic processing wherein no single region exclusively handles any particular linguistic phenomenon, whereas neuroimaging evidence appears to support a more localized view. For example, some research, such as Grodzinsky (1986, 2000) has claimed that there is relatively direct evidence for a neural module in Broca's area that is responsible for syntactic operations like MOVE. Kay (2000) and others point out that such experimental results are also compatible with non-movement-based accounts, and Wilson and Saygın (2004) and others provide evidence which challenges Grodzinsky's claims, by showing that no particular brain region is involved. Many other studies have arrived at the same conclusion, that filler-gap processing is not exclusive to any specific brain region. A closer look at the neuroimaging results on sentence comprehension suggests that the activation profile of the posterior temporal lobe is almost always coupled with Broca's area, weakening the proposed unique role of Broca's area in syntactic processing (Matchin et al., 2017).

For example, Wartenburger et al. (2003) report an event-related functional magnetic resonance imaging (fMRI) experiment in which healthy subjects were asked to judge the acceptability of visually presented sentences with and without extraction of phrasal constituents. During both kinds of sentences, there was activation in language-related brain regions, but comparing both kinds of sentences did not result in differential brain activation of left frontal or temporal regions. In particular, Broca's area was similarly activated in processing sentences with UDCs and without. Analogously, Matchin (2014) reports evidence showing that Broca's region is not selectively sensitive to movement phenomena. Rather, Broca's area seems sensitive to the processing of dependencies that involve active prediction, which includes but is not exclusive to the kind of prediction concerning gap sites during the processing of UDCs. Matchin (2014) concludes that there are as yet no clearly localized neurobiological correlates of movement, nor of syntax in general. Similarly, Rogalsky et al. (2015) used within-subject fMRI to detect movement distance effects in Broca's area, but no difference was found between movement and non-movement sentences.

As Balewski et al. (2016) note, further support for syntactic processing being distributed rather than localized is the fact that it is robust: brain lesions to many different parts of the language system other than Broca's can cause similar syntactic comprehension difficulties to those attributed to Broca's in prior studies. In fact, there is evidence that if brain damage to critical language areas occurs sufficiently early in childhood, language acquisition is not hampered (Dąbrowska, 2004, §4.1), which argues against strong localized modularity in the language faculty.

Nieto-Castañón and Fedorenko (2012) provide evidence that prior neurolinguistic research which identified a localized rather than distributed syntactic processing, such as that of Santi and Grodzinsky (2007a,b), has very likely suffered from a methodological flaw caused by the poor sensitivity of traditional group-based analyses, which overestimated the importance of Broca's area in the processing of syntax in general and UDCs in particular; see Rogalsky and Hickok (2011) for an overview.

Balewski et al. (2016) similarly find that the processing of syntactic structures involves multiple streams of information in multiple regions of both hemispheres of the brain. Syntax appears to be predominantly processed in the left temporo-parietal region, the left posterior superior temporal sulcus, and multiple regions in the right temporo-parietal cortex. The regions found in the bilateral temporal cortices are related to both dependency role and part of speech features. Activation in more posterior regions corresponds to part-of-speech features, and in more anterior regions, corresponds to dependency roles (i.e. word integration and sentence structure building). Overall, the extant evidence has not identified a locus for processing extraction, and it is rather unclear whether there is any localized area solely responsible for filler-gap dependencies. More likely, UDC processing is robustly distributed across multiple regions, permeating different types of linguistic representation. There is currently no behavioral evidence for anything like the MOVE operation.

4.4.1 Three views of movement

According to Phillips and Lewis (2013), there are three views that one can adopt in describing the relationship between grammar and the language processor. In the first view, called **extensionist**, there is no connection between the movement operation as defined by linguistic theory and the actual operations deployed during language processing. In other words, movement is little more than a mathematical abstraction, and as such it is under no expectation that its psycholinguistic effect is measurable. In the **literalist** view, in contrast, any operations that are postulated by the grammatical theory are the reflection of analogue cognitive processes in the minds of speakers. Thus, if a theory of UDCs is based on MOVE, then it should—in principle—be possible to find behavioral evidence of its neural correlate that is not consistent with non-movement-based accounts of UDCs. Finally, in the **formalist** view the link between the grammatical theory and the cognitive processes involved in language use is only partial. We discuss below how these views fare in resolving the fundamental disconnect between movement theories of UDC and the behavioral facts of incremental human language processing.

4.4.1.1 The extensionist view

The extensionist view assumes that grammars simply provide a characterization of the grammatical and ungrammatical sentences of a language, with little further significance attributed to the individual components of a grammatical theory, or to the computations that these carry out.

Various central tenets in the MP strike us as inconsistent with the extensionist view, since their main motivation comes from performance considerations, such as the rationale for Multiple Spell-Out, as given by Chomsky (2000a, 106), for the Phase Impenetrability Condition (Chomsky, 2001), and for the Edge Condition (Chomsky, 2008, 148). All of these are supposed to reduce the computational and working memory burden, which is a psycholinguistic consideration. Finally, recall also that Berwick and Chomsky (2016), Bolhuis et al. (2014), and Berwick et al. (2013) argue that MOVE is the result of a single genetic mutation that endowed one individual with the necessary biological equipment for language. For all of these reasons, it is not clear in what sense the MP is an extensionist approach to grammar.

According to the extensionist view, MOVE is nothing but an idealized mathematical abstraction over the actual psychological devices that are responsible for syntactic displacement. Indeed, it is known since McCawley (1968), Lakoff (1971), and Thomson (1975) that transformational operations can be reconceptualized as relational constraints between tree structures rather than as a procedural operation. This was perhaps what Chomsky (2001) had in mind when he wrote:

> displacement is implemented by selecting a target and a related category to be moved to a position determined by the target ... Terminology is often **metaphoric** [emphasis added] here and below, adopted for expository convenience.
>
> (Chomsky, 2001, 4, 42, n. 4)

According to Chomsky (1995, 52), movement-based grammar belongs to the computational level of grammatical description, rather than the algorithmic or implementation levels, as borrowed from David Marr's famous levels of analysis. Marr (1982, 25) proposed that the study of any complex system or human behavior can be factored into three different levels:

- The **computational level** concerns a description of what the system does, and why it does it. In the language domain, this is the goal of linguistics.
- The **algorithmic level** concerns how the system does what it does—specifically, what representations it uses and what processes it employs in order to build and manipulate the representations. In the language domain, this corresponds to the object of the study of psycholinguistics.
- The **implementational level** concerns how the system and its computations are physically carried out in the brain. In the language domain, this corresponds to neurolinguistics.

Each level imposes a series of constraints on the theory. The problem is first defined at a logical level, and methods of solving it are ignored. The algorithm specifies how the logical problem is solved, without concern for how the algorithm is biologically implemented. Finally, the implementational level establishes a correspondence between the algorithmic abstractions and physical, biological mechanisms. Marr's approach is essentially a triage method to help researchers reverse-engineer any complex system.

If MOVE is merely a computational-level metaphor, with no logical connection to how brains compute UDCs, then its value is diminished. The blind enumeration of all the strings (i.e. the generation of LF and PF pairs) of a language is not a computation that is ever carried out by speakers, and therefore it is arguably uncalled for.

As Marr stressed, the logical idealizations of the computational level must be close enough to the actual nature of the system; otherwise there is no link between the levels, and the reverse engineering process breaks down. A similar sentiment is expressed by Phillips and Lewis (2013):

> A grammatical theory that achieves impressive descriptive adequacy using mechanisms that are opaque to real time implementation is an interesting theory nonetheless. However, the descriptive success of such a theory begs for further analysis of why it works so well, and whether its success crucially depends on the opaque mechanisms. This analysis should ideally lead to development of a more psychologically transparent version of the theory.
>
> (Phillips and Lewis, 2013)

In order to progress into lower zones of Marr's description level, linguistic theory must be increasingly consistent with experimental evidence. Crucially, it is difficult to see how movement-based conceptions of grammar can be reconciled with the basic facts of incremental real-time language processing (Pollard and Sag, 1994; Johnson and Lappin, 1999; Edelman and Christiansen, 2003; Seuren, 2004; Labelle, 2007; Sag and Wasow, 2011, 2015; Ferreira, 2005; Phillips, 2017; Branigan and Pickering, 2017). Linguistic expressions are clearly not processed 'bottom-up-right-to-left', as generally required by MP derivations.

The MP's goal of optimizing for theories of language without regard for how this system interacts with others in real time leads to approaches that are fundamentally inconsistent with cognitive science more broadly (Edelman and Christiansen, 2003; Ferreira, 2005; Phillips, 2017):

> Why haven't the fields reestablished their closer relationship? I would argue that a fundamental reason is the theoretical shift in formal syntax from GB to the Minimalist Program (MP). Unfortunately, the MP is highly unappealing from the point of view of human sentence processing.
>
> (Ferreira, 2005, 370)

There is no guarantee that the 'simplest', most 'elegant', and descriptively adequate theory available has anything to do with the categories, structures, and rules that speakers actually acquire and use during real-time sentence processing. Even if the simplest theory that can be formulated is descriptively adequate and predicts all the facts exactly correctly, its value and credibility are undermined if it turns out to be deeply incompatible with what is known about human cognition, child language acquisition, and computational tractability.

4.4.1.2 The literalist view

According to Phillips and Lewis (2013), the literalist view holds that the construction of grammatical representations as described by the linguistic theory is a direct reflection of mental processes. Berwick and Weinberg (1984) call such theories **type-transparent**. As already noted throughout this chapter, it is difficult to see how the MP can be reconciled with the literalist view. Indeed, the MP has been much criticized for being fundamentally incompatible with what happens in real-time language processing (Johnson and Lappin, 1999; Jackendoff, 2002; Seuren, 2004; Ferreira, 2005; Labelle, 2007).

One attempt to rescue the literalist approach is the **two-system architecture** proposed by Berwick and Weinberg (1984); see also Townsend and Bever (2001). The two-system architecture assumes that there is a more abstract relationship between the competence grammar and human language processing, weaker in some respects and stronger in others. For Berwick and Weinberg, the parsing model is parallel, and explicitly contains a subset of the operations required by the competence grammar, so that the rules of the grammar are 'mirrored rather exactly' (Berwick and Weinberg, 1984, 29) in the parsing module. The result is that a dual-system model of sentence parsing analyzes all sentences using two different syntactic systems, one at a time. But there are several problems with the two-system architecture. First, no psychological evidence exists for this mirroring process that Berwick and Weinberg (1984) and Townsend and Bever (2001) propose. Second, no details are provided about what exactly this mirroring process is, or how the language processing system is informed by grammatical constraints. What is more, the two-system architecture renders movement-based grammar undetectable to experimental confirmation, and is, as far as we can tell, impossible to falsify. For further criticism of the two-system architecture, see Lewis and Phillips (2015).

There are some attempts to reconceptualize MOVE within the MP so as to allow incremental top-down processing (Phillips, 1996; Richards, 1999; Guilliot, 2006): constituents are base-generated in their surface position, and can be moved downwards, into deeper syntactic levels, creating copies.[14] But such accounts are not fully formalized, and furthermore are faced with a fundamental problem: how to decide which branching nodes are possible at any given point, and which features are present at any given parsing step. There are myriad different ways for any phrasal node to branch into. The total number of distinct and grammatical local trees is very large, as is the number of distinct ungrammatical local trees. Somehow, the parser must know which are which, and make educated guesses about the most likely upcoming structure, if it is to be consistent with the behavioral facts of incremental human sentence processing. This creates a large set of potential derivational histories, not all of which are psycholinguistically plausible.

To our knowledge, the only explicit attempts to reconcile Minimalism with the facts of incremental processing are Chesi (2007, 2015), Stabler (2013), and Hunter (forthcoming). Their models involve top-down processing, but in order to achieve this, Chesi and Hunter must go against one of the basic tenets of Minimalism, i.e. the claim that constructions are epiphenomenal rather than part of the grammar. Without constructional knowledge, there is no way to create top-down structural predictions without knowledge of which structures can exist, and how they can branch (i.e. which phrasal categories can be merged with what, and which features are therein).

---

[14] Phillips and Lewis (2013) reject this literalist view on the grounds that it is too rigid in identifying the grammar with the task of language comprehension.

It is important to note that Chesi and Hunter's accounts are not cast in the MP, but rather in a related framework put forth by Stabler (1997) and Stabler and Keenan (2003), known as **minimalist grammar**. This point is worth stressing because Stabler's conception of the MP is quite different from what is standardly assumed in the mainstream. In Stabler's model, for instance, there are at least three kinds of MERGE (COMP-MERGE, SPEC-MERGE, and NONFINAL-MERGE), as well as several flavors of MOVE (e.g. SPEC-MOVE and NONFINAL-MOVE). Second, Stabler's minimalist grammars are provably equivalent to a certain kind of CFG (Kobele et al., 2007; Michaelis, 2001), and are parsable in top-down fashion using standard top-down CFG parsing algorithms (Stabler, 2013). The equivalence to CFGs allows this type of grammar to be compatible with probabilistic extensions (Hunter and Dyer, 2013), which is a most welcome property that standard Minimalism lacks.

The adoption of a small repertoire of phrase-structure rules is not unlike the rules of X'-Theory, or the immediate dominance schemata of Head-driven Phrase-Structure Grammar (Pollard and Sag, 1994), and very much inconsistent with Chomsky's claim that all phrase-structural patterns are purely epiphenomenal and not part of the grammar.[15]

In Chesi (2004, 2007, 2015) and Bianchi and Chesi (2014), computation proceeds top-down, by projecting a verbal phrase with certain features and creating binary branches via MERGE, until the correct leaves are reached. There are many different features that a phrase can have, however, and therefore it is not clear how computationally tractable this top-down parsing conception of Minimalism is in practice. Nodes that would be due to movement in standard Minimalism correspond to features that are unexpected in the initial position at the left periphery of the clause.[16] This approach is illustrated in Figure 4.14, using Stabler's (1997) minimalist grammar notation. The subscript elements in square brackets are features to be checked. Beginning at the top, an expectation for an interrogative phrase is generated, i.e. an extended V projection with +wh feature expressed. The first feature [+wh] is processed and a compatible wh-item is retrieved and merged—in this case the nominal *who*. Because the features [+D N] are unselected, and therefore unexpected, a copy of *who* is placed into a memory buffer. The curved brackets indicate that the copy will be silent, and thus not pronounced. Later in the derivation, *John* is inserted in the subject position, but similarly is placed in the buffer because of its unselected [+D N] features. Then, the VP node branches into a transitive verb and a complement, which can check the subject NP feature. At this point, the verbal head *call* is processed and projects two DP expectations compatible with the [N +D N] features. Later, the complement DP is predicted, and the copy of *who* in the buffer is inserted into the last node.

It is unclear how Chesi's account avoids recursive structures processed top-down resulting in infinite loops, such as those created by adjunction, or what guides the decision between alternative derivational top-down expansions. There are many alternative expectations that can be used to construct the top branching node. The knowledge about which

---

[15] Torr et al. (2019) reports a large-scale implementation of Stabler's minimalist grammars. However, it crucially relies on a very large bidirectional Long-Short-Term Memory neural network to create supertags (tree fragments) that a dedicated A* search algorithm can use to arrive at parsings. None of this machinery is native to the MP, or in the spirit of Minimalism. Moreover, the parsing performance results reported in Torr et al. (2019) lag far behind the state of the art in CCG, HPSG, and LFG parsing. Fong (2014) attempts a more faithful (toy) implementation of the MP, but is nonetheless forced to rely on a CFG backbone to make it work.

[16] See Stroik and Putnam (2013) for a similar proposal.

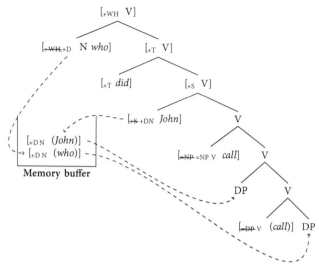

Figure 4.14 A buffer-based account of UDCs

expectations are possible and which are not amounts to a CFG, i.e. the knowledge that a CP node can have as immediate daughters DP[wh] and C̄[+wh], in that order, and that DP[wh] can have as immediate daughters DP[wh] and N, and so on. The need for such a CFG backbone is particularly clear in a cartographic approach such as Rizzi (1997), where there are many such local structures (supposedly part of the human biological endowment, in some way or other). Hunter (forthcoming) is more explicit than Chesi, and directly addresses this problem by relying on phrase-structure grammar information heavily reminiscent of Gazdar (1981) and Gazdar et al. (1985) in order to make judicious top-down predictions.

There are no movement operations of any kind in Chesi's approach. Rather, ex situ phrases are copied to a memory buffer, and reaccessed later downstream. Chesi (2015) proposes that buffers are limited by phases in particular ways in order to obtain CED island effects. However, like all other accounts surveyed in this chapter, neither Chesi (2015) nor Hunter (forthcoming) predicts the CED exceptions listed in Chapter 3, nor the existence of convergent and cumulative UDCs.

Chesi's account also suffers from a number of other conceptual issues. For example, it is unclear how semantic composition and phonological composition are supposed to proceed, since the point of phases is to unburden working memory by shipping off syntactic representations to LF and PF. Second, the existence of a filler-gap dependency is recorded in the buffer, outside the syntactic tree, and therefore extraction pathway phenomena like Irish complementizer alternations are not predicted, and must be stipulated with additional machinery. For more criticism, see Den Dikken (2018, §2.4.2).

Den Dikken (2018) also proposes a top-down structure-building strategy and employs a stack mechanism rather than MOVE to model filler-gap dependencies. Although Den Dikken (2018) is too informal to evaluate, the basic idea is clear: fronted *wh*-phrases are placed in a stack, the stack is propagated in phrase structure, and the search for the respective gap proceeds via dedicated structural relations. As in Chesi's account, it is unclear how the combinatorial explosion of possible top-down subtrees is handled in a computationally efficient and cognitively plausible way, without assuming phrase-structure grammar knowledge. Unlike Chesi, however, Den Dikken (2018) represents UDCs as part of the syntactic tree, and therefore can straightforwardly account for the existence of extraction pathway phenomena.

Den Dikken (2009, 2018) reject successive-cyclic movement entirely, and argues that *phases* have no bearing on island effects, along with others like Abels (2012) and Boeckx (2008, ch. 3). By eliminating movement from the MP entirely, Den Dikken (2018) avoids Müller's (2011) criticism concerning the potential incompatibility of cyclic movement and AGREE-based syntactic boundaries for extraction, but this results in an account of UDCs that resembles Gazdar (1981) in that filler-gap dependencies are registered in phrasal nodes, and CFG-like knowledge must be deployed in order to determine which features are present in which branches, and how they propagate down the tree.

The top-down conceptions of the MP just discussed are a step in the right direction: they acknowledge the existence of the problem created by MOVE and attempt to improve on the standard model of UDCs by abandoning bottom-up derivations. However, in the process, such models abandon MOVE and must resort to a CFG backbone that guides top-down prediction. In this sense, Chesi (2007), Stabler (2013), Hunter (forthcoming), and Den Dikken (2018) have all but rediscovered the main insight of Gazdar (1981). But there is still a major difference. Chesi (2007), Stabler (2013), Hunter (forthcoming), and Den Dikken (2018) are intrinsically procedural sentence-parsing mechanisms: the input consists of surface forms and the output consists of logical forms. Such grammars are therefore not compatible with the behavioral facts of incremental sentence production, where the input must be logical forms and the output must be phonological forms. Hence, it remains unclear how the MP can be made compatible with both production and comprehension. We suspect that correcting this problem will inevitably lead the MP to move even closer to the declarative and processing-neutral phrase-structure system of Gazdar (1981), and its more recent formulations discussed in Chapter 5.

4.4.1.3 The formalist view

The formalist view holds that the construction of grammatical representations does not necessarily mirror the temporal sequence of elements during language processing (Phillips and Lewis, 2013; Phillips, 2017). Pinpointing the exact computational steps involved in processing linguistic structure is difficult, as our knowledge of mental representations and cognitive processes related to language is still incomplete. Thus, the grammatical theory does not perfectly align with the mental processes that arise during comprehension and production.

The formalist view allows MOVE to remain a central component of human grammar because its mental correlates may be out of sync with the time course of UDC processing. This dissociation between performance and competence makes it difficult to link linguistic operations and linguistic representations to specific processing effects. In particular, it makes implausible grammatical mechanisms impossible to experimentally falsify, since a negative result can be taken to mean that the effect predicted by the grammar is not time-locked with online processing because of the interference with some unknown factor.

Recall that the very point of Marr's levels of analysis is to reverse-engineer the implementation level, by characterizing how the system works at varying degrees of granularity, such that the more abstract levels inform the characterization of the lower levels. Thus, grammatical theory should be accountable to a much richer body of evidence, particularly behavioral evidence about online language processing. We conclude that, as it stands, the MP falls short of this desideratum (Ferreira, 2005; Sag and Wasow, 2011, 2015; Phillips and Lewis, 2013).

4.5 Summary

The concept of transformations was the precursor of movement as a way to model a wide range of phenomena, including UDCs. This was a pivotal development in the history of theoretical linguistics, as subsequent revisions of the theory sought to unify all structure-building in terms of a single operation, abandoning phrase-structural rules of any kind. The MP seeks to discover the role that particular local relations play in understanding a wide range of phenomena, using economy as one of the main guiding principles. We have identified two major problems. The first one is whether or not economy and related concepts can actually explain the full range of empirical and behavioral facts. The second is that optimizing for a language design solution that is maximally general without regard for how this system actually interacts with others in real time has arguably led to conceptions of grammar that are problematic in the broader context of the cognitive architecture, including the functions that crucially interact with language, such as comprehension, production, and acquisition.

At the present time, modeling filler-gap dependencies via operations such as MOVE faces significant theoretical and empirical issues. For example, there is no parsimonious account of successive-cyclic movement in the MP because of the Triggering Problem. This makes it unclear how any UDCs are to be derived in accordance with economy principles, let alone convergent and cumulative UDCs. Extra machinery can be introduced in order to avoid these problems, but as Borsley (2012) notes, the key question is whether the need for such additions provides evidence that movement-based accounts are wrong-headed, given their lack of independent empirical justification.

Other problems for the MP come from island phenomena, argued to follow from core architectural economy constraints such as structural proximity (e.g. Attract, Minimal Link), chain complexity (Chain Uniformity), and cyclic movement bounded by phases (Phrase Impenetrability). But such syntactic constraints on extraction make incorrect predictions not only about islands, but also about UDCs more generally (e.g. wrongly ruling out complex chains and crossing dependencies). Unsurprisingly, there is a growing consensus that an exclusively syntactic approach to islands is overly ambitious (Boeckx, 2012; Newmeyer, 2016).

The MP has also been difficult to reconcile with extant psycholinguistic and neurolinguistic evidence about language processing, and of UDCs in particular (Seuren, 2004; Labelle, 2007; Sag and Wasow, 2011, 2015; Ferreira, 2005; Phillips, 2017; Branigan and Pickering, 2017). There is no evidence for MOVE operations in psycholinguistic or neurolinguistic research. In fact, all recent attempts to make the MP consistent with incremental sentence processing that we are aware of adopt phrase-structural information, and abandon MOVE altogether. The end result is a grammar that shares key commonalities with Gazdar (1981), first proposed as an alternative to movement, but dismissed by Chomsky (1981, 1995) and many others since as a mere notational variant. In the next chapter we will show that Gazdar's approach to UDCs and more modern reconceptualizations thereof are superior to movement-based accounts.

5

Non-movement-based approaches

The idea that Context-Free Phrase-Structure Grammars (CFGs) could not describe UDCs was widely accepted by the early 1980s, and had made it to introductory textbooks such as Radford (1981, 149–52). This view was upended when Gazdar (1981) showed that CFGs could not only account for UDCs, but in fact offered a straightforward analysis of a broader range of filler-gap dependency patterns than movement-based approaches, including convergent UDCs. Gazdar (1981) was subsequently adapted to Generalized Phrase-Structure Grammar (Gazdar et al., 1985), Head-driven Phrase-Structure Grammar (Pollard and Sag, 1994; Ginzburg and Sag, 2000; Levine and Hukari, 2006; Sag, 2010), Combinatorial Categorial Grammar (Steedman, 1985, 1996, 2001), and Simpler Syntax (Culicover and Jackendoff, 2005).

Chomsky (1981, 91) dismissed Gazdar's account as virtually indistinguishable from movement, reaffirming (in Chomsky, 1995, 403) that such accounts and their more modern kin were transformational theories, whether one chose to call them that or not. See Hornstein (2009, 6, n. 11; 2019, 191, n. 5) for more recent expressions of the same sentiment. As we shall see, the claim that non-movement grammars are nothing but notational variants of movement-based grammars is unwarranted.

For Chomsky and others, phrase-structural approaches miss a deep generalization by relying on a large number of phrase-structural rules rather than on a more abstract unitary operation MERGE (Chomsky, 2000b, 13). On the contrary, we argue that a phrase-structural component offers a range of empirical and psycholinguistic advantages, once a broader picture of empirical and behavioral evidence is considered. For example, it is not clear how an epiphenomenal approach to constructions can account for the full range of structural idiosyncrasies observed in natural language, such as those surveyed in §2.1. Moreover, recent attempts to make the MP more consistent with the behavioral facts of incremental language processing are forced to replace movement with a stack mechanism analogous to Gazdar's (1981) '/' operator, and to rely on (CFG-like) phrase-structural knowledge in order to guide and prune top-down structural prediction; see §4.4.1. In sum, we see no a priori reasons for dismissing constructivist models of grammar.

This chapter provides an overview of the strengths and weaknesses of Gazdar (1981) and describes a more modern formulation of this approach. As we shall see, the result is a feature-based phrase-structural account of UDCs that is empirically and psycholinguistically superior to movement-based approaches. In the unification- and feature-based theory we will focus on during the remainder of this chapter, virtually all that goes on in the grammar boils down to a general and simple operation: feature identity. In other words, agreement, subcategorization, semantic composition, anaphora, case assignment, UDCs, etc. all reduce to equating feature values. In this sense—at least—phrase-structure feature-based grammars are quite minimalist.

Unbounded Dependency Constructions: Theoretical and Experimental Perspectives. Rui P. Chaves and Michael T. Putnam,
Oxford University Press (2020). © Rui P. Chaves and Michael T. Putnam.
DOI: 10.1093/oso/9780198784999.001.0001

5.1 Gazdar's (1981) phrase-structure model

CFGs can be viewed procedurally as string rewriting systems (Harwood, 1955; Chomsky, 1956) or declaratively as node admissibility constraints (McCawley, 1968; Peters and Ritchie, 1973; Perrault, 1984). In the latter interpretation the grammar does not dictate any particular derivational procedure, and the symbol '→' is nothing but a relation between a (mother) node and an ordered sequence of (daughter) nodes. Consider the mini CFG in (1), for example.

(1)   S → NP VP
    VP → V NP
    NP → *Ed*
    NP → *Jo*
    V → *likes*

Each rule is nothing but a template relating certain mother nodes to their respective daughters. We omit the semantic and pragmatic components from these rules for exposition purposes here and throughout, but stress that in Gazdar's system meaning and pragmatic composition work in tandem with the syntactic component. Phonological composition works this way as well, in tandem with the other modalities of linguistic information. See, for example, Klein and Sag (1985) for a rather straightforward account of semantic composition with CFGs.

Declaratively conceptualized, CFGs are compatible with any model of sentence comprehension or production. Suppose, for example, that one adopts a hybrid top-down and bottom-up parsing model, like the Left-Corner (LC) algorithm (Aho and Ullman, 1972). As Johnson-Laird (1983), Resnik (1992), and many others have noted, the Left-Corner parser is particularly well suited as a model of human sentence processing, since it is driven by predictions triggered by top-down and bottom-up steps.[1] An LC parse using the grammar in (1) is shown in Table 5.1.

Table 5.1 Tracing the LC parse of *Jo likes Ed*

	Stack	Input	Rule used
1	–	*Jo likes Ed*	–
2	NP → *Jo•*	*likes Ed*	NP → *Jo*
3	S → NP•VP	*likes Ed*	S → NP VP
4	V → *likes•*, S → NP•VP	*Ed*	V → *likes*
5	VP → V•NP, S → NP•VP	*Ed*	VP → V NP
6	NP → *Ed•*, VP → V•NP, S → NP•VP	–	NP → *Ed*
7	VP → V NP•, S → NP•VP	–	Complete
8	S → NP VP•	–	Complete

[1] More recently, Lewis and Vasishth (2005) combine Left-Corner parsing with a CFG in the ACT-R model of sentence processing, showing that it aligns well with behavioral data, and similarly Rasmussen and Schuler (2017) show that surprisal and locality effects are predicted by Left-Corner parsing. On the behavioral side, see Federmeier (2007), Brennan and Pylkkänen (2017), and Brothers et al. (2017) for ERP evidence suggesting that both top-down and bottom-up predictive processes are active during language processing; top-down predictions are processed in the left brain hemisphere, while bottom-up integration processes take place in the right hemisphere.

Here the symbol '•' distinguishes sub structures that have actually been parsed from those that are merely predicted. Thus, when the input *Sam* is recognized as an NP, that structure is completely processed, and the '•' is placed at the very end to indicate exactly that. Starting with an empty parsing stack '–', the parser begins processing by recognizing that the word *Jo* is a noun phrase via the rule 'NP → *Jo*'. Once the NP is parsed, a prediction about an upcoming VP can be created via the rule 'S → NP VP'. Similarly, once the verb is parsed, a prediction is created about an upcoming NP via the rule 'VP → V NP'. Once the upcoming NP is parsed, the partially processed structure 'VP → V • NP' and the structure 'NP → *Jo*•' at the top of the stack are combined with each other and reduced to 'VP → V NP•', completing the parse of the VP. The same happens to the remainder elements in the stack, namely the subject *Sam* and the main clause structure 'S → NP • VP'. The two combine and reduce to 'S → NP VP•', completing the parse of the S. The tree structure in Figure 5.1 is a convenient way to render the history of rule applications that the parser successfully employed.

Figure 5.1 A declarative clause *Jo likes Ed*

As Pereira and Warren (1983) show, there are countless possible parsing algorithms, of which the Left-Corner parser is but a special case. There is no shortage of models of sentence parsing, once one adopts a CFG framework. This welcome result carries over to any phrase-structural framework that models UDCs without movement, including models where nodes are complex feature sets, and no longer strictly speaking in the realm of context-free languages. We use the term **phrase-structure grammar** (PSG) to very broadly describe any system of rules composed of templates or schemata that have an immediate-dominance CFG-like format $\alpha \rightarrow \beta_1 \ldots \beta_n$ ($n \geq 1$), regardless of whether $\alpha, \beta_1, \ldots, \beta_n$ are atomic symbols or not. In this sense, Chomsky (1981) and most grammatical formalisms have a phrase-structure grammar component, albeit with notational differences and varying degrees of abstraction. See Blevins and Sag (2012) for a history of phrase-structure grammar.

Gazdar (1981) proposed to model UDCs by directly encoding the presence of filler-gap dependencies in local syntactic nodes, as shown in (2). Each rule was paired with a semantic composition rule as well, which we omit for exposition purposes. The 'α/β' notation indicates that α has a gap of type β. The symbol '∅' indicates null phonology, i.e. a trace for a phrase that is ex situ; we use a subscript to make extracted categories more obvious.

(2) NP → *Ed*
     NP → *Jo*
     VP → V NP
     V → *likes*
     S → NP VP

$NP_i/NP_i \rightarrow \emptyset$
$VP/NP_i \rightarrow V\ NP/NP_i$
$S/NP_i \rightarrow NP/NP_i\ VP/NP_i$
$S/NP_i \rightarrow NP/NP_i\ VP$
$S \rightarrow NP_i\ S/NP_i$

Crucially, the rules containing 'slashed' categories were derived automatically from the base CFG, and were in every way used and interpreted like canonical CFG rules. Nothing else needs to be said about how the grammar works in order to model UDCs. Just like any other CFG, the one in (2) is compatible with any standard parsing algorithm: it can be processed bottom-up, top-down, or any combination thereof. Consider the topicalization in Figure 5.2.

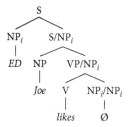

Figure 5.2 The Topicalization *ED, Joe likes!*

Here, the fronted NP is an ex situ phrase which is linked to the object of the verb. This linkage is achieved by the phrase-structure rules themselves, which propagate the information about the corresponding NP gap via '/' categories and rules in syntactic structure, just as part-of-speech information is propagated, for example.

Gazdar's (1981) account has a number of welcome properties. First, the existence of filler-gap dependencies is registered in the extraction pathway, and therefore it is predicted that at least some languages will contain words or constructions that are sensitive to that locally available information. In other words, Gazdar's account predicts the existence of extraction pathway phenomena languages. Second, there is nothing fundamentally problematic with UDCs that lack fillers. Consider, for example, object relatives like *I read the paper$_i$ you wrote ___$_i$*, discussed in §2.1. These UDCs can trivially be modeled by a rule like (3), without the need to assume the presence of otherwise unmotivated invisible filler phrases.

(3) $N_i \rightarrow AUX\ N_i\ S/NP_i$

The resulting representation for this kind of UDC is shown in Figure 5.3. Similar rules can handle other filler-less UDCs, such as those in comparatives (e.g. *You made more mistakes$_i$ than Robin made ___*), missing object constructions (e.g. *Being difficult to reach ___ has its advantages*), and *Not*-fragments (e.g. *No, not that I can think of ___*).

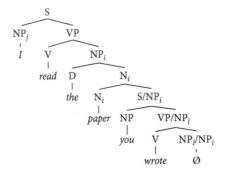

Figure 5.3 A filler-less UDC in Gazdar's model

Gazdar (1981) also provides a straightforward account of convergent filler-gap dependencies. For example, rules like (4) allow a subject NP-internal gap to be linked with a VP-internal gap to form a convergent dependency, as in Figure 5.4. Similar rules license other instances of convergent filler-gap dependencies, such as ATB extraction in coordination.

(4) $S/NP_i \rightarrow NP/NP_i\ VP/NP_i$

Just as in early transformational grammar (Chomsky, 1957, 1965, 1975), there isn't a single unitary operation that is responsible for filler-gap dependencies in Gazdar's approach. Rather, UDCs are distributed across the grammar, and propagate throughout syntactic structure like any other kind of morphosyntactic information. The key insight in Gazdar's analysis is to assume that phrasal categories include information indicating ex situ dependents, a strategy that can be adopted by any theory of grammar, in principle. From a psycholinguistic perspective, Gazdar's account has several advantages over movement-based grammar precisely because of the CFG component, listed below; for a more extensive discussion, see Wasow (2020).

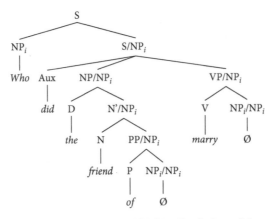

Figure 5.4 A convergent UDC in Gazdar's model

- *Constructional effects*

  Phrase-structure models of grammar are consistent with the fact that specific constructions can be primed (Gries, 2005; Szmrecsanyi, 2005), as can specific syntactic rules (Reitter et al., 2006a,b; Reitter and More, 2014). See also Gruberg et al. (2019) for evidence that syntactic structures are associated with particular semantic content, i.e. construction-specific meaning.

- *Process-neutrality*

  Although production and comprehension are very different tasks, there is evidence that they tap into common linguistic knowledge (Pickering and Garrod, 2013; Momma and Phillips, 2018; Matchin and Hickok, 2019). This suggests a constraint-based or declarative characterization of linguistic information (Kaplan and Bresnan, 1982; Sag and Wasow, 2011, 2015). The fact that CFGs can be interpreted declaratively (McCawley, 1968; Peters and Ritchie, 1973; Perrault, 1984) makes them suitable to serve both language production and language comprehension models. See, for example, Neumann (1998) for an efficient interleaved computational PSG model of parsing and generation.

- *Constraint-based parallelism*

  Constructing an interpretation for a sentence involves word-by-word integration of a variety of different information sources, including lexical constraints, plausibility constraints, and discourse context (MacDonald, 1994; Konieczny and Hemforth, 1994; Tanenhaus et al., 1995; Tabor and Hutchins, 2004); for a recent overview, see Spevac et al. (2018). In PSGs like the ones we discuss in this chapter, there is no autonomy of syntax, and all levels of description (including semantics, pragmatics, and phonology) are locally and simultaneously available; this is consistent with the available neurolinguistic evidence (Pylkkänen, 2019); see Hagoort (2003, 2005) for electrophysiological and neuroimaging evidence suggestive of a unification-based process that acts on syntactic, semantic, and phonological representations simultaneously, and see Vosse and Kempen (2000) for simulation results concerning a unification-based PSG psycholinguistic model of human syntactic processing.

- *Distributed UDC processing*

  According to Gazdar's (1981) model, one would not expect to find localized psycholinguistic evidence of UDC processing, as the computation of filler-gap linkages is distributed across the grammar rules. As already discussed in §4.4, the available neurophysiological evidence suggests that the computation of UDCs is distributed in the language system, rather than localized (Wartenburger et al., 2003; Matchin, 2014; Rogalsky et al., 2015; Balewski et al., 2016).

- *Learnability*

  CFGs are simpler to learn than grammars where the surface order does not directly match the underlying syntactic structure, as is the case with movement-based grammars (Sakas and Fodor, 2001; Newmeyer, 2004). For unsupervised grammar algorithms, see Bod (2009), Clark and Lappin (2011), and references cited. Constructional models have also received support from language acquisition research (Clark and Kelly, 2006). For a demonstration of a Bayesian framework of phrase-structure grammar induction on typical child-directed speech that can learn hierarchical syntax, see Perfors et al. (2011).

- *Incremental and probabilistic processing models*

  The ability to include probabilistic information is crucial for the modeling of a wealth of behavioral phenomena that are tied to frequency (Jurafsky, 1996, 2003; Manning, 2003; Gahl and Garnsey, 2004). High-probability structures are accessed faster, and more easily, which enables syntactic ambiguities to be resolved by picking the most likely resolution. All of this follows if grammars have a phrase-structure component. Well-understood and efficient algorithms exist for finding and refining Probabilistic PSGs from data (Petrov et al., 2006, Clark and Fijalkow 2020), and for parsing CFGs in a way that correlates well with incremental human language processing (Resnik, 1992; Hale, 2001, 2006, 2014; Levy, 2008), including information-theoretic accounts of garden-path effects and reading time delays, among other phenomena (Jurafsky, 1996; Manning, 2003; Keller, 2003; Lewis and Vasishth, 2005; Bresnan, 2007; Brennan and Pylkkänen, 2017). See in particular van Schijndel et al. (2014) and Hale (2014, 16,17) for probabilistic phrase-structure models of human language processing that adopt Gazdar's '/' approach to UDCs.

One problem with Gazdar's account is, of course, that natural languages aren't strictly context-free, but this is an easy problem to solve. Once CFG symbols like 'S', 'VP', 'V', and so on are replaced with sets of features, the expressiveness of the model increases significantly and context-dependent linguistic phenomena can be accounted for. See Francez and Wintner (2012, ch. 6) for an accessible discussion of the expressiveness of feature- and unification-based PSGs. But although the resulting formalism is much more powerful than CFGs, the grammars that linguists actually construct are typically weakly equivalent to far less expressive formalisms, which ends up striking a balance between the systems' expressiveness and the patterns that the grammar is required to model. For example, Carroll (1994) showed that in realistic large-scale Head-driven Phrase-Structure Grammar (henceforth HPSG) models the relationship between sentence length and parse time is merely quadratic $O(n^2)$, and more modern implementations achieve faster results. The point here is that the expressiveness of a formalism in which a theory is expressed should not be confused with the expressiveness of the theory itself. Thus, although Stabler and Keenan (2003) and Stabler (2013) employ extremely expressive formalisms such as abstract algebra, set theory, and first-order logic in the formalization of the Minimalist Program, the theory that is expressed is severely restricted. Likewise, feature- and unification-based PSGs like the one described in this chapter make use of a restricted set of features that greatly restrict the linguistic patterns that the grammar rules can express, and therefore can be parsed very efficiently. For more on this rather pervasive formalism/theory confusion, see Givón (1979), Pollard (1996), and Müller (2017, 21).

A more serious problem with Gazdar (1981) is that in order for the grammar to be able to handle any number of gaps, of any kind, in a given sentence, it requires a combinatorial explosion of PSG rules. For example, since adjectival phrases, prepositional phrases, and adverbial phrases can be extracted, in addition to NPs, we need not only the rule 'S/NP → NP VP/NP', but also all of its counterparts bearing a distinct extracted category, e.g. 'S/AP → NP VP/AP', 'S/PP → NP VP/PP', and so on. What's worse, we need rules to allow multiple gaps in a given sentence, leading to a combinatorial explosion of rules. See, for example, Hukari and Levine (1991) and Pollard and Sag (1994, 169) for more detailed discussion.

Modern theories of grammar that adopt Gazdar's approach to UDCs have solved this combinatorial explosion problem by encoding filler-gap dependencies in a slightly different way, using grammar rules with variables over categories, including complex 'slashed' categories. For example, in HPSG (Pollard and Sag, 1994), ex situ phrases are registered via a list-valued feature called GAP (Sag et al., 2003; Sag, 2010), as illustrated in Figure 5.5. Each node in the tree consists of a set of features, one of which is GAP. The ex situ phrase and its corresponding 'gap' are highlighted for exposition purposes.

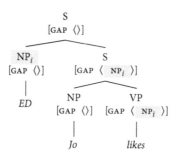

Figure 5.5 A feature-based account of topicalization (abbreviated)

There is no trace at the bottom of the dependency, and so the fact that the verb subcategorizes for an ex situ complement is directly registered in GAP. This is consistent with the online experimental findings of Pickering and Barry (1991), Pickering (1993), Pickering et al. (1994), Boland et al. (1995), and Traxler and Pickering (1996), which suggest that fillers are linked to the subcategorization frame of the head.[2]

The approach pursued by Steedman (1996) within the Combinatorial Categorial Grammar (CCG) framework is very close to Gazdar's (1981), but there are several differences between HPSG and CCG that in our view tip the balance in favor of the former. Steedman (2002, 59–66) makes excessively strong claims about the syntactic nature of islands. Thus, the Adjunct Constraint, the Clause Non-Final Incomplete Constituent Constraint, the Complementizer Constraint, the Complex NP Constraint, and the Coordinate Structure Constraint all fall out as consequences of CCG's combinatorial rules. But as we have seen in §3.2, all such islands have robust exceptions and are therefore unlikely to be purely syntactic, *contra* Steedman (2002). Take, for example, the CCG coordination rule in (5), which requires the daughters and the mother node to share the same X category.

(5) X COORD $X \Rightarrow X$

We say variables like X are **unified** when there are multiple occurrences of the same variable, as in (5). Thus if X = S/NP for the first variable, then all occurrences of X are similarly resolved as S/NP. Like Gazdar (1981), the coordination rule in (5) predicts the Coordinate Structure Constraint (CSC) and its ATB exception because if one conjunct has a gap, then so must all others. However, this does not allow for asymmetric exceptions like those discussed in §3.2. Recall also that ATB extraction in asymmetric coordination does not require a convergent filler-gap dependency. For example, it is possible to have overlapping singleton dependencies, in which case the gaps are completely independent from each other:

---

[2] See, however, Levine and Hukari (2006) for a trace-based HPSG account, analogous to Gazdar's (1981). This goes to show that whether a theory adopts traces or not is independent from whether movement is adopted.

(6) [A bird THIS RARE]$_i$ – [how many years]$_j$ could someone spend $\_j$ and never actually
     see $\_i$?
     (Chaves, 2012b)

As we have argued in §3.2, there is strong evidence that the CSC is semantic-pragmatic in
nature, not syntactic. The problem with the CCG approach is that additional stipulations
are needed to factor out the arguments that are extracted, in order to compute the category
of the mother node. For example, a feature must be added in order to allow the coordination
rule to separate the in situ arguments that must be unified across conjuncts from the
ex situ arguments that may or may not be unified across conjuncts. In HPSG, however,
ex situ arguments are naturally separated from in situ arguments: the former are lists in
GAP, and the latter are listed in VAL. So, the coordination rule can be stated as in (7)
without any commitment to the coordination's being interpreted either symmetrically or
asymmetrically (Chaves, 2012b). The CSC follows from orthogonal semantic-pragmatic
parallelism constraints (Kehler, 2002).

(7) [VAL X] → [VAL X] COORD [VAL X]

Another difference between HPSG and CCG lies in which sequences each theory considers
to be a constituent. Indeed, one of the major motivations for CCG comes from Right-Node
Raising, and Gapping phenomena, and related 'non-constituent' phenomena. Although
nothing prevents HPSG from being reformulated in order to allow for a broader notion
of constituency, if desired, Chaves (2014) and Park (2019) provide empirical evidence that
an HPSG account is preferable. Finally, we find the PSG approach in Figure 5.5 more
intuitive than CCG, and closer to Gazdar's (1981). We therefore focus on phrase-structural
approaches in the remainder of this book.

5.2 A constructional HPSG approach

In what follows, we describe how Gazdar's model of UDCs is incorporated into modern
PSG models. We opt for the antithesis of Chomsky's MERGE-based approach: **construction
grammar** (Fillmore et al., 1988; Goldberg, 1995; Fillmore and Kay, 1996; Kay and Fillmore,
1999; Croft, 2001; Bergen and Chang, 2005; Feldman et al., 2009; Michaelis, 2012; Sag,
2012):

> The [Construction Grammar] approach supposes a grammar to consist of a repertory
> of conventional associations of lexical, syntactic, and pragmatic information called con-
> structions. Familiar grammar rules are constructions that are deficient in not containing
> any lexical information except for specification of rather gross syntactic categories and, in
> some cases, lacking any pragmatic values as well. Every such conventional association that
> must be learned or recognized separately by the speaker of a language is a construction.
> This includes all idioms and partially productive lexico-grammatical patterns.
>
> (Kay, 1992, 310)

The idea that grammars contain very large inventories of phrasal constructions may appear
to be a step backward, away from deeper generalizations. But there are several flaws

with such a conclusion. The number of lemmas that the average adult native speaker of American English knows has been estimated to be around 40,000 (Brysbaert et al., 2016), and therefore it is not unreasonable that speakers also learn a few hundred constructions. As already discussed, a grammar consisting of a rich repertoire of constructions is arguably a more cognitively plausible model of the linguistic knowledge that speakers acquire and use during language processing; see, for example, Bybee, 2013; Diessel, 2015. We thus adopt a rather broad definition for what a construction is:

> Any linguistic pattern is recognized as a construction as long as some aspect of its form or function is not strictly predictable from its component parts or from other constructions recognized to exist. In addition, patterns are stored as constructions even if they are fully predictable as long as they occur with sufficient frequency.
>
> (Goldberg, 2006, 5)

There are many different variants of Construction Grammar, formalized to varying degrees, and not all provide an explicit account of UDCs. In this chapter we draw from a recent version of HPSG detailed in Boas and Sag (2012), known as Sign-Based Construction Grammar (SBCG), which is closer to Gazdar (1981) than standard HPSG, and ideally suited for our purposes. We generally follow HPSG/SCBG, except when otherwise noted. For a comprehensive survey of mainstream HPSG, see Müller et al. (2020).

5.2.1 Lexical constructions

As form-meaning pairings, lexical expressions are themselves constructions. Indeed, the survey of a wide range of psycholinguistic studies made by MacDonald et al. (1994) concludes that lexical representation includes a representation of the word's phonological form, semantics, morpho-grammatical features, and argument structure. This is essentially the kind of information that is present in HPSG's lexical entries, where linguistic signs are composed of the following features:

- PHON(OLOGY): contains phonological information (segments, syllables, prosodic words, intonational phrases, etc.), which we abbreviate by showing only the phonological segments. See Bird (1995), Höhle (1999), Bonami and Delais-Roussarie (2006), Tseng (2008), and references cited for a more detailed discussion of Phonology within HPSG, and Riehemann (1998), Koenig (1999), Bonami and Crysmann (2013), and references cited for more on HPSG's account of morphology.
- CAT(EGORY): contains information specific to parts of speech. Thus, nouns come with a CASE feature for case information and an AGR(EEMENT) feature for agreement. For a detailed treatment of agreement in HPSG, see Wechsler and Zlatic (2003). In contrast, verbs come with a FORM feature for distinguishing between verb forms (finite, infinitival, etc.) and an INV(ERTED) feature for distinguishing invertable verbs from non-invertable verbs.
- ARG(UMENT) ST(RUCURE): contains the morphosyntactic categories of the arguments of the verb (e.g. NP, VP, PP, S, etc.), regardless of how they are overtly realized.

Thus, verbs like *mention, confess, say,* and *report* can be specified as [ARG-ST ⟨NP$_i$, PP$_j$, S$_e$⟩] (e.g. [$_{NP_i}$ You] mentioned [$_{PP_j}$ to me] [$_{S_e}$ it had snowed]), among others, whereas semantically very similar verbs like *tell, inform, notify,* and *warn* can instead be specified [ARG-ST ⟨NP$_i$, NP$_j$, S$_e$⟩] (e.g. [$_{NP_i}$ You] told [$_{NP_j}$ me] [$_{S_e}$ it had snowed]), among others. The same verb is compatible with a wide range of different ARG-ST elements, and variations thereof; see Davis (2001) and Chaves (2019).[3]

- VAL(ENCE): lists the features SUBJ(ECT) and COMP(LEMENT)s, which are responsible for specifying which members of ARG-ST are realized in situ, as complements, or as subjects, if any. Thus, a preposition like *to* is specified as [SUBJ ⟨ ⟩] and [COMPS ⟨NP⟩], whereas the intransitive use of verbs like *laugh* is specified [SUBJ ⟨NP⟩] and [COMPS ⟨ ⟩].
- GAP: is the featural analogue of Gazdar's '/' which lists the ex situ arguments (for this reason this feature is sometimes called SLASH in some versions of HPSG). The feature GAP lists the members of ARG-ST which are extracted, and therefore not in VAL. For example, the canonical use of the preposition *to* is specified as [SUBJ ⟨ ⟩], [COMPS ⟨NP⟩], and [GAP ⟨ ⟩], whereas the stranded counterpart use is specified as [SUBJ ⟨ ⟩], [COMPS ⟨ ⟩] [GAP ⟨NP⟩]. The two uses are systematically related, as we shall see.
- SEM(ANTICS): contains the features INDEX and RESTR(ICTIONS). The former singles out the variable that is relevant for semantic composition, and the latter introduces a list of semantic representations. Thus, the value of RESTR for a sentence like *Every house is blue* consists of a feature-based representation equivalent to $\forall_x(house(x) \rightarrow blue(x))$; see Ginzburg and Sag (2000), Richter and Sailer (2004), Copestake et al. (2005), and Sag (2010, 2012) for a number of different semantic approaches within HPSG.
- C(O)NT(E)XT: contains contextual-pragmatic constraints, including constraints on the Focus and the Background, as well as constraints on the speaker and hearer indices; see Kuhn (1996), Engdahl and Vallduví (1996), Wilcock (2005), Lee-Goldman (2011), Song and Bender (2012), and Song (2017) for more on pragmatics in HPSG; and §7.1.1 for some more discussion. For example, the CNTXT information of an honorific expression is such that the (contextual) index of the speaker is in a hierarchical relation to the (contextual) index of the addressee.

All information (lexical or otherwise) is consistently represented in terms of (typed) feature structures, using standard techniques from Knowledge Representation systems; see Carpenter (1992) for a comprehensive discussion. Features appear in uppercase and their values are types, which appear in lowercase italics and may themselves introduce other features. Lists are depicted with angle brackets '⟨' and '⟩', but this is but a matter of exposition, since lists are themselves encoded as feature structures (Carpenter, 1997, 97–8). The 'feature geometry' for feature structures of type *word* is shown in Figure 5.6. This is the basic template that all words are required to have, and is usually assumed to hold for all languages.[4] Thus, lexical items are themselves constructions.

---

[3] The ARG-ST feature is also where Keenan and Comrie's (1977) Accessibility Hierarchy phenomena are captured; see (Sag et al., 2003, ch. 7) for more discussion.

[4] Usually, CAT, VAL and GAP are further organized inside a feature SYN, which we omit for exposition purposes. See, however, Koenig and Michelson (2015) for arguments suggesting that Iroquoian languages may lack many of the standard syntactic features found in languages like English.

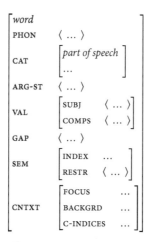

Figure 5.6 Feature geometry for all lexical signs

A common assumption in construction grammar is that lexical entries are usually neutral with regard to their possible syntactic realizations, and it is the interaction between their lexically specified information and the constructions they combine with that gives rise to the observed syntactic patterns. See, for example, Goldberg (1995, 50, 99), Croft (2001, 54, 168), Fillmore (2009, 120), Davis (2001), Koenig and Davis (2006), Sag (2012, 133–9), and Chaves (2019). In effect, what this means is that the value of the ARG-ST of a given word can be instantiated in many different ways, each of which characterizes the types of argument that are allowed, their agreement and case, their order, and their thematic roles. Different versions of Construction Grammar achieve this in different ways, but, regardless, such a view is consistent with evidence that thematic roles and subcategorization structures associated with a verb are available shortly after that verb is accessed, as experimentally shown by Boland (1993) and Trueswell and Kim (1998).

Thus, even an apparently intransitive verb like *laugh* is consistent with a wide range of alternative ARG-ST values, as the small sample in (8) illustrates. In Construction Grammar, each of these variants results from combining a lexical entry with a specific argument-structure construction that instantiates the value of ARG-ST and links its members to the respective variables in the semantics of the verb.

(8) a. Sam laughed.   *(strict intransitive)*
     b. Sam laughed her throat hoarse.   *(resultative)*
     c. Sam laughed the kids off the stage.   *(caused motion)*
     d. Sam laughed her way out of the room.   *(way-manner)*
     e. Sam laughed and laughed. . .   *(X-and-X intensification)*

Many of these examples involve idiosyncratic meaning and structure, both of which must be stipulated somewhere in the grammar, regardless of which theory one adopts. Thus, any of the uses in (8) have UDC counterparts, illustrated in (9), because the ARG-ST information is independent from whether the arguments are in situ or not.

(9) a. It was THE KIDS$_i$ [who]$_i$ Sam supposedly tried to laugh off_$_i$ the stage.

    b. [What]$_i$ Sam seemed to be laughing _$_i$ were the lyrics.

According to Manning et al. (1999), Bouma et al. (2001), and various others, post-verbal phrases that are traditionally considered adjuncts are, in fact, optional members of ARG-ST. This explains why post-verbal adverbials can be extracted and behave like complements in a number of ways, as detailed in §3.2.7. There are two approaches for allowing adverbials into ARG-ST in HPSG. One achieves this via a special lexical rule (Manning et al., 1999; Bouma et al., 2001) and the other simply takes such phrases to be optional complements, as in Chaves (2019), which is analogous to the situation in other varieties of Construction Grammar. Let us consider the latter approach in more detail.

Sag (2012) and Chaves (2019) incorporate Frame Semantics (Fillmore, 1977, 1982) into HPSG/SBCG. One consequence of this approach is that many expressions traditionally regarded as modifiers should instead be analyzed as (non-core) arguments; see FRAMENET (Fillmore et al., 2003) for more details and examples. In HPSG terms, this means that a broader range of dependents can be members of ARG-ST because such expressions are part of the broader conceptual representation of verbs. Consider, for example, the intransitive use of the lexeme *laugh* in (8a), as formalized in (10). Thus, even a simple intransitive verb such as *laugh* includes information about manner, reason, spacial location, and temporal location, any of which may correspond to an ARG-ST member over and above the one listed in (8). In the extreme case, all of these frame elements are also syntactic dependents of the verb, as in [ARG-ST ⟨NP$_i$, NP$_n$, XP$_r$, XP$_l$, XP$_t$⟩].

(10)
$$
\begin{bmatrix}
\text{word} \\
\text{PHON } \langle \text{læft} \rangle \\
\text{CAT} \begin{bmatrix} \text{VERB} \\ \text{INV} \quad - \\ \text{FORM} \quad \textit{finite} \end{bmatrix} \\
\text{ARG-ST} \left\langle \begin{bmatrix} \text{NP}_i \\ \text{PER} \quad \textit{3rd} \\ \text{NUM} \quad \textit{sing} \\ \text{CASE} \quad \textit{nom} \end{bmatrix} \right\rangle \\
\text{SEM} \begin{bmatrix} \text{INDEX} \quad e \\ \text{RESTR} \left\langle \begin{bmatrix} \textit{laugh} \\ \text{SIT} \quad e \\ \text{ACTOR } i \end{bmatrix}, \begin{bmatrix} \textit{manner} \\ \text{FORM } n \\ \text{SIT} \quad e \end{bmatrix}, \begin{bmatrix} \textit{reason} \\ \text{CAUSE } r \\ \text{SIT} \quad e \end{bmatrix}, \begin{bmatrix} \textit{location} \\ \text{PLACE} \quad l \\ \text{THEME} \quad e \end{bmatrix}, \begin{bmatrix} \textit{time} \\ \text{PAST } t \\ \text{SIT} \quad e \end{bmatrix} \right\rangle \end{bmatrix}
\end{bmatrix}
$$

In (10), the ARG-ST list specifies that the verb subcategorizes exactly one dependent, a nominative third-person singular NP corresponding to the actor of the described situation. The value of the VAL feature is underspecified, as other constraints are responsible for determining whether the members of ARG-ST are locally realized or not.

The symbol 'NP' is nothing but an abbreviation for any feature structure of nominal category (lexical or phrasal) with empty VAL lists, and which describes a quantified referent, as illustrated in Figure 5.7. Thus, any features that are of direct relevance for the exposition are added to the abbreviation, and those that are not directly relevant are left out, for ease of exposition. This word's lexical entry can be abbreviated as 'NP' because its CAT value is nominal, its COMPS list is empty, and at the very top of the frame semantics list

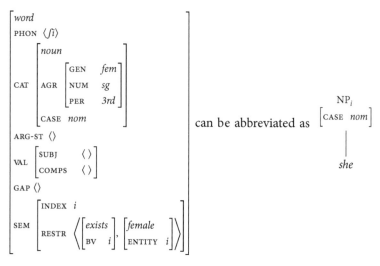

Figure 5.7 The symbol 'NP' as a shorthand

is an existential quantifier. The last of these binds the variable (via the B(OUND)V(ARIABLE) feature) introduced by the *female* frame.[5] The frame semantics of *she* is equivalent to $\exists i$ *female*(*i*).

When constructions combine with each other—lexical or otherwise—partially specified lexical feature structures obtain richer ones, where certain features are resolved in particular ways. The mechanism which combines feature structures in general is the '⊔' **unification** function (Shieber, 1986; Pollard and Sag, 1987; Carpenter, 1992), illustrated in Figure 5.8. In this example, two feature structures that describe agreement information are unified into a single feature structure. Unification amounts to the incremental and monotonic combination of information by the pairwise equation of feature values, a pervasive operation which is responsible for virtually all the computation that happens in the grammar in many variants of PSG (Pollard and Sag, 1987; Kay, 2002; Bergen and Chang, 2005; Steels and Beule, 2006; Fillmore, 2009).[6]

$$
\begin{bmatrix} agr \\ \text{NUM} & sg \\ \text{GEN} & fem \\ \text{PER} & ... \end{bmatrix}
\sqcup
\begin{bmatrix} agr \\ \text{NUM} & sg \\ \text{GEN} & ... \\ \text{PER} & 3rd \end{bmatrix}
=
\begin{bmatrix} agr \\ \text{NUM} & sg \\ \text{GEN} & fem \\ \text{PER} & 3rd \end{bmatrix}
$$

Figure 5.8 Feature Structure Unification of agreement features

Sometimes it is important to require that two features have the same value. This is achieved via variables (over typed feature structures), represented as italicized capital letters like X, Y, and Z.[7] For example, the lexical construction responsible for resolving the value of

---

[5] Bare NPs are the result of a unary branching rule that adds the (covert) quantifier (Fillmore and Kay, 1996; Michaelis, 2003; Fillmore, 2009).

[6] In Pollard and Sag (1994) the grammar is taken to be model-theoretic instead, but in this chapter we adopt a more computationally inclined interpretation, closer to that of Pollard and Sag (1987) and certain varieties of Construction Grammar.

[7] Although HPSG traditionally employs boxed tags like ⓵, nothing hinges on this choice, and we have here opted for a notation closer to that of Sag (2012).

VAL is the Argument Realization construction shown in (11), adapted from Sag et al. (2003) and Chaves (2012b). This construction unifies with words in order to map elements in ARG-ST into either VAL or GAP, by splitting the list value of AGR-ST into three sub-lists: S (which lists subjects), C (which lists complements), and G (which lists extracted dependents).

(11)   ARGUMENT REALIZATION Cx

$$\begin{bmatrix} word \\ \text{ARG-ST} & (S \oplus C) \bigcirc G \\ \text{VAL} & \begin{bmatrix} \text{SUBJ} & S \\ \text{COMPS} & C \end{bmatrix} \\ \text{GAP} & G \end{bmatrix}$$

Before going into detail about how the ARGUMENT REALIZATION Cx works, we must stress that it can be seen as a highly articulated and abstract description of a large number of more specific constructions, each linking members of ARG-ST to VAL and GAP lists differently, without appeal to list operations like '$\oplus$' and '$\bigcirc$'; see §7.2 for more discussion.

Let us consider the formulation (11) in more detail. Whereas the **append** '$\oplus$' function merely concatenates lists (e.g. $\langle \text{NP} \rangle \oplus \langle \text{PP} \rangle = \langle \text{NP}, \text{PP} \rangle$, and so on), the **sequence union** relation '$\bigcirc$' (Reape, 1996) allows for the computation of sub-lists composed of elements that need not be adjacent, and in a sense treats lists as if they were ordered sets.[8] The effect of (11) is that any arguments in sub-list S or C are registered in VAL as subjects or complements, respectively, and will be required to appear in situ. Any arguments in sub-list G are registered in GAP and therefore will be required to not appear in situ. Sequence union is defined in (12).

(12)   **Sequence union:**

    a. $(\langle \rangle \bigcirc \langle \rangle) = \langle \rangle$ (base case)

    b. $(\langle X \rangle \oplus L_1) \bigcirc L_2 = \langle X \rangle \oplus (L1 \bigcirc L2)$ (left append)

    c. $L_1 \bigcirc (\langle X \rangle \oplus L_2) = \langle X \rangle \oplus (L1 \bigcirc L2)$ (right append)

The base case in (12a) states that the sequence union of empty lists is the empty list, the left append case in (12b) recursively takes the top element of the first list and appends it to the top of the result list, and the right append case in (12c) recursively takes the top element of the second list and appends it to the top of the result list. The left and right append cases are non-deterministic, allowing '$\bigcirc$' constraints to be resolved in different ways.

To illustrate the ARGUMENT REALIZATION Cx at work, suppose that the transitive verb *trust* selects two NP arguments and is unified with the Argument Realization construction in (11). The value of ARG-ST is $\langle \text{NP}_i, \text{NP}_j \rangle$, and if $S = \langle \text{NP}_i \rangle$, $C = \langle \text{NP}_j \rangle$, $G = \langle \rangle$, then we obtain uses like (13), where neither argument is ex situ. Here we omit all PHON, CAT, and SEM information for ease of exposition, given that such features are unaffected by (11). Such a VAL specification will ultimately be responsible for licensing sentences like *Sam likes Kim*, for instance. From now on, we omit case information, for exposition purposes.

---

[8] Note that the '$\oplus$' operation is not a primitive, as it can be efficiently defined as feature unification using 'difference lists' (Copestake et al., 2001). The non-deterministic '$\bigcirc$' relation allows lists to be combined in many different ways, e.g. $\langle \text{NP}, \text{PP} \rangle \bigcirc \langle \text{VP} \rangle$ has a total of exactly three possible resolutions: (i) $\langle \text{NP}, \text{PP}, \text{VP} \rangle$, (ii) $\langle \text{NP}, \text{VP}, \text{PP} \rangle$, and (iii) $\langle \text{VP}, \text{NP}, \text{VP} \rangle$. The sequence union thus allows (11) to split lists in many different ways.

(13)
$$
\begin{bmatrix}
word \\
\text{ARG-ST} & \langle\, \text{NP}_i, \text{NP}_j\,\rangle \\
\text{VAL} & \begin{bmatrix} \text{SUBJ} & \langle\,\text{NP}_i\,\rangle \\ \text{COMPS} & \langle\,\text{NP}_j\,\rangle \end{bmatrix} \\
\text{GAP} & \langle\,\rangle
\end{bmatrix}
$$

If instead $S = \langle\text{NP}_i\rangle$, $C = \langle\,\rangle$ $G = \langle\text{NP}_j\rangle$, then we obtain uses like (14), where the complement is ex situ, as in *It was Kim who Sam likes __.*

(14)
$$
\begin{bmatrix}
word \\
\text{ARG-ST} & \langle\, \text{NP}_i, \text{NP}_j\,\rangle \\
\text{VAL} & \begin{bmatrix} \text{SUBJ} & \langle\,\text{NP}_i\,\rangle \\ \text{COMPS} & \langle\,\rangle \end{bmatrix} \\
\text{GAP} & \langle\,\text{NP}_j\,\rangle
\end{bmatrix}
$$

If instead $S = \langle\,\rangle$, $C = \langle\text{NP}_j\rangle$, and $G = \langle\text{NP}_i\rangle$, we obtain uses like (15), where the subject is ex situ, as in *Who did you say __ likes Kim?*

(15)
$$
\begin{bmatrix}
word \\
\text{ARG-ST} & \langle\, \text{NP}_i, \text{NP}_j\,\rangle \\
\text{VAL} & \begin{bmatrix} \text{SUBJ} & \langle\,\rangle \\ \text{COMPS} & \langle\,\text{NP}_j\,\rangle \end{bmatrix} \\
\text{GAP} & \langle\,\text{NP}_i\,\rangle
\end{bmatrix}
$$

Finally, if $S = \langle\,\rangle$, $C = \langle\,\rangle$, and $G = \langle\text{NP}_i, \text{NP}_j\rangle$, then we obtain uses like (16), where both valents are ex situ, as in *Which toy did you forget which kid __ likes __?*; see §2.2.1.1 for more co-argument gap examples.

(16)
$$
\begin{bmatrix}
word \\
\text{ARG-ST} & \langle\, \text{NP}_i, \text{NP}_j\,\rangle \\
\text{VAL} & \begin{bmatrix} \text{SUBJ} & \langle\,\rangle \\ \text{COMPS} & \langle\,\rangle \end{bmatrix} \\
\text{GAP} & \langle\,\text{NP}_i, \text{NP}_j\,\rangle
\end{bmatrix}
$$

No other resolutions are licit because they are inconsistent with other grammatical constraints. For example, $S = \langle\text{NP}_i, \text{NP}_j\rangle$, $C = \langle\,\rangle$, $G = \langle\,\rangle$ is not allowed because the phrasal construction that models head-subject constructions allows exactly one subject only; see §5.2.2. Similarly, $S = \langle\,\rangle$, $C = \langle\text{NP}_i, \text{NP}_j\rangle$, $G = \langle\,\rangle$ is not licit because only the first member of ARG-ST (the highest argument in the Keenan-Comrie Accessibility hierarchy) is allowed to appear in SUBJ.

In addition to argument structure, ARG-ST is also where Binding Theory is stated: anaphoric dependencies are captured as the co-indexing of pronouns according to their order of appearance in ARG-ST (Pollard and Sag, 1994, ch. 6). For example, a reflexive pronoun such as *herself* is required to be co-indexed with a non-reflexive preceding antecedent in the same ARG-ST. As a consequence, so-called reconstruction phenomena as in (17) are automatic and unavoidable, since HPSG's Binding Theory applies to the members of the ARG-ST, regardless of whether the arguments are in situ or ex situ; see Sag et al. (2003, ch. 7) for more discussion.

(17)   It was HIMSELF$_i$ [who]$_i$ Roger didn't trust ___$_i$

Since ARG-ST optionally contains adverbial arguments, then Binding Theory can predict the oddness of examples like (18), as Levine and Hukari (2006, 84) note; see also Reinhart (1983, 102) and Hukari and Levine (1996).

(18)   *They$_i$ went into the city [without the twins$_i$ being noticed].
       (Hukari and Levine, 1996)

The Argument Realization construction in (11) is not restricted to application to verbal signs. Any word that has a non-empty argument structure in principle has uses where some or all of its arguments are either in situ or ex situ, unless it already comes with specific values for VAL and/or GAP, such as certain uses of verbs like *assure* and *suggest*, as discussed in §2.3, repeated below in (19). Such uses lexically force the object to be in GAP, which has the effect of the UDC being obligatory.

(19)   a.   *I assure you Chris to be the most competent.
       b.   ?[Who]$_i$ can you assure me ___$_i$ to be the most competent?

Thus, some verbs are underspecified and allow a wide range of possible mappings between ARG-ST, VAL, and GAP, while other verbs do not. Similarly, prepositions impose no lexical constraints on their COMPS or GAP lists, and therefore the accusative NP they subcategorize via ARG-ST can appear in either list, as illustrated in (20) for the argument-marking use of the preposition *on*.

(20)
$$
\begin{bmatrix}
\textit{word} \\
\text{PHON} & \langle \textit{ɔn} \rangle \\
\text{CAT} & \begin{bmatrix} \textit{prep} \\ \text{FORM } \textit{on} \end{bmatrix} \\
\text{ARG-ST} & \langle \text{NP}_i \rangle \\
\text{VAL} & \begin{bmatrix} \text{SUBJ} & \langle\,\rangle \\ \text{COMPS} & \langle \ldots \rangle \end{bmatrix} \\
\text{GAP} & \langle \ldots \rangle \\
\text{SEM} & \begin{bmatrix} \text{INDEX} & i \\ \text{RESTR} & \langle\,\rangle \end{bmatrix}
\end{bmatrix}
$$

Once the preposition in (20) and the Argument Realization construction in (11) are unified with each other, exactly two resolutions are possible, shown in (21a, b). The former requires the NP to be in situ, and the latter requires it to be ex situ, stranding the preposition as in *Who did you rely on ___?*[9]

---

[9] Note also that according to Wechsler (1995) and Davis (2001), even argument-marking prepositions like (21b) assign a thematic role to their complements.

(21) a.
$$
\begin{bmatrix}
word \\
\text{PHON} \quad \langle \text{ɔn} \rangle \\
\text{CAT} \quad \begin{bmatrix} prep \\ \text{FORM} \quad on \end{bmatrix} \\
\text{ARG-ST} \quad \langle \text{NP}_i \rangle \\
\text{VAL} \quad \begin{bmatrix} \text{SUBJ} \quad \langle \rangle \\ \text{COMPS} \quad \langle \text{NP}_i \rangle \end{bmatrix} \\
\text{GAP} \quad \langle \rangle \\
\text{SEM} \quad \begin{bmatrix} \text{INDEX} \quad i \\ \text{RESTR} \quad \langle \rangle \end{bmatrix}
\end{bmatrix}
$$

b.
$$
\begin{bmatrix}
word \\
\text{PHON} \quad \langle \text{ɔn} \rangle \\
\text{CAT} \quad \begin{bmatrix} prep \\ \text{FORM} \quad on \end{bmatrix} \\
\text{ARG-ST} \quad \langle \text{NP}_i \rangle \\
\text{VAL} \quad \begin{bmatrix} \text{SUBJ} \quad \langle \rangle \\ \text{COMPS} \quad \langle \rangle \end{bmatrix} \\
\text{GAP} \quad \langle \text{NP}_i \rangle \\
\text{SEM} \quad \begin{bmatrix} \text{INDEX} \quad i \\ \text{RESTR} \quad \langle \rangle \end{bmatrix}
\end{bmatrix}
$$

In languages where no preposition stranding is allowed, the non-English counterpart of (20) can be lexically specified as [GAP $\langle \rangle$], thus preventing the preposition from being stranded by the Argument Realization construction. See, however, §5.2.4 for an alternative account.

5.2.2 Phrasal constructions

We now turn to how the lexical representations just discussed give rise to phrasal structures. In their survey of priming evidence, Branigan and Pickering (2017) conclude that syntactic representations capture local relationships between a mother and its immediate constituent daughter(s), and involve a range of mappings between information encoded in the semantic representation and information encoded in the syntactic representation. HPSG phrasal constructions consist of exactly this kind of information.

Phrasal signs differ from lexical signs in that the former have at least one daughter and the feature ARG-ST is absent. For example, verbal heads combine with the arguments they subcategorize via a phrasal construction like that shown in (22), here represented in a familiar PSG format, for legibility. For now, this construction says nothing about the feature GAP.

(22)   PREDICATIONAL HEAD-COMPLEMENT Cx (preliminary)

$$
\begin{bmatrix}
phrase \\
\text{CAT } Y \\
\text{VAL} \begin{bmatrix} \text{SUBJ} & L \\ \text{COMPS} & \langle\rangle \end{bmatrix} \\
\text{SEM} \begin{bmatrix} \text{INDEX } e \end{bmatrix}
\end{bmatrix}
\rightarrow
\begin{bmatrix}
word \\
\text{CAT } Y : \begin{bmatrix} verb \\ \text{INV } - \end{bmatrix} \\
\text{VAL} \begin{bmatrix} \text{SUBJ} & L \\ \text{COMPS} & \langle X_1, \ldots, X_n \rangle \end{bmatrix} \\
\text{SEM} \begin{bmatrix} \text{INDEX } e \end{bmatrix}
\end{bmatrix}
X_1 \ldots X_n
$$

Constraints of the form $V{:}F$ mean that the value of the variable V is a feature structure with at least the information that is explicitly shown in F. Thus, (22) states that the first daughter is required to be a non-inverted verb (auxiliary or otherwise), and that both the mother node and the first daughter have the same information for CAT and SUBJ. In addition, the semantic index e of the mother and that of the head daughter are the same.

Once a verb is unified with the first daughter of (22), the latter's COMPS value becomes instantiated with whatever constraints the verb imposes on COMPS. And as the rules' COMPS list is instantiated with the word's COMPS list, so are the n sisters of the verbal daughter. The Predicational Head-Complement construction is thus responsible for licensing all VP structures. For example, the use of *like* shown in Figure 5.9 lexically requires only one accusative NP, and, thus, this is what is licensed by (22).

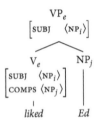

$$
\begin{array}{c}
\text{VP}_e \\
\begin{bmatrix} \text{SUBJ} & \langle \text{NP}_i \rangle \end{bmatrix}
\end{array}
$$

$$
\begin{array}{cc}
\text{V}_e & \text{NP}_j \\
\begin{bmatrix} \text{SUBJ} & \langle \text{NP}_i \rangle \\ \text{COMPS} & \langle \text{NP}_j \rangle \end{bmatrix} & \\
liked & Ed
\end{array}
$$

Figure 5.9 Verb phrase *liked Ed*

Although it is not shown here, the content of the mother's RESTR list is defined as the concatenation of all the (non-quantificational) content of the daughters' RESTR lists plus whatever semantic contribution is made by the phrasal construction itself; see Sag (2010, 2012) for example. A similar constraint should apply to CNTXT, combining the pragmatic contributions of the daughter, also via list concatenation.[10] Since in this chapter we are mostly concerned with the syntactic mechanism responsible for filler-gap dependencies, we usually omit PHON, SEM, and CNTXT from our examples. Nonetheless, we stress that these are crucial levels of representation that are locally available in every node and that often interact with the rest of the grammar, including UDCs; see §7.2 and §7.1.1.

Following standard practice, 'VP$_e$' is used as a shorthand that abbreviates any verbal expression (lexical or otherwise) with an empty COMPS list and non-empty SUBJ list, as

---

[10] See §3.4.2 for more discussion about quantifier scope, as well as interrogative scope.

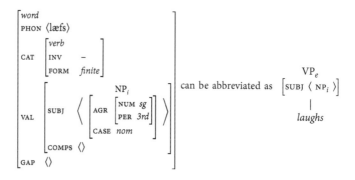

Figure 5.10 The symbol 'VP' as a shorthand

seen in Figure 5.10. The subscript *e* corresponds to the value of INDEX. Features explicitly shown in abbreviations are just those relevant for exposition purposes. Analogously, 'S$_e$' abbreviates any verbal expression (lexical or phrasal) that has empty VAL features and [INDEX *e*]. So, even an intransitive verb is consistent with the VP abbreviation, and an imperative like *Read!* is consistent with the S abbreviation.

Prepositions, nouns, adjectives, and so on combine with their complements via analogous rules, which allow them to project phrases of the same part of speech as the first daughter. Take, for instance, the PP rule in (23), as formulated in Sag (2012).

(23) SATURATIONAL HEAD-COMPLEMENT Cx (preliminary)

$$
\begin{bmatrix}
\textit{phrase} \\
\text{CAT} & Y \\
\text{VAL} & \begin{bmatrix} \text{SUBJ} & \langle\,\rangle \\ \text{COMPS} & \langle\,\rangle \end{bmatrix} \\
\text{SEM} & \begin{bmatrix} \text{INDEX } i \end{bmatrix}
\end{bmatrix}
\rightarrow
\begin{bmatrix}
\text{CAT} & Y{:}prep \\
\text{VAL} & \begin{bmatrix} \text{SUBJ} & \langle\,\rangle \\ \text{COMPS} & \langle X\rangle \end{bmatrix} \\
\text{SEM} & \begin{bmatrix} \text{INDEX } i \end{bmatrix}
\end{bmatrix}
\; X
$$

Consequently, PPs like the one in Figure 5.11 are licensed. Here and throughout the symbol 'PP' is used as an abbreviation for any prepositional expression, lexical or phrasal, that bears empty valence specifications.

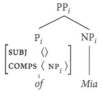

Figure 5.11 Prepositional phrase *of Mia*

The phrasal rule that allows verbal expressions (lexical or otherwise) to combine with their subcategorized subject is (24), from Sag (2012).

(24) SUBJECT-PREDICATE Cx (preliminary)

$$
\begin{bmatrix}
\textit{phrase} \\
\text{CAT} & Y \\
\text{VAL} & \begin{bmatrix} \text{SUBJ} & \langle\,\rangle \\ \text{COMPS} & \langle\,\rangle \end{bmatrix} \\
\text{SEM} & \begin{bmatrix} \text{INDEX } e \end{bmatrix}
\end{bmatrix}
\rightarrow
X
\begin{bmatrix}
\text{CAT} & Y{:}\begin{bmatrix} \textit{verb} \\ \text{INV} - \end{bmatrix} \\
\text{VAL} & \begin{bmatrix} \text{SUBJ} & \langle X\rangle \\ \text{COMPS} & \langle\,\rangle \end{bmatrix} \\
\text{SEM} & \begin{bmatrix} \text{INDEX } e \end{bmatrix}
\end{bmatrix}
$$

The category of the subject is determined by the head, so that if the verb lexically requires a CP subject or a PP subject, for example, then X must be instantiated accordingly. This rule licenses VPs like those in Figure 5.12.

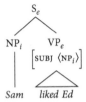

$$S_e$$

$$NP_i \qquad VP_e$$
$$\qquad \left[\text{SUBJ} \langle NP_i \rangle \right]$$

$$Sam \qquad liked\ Ed$$

Figure 5.12 Clause *Sam liked Ed*

The semantics of the S node of Figure 5.12 is omitted here, but it is exactly the same as that in (25). Recall that the value of RESTR of any given mother node is the concatenation of the RESTR values.

(25)
$$
\begin{bmatrix}
\text{INDEX } e \\
\text{RESTR} \left\langle
\begin{bmatrix} name \\ \text{NAMED} \quad Sam \\ \text{ENTITY} \quad i \end{bmatrix},
\begin{bmatrix} like \\ \text{SIT} \quad e \\ \text{ACTOR } i \\ \text{THEME } j \end{bmatrix},
\begin{bmatrix} manner \\ \text{FORM } n \\ \text{SIT} \quad e \end{bmatrix},
\begin{bmatrix} reason \\ \text{CAUSE } r \\ \text{SIT} \quad e \end{bmatrix},
\begin{bmatrix} location \\ \text{PLACE} \quad l \\ \text{THEME} \quad e \end{bmatrix},
\begin{bmatrix} time \\ \text{PAST } t \\ \text{SIT} \quad e \end{bmatrix},
\begin{bmatrix} name \\ \text{NAMED} \quad Ed \\ \text{ENTITY} \quad j \end{bmatrix}
\right\rangle
\end{bmatrix}
$$

The Subject-Auxiliary Inversion (SAI) construction in (26) allows auxiliary verbs that are compatible with the INV+ feature to precede all their valents. The value of INV is underspecified for most auxiliaries, but some, like deontic *shall*, are lexically specified as INV+ and therefore can only occur in SAI constructions, whereas others, like *better*, are lexically specified as INV− and therefore have to occur in non-inverted constructions like (24); see Sag et al. (2020) for a detailed discussion.

(26)   SUBJECT-AUXILIARY INVERSION Cx (preliminary)

$$
\begin{bmatrix}
phrase \\
\text{CAT } Y \\
\text{VAL} \begin{bmatrix} \text{SUBJ } \langle \rangle \\ \text{COMPS } \langle \rangle \end{bmatrix} \\
\text{SEM} \begin{bmatrix} \text{INDEX } e \end{bmatrix}
\end{bmatrix}
\rightarrow
\begin{bmatrix}
word \\
\text{CAT } Y: \begin{bmatrix} verb \\ \text{INV } + \end{bmatrix} \\
\text{VAL} \begin{bmatrix} \text{SUBJ } \langle X_0 \rangle \\ \text{COMPS } \langle X_1, \dots, X_n \rangle \end{bmatrix} \\
\text{SEM} \begin{bmatrix} \text{INDEX } e \end{bmatrix}
\end{bmatrix}
\quad X_0 \ X_1 \ \dots \ X_n
$$

All non-auxiliary verbs are specified as INV−, which means they cannot head (26). This constraint rules out SAIs like *Saw he her?*, and licenses structures like that set out in Figure 5.13. Note how the complement VP_{e_2} of the auxiliary is required to subcategorize the same subject-dependent NP as the first member of the ARG-ST list of the auxiliary, i.e. the auxiliary's subject. Hence, *She* is both the actor of *meet* and the nominative subject of *did*. From now on we will abbreviate the COMPS value of auxiliary verbs as simply VP.

Note that the construction in (26) is an oversimplification. Different kinds of SAI constructions have radically different syntactic, semantic, pragmatic, and prosodic constraints,

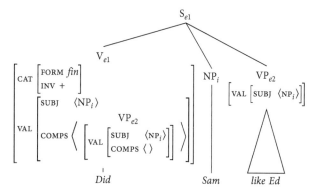

Figure 5.13 SAI clause *Did Sam like Ed?*

as the small sample in (27) illustrates. There is no single SAI construction, but, rather, a family or cluster of SAI constructions of which (26) is the common syntactic template (Culicover, 1971; Goldberg, 1995; Fillmore, 1999; Newmeyer, 1998; Ginzburg and Sag, 2000).

(27)   a. [[Can] [we] [go home]]?
           (Polar Interrogative SAI)

       b. Where [[did] [they] [go _]]?
           (*wh*-Interrogative SAI)

       c. [[Didn't] [you] [fly first class]]?
           (Expectation confirmation SAI)

       d. (Wow/Boy,) [[can] [she] [sing]]!
           (Exclamative SAI)

       e. (Oh) [[don't] [I] [know it]] …
           (Declarative SAI)

       f. [[Don't] [you] [be late]]!
           (Negative Imperative SAI)

       g. [[May] [all your teeth] [fall out]].
           (Blessings/Curses SAI)

       h. [[Had] [you] [warned me]], we would be ready by now.
           (Conditional SAI)

       i. Rarely/Never [[had] [we] [seen them laugh so hard]].
           (Negative fronting SAI)

Chomsky (2010, 9) criticizes constructional analyses of SAI precisely because they resort to multiple SAI constructions, but this criticism ignores the fact that there are syntactic, semantic, and pragmatic idiosyncrasies occurring in the various SAI types. Every theory must be able to account for these idiosyncratic facts, and constructional frameworks can capture them directly, in terms of the specific constraints introduced by each kind of SAI rule.

The case for constructions can be made even stronger. As Kay (2002) points out, over-arching constructional generalizations like those discussed so far are best seen as a (non-redundant) taxonomic characterization of the constructional knowledge shared by a cluster of constructions. In practice, it is the cluster of constructions that matters for speakers, not abstract taxonomies. The latter capture all the generalizations potentially available to the speaker of a language, though that does not entail that the internal representation of the language in the mind of each speaker effectively contains every generalization inherent in the data. Language users are under pressure to acquire and use language efficiently and robustly, and such functional pressures are likely to require the sacrifice of elegance and favor redundancy.

5.2.3 Constructional GAP propagation

According to §2.2 there are six distinct filler-gap dependency patterns to consider, illustrated in (28). Of course, the number and category of the extracted phrases can vary, and different filler-gap dependency types can be overlaid on top of each other.

(28)   a. I like Ed.
        (No filler-gap dependency)

      b. It was Ed [who]$_i$ I hired __$_i$.
        (Singleton dependency)

      c. Ed is someone [who]$_i$ I never know [what]$_j$ to say __$_j$ to __$_i$.
        (Overlapping dependencies)

      d. [Which brand of energy bar]$_i$ did you forget [how many boxes of __$_i$]$_j$ Ed ordered __$_j$ online?'
        (Chaining dependencies)

      e. [Which candidate]$_i$ did you neglect to inform __$_i$ that Ed wanted to interview __$_i$?
        (Convergent dependencies)

      f. [What]$_{\{i,j\}}$ do you think Ed ate __$_i$ and drank __$_j$ at the party?'
        (Cumulative dependencies)

Drawing from Grover (1995, 221), Sag et al. (2003, 447), and Chaves (2012a), we use a '$\otimes$' relation to compute how GAP lists of any given mother node are related to the GAP lists of its local daughters. Suppose for example that a phrasal node is specified as [GAP G], where $G = \langle \text{NP}_i \rangle$, and that phrasal structures are binary-branching, for ease of exposition. In general, we state that the left daughter is specified as [GAP G_1] and the right daughter as [GAP G_2] such that $G = G_1 \otimes G_2$. The constraint $G = G_1 \otimes G_2$ can be resolved in multiple ways. If the resolution is $G_1 = \langle \rangle$ and $G = G_2$, then the extraction pathway percolates through the right daughter, as in Figure 5.14:

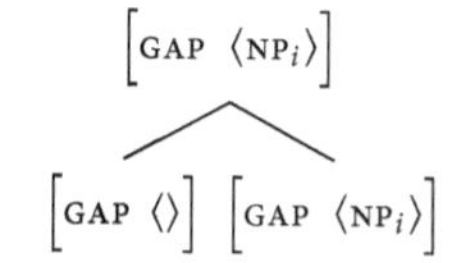

$$\left[\text{GAP } \langle \text{NP}_i \rangle\right]$$

$$\left[\text{GAP } \langle \rangle\right] \quad \left[\text{GAP } \langle \text{NP}_i \rangle\right]$$

Figure 5.14 GAP (rightward) percolation

If instead we have the resolution $G = G_1$ and $G_2 = \langle \rangle$, then the extraction pathway percolates through the left daughter, as in Figure 5.15:

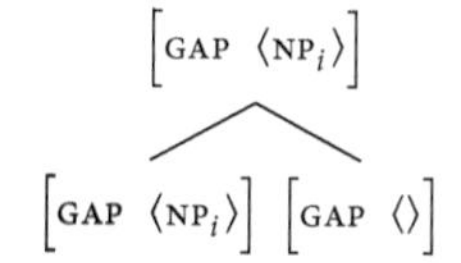

$$\left[\text{GAP } \langle \text{NP}_i \rangle\right]$$

$$\left[\text{GAP } \langle \text{NP}_i \rangle\right] \quad \left[\text{GAP } \langle \rangle\right]$$

Figure 5.15 GAP (leftward) percolation

If instead we have the resolution $G = G_1 = G_2$, then we have a convergent dependency, and the extraction pathway splits into both daughters, as in Figure 5.16:

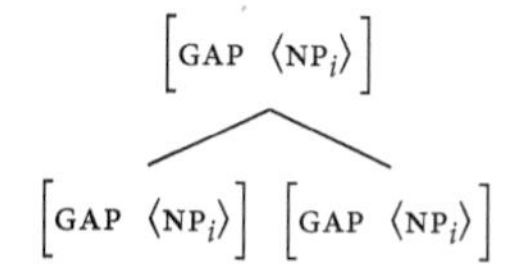

$$\left[\text{GAP } \langle \text{NP}_i \rangle\right]$$

$$\left[\text{GAP } \langle \text{NP}_i \rangle\right] \quad \left[\text{GAP } \langle \text{NP}_i \rangle\right]$$

Figure 5.16 Convergent GAP percolation

The sharing of non-empty GAP specifications across local nodes may be taken to correspond to the anticipation of a gap and to result in increasing working-memory load (Wanner and Maratsos, 1978; Kluender, 1998; Gibson, 1998; Sag, 1992; Culicover and Jackendoff, 2005; Sag and Wasow, 2011, 2015).

If instead we have a resolution where $G = \langle \text{NP}_i \rangle$ such that $i = \{i, j\}$, then $G_1 = \langle \text{NP}_i \rangle$ and $G_2 = \langle \text{NP}_j \rangle$. This yields a cumulative extraction, as in Figure 5.17:

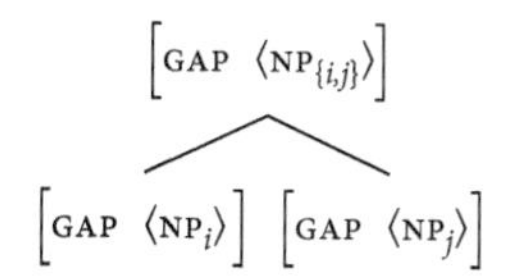

$$\left[\text{GAP } \langle \text{NP}_{\{i,j\}} \rangle\right]$$

$$\left[\text{GAP } \langle \text{NP}_i \rangle\right] \quad \left[\text{GAP } \langle \text{NP}_j \rangle\right]$$

Figure 5.17 Cumulative GAP percolation

Since nothing requires G to be singleton in the first place, we should allow for multiple gaps, in which case we can have overlapping dependencies, and combinations of overlapping and cumulative or convergent UDCs. In sum, what is needed in general is a definition for '$\otimes$' such that the aforementioned resolutions are allowed, for whatever the number of branching daughters, as illustrated in Figure 5.18.

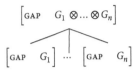

Figure 5.18 GAP list joining (schematic)

The list-join relation is defined in (29). The append case is stated in terms of the list concatenation '$\oplus$' function, whereas the union case is stated in terms of a Linkean i-sum operation '+' (Link, 1983).

(29) **List-join:**

    a. $(G_1 \otimes G_2) = G_1 \oplus G_2$ (append case)

    b. $((\langle X_i \rangle \otimes \langle X_j \rangle) = \langle X_{i+j} \rangle$ (union case)

This definition is non-deterministic by design, so that different resolutions are sometimes possible for the same input. The condition in (29a) states that list-joining any list G_1 (empty or otherwise) with any other list G_2 (empty or otherwise) can simply reduce to list concatenation. This allows different gaps to remain independent, as in overlapping UDCs: for example, $\langle NP_i \rangle \otimes \langle NP_j \rangle = \langle NP_i, NP_j \rangle$. In this case, (29a) would resolve as $G_1 = \langle \rangle$ and $G_2 = \langle NP_j \rangle$. Of course, (29a) also allows cases where there are no gaps $\langle \rangle \otimes \langle \rangle = \langle \rangle$, as well as mixed cases like $\langle NP_i \rangle \otimes \langle \rangle = \langle NP_i \rangle$ and so on, for any number or category of gaps.

In contrast, the union case in (29b) states that it is possible to combine two gaps into a single gap, licensing UDCs where multiple gaps are linked to the same filler, e.g., $\langle NP_i \rangle \otimes \langle NP_j \rangle = \langle NP_{i+j} \rangle$. Following Chaves (2014), the '+' operator is a Linkean i-sum (Link, 1983), which in effect means that if $i = j$, then $i + j = i = j$ and we obtain a convergent UDC like (28e) where the gaps are co-indexed to each other and to the filler phrase. This is only possible because Linkean sums are idempotent: $\forall i (i + i = i)$. If, on the other hand, $i \neq j$, then the union obtains a cumulative UDC where the filler phrase refers to a plurality consisting of i and j, i.e., $\{i, j\}$.

Given the neurolinguistic evidence suggesting that the computation of UDCs is distributed across the language areas, we follow Gazdar (1981) in assuming that phrasal constructions are themselves responsible for the propagation of any extant filler-gap dependencies. We therefore directly incorporate '$\otimes$' into all of the phrasal rules discussed in the previous section, as illustrated in (30) and (31).

(30) PREDICATIONAL HEAD-COMPLEMENT CX (revised)

$$
\begin{bmatrix} phrase \\ \text{CAT } Y \\ \text{VAL} \begin{bmatrix} \text{SUBJ } L \\ \text{COMPS } \langle \rangle \end{bmatrix} \\ \text{GAP } G_0 \otimes \ldots \otimes G_n \\ \text{SEM} \begin{bmatrix} \text{INDEX } v \end{bmatrix} \end{bmatrix} \rightarrow \begin{bmatrix} word \\ \text{CAT } Y: \begin{bmatrix} verb \\ \text{INV } - \end{bmatrix} \\ \text{VAL} \begin{bmatrix} \text{SUBJ } L \\ \text{COMPS } \langle X_1, \ldots, X_n \rangle \end{bmatrix} \\ \text{GAP } G_0 \\ \text{SEM} \begin{bmatrix} \text{INDEX } v \end{bmatrix} \end{bmatrix} X_1 : \begin{bmatrix} \text{GAP } G_1 \end{bmatrix} \ldots X_n : \begin{bmatrix} \text{GAP } G_n \end{bmatrix}
$$

(31)   SUBJECT-PREDICATE Cx (revised)

$$\begin{bmatrix} phrase \\ \text{CAT} \quad Y \\ \text{VAL} \quad \begin{bmatrix} \text{SUBJ} & \langle\,\rangle \\ \text{COMPS} & \langle\,\rangle \end{bmatrix} \\ \text{GAP} \quad G_1 \otimes G_n \\ \text{SEM} \quad \begin{bmatrix} \text{INDEX } v \end{bmatrix} \end{bmatrix} \rightarrow X{:}\begin{bmatrix} \text{GAP } G_1 \end{bmatrix} \; \begin{bmatrix} \text{CAT} \quad Y{:}\begin{bmatrix} verb \\ \text{INV } - \end{bmatrix} \\ \text{VAL} \quad \begin{bmatrix} \text{SUBJ} & \langle X \rangle \\ \text{COMPS} & \langle\,\rangle \end{bmatrix} \\ \text{GAP} \quad G_2 \\ \text{SEM} \quad \begin{bmatrix} \text{INDEX } v \end{bmatrix} \end{bmatrix}$$

The grammar accounts for sentences without UDCs, as illustrated in Figure 5.19. Every word has an empty list value for GAP, and therefore no extraction.

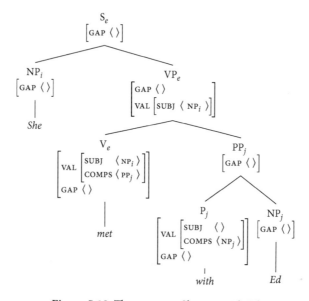

Figure 5.19 The sentence *She met with Ed*

The Argument Realization Construction has resolved the $S \bigcirc C \bigcirc G$ constraint so that all members of the verb's ARG-ST appear in VAL, which means GAP is empty. The subject phrase combines with the verb phrase via (31), and the verb and preposition combine with their subcategorized complements via (30). As in Gazdar's CFG, the rules can be applied in any order, depending on the parsing model of choice.

In a Left-Corner strategy, for instance, the presence of an NP can lead to the expectation of S with an upcoming VP structure via the construction in (31). Because pronouns have by definition empty ARG-ST, it follows that they also have empty VAL and GAP lists. Thus, the expected S has GAP value $\langle\,\rangle \otimes G_2$, where G_2 is the value of GAP for the upcoming VP, as in Figure 5.20. Here, there is no filler in memory and no active gap search. Processing proceeds in the usual way according to the Left-Corner strategy: the verb is scanned, confirming the VP expectation, and the valence of the verb creates an expectation about an upcoming PP complement, and so on. G_2 must ultimately be resolved as the empty list $\langle\,\rangle$, given that every word in the utterance is specified as [GAP $\langle\,\rangle$].

The construction in (32) is responsible for linking a filler phrase X to the corresponding member of the GAP list in its clausal sister; cf. Sag (2012). In particular, the constraint [GAP $\langle X \rangle \bigcirc G_2$] has the effect of unifying the GAP list of the second daughter with two sub-lists: $\langle X \rangle$ and G_2. Because '$\bigcirc$' is used instead of '$\oplus$', the element X could be anywhere in the GAP list, and G_2 is the remainder list.

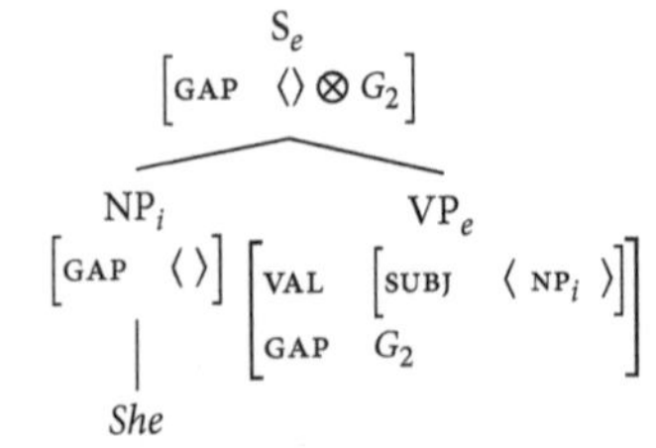

$$S_e \quad [\text{GAP} \ \langle\rangle \otimes G_2]$$

Tree: $S_e\,[\text{GAP}\ \langle\rangle \otimes G_2]$ branches into:
- $NP_i\,[\text{GAP}\ \langle\rangle]$ — *She*
- $VP_e\begin{bmatrix}\text{VAL} & [\text{SUBJ}\ \langle NP_i\rangle] \\ \text{GAP} & G_2\end{bmatrix}$

Figure 5.20 A Left-Corner prediction after processing *She*

(32) HEAD-FILLER CX

$$\begin{bmatrix}\text{phrase} \\ \text{CAT} & Y \\ \text{VAL} & \begin{bmatrix}\text{SUBJ} & \langle\rangle \\ \text{COMPS} & \langle\rangle\end{bmatrix} \\ \text{GAP} & G_1 \otimes G_2 \\ \text{SEM} & [\text{INDEX } v]\end{bmatrix} \rightarrow X{:}\big[\text{GAP } G_1\big]\ \begin{bmatrix}\text{CAT} & Y : verb \\ & \begin{bmatrix}\text{SUBJ} & \langle\rangle \\ \text{COMPS} & \langle\rangle\end{bmatrix} \\ \text{GAP} & \langle X\rangle \bigcirc G_2 \\ \text{SEM} & [\text{INDEX } v]\end{bmatrix}$$

Since the grammar is a set of declarative constraints, all that (32) actually requires is that the daughter *i* must unify with one of the elements of the S node's GAP list and that *i* does not appear in the mother's GAP list. From a top-down perspective, the construction in (32) has the effect of adding the 'fronted' phrase to the GAP list of the S node. Hence, there is an active filler phrase (the GAP member) and a search for the corresponding gap site. From a bottom-up perspective, (32) has the effect of removing an element in GAP and unifying it with the 'fronted' phrase. Regardless of how the grammar is used by the parser, (32) has the effect of licensing the top branching node of Figure 5.21.[11] The ex situ argument is highlighted for perspicuity.

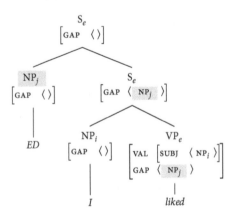

Figure 5.21 A Topicalization *ED I liked __*

None of these discussed phrasal rules can prevent GAP values from propagating in the syntactic tree, with the exception of head-filler rules. Thus, filler-gap dependencies cross clausal boundaries until they can be resolved, as in Figure 5.22. The top branching node

---

[11] Recall that semantic composition essentially amounts to appending '⊕' to RESTR lists. As a result, the semantics of the UDC in Figure 5.21 is the same as that of its non-extraction counterpart in Figure 5.12; more specifically (25).

is licensed by the Head-Filler construction, and the rest is licensed by the Head-Subject construction and the Predicational Head-Complement construction.

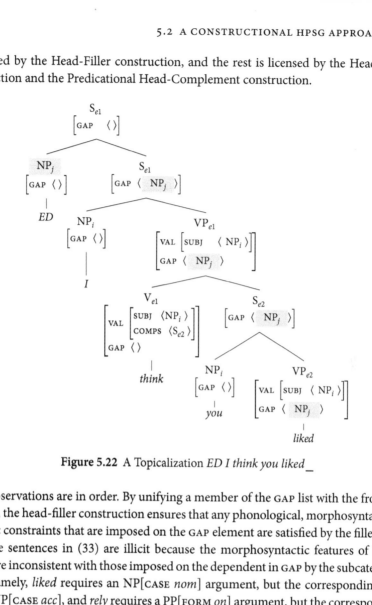

Figure 5.22 A Topicalization *ED I think you liked___*

A few observations are in order. By unifying a member of the GAP list with the fronted expression, the head-filler construction ensures that any phonological, morphosyntactic, and semantic constraints that are imposed on the GAP element are satisfied by the filler phrase. Thus, the sentences in (33) are illicit because the morphosyntactic features of the filler phrase are inconsistent with those imposed on the dependent in GAP by the subcategorizing head. Namely, *liked* requires an NP[CASE *nom*] argument, but the corresponding ex situ filler is NP[CASE *acc*], and *rely* requires a PP[FORM *on*] argument, but the corresponding ex situ filler is PP[FORM *to*]. Analogous agreement or part-of-speech mismatches are similarly ruled out when the filler is unified with the corresponding member of ARG-ST.

(33)   a. *[HER]$_i$ I think ___$_i$ liked the movie.
       b. *[TO ROBIN]$_i$ I would never rely ___$_i$.

Moreover, the fact that fillers are required to combine with clauses predicts contrasts like (34) and (35). In the acceptable cases the filler phrase combines with S, but in the unacceptable cases it does not.

(34)   a. [HIM]$_i$ she could hire ___$_i$. (The other candidates, she couldn't.)
       b. *She [HIM]$_i$ hired ___$_i$. (The other candidates, she couldn't.)

(35)   a.   I know [who]$_i$ Kim tried to hire __$_i$.
     b.   *I know Kim tried who to hire __$_i$.

Finally, the fact that the subcategorization of ex situ arguments is locally registered in the syntactic node itself allows for a straightforward account of extraction pathway phenomena (Hukari and Levine, 1995; Bouma et al., 2001; Levine and Hukari, 2006; Sag, 2010). For example, the Irish complementizer *goN* can be assumed to select S complements bearing the feature [GAP ⟨⟩]. Thus, *goN* cannot occur between a filler and a gap, because the value of GAP is required to be the empty list (Vaillette, 2002; Assmann et al., 2010). Conversely, the complementizer *aL* can be assumed to instead select S complements bearing a non-empty gap set specification [GAP ⟨X, ... ⟩]. If instead one opts to analyze *goN* and *aL* as verb particles rather than complementizers, the account is still straightforward, as Vaillette (2002) shows. For GAP-based HPSG accounts of resumption in various languages, see Borsley (2010), Alotaibi and Borsley (2013), Crysmann (2016), and references cited.

It should be stressed that the Head-Filler construction in (32) is an oversimplification, since there are many such constructions, not just one. All head-filler constructions share the same basic syntactic template but impose slightly different syntactic, semantic, pragmatic, and prosodic components (Sag, 2010). For example, as detailed in §2.1, in Topicalization the filler phrase is required to bear a Topic relation to the presupposed open proposition expressed by the remainder of the sentence, modulo whatever is in Focus. By adding a feature with pragmatic information, such constraints can be directly stated in (32) to impose the correct contextual constraints on examples like (36a); see Prince (1981) for a survey of declarative frontings.

(36)   A: Where do his cousins live nowadays?
     B: [SAM]$_i$ I think __$_i$ moved to TORONTO, and [ROBIN]$_j$ I suspect __$_j$ is still in OTTAWA.

Conversely, in Focus Movement the filler is instead required to bear a Focus with regard to the presupposed open proposition expressed by the remainder of the utterance. Again, a variant of (32) augmented with the proper pragmatic information can directly capture the contextual constraints required by different kinds of frontings, as in (37).[12]

(37)   a.   I didn't have any weekends all for myself when I was working at the diner. [THREE MEALS A DAY]$_i$ I cooked __$_i$ on Sundays.
       (Focus Movement)

     b.   A: John wants to eat some more.
       B: [Not ANOTHER BURGER]$_i$ he won't (eat __$_i$).
       (Not-Topicalization)

     c.   [A FINGER]$_i$ I wouldn't lift __$_i$ for him.
       (Yiddish Movement)

---

[12] In the case of (37b) additional syntactic constraints are needed in order to ensure that the fronted phrase is negative and the presuppositional phrase can be elliptical. See Culicover (1999, 182–6) for more discussion about this particular type of UDC.

Interrogative constructions similarly involve a cluster of constructions that share the same basic syntactic template as that shown in (32), but which impose additional constraints. This is necessary to capture the fact that a wide range of interrogative constructions exists, as surveyed in §2.1, ranging from echo questions and reprise questions to various kinds of direct interrogatives. For example, even a simple question like (38) can instantiate various kinds of interrogative inquiry, including a rhetorical question (in which case the Question Under Discussion is whether the hearer knows the answer or not), a self-addressed question (with a falling intonation), a standard information request, or an echo or reprise question.

(38)   [What]$_i$ was her name __$_i$?

Other interrogative UDCs are more idiomatic and similarly require idiosyncratic instantiations of (32). Recall the case of reason interrogatives like (39a) (Kay and Fillmore, 1999), and sarcastic questions like (39b) (Michaelis and Feng, 2015). These are special constructions that share approximately the same syntactic constraints as standard questions, but come with unique semantic and pragmatic restrictions.

(39)   a. [What]$_i$ am I doing __$_i$ reading this book?
        b. [What]$_i$ are you __$_i$, a monk?

Other instances of (32) are necessary in order to capture degree exclamatives like (40); see Ginzburg and Sag (2000, ch. 6) and Sag (2010) for an account of these and various other UDC types.

(40)   a. [What a fool]$_i$ this guy is __$_i$!
        b. [The fool]$_i$ that I have been __$_i$!

Analogously, relative clauses and clefts are also families of constructions, each of which imposes different syntactic, semantic, and pragmatic peculiarities, as detailed in §2.1. Take, for example, Free Relatives like (41). Recall that such UDCs are remarkable in that the filler phrase is also the head of the entire clause. But this peculiarity poses no problem for a constructivist framework, since this particular construction is captured via a dedicated rule (Sag, 1997, 2010).

(41)   a. Kim was [[who]$_i$ I invited __$_i$]$_{NP_i}$.
        b. [[Who]$_i$ I invited __$_i$]$_{NP_i}$ was Kim.

We illustrate the account with (42). This rule requires some phrase X to be identified as the gap Y of a non-inverted clause. Crucially, the mother node is of the same category as X, and shares the same index v. Thus, the filler Y is also the head of the entire structure.

(42)   FREE RELATIVE CLAUSE CX

$$
\begin{bmatrix} \text{CAT } X \\ \text{VAL } K \\ \text{GAP } G_1 \otimes G_2 \\ \text{SEM } [\text{INDEX } v] \end{bmatrix} \rightarrow Y : \begin{bmatrix} \text{CAT } X \\ \text{VAL } K : [\text{COMPS } \langle \rangle] \\ \text{GAP } G_1 \\ \text{SEM } [\text{INDEX } v] \end{bmatrix} \begin{bmatrix} \text{CAT } \begin{bmatrix} verb \\ \text{INV } - \end{bmatrix} \\ \text{VAL } \begin{bmatrix} \text{SUBJ } \langle \rangle \\ \text{COMPS } \langle \rangle \end{bmatrix} \\ \text{GAP } \langle Y \rangle \ominus G_2 \end{bmatrix}
$$

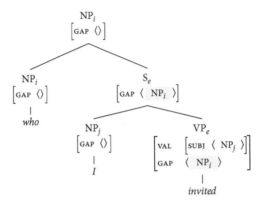

Figure 5.23 Subject-embedded relative *The person I invited*

If the variable v of the adjoined phrasal head (i.e. the first daughter) denotes an entity, then the gap is required also to denote an entity, since both have the same variable v. In that case we have an adnominal relative. Similarly, if the variable v denotes an eventuality, then we have an adverbial relative clause. The effect of (42) is illustrated in Figure 5.23.

In contrast, Bare Relative clauses boil down to a template in which the element in the clause's GAP list is co-indexed with the adjoined head, but not with any filler phrase, as in (43). Notice that here the second daughter, the clause, is the head X of the entire structure, and that the gap Y is simply co-indexed with the sister node, not equated to it. Since the nominal head and the gap are simply co-indexed, they are free to exhibit different morphosyntactic information, including different case.

(43)   BARE RELATIVE CLAUSE CX

$$
\begin{bmatrix} \text{CAT } X \\ \text{VAL } K \\ \text{GAP } G_1 \otimes G_2 \\ \text{SEM} \begin{bmatrix} \text{INDEX } v \end{bmatrix} \end{bmatrix} \rightarrow \begin{bmatrix} \text{VAL} \begin{bmatrix} \text{COMPS } \langle\rangle \end{bmatrix} \\ \text{GAP } G_1 \\ \text{SEM} \begin{bmatrix} \text{INDEX } v \end{bmatrix} \end{bmatrix} \begin{bmatrix} \text{CAT } X : \begin{bmatrix} verb \\ \text{INV } - \end{bmatrix} \\ \text{VAL } K : \begin{bmatrix} \text{SUBJ } \langle\rangle \\ \text{COMPS } \langle\rangle \end{bmatrix} \\ \text{GAP } \langle Y_v \rangle \bigcirc G_2 \end{bmatrix}
$$

The effect of (43) is illustrated in Figure 5.24. The relative clause adjoins the nominal antecedent *person* via a (post)head-modifier construction, and the feature SELECT; see §5.2.4 for some discussion about adjunction in HPSG, and see Sag (2010) for a more in-depth exposition.

5.2.3.1 Multiple-gap UDCs

We now turn to UDCs that involve multiple filler-gap dependencies, and show how the grammar handles all the patterns identified in §2.2. Overlapping filler-gap dependencies arise when multiple words list one of their ARG-ST members in GAP, linked to different fillers. This is shown in Figure 5.25.

Suppose the grammar is coupled with a Left-Corner parser. The Head-Filler Construction has the effect of entering the phrase *someone that inept* into the GAP list of the clausal node. Next, the Head-Filler Construction applies again to enter a second filler phrase into the GAP list of the second clausal node. The value of GAP is then propagated as the

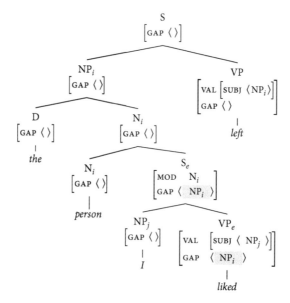

Figure 5.24 Subject-embedded relative *The person I liked __ left*

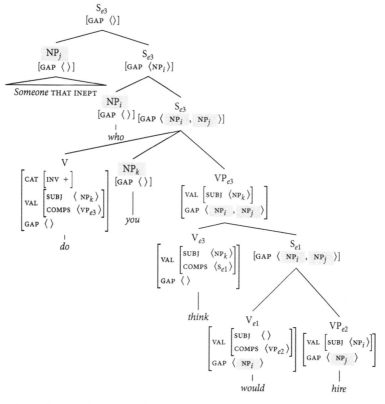

Figure 5.25 Overlapping UDCs *Someone that inept, who do you think __ would hire __?*

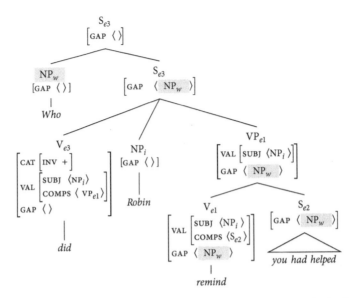

Figure 5.26 Convergent UDC *Who did Robin remind__ you had helped__?*

remaining structures are processed until its members can be unified with an element of ARG-ST of some lexical item. The key step for the overlapping UDC occurs at the VP node, where the subject-gapped auxiliary *would* combines with the object-gapped *hire* verb. Here, the constraint $G = \langle NP_i, NP_j \rangle = G_1 \otimes G_2$ that is imposed by the Predicational Head-Complement construction is resolved as $G_1 = \langle NP_i \rangle$ and $G_2 = \langle NP_j \rangle$. The union case of '$\otimes$' alternatively allows the same filler phrase to be linked to two different gaps, as in the convergent UDC in Figure 5.26.

The key step occurs at the VP node, where the object-gapped verb *remind* combines with its object-gapped clausal complement, and $G = \langle NP_w \rangle = G_1 \otimes G_1$ is resolved such that $G_1 = \langle NP_w \rangle$ and $G_2 = \langle NP_w \rangle$.[13]

Gaps can be contributed by the ARG-ST of any word. In the convergent UDC in Figure 5.27, one gap is subject-internal and the other is object-internal. For more about how complex NPs are licensed, see §5.2.4.

Nothing requires convergent dependencies involving subject-embedded gaps to come from the same clause, and so patterns like (44) are predicted.

(44)   [Who]$_i$ did you say the criticism of __$_i$ would make us think __$_i$ was stupid?
       (Engdahl, 1983)

Nothing in the Head-Subject construction forces convergent UDCs, and therefore putative Subject Island violations like (45a–c) are allowed by the grammar, including double Subject Island violations like (45d).

---

[13] For an HPSG underspecification account of case syncretism in convergent UDCs like (i), see Levine et al. (2001). In a nutshell, Levine et al. propose that there are three kinds of structural case in English: nominative, structural accusative, and syncretic. With the exception of *whom*, all nominals are allowed to fall in any of these categories.

i   [Who] did the judge have to remind __$_{ACC}$__$_{NOM}$ was still under oath?

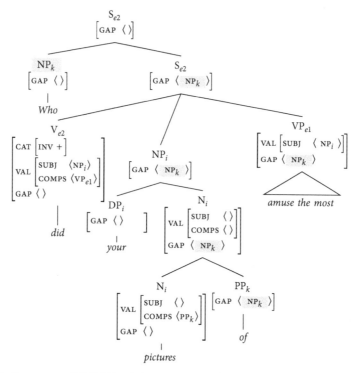

Figure 5.27 Convergent UDC *Who did your pictures of_ amuse_ the most?*

(45) a. [Which student]$_i$ are [the parents of _$_i$] picking up _$_i$ around noon?

    b. This is a man [who]$_i$ [[friends of _$_i$] think that [enemies of_$_i$] [are everywhere]].
(adapted from Culicover (2013, 161))

    c. [What]$_i$ did [[the attempt to find _$_i$] end in failure]?
(Hofmeister and Sag, 2010)

    d. This is something [which]$_i$ [[for you to try to understand _$_i$] would be futile].
(Kuno and Takami, 1993)

The Filler-Head construction does not prevent the filler phrase from itself hosting a gap, thus licensing chaining UDCs like the one in Figure 5.28. Here the filler *which document* is linked to a gap inside the second filler *how many copies of*, which is in turn linked to the object of the verb *print*. Ginzburg and Sag (2000, 174, n. 11), Bouma et al. (2001), and Levine and Hukari (2006, 94) assume that chaining constructions are ungrammatical in general, and therefore stipulate that filler phrases be specified as GAP ⟨ ⟩. But given examples like (46), discussed in §2.2.1.2, no such stipulation is required.

(46) a. This is the wine [which]$_i$ I can't remember [how many bottles of _$_i$] we decided to order _$_i$.

    b. This is the type of person [who]$_i$ [even the seemingly good advice of_$_i$]$_j$ I would not trust _$_j$.

    c. This is an animal [which]$_i$ – [for us to STUDY _$_i$ up close]$_j$ – we would need MONTHS of planning _$_j$.

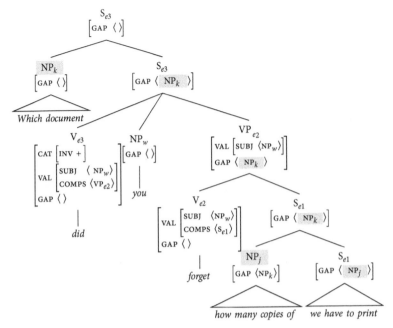

Figure 5.28 Chaining UDC *Which document did you forget how many copies of_ we have to print_?*

Under the assumption that post-verbal adverbs are (optional) members of ARG-ST, as discussed in §2.2.1, it follows that the Argument Realization Construction allows them to appear in COMPS or GAP. If they appear in GAP, then extractions like (47) are licensed.[14]

(47) a. [YESTERDAY]$_i$ it seems that [Kim arrived home very early $_{\_i}$].

   b. [How often]$_i$ do you think that [Fred was late this week $_{\_i}$]?

   c. [Without reading these books]$_i$ I don't think I would have passed this course $_{\_i}$.

As such, convergent UDCs like the one in Figure 5.29 are obtained in exactly the same way as convergent UDCs involving canonical complements. Here, one gap corresponds to the object of *sign* and the other corresponds to the object of *reading*, inside an oblique complement.

No special GAP constraints are imposed on such adverbials by the grammar, and therefore extractions like (48a,b) are allowed, as are overlapping UDCs like (48c), and convergent UDCs like (48d).

(48) a. [Who]$_i$ does Robin claim that Sandy sang a song [for $_{\_i}$]?
   (Bouma et al., 2001)

   b. This is the watch$_i$ that I got upset [when I lost $_{\_}$].
   (attributed to Ivan A. Sag (pers. comm.) in Truswell (2011, 175, n. 1))

---

[14] This assumption also dispenses with special augmentation rules like those of Manning et al. (1999) or Bouma et al. (2001).

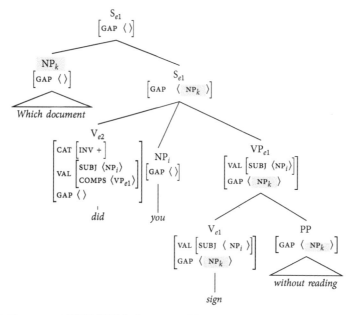

Figure 5.29 Convergent UDC *Which document did you sign___ without reading___?*

   c. [A project THIS COMPLEX]$_i$, [how much time]$_j$ would you spend $\_\_j$ on $\_\_i$ before finishing $\_\_i$?
   (Chaves, 2012b)

   d. [Which AC unit]$_i$ did you drive Ed crazy [complaining about $\_\_i$] yesterday [after buying $\_\_i$ from Craigslist]?

The quintessential construction that allows multiple gaps is the coordination construction, formalized in (49). This rule combines any number of phrases with the same VAL specifications into a single phrase. Thus, VPs coordinate with VPs, Ss coordinate with Ss, NPs coordinate with NPs, and so on, for all categories, lexical or otherwise. Crucially, the construction imposes the usual '$\otimes$' constraints on GAP lists (Chaves, 2012b).

(49) COORDINATION CX

$$
\begin{bmatrix} \text{CAT } X \\ \text{VAL } Y \\ \text{GAP } G_1 \otimes \ldots \otimes G_n \end{bmatrix} \rightarrow \begin{bmatrix} \text{CAT } X \\ \text{VAL } Y \\ \text{GAP } G_1 \end{bmatrix} \ldots \begin{bmatrix} \text{CAT } X \\ \text{VAL } Y \\ \text{GAP } G_{n-1} \end{bmatrix} \text{COORD} \begin{bmatrix} \text{CAT } X \\ \text{VAL } Y \\ \text{GAP } G_n \end{bmatrix}
$$

This rule's effect is illustrated in Figure 5.30. The key juncture for GAP is at the S coordination node, where a subject-gapped clause is conjoined with another subject-gapped clause and their gaps are unioned by '$\otimes$'. Thus, $G = \langle \text{NP}_i \rangle = G_1 \otimes G_2$ at the S_{e_3} node is resolved as $\langle \text{NP}_i \rangle \otimes \langle \text{NP}_i \rangle$.

Like many of the constructions discussed so far, (49) should be regarded as a schematic abbreviation of various types of coordination construction. This is because some coordination constructions impose peculiar prosodic, syntactic, semantic, and/or pragmatic constraints, as (50) illustrates. See also §3.2.5 for coordination constructions in which a conjunct describes the main action, while the other(s) describe(s) secondary or preparatory action(s).

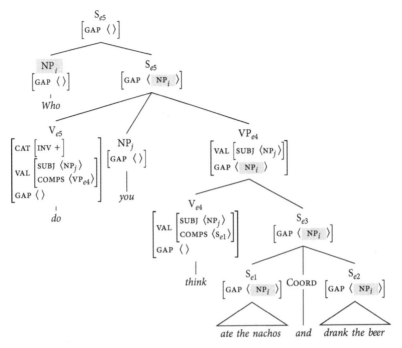

Figure 5.30 Convergent UDC *Who do you think __ ate the nachos and __ drank the beer?*

(50) a. [Open the windows↑ and the wasp will fly away↓].
(Conditional coordination)

b. We [washed the windows, cleaned the counters, dusted the shelves . . .] we did everything.
(Enumerative coordination)

c. We [pushed it and pushed it and pushed it] until it finally cracked open!
(Intensification conjunction)

d. The North Koreans were developing nuclear weapons anyway, [Iraq war or no Iraq war].
(Negative reduplicative disjunction)

As discussed in §3.2.5, it is up to pragmatics to impose constraints on the GAP values in coordination, not syntax (Kehler, 2002; Chaves, 2012b; Kubota and Lee, 2015). The Element Constraint and its symmetric and asymmetric exceptions are governed by discourse coherence constraints between the conjuncts. Thus, if coordination is interpreted symmetrically, then we obtain converged ATB extraction (i.e. all conjuncts have the same non-empty GAP specification); if interpreted asymmetrically, then the conjunct that expresses the preparatory action need not have a gap, as (51) illustrates. Of course, this means that asymmetric coordinations can involve multiple filler-gap dependencies, either convergent (52a) or overlapping (52b), repeated from §3.2.5.

(51) a. Here's the whiskey [which]$_i$ I [went to the store and bought __$_i$].
b. [How much]$_i$ can you [drink __$_i$ and still stay sober]?

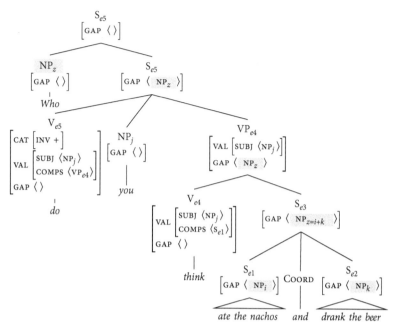

Figure 5.31 Cumulative UDC *Who do you think_ ate the nachos and_ drank the beer?*

(52) a. [What]$_i$ did Harry buy _$_i$, come home, and devour _$_i$ in thirty seconds?

   b. [A bird THIS RARE]$_i$ – [how many years]$_i$ could someone spend _$_j$ and never actually see_$_i$?

Finally, cumulative interpretations arise from list-join resolutions at the coordination phrase where different indices form a plurality. More specifically, $G = \langle NP_z \rangle = G_1 \otimes G_2$ at the S_{e_3} node is resolved as $\langle NP_i \rangle \otimes \langle NP_j \rangle$, where $i \neq j$, and therefore $z = i + j$ forms a plurality. This is illustrated in Figure 5.31. Although such cumulative readings are in principle possible in any convergent UDC discussed so far, it so happens that these are more easily elicited in coordinate structures, perhaps because of the parallelism constraints associated with symmetric coordination.

5.2.3.2 Missing object constructions
In MOCs, the index of a gap in the infinitival VP is co-indexed to the index of the subject of the clause, not to a filler. Since only the index is shared, the morphosyntactic features of the gap and the respective antecedent need not match. Thus, object gaps can be co-indexed with the subject, as in (53).

(53) Alex$_i$ is difficult [(for anyone) to please _$_i$].

In what follows we depart from standard HPSG in particular aspects, and describe an account that is more in line with Gazdar's analysis. The lexical entry for adjectives like *easy* can be assumed to be underspecified, as shown in (54). The adjective selects an infinitival phrase, and binds the latter's external argument to the experiencer role introduced by the adjective. According to Levine (2001b), the infinitival phrase is a clause. In cases where only a VP is overt, as in *Kim is easy to please*, the VP can be assumed to have been coerced to an S which has a generically quantified subject referent.

(54) $$\begin{bmatrix} word \\ \text{PHON } \langle IZI \rangle \\ \text{CAT } adj \\ \text{VAL} \begin{bmatrix} \text{SUBJ } \langle XP \rangle \\ \text{COMPS} \left\langle \begin{bmatrix} \text{CAT} \begin{bmatrix} verb \\ \text{XARG } j \\ \text{FORM } inf \end{bmatrix} \\ \text{VAL} \begin{bmatrix} \text{SUBJ } \langle \rangle \\ \text{COMPS } \langle \rangle \end{bmatrix} \end{bmatrix} \right\rangle \end{bmatrix} \\ \text{SEM} \begin{bmatrix} \text{INDEX } e \\ \text{RESTR} \left\langle \begin{bmatrix} easy \\ \text{SIT } \quad e \\ \text{EXPR } j \end{bmatrix} \right\rangle \end{bmatrix} \end{bmatrix}$$

The (E)X(TERNAL-)ARG(UMENT) *j* of the verbal complement is co-indexed with an experiencer role. The feature XARG of a verb is assumed to always be co-indexed with that sign's subject, in order to allow the grammar rules access to the subject of a clause. This is used to model tag questions (cf. *Sarah$_i$ read the book$_j$, didn't she$_i$/*it$_i$?* with *The book$_j$ was read by Sarah$_i$, wasn't it$_j$/*she$_i$*), dangling modifiers (cf. *Furious$_i$, the woman$_i$ threw the TV out the window* with **Furious$_i$, the TV was thrown out the window by the woman$_i$*. For more on XARG, see Sag and Pollard (1991), Bender and Flickinger (1999), Meurers (1999), and Boas and Sag (2012).

If the adjective is instantiated with the MOC construction in (55), then the infinitival complement must contain at least one gap and that gap must be co-indexed with the adjectives' subject, as in Gazdar (1981). This construction also prevents the gap that is linked to the subject from being present in the mother node's GAP value. Further semantic constraints must be added to (55), so that only the right kind of adjective is allowed in the rule, e.g. the adjective must assign no thematic role to *i*, and so that the index of the gap is the (local) Topic relative to the infinitival (Mair, 1990, 72).

(55)   ADJECTIVEMOC CONSTRUCTION

$$\begin{bmatrix} \text{CAT } Y \\ \text{VAL } K \\ \text{GAP } G_1 \otimes G_2 \\ \text{SEM } \begin{bmatrix} \text{INDEX } e \end{bmatrix} \end{bmatrix} \rightarrow \begin{bmatrix} \text{CAT } Y{:}adj \\ \text{VAL } K{:} \begin{bmatrix} \text{SUBJ } \langle XP_i \rangle \\ \text{COMPS } \langle K \rangle \end{bmatrix} \\ \text{GAP } G_1 \\ \text{SEM } \begin{bmatrix} \text{INDEX } e \end{bmatrix} \end{bmatrix} \quad K{:} \begin{bmatrix} \text{CAT} \begin{bmatrix} verb \\ \text{FORM } inf \end{bmatrix} \\ \text{VAL } \begin{bmatrix} \text{COMPS } \langle \rangle \end{bmatrix} \\ \text{GAP } \langle XP_i \rangle \bigcirc G_2 \end{bmatrix}$$

In Figure 5.32, the adjective combines with a gapped verbal complement, and co-indexes that gap with the adjective's subject. The raising verb *is* co-indexes its subject to the NP in its complements' SUBJ list.

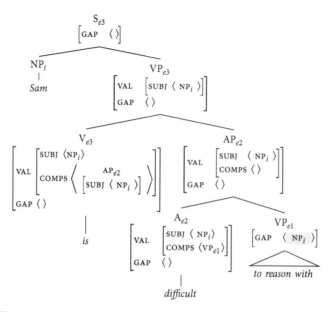

Figure 5.32 A Missing Object UDC *Sam is difficult to reason with___.*

Examples like (56a) are illicit because the infinitival phrase is gapless, and (56b) is illicit because the gap has propagated beyond the adjectival phrase node, which (55) expressly forbids. Finally, (56c) is possible because the gap that is linked to the subject is independent from the gap that is linked to the higher filler phrase.

(56) a. *Kim is easy to talk to him.
      b. *[Who]$_i$ did you say Sam is difficult to reason with___$_i$?
      c. Who$_j$ did you say Sam$_i$ is difficult to compare___$_i$ with___$_j$?

Since the GAP value of the adjective and the gap value of the infinitival are list-unioned, then cases like (57) are captured. See §2.1.3.5 for many other examples, all of which are accounted for by the present grammar fragment.

(57) [Who]$_i$ did you find [the stories about___$_i$]$_j$ difficult to believe___$_j$?

If, instead, the adjective in (54) is instantiated in a construction which requires that the adjective's SUBJ value be an expletive *it*, and simply list-joins the GAP values of the daughters, then the counterpart in (58a) is obtained. UDCs are still possible, of course, but they exhibit a canonical UDC behavior, as seen in (58b, c).

(58) a. It is easy to talk to Kim.
      b. [Who]$_i$ did you say it is easy to talk to___$_i$?
      c. *It is easy to talk to___.

5.2.4 Predicted island effects

The construction-based approach to UDCs described in this chapter does not prevent extraction from subjects or complements in any way. This is a welcome state of affairs according to the survey in §3.2, given that the island effects associated with such syntactic environments are often graded, sensitive to small changes in wording, prone to contextualization effects, and sometimes attenuated by repeated exposure. Thus, any acceptability differences between very deep NP Constraint or Subject Island violations like (59a, b) come from non-syntactic factors, including the likelihood of the particular pragmatic interpretation that is required of the filler and its open proposition, how easy it is to process the utterance, the frequency of the structures involved, and the prosodic phrasing (e.g. whether the phrasing is natural and cues the gap via a pause), as detailed in Chapter 3.

(59)   a. [Which US president]$_i$ did you say you were thinking of writing [a book about the impeachment of _$_i$]?

   b. I have a question [which]$_i$ [the probability of you knowing the answer to _$_i$] is ZERO.
   (Chaves, 2013)

That said, the present theory makes various predictions about what can and cannot be extracted, without the need for stipulating filtering constraints of any kind. To our knowledge, none of the following island phenomena has known exceptions, or is susceptible to contextualization or habituation effects of any kind, which suggests that they are syntactic in nature. For example, according to the Coordination Construction in (42), words like *and* are not heads and therefore do not select any arguments. Rather, they are markers (Borsley, 1994; Bouma et al., 2001; Borsley, 2005; Chaves, 2007). Thus, if *and* combines with NPs, the result is a coordinate NP; if *and* combines with VPs, the result is a coordinate VP, and so on. But since only elements of ARG-ST can be extracted, as per the Argument Realization construction, the present account predicts the Element Constraint discussed in §3.2, illustrated again in (60). Thus, conjuncts in general cannot be extracted.

(60)   a. *[Who]$_i$ did you see Robin and _$_i$ yesterday?
   b. *[AND ROBIN] I think I saw Alex _$_i$.
   c. *[Who]$_i$ did you see [_$_i$ and Robin] yesterday?
   d. *[Which of her books] did you find both [a review of _$_i$ and _$_i$]?
   e. *[Which of her books] did you find [_$_i$ and a review of _$_i$]?

In practice, this is a syntactic account of the Conjunct Constraint, but in a sense, the phenomenon is ultimately semantic rather than syntactic. It is the notion of semantic argument that is key in determining whether something is a syntactic argument or not. The same is true for all other island phenomena discussed in the remainder of this section.

   For example, another UDC constraint that is predicted in exactly the same way as the Conjunct Constraint is the Left Branch Condition and some other related constraints: determiners are not arguments of nominal heads in any way, and therefore are not listed in the ARG-ST of the nominal heads. Consider, for example, the lexical entry of the determiner *these* in (61).

(61)

$$
\begin{bmatrix}
word \\
\text{PHON} & \langle \partial \text{IZ} \rangle \\
\text{CAT} & \begin{bmatrix} det \\ \text{AGR} & \begin{bmatrix} \text{NUM} & pl \\ \text{PER} & 3rd \end{bmatrix} \end{bmatrix} \\
\text{VAL} & \begin{bmatrix} \text{SUBJ} & \langle \, \rangle \\ \text{COMPS} & \langle \, \rangle \end{bmatrix} \\
\text{GAP} & \langle \, \rangle \\
\text{SEM} & \begin{bmatrix} \text{INDEX} & i \\ \text{RESTR} & \left\langle \begin{bmatrix} these \\ \text{BV} & i \end{bmatrix} \right\rangle \end{bmatrix} \\
\text{ARG-ST} & \langle \, \rangle
\end{bmatrix}
$$

Following Fillmore and Kay (1996) and Bergen and Chang (2005), the Determination Construction rule in (62) allows determiners to combine with nominal heads. The agreement information must be unified between the determiner and the nominal head, and the quantifier expressed by the determiner binds the nominal index. For arguments in favor of the NP analysis and against the DP analysis, see Van Eynde (2006).

(62) DETERMINATION Cx

$$
\begin{bmatrix}
phrase \\
\text{CAT } X \\
\text{VAL } Y \\
\text{SEM} \begin{bmatrix} \text{INDEX } x \end{bmatrix}
\end{bmatrix}
\rightarrow
\begin{bmatrix}
\text{CAT} \begin{bmatrix} det \\ \text{AGR } K \end{bmatrix} \\
\text{SEM} \begin{bmatrix} \text{INDEX } x \end{bmatrix}
\end{bmatrix}
\begin{bmatrix}
\text{CAT } X : \begin{bmatrix} noun \\ \text{AGR } K \end{bmatrix} \\
\text{VAL } Y : \begin{bmatrix} \text{SUBJ} & \langle \, \rangle \\ \text{COMPS} & \langle \, \rangle \end{bmatrix} \\
\text{SEM} \begin{bmatrix} \text{INDEX } x \end{bmatrix}
\end{bmatrix}
$$

The determiner is not a member of the nominal's ARG-ST, as in Sag (2012), since there is no semantic sense in which the determiner is an argument of the nominal head. Rather, the function of the determiner is to add information about the nominal head, such as quantificational information. The effect of this construction is illustrated in Figure 5.33. The symbol 'N' abbreviates a nominal expression with empty valence that is not yet quantificationally bound, and 'NP' abbreviates a nominal with empty valence and a quantificationally bound index.

Figure 5.33 Noun phrase *these cats*

The function of a determiner is to characterize the reference of a nominal head. They are not predicates that assign a thematic role of any kind. Consequently, determiners' ARG-ST lists are always empty, and so are their VAL and GAP lists. This in turn means that the nominal head is not a member of the ARG-ST of the determiner and therefore cannot be extracted:

(63)   a.   *[MUSIC]$_i$ I don't think I heard [the _$_i$].
     b.   *[What]$_i$ did you say you heard [my_$_i$]?

Analogously, the ARG-ST list of the N head does not list the DP as an argument, as it too is not a thematic argument of the nominal head. Therefore, DPs do not appear in the ARG-ST of the nominal, and thus cannot appear in GAP either, predicting Left Branch Condition effects:

(64)   a.   *[HER]$_i$ I don't think you liked [_$_i$ book].
     b.   *[MIA's]$_i$ I don't think you liked [_$_i$ book].
     c.   *[Whose]$_i$ did you say you liked [_$_i$ book]?

Possessive determiner phrases like *Kim's* in (65) are obtained by a unary-branching construction that adds the possessive clitic *s* to an NP to yield a DP (Sag, 2012, 131–3). Again, the relation between the DP and the nominal head it attaches to is not a predicate-argument relation of any kind, and therefore the possessive NP is not extractable:[15]

(65)   a.   You saw [[Kim's] car].
     b.   *[KIM's]$_i$ you saw_$_i$ car.
     c.   *[Whose]$_i$ did you see_$_i$ car?

The extraction of modifiers (as opposed to optional non-core complements) is impossible because these are by definition not arguments of any head. Therefore, they are not listed in any head's ARG-ST, and consequently cannot appear in any head's VAL or GAP list. Modifiers in general select the heads they attach to via a feature MOD(IFIED) rather than via VAL. The latter is reserved for arguments of the modifier, if any. This analysis is illustrated in the lexical entry of the adjective *old*.

(66)
$$
\begin{bmatrix}
word \\
\text{PHON} & \langle old \rangle \\
\text{CAT} & \begin{bmatrix} adj \\ \text{MOD } N_i \end{bmatrix} \\
\text{VAL} & \langle \rangle \\
\text{GAP} & \langle \rangle \\
\text{SEM} & \begin{bmatrix} \text{INDEX} & e \\ \text{RESTR} & \left\langle \begin{bmatrix} old \\ \text{SIT} & e \\ \text{THEME} & i \end{bmatrix} \right\rangle \end{bmatrix} \\
\text{ARG-ST} & \langle \rangle
\end{bmatrix}
$$

The feature MOD thus allows modifiers to impose constraints on the head they adjoin. Thus, adnominal adjectives can select N nodes, some adverbial modifiers select verbal phrases, others select adjectival phrases, and so on. The relevant adjunction rule is shown in (67). Here, the first daughter is the modifier that selects the head *X* sister.

---

[15] In the case of French *combien*, which can be extracted, as discussed in §3.2.12, we assume that it corresponds to an implicitly quantified nominal that is selected as a specifier by *de*, and therefore is a member of ARG-ST and can be extracted. For an account along these lines, see Abeillé et al. (2004).

(67)   HEAD-MODIFIER CX

$$\begin{bmatrix} phrase \\ \text{CAT} & K \\ \text{GAP} & G_1 \otimes G_2 \\ \text{SEM} & [\text{INDEX } v] \end{bmatrix} \rightarrow \begin{bmatrix} \text{CAT} & [\text{MOD } X] \\ \text{VAL} & \begin{bmatrix} \text{SUBJ} \langle \rangle \\ \text{COMPS} \langle \rangle \end{bmatrix} \\ \text{GAP} & G_2 \end{bmatrix} \quad X: \begin{bmatrix} \text{CAT} & K \\ \text{GAP} & G_1 \\ \text{SEM} & [\text{INDEX } v] \end{bmatrix}$$

The effect of this rule is illustrated in Figure 5.34. Note that the second daughter is the modified head, and therefore its CAT information remains unchanged in the mother node.[16]

Figure 5.34 Nominal phrase *old tree*

As a consequence of the fact that modified heads are not thematic arguments of the modifier, as in (68), their extraction is impossible, since only members of ARG-ST are generally allowed in GAP.

(68)   *[What]$_i$ do you think old $\_\_i$ were cut down?
       (cf. *Do you think old trees were cut down?*)

And, because the adjective is not a thematic predicate of the nominal either, it likewise cannot be extracted, as (69) illustrates. Again, this is because only members of ARG-ST are generally allowed in GAP. Exactly the same explanation applies to the impossibility of extracting preverbal adverbials (Bouma et al., 2001).

(69)   *[How old] did you see the $\_\_i$ trees?
       (cf. *Did you see the very old trees?*)

This does not mean that adjectives and adverbs can never be extracted, of course. When they appear as complements, then they are extractable. For example, linking verbs select predicative phrases as complements (including adjectives); such predicative phrases are members of ARG-ST, and as such can be mapped into VAL features or into GAP. Thus, predicative phrases are usually extractable, as (70) shows. For more details on the syntax and semantics of linking verbs, see Van Eynde (2015).

(70)   a.   Do you think the trees were old?
       b.   [How old] do you think the trees were $\_\_i$?

The adverbial Left Branch violation in (71a) is predicted in exactly the same way. By itself, the adverb *right* is not the argument of any head. Rather, the adverb *right* modifies a PP

[16] Sag (2012) follows Van Eynde (2003) in collapsing (62) and (67) into the same rule. Though this is descriptively appealing, it causes the rule to be more abstract and arguably harder for learners to acquire. To remain as close as possible to the spirit of Gazdar (1981), we follow earlier versions of HPSG like that in Pollard and Sag (1994)—and other traditions of construction-based grammar, like those given in Fillmore and Kay (1996) and Bergen and Chang (2005)—in keeping the two rules separate.

head, and the resulting phrase is an optional locative argument of the main verb. Thus, the PP cannot be extracted, as in (71b), because it is not a complement of the adverb, but the entire phrase can be extracted, as in (71c).

(71)   a. * ... and [RIGHT]$_i$ it plunged __$_i$ into the water.
      b. * ... and [INTO THE WATER]$_i$ it plunged right __$_i$.
      c. ... and [RIGHT into the water]$_i$ it plunged __$_i$.

Since only ARG-ST elements can be extracted, it is also impossible to extract the clausal sister of a complementizer, as in (72), assuming that complementizers are markers rather than heads (Pollard and Sag, 1994). Similarly, preposition stranding is (perhaps) not possible in most languages of the world because such prepositions are markers, not heads, and therefore combine with NPs rather as conjunctions combine with conjuncts, and complementizers combine with clauses.

(72)   *[This was ILLEGAL]$_i$, I had no idea that __$_i$.
      (cf. [*That this was illegal*]$_i$, I had no idea __$_i$)

5.3 Models of processing

Declarative feature- and construction-based grammars like the one presented in this chapter make no assumptions about how derivations are constructed. Consequently, such models are more consistent with incremental and probabilistic models of sentence comprehension and production than movement-based approaches (Sag, 1992; Sag and Wasow, 2011, 2015). For example, Konieczny (1996) proposes a model of human language processing that combines HPSG with a parser that can model preferential head attachment bias. More recently, Bergen and Chang (2005) integrate Embodied Construction Grammar (a close feature- and unification-based variant of HPSG/SBCG) with a simulation-based model of language understanding. Another example is Bryant (2008), where a psychologically plausible best-fit probabilistic construction-based model of parsing and interpretation is proposed, which aligns well with behavioral sentence-processing data. Finally, see Mellow (2004) for a connectionist reconceptualization of HPSG in order to model language acquisition phenomena.

Modern and large-scale computational implementations of HPSG are coupled with Maximum Entropy models (Abney, 1997; Toutanova et al., 2005; Miyao and Tsujii, 2005, 2008; Nakanishi et al., 2005; Zhang and Kordoni, 2008; Ytrestøl, 2011; Zhang and Krieger, 2011), enabling not only efficient and robust state-of-the-art parsing and generation for large-scale grammars, but also the modeling of frequency effects in incremental sentence processing. To illustrate, let s be a sentence with possible parses $t_1 \ldots t_n$. The conditional probability for a given parse t_i is given by:

$$(73) \quad P(t_i|s) = \frac{exp \sum_{j=1,\ldots,m} f_j(t_i)\lambda_j}{\sum_{i'=1,\ldots,k} exp \sum_{j=1,\ldots,m} f_j(t_{i'})\lambda_j}$$

where $f_1, \ldots, f_n$ are features over analyses and $\lambda_i, \ldots, \lambda_j$ are their corresponding weights. A given feature f can be, for example, a particular arrangement of categorical and agreement information across the mother and the head daughter. Such models are trained with HPSG treebanks like the Redwoods Treebank (Oepen et al., 2004) and others, by maximizing the conditional likelihood of the preferred analyses and using a Gaussian prior for smoothing. In particular, the objective being maximized is:

$$(74) \quad L(D, \Lambda) = \sum_{i=1,\ldots,n} log(P(t_1|s_i)) - \frac{1}{2\sigma^2} \sum_{j=1,\ldots,m} \lambda_j^2$$

D is the training data set, i ranges over all sentences, t_i is the correct analysis for a sentence, and σ is the standard deviation of the Gaussian prior. The point is that such models are compatible with incremental probabilistic modeling, and efficient large-scale language processing, which makes for an easier bridging between the computational, algorithmic, and implementation levels, using Marr's terminology. Although the PSG backbone of HPSG is strictly more expressive than a classic CFG, it can be efficiently parsed, at scale, with basically the same algorithms that parse CFGs, since they can be applied bottom-up or top-down, or some combination thereof, depending on the parsing strategy that the grammar rules are coupled with. See also the DELPH-IN consortium at http://www.delph-in.net/wiki/index.php/Home for large grammars for various languages, and the PET system at http://pet.opendfki.de/ for state-of-the-art HPSG parsing.

In Chapter 7 we describe how the grammar fragment discussed so far can be recast in terms of an exemplar-based model which can explain the island phenomena discussed in Chapter 6. In a nutshell, we will reconceptualize the grammar in terms of a collection of chunks of varying complexity, containing phonological, morphosyntactic, semantic, and pragmatic constraints. Thus, we arrive at an incremental grammar model where the processing of UDCs is distributed and sensitive to fine-grained probabilistic expectations about the propagation of filler-gap information.

5.4 Summary

Gazdar (1981) and its more modern kin provide a better handle of UDC phenomena than the MP, not only from a linguistic perspective, but also from a psycholinguistic point of view. The flexibility offered by non-movement-based accounts allows a much wider and much more complex array of unbounded dependency patterns because it rejects the basic idea that extracted phrases start out embedded in sentence structure, and instead views the propagation of UDC information in sentence structure as a local and distributed process.

A broad range of convergent, cumulative, overlapping, and chaining dependencies are allowed, and a broad range of dependents are considered to be extractable arguments. This predicts various kinds of island phenomena, such as the unextractability of (true) adjuncts, as well as the Left Branch Condition, and the Conjunct Constraint, among others. In a sense, such islands are semantic rather than syntactic, since it is the notion of semantic argument that is key in determining whether something is a syntactic argument or not. This contrasts with movement-based explanations of UDCs, which traditionally impose a series of additional constraints and filters to handle island effects. As we have seen, purely structural constraints fail to capture the full range of empirical facts.

The grammatical theory discussed in this chapter is also more consistent with extant models of human language processing than the MP, and demonstrably allows for incremental and probabilistic language comprehension and production. Moreover, as we shall see in §7.2, the present model also allows for a more usage-based conception of the grammar, whereby frequent chunks are stored in memory, form clusters, and are profitably used during language processing to make predictions about upcoming linguistic information.

6
Experience-based effects

In Chapter 3 we discussed multiple grammatical and extra-grammatical factors that affect the processing and acceptability of UDCs, and argued that different types of island phenomena are due to different arrangements of such factors. This interpretation of the linguistic and behavioral evidence explains why some island effects are stronger than others, across and within UDC types. For example, whereas the Left Branch Condition and the Conjunct Constraint are absolute and due to the syntactic mechanism responsible for extraction, Negative Islands and Factive Islands have principled exceptions and are plausibly due to semantic-pragmatic conflicts. In contrast, the largest group of island phenomena—which we refer to as Relevance Islands—was argued to result from the violation of a general semantic-pragmatic constraint that all UDCs are required to satisfy.

Drawing from Erteschik-Shir and Lappin (1979), Reinhart (1981), Lakoff (1986), Kuno (1987), Deane (1991), and Van Valin (2005, 288), we proposed that the only constraint that is common to all UDCs boils down to a general Gricean Relevance presupposition: speakers can felicitously draw attention to a referent by using a non-canonical construction such as a UDC only if the referent is sufficiently relevant to the main action that the utterance describes, i.e. if the referent is taken to be the center of current interest relative to the proposition in which it occurs. This raises the following question: what does it mean for a referent to be relevant relative to a proposition? We believe that Deane (1991) was on the right track in proposing that the answer to this question is intimately tied to world knowledge and to how linguistic and non-linguistic experience shape the mental representation of situations and relations between situations.

The Relevance constraint, which we assume governs the pragmatic well-formedness of UDCs, ultimately comes from experience: which predicates come with which event participants in particular situation types. As we shall see, the range of participants that a given situation evokes can be quite large, because complex situations can be **chunked**, if they are useful enough (see Chapter 7 for more about chunking), or at the very least be highly associated to each other. As a consequence, some islands vanish because the situation that is described is prototypical enough to be regarded as a complex unit. In the present account, experience will play two very different and important roles in the acceptability of extraction, one more syntactic, and the other more semantic:

- Syntactically, more commonly occurring structures are easier to process and predict, as opposed to those where a gap site would be unusual. If the frequency of such structures increases, however, speakers can adapt, provided that no other sources of difficulty or anomaly interfere.
- Semantically, sentences are more acceptable if they express more likely situations according to the speaker's world-knowledge experience, which means that the entities referenced in the proposition must be highly plausible participants in the overall scene that the utterance describes.

Unbounded Dependency Constructions: Theoretical and Experimental Perspectives. Rui P. Chaves and Michael T. Putnam, Oxford University Press (2020). © Rui P. Chaves and Michael T. Putnam.
DOI: 10.1093/oso/9780198784999.001.0001

Thus, the more collocational a structure is, the more coherent the referents therein must be semantically, and therefore the easier it is for extraction to take place from an otherwise deeply embedded position. In §7.2 we will describe an exemplar-based reconceptualization of construction grammar which is consistent with the present experience-driven effects.

6.1 Setting the stage

The conventionalized world knowledge that is evoked during sentence processing is referred to as a **frame** (Goffman, 1974; Minsky, 1975; Fillmore, 1977, 1982; Langacker, 1987), but sometimes goes by other names in different branches of cognitive science, such as schemas (Barlett, 1932; Rumelhart, 1975), idealized cognitive models (Lakoff, 1987), scripts (Schank and Abelson, 1977), and scenarios (Sanford and Garrod, 1981, 1998). It is now clear that general encyclopedic knowledge about events is activated during language processing, and likely drives the generation of linguistic expectations (Metusalem et al., 2012). For example, the meaning of the word *sell* cannot be understood without knowing about the situation of commercial transfer, which involves not only a seller, a buyer, goods, money, but also the relations between the money, the goods, the seller, and the buyer. This is what allows the two sentences in (1) to be interpreted in a coherent way. Comprehenders familiar with this kind of situation readily recognize that the subject of the second clause is the seller and the dollar amount is the money that the speaker paid for the portrait.

(1)   I bought this portrait at a garage sale. The guy was quite happy with $1, can you believe that?

Another example is (2), where the word *married* evokes knowledge about spouses and thus Fred can easily be integrated into the situation that the first sentence evokes.

(2)   Sue got married last week. Fred is such a lucky guy.

The intra-clausal resolution of referential dependencies as a function of discourse relations is sometimes referred to as **bridging**. See Asher and Lascarides (2003) for a detailed discussion and formalization. The main action described by the first sentence is that Sue got married in the previous week (and in a given location and manner, and for a certain reason), which, using the FrameNet-based semantic representation adopted in §5.2, would be as shown in (3). The second clause is felicitous because Fred can be understood as the theme j of *married*, in which case the speaker is expressing supplemental information about Sue and her marriage.

(3)
$$
\begin{bmatrix}
\text{INDEX } e \\[2pt]
\text{RESTR} \left\langle
\begin{bmatrix} name \\ \text{NAMED} \quad Sue \\ \text{ENTITY} \quad i \end{bmatrix},
\begin{bmatrix} marry \\ \text{SIT} \quad e \\ \text{ACTOR } i \\ \text{THEME } j \end{bmatrix},
\begin{bmatrix} manner \\ \text{FORM } n \\ \text{SIT} \quad e \end{bmatrix},
\begin{bmatrix} reason \\ \text{CAUSE } r \\ \text{SIT} \quad e \end{bmatrix},
\begin{bmatrix} space \\ \text{LOC } l \\ \text{SIT } e \end{bmatrix},
\begin{bmatrix} time \\ \text{PAST } t \\ \text{SIT } e \end{bmatrix},
\begin{bmatrix} last\text{-}week \\ \text{TIME } t \end{bmatrix}
\right\rangle
\end{bmatrix}
$$

The same phenomenon is seen in (4). Here, the first sentence evokes knowledge that people pay rent to live in buildings, and the second sentence can therefore easily instantiate further information already implicitly salient. In this case, the second sentence explains why John decided to move.

(4)   John moved from Manhattan to the Bronx. The rent was less expensive.

Thus, frame knowledge does not exist in a vacuum, as there are complex relations between frames that allow speakers to understand how different utterances cohere with each other. Moreover, some constructions come with pragmatic constraints which further restrict how different entities can be linked to each other in a given situation. For example, the acceptability of (5) from §3.2 results from the fact that books contain information, and that information is usually coherently organized around a topic. Furthermore, people read books because of their content, and a famous historical figure is a plausible topic for a book. For all these reasons, (5) is felicitous.

(5)   Speaking of Napoleon, I just read a book about him.

The fact that people read books because of their topics is not strictly part of the semantics of *read*, but rather, part of world knowledge. In the seminal framework laid out by Hobbs (1979) the mechanism that links two states of affairs is a form of abduction over world knowledge along with a specialized set of coherence relations. For our purposes it suffices to assume that if the verb *read* is activated, then it follows that a theme expressing a source of information is also activated, along with the topic of that information.

   Examples like (6) are less felicitous because the verb *drop* evokes a theme denoting some physical object, but does not evoke any information source, like a book, and consequently no information topic. Hence, it is unclear in what sense Napoleon has anything to do with the main action expressed by the proposition, i.e. that a book was dropped. The content of the book and its topic is irrelevant, unless the discourse context can contribute the relevant information, as noted by Kuno (1987).

(6)   ?Speaking of Napoleon, I just dropped a book about him.

We note, however, that the linkage between the nominal in the preposed phrase and the subsequent proposition need not be direct in *speaking of* constructions. It is possible for an intermediate discourse relation to bridge the reference to Napoleon and the matrix clause. This is the case in (7), which is felicitous in a context where Robin needs to discuss a pressing matter with Sam.

(7)   Speaking of Robin, has Sam arrived yet?

It is not our goal to formalize how world knowledge interacts with linguistic meaning.[1] Our purpose is simply to point out that there is ample empirical and experimental motivation for background world knowledge playing a critical role in sentence processing, which leads us to make the following conjecture:

---

[1] For a computational model of discourse comprehension based on coherence and world knowledge, see Hobbs et al. (1993), and see Asher and Lascarides (2003) for a formalized and broader-scale theory of discourse based on Hobbs work. For a more experimental perspective of this kind of phenomenon, we refer the reader to Kehler et al. (2008).

EVENT PARTICIPANT SALIENCE CONDITION: event participants that are part of the conventionalized world knowledge directly or indirectly evoked by the main action that the
sentence describes are salient and, by definition, relevant for the utterance (though not
necessarily equally relevant).

In other words, the event participants evoked by the background frame are all salient and
relevant for discourse. Thus, the arguments of a verb (core or non-core) are by definition
relevant to what the verb describes. For example, the main action expressed by (8a) is a
talking event, which evokes a talker, a hearer, a topic of information, a location, a duration,
etc. In the case of (8a) the hearer and the location are not overtly realized, for example, but
subsequent discourse can supply further information about them. In (8b) the finite verb
is semantically light, and does not evoke any significant background frame information.
Rather, it is still the verb *talked* that describes the main action and evokes the relevant
background knowledge, just as in (8a)

(8) a. Mia talked about Alex all night.
     b. Mia had talked about Alex.

This is not to say that all event participants are equally relevant for the action that the verb
evokes. For example, agents are by default more relevant than patients, and patients are
more relevant than non-core event components such as manner, location, and time. After
all, agents are the ones that control or initiate the action, and thus cannot easily be deemed
irrelevant for what the sentence describes.[2] Language also has specific means for signaling
low relevance of an agent, such as the passive voice or the middle voice. Thus, if a referent
is not part of the frame evoked by the main action, its very mention is not felicitous:

(9) ?Fred bought a book online near a chair.

Nothing in the grammar of English prevents a locative PP like *near a chair* from combining
with a verb phrase, and yet the particular combination in (9) is odd. This is simply
because there is no obvious reason why the mention of the location is noteworthy. In
other words, there is no typical situation that comes to mind that includes this kind of
information.

We can now link event participant salience to relevance in UDC constructions. Drawing
from insights due to Kuno (1987), Deane (1991), Lambrecht (1994, 53), Van Valin (2005,
288), and Goldberg (2006, 135), we argue that all filler-gap dependencies are subject to the
following general pragmatic constraint:

RELEVANCE PRESUPPOSITION CONDITION: the referent that is singled out for extraction in
a UDC must be highly relevant (e.g. part of the evoked conventionalized world knowledge)
relative to the main action that the sentence describes. Otherwise, extraction makes no
sense from a Gricean perspective, as there is no reason for the speaker to draw attention
to a referent that is irrelevant for the main contribution of the sentence to the discourse.

---

[2] See Deane (1992, §5.2) for a different exploration of this idea, in terms of entrenchment.

For example, consider the UDC in (10). A claim is the sort of thing that one makes concerning certain information topics. As comprehenders process *make a claim*, they are also activating, through inference, the existence of a claim, and therefore the subextraction is licit simply because the referent for *who* is part of the overall frame knowledge evoked by the predication. From now on we refrain from explicitly signaling fillers and gaps.

(10)   Who did you make a claim about?

If the verb and the noun are not as intimately associated with each other, the extraction is less acceptable, as in (11). Clearly, claims are usually heard, but the link between *hear* and *claim* in (11) is not as automatic as the link between *make* and *claim* in (10).

(11)   ?Who did you hear a claim about?

Contrasts like (12) follow from the fact that in (12a) the extracted referent is part of the frame evoked by the verb, but not in (12b).

(12)   a.   What did you read a book about?
       b.   *What did you drop a book about?

Mentioning the content of a book is more felicitous in a sentence like *I read a book about chemistry* than, say, *I dropped a book about chemistry* because the content of a book is relevant for understanding a book-reading scene, but not so much for understanding a book-dropping scene. This is because information about the book content has no bearing on the action. The oddness of examples like (13) is analogously because whether or not an article is coffee-stained is irrelevant for whether someone is reading an article.

(13)   *Who are you reading a coffee-stained article about?
       (Davies and Dubinsky, 2003)

Similarly, even though both declaratives in (14) are highly acceptable, the referent for *Paris* is more relevant for the utterance in (14a) than in (14b) because trips are generally booked because of the destination, whereas trips are routinely cancelled for reasons having nothing to do with the destination. Thus, the mention of the trip's destination in (14a) is easier to contextualize than that in (14b).

(14)   a.   Kayla booked a trip to Paris.
       b.   Kayla cancelled a trip to Paris.

A similar pattern arises in extractions from adverbial phrases that express circumstantial (not at-issue) information like (15), based on Deane (1991, 31). The extraction in (15a) is infelicitous because there is no obvious connection between the action of burying a letter and a given party without a suitable context. The reference to a party is not easy to accommodate into the background frame information that the main verb evokes.

(15)   a. *Which party did John bury the letter after?
           (cf. *Did John bury his resignation letter after his birthday party?*)

       b. *Which house did you sell the car near?
           (cf. *Did you sell the car near my house?*)

Analogously, (15b) is not felicitous because the action of selling a car does not evoke a frame that includes a geographical location situated *near* the transaction site. A geographical site for the location is expected, and therefore extractions like *Which car dealer did you sell the Honda at?* are more felicitous, but not some other nearby site, as in (15b).

Long-distance extractions like (16a) are more felicitous than those in (16b) because the verbs *say* and *think* are semantically very abstract (and very common), which means that they do not evoke a rich background frame that the speaker can use to interpret the utterance.

(16)   a. Who did you say / think / hear that Robin was writing a book about?

       b. ?Who did you deny / doubt / hiss that Robin was writing a book about?
           (Deane, 1992, 245)

Thus, the main action of (16a) is conveyed by the complement clause, as it is the latter that provides the key background frame information with which to interpret the utterance. In contrast, *deny* or *doubt* are semantically richer (and much less frequent), and therefore evoke a richer background frame. Consequently, they are more likely to describe the main action of the utterance in (16b).

In some cases, the construction itself forces one of the daughters to express the main action. For example, presentational relatives are required to express at-issue (i.e. asserted) information, as discussed in §2.1.3.1, and therefore it is the frame evoked by the relative that is active and key for interpreting the situation expressed by the utterance. As a consequence, restrictive relatives are island environments but presentational relatives are not, as discussed in §3.2.3. Similarly, coordinated phrases structures can cohere in various ways, as detailed in §3.2.5. If the main action is expressed by the first conjunct, then non-ATB extractions like (17) are permitted because the active frame against which the utterance is being interpreted is the one evoked by the main action. When conjuncts are interpreted as conveying a parallel coherence relation, then the two conjuncts together evoke a complex of two equally active frames.

(17)   How much can you drink and still stay sober?

The oddness associated with the NP Constraint (§3.2.1), the Complex NP Constraint (§3.2.3), the Bridge Island Constraint (§3.2.4), the Element Constraint (§3.2.5), the Subject Constraint (§3.2.6), and the Adjunct Constraint (§3.2.7) is predominately due to a Relevance Presupposition Condition violation, whereby the referent that is singled out to be fronted has low relevance for the main action described by the proposition. This explains why Complex NP Constraint effects vanish in relative clauses that express assertions (the extracted referent is predicated by the main action, as opposed to non-at-issue content), and why Subject Island effects vanish in relative clauses (the relative subject can have whatever pragmatic function the matrix clause requires). Finally, this also explains why the NP Constraint, the Bridge Constraint, and the Adjunct Constraint are extremely sensitive to the particular proposition that is expressed: their acceptability hinges on whether the extracted referent is of relevance to the main action. All of these island effects become stronger when the proposition itself is unusual, requires peculiar contexts, or when there are additional sources of oddness or processing difficulty in the sentence. Relevance Islands should, therefore, be sensitive to the particular proposition that is expressed, such that syntactically isomorphic UDCs differ in acceptability as a function of how relevant the extracted referent is for the main action in the proposition.

6.2 Experimental evidence

All participants in the experiments reported in this section were recruited online via the Amazon.com's Mechanical Turk (AMT) crowd sourcing marketplace, and all had IP addresses located in the United States. At the very end of the experiment, all participants were asked to report if they happened to be native speakers after the experiment (i.e. 'Did you grow up speaking English as a first language?'), while being informed that their answer would not jeopardize their compensation for participating. All the experimental materials for all experiments discussed are available for download at https://github.com/ RuiPChaves/Materials.

Throughout this chapter we follow the American Psychological Association guidelines (VandenBos, 2010, §2.07) in using raw values rather than z-scores, as the former are easier to interpret relative to the original scale, and since we do not wish to compare the results across experiments. All Linear Mixed-Effect Regression Models were fitted with the LME4 package (Bates et al., 2014), and the p-values were calculated by Satterthwaite approximation, using the LMERTEST package (Kuznetsova et al., 2015). On occasion, we supplement these results with Bayesian Logistic Regression models by using the BRMS package (Bürkner, 2017), a high-level R interface to Stan (Carpenter et al., 2017).

6.2.1 Adaptation in extraction from subject NPs

One of the main points made by Hofmeister and Sag (2010, 381, 385), Hofmeister et al. (2012, 396), and Chaves and Dery (2014) is that research on islands has not systematically controlled for factors affecting acceptability that are orthogonal to the filler-gap dependency, such as unnecessarily complex items and lack of discourse felicity (i.e. pragmatically unusual propositions requiring peculiar contexts). In order to avoid comparing the acceptability of sentences that express radically different propositions, Chaves and Dery (2019) (Experiment 1) compare the acceptability of twenty-two near-truth-conditionally equivalent sentence pairs like those in (18) and (19). In the (a) examples we have subextraction from the direct object (an NP Constraint violation) and in the (b) examples we have subextraction from the subject (a Subject Island violation). In this chapter we omit diacritics signaling fillers, gaps, and island environments from the prose, for ease of exposition.

(18)   a. Which stock does the value of the dollar often parallel the price of?
       [object subextraction condition]

       b. Which stock does the value of often parallel the price of the dollar?
       [subject subextraction condition]

(19)   a. Which song does the beat of 'Ice, Ice Baby' supposedly coincide with the melody of?
       [object subextraction condition]

       b. Which song does the beat of supposedly coincide with the melody of 'Ice, Ice Baby'?
       [subject subextraction condition]

What is special about such example pairs is that the order of the subject and the object can be switched without a radical difference in interpretation because the main verb is a symmetric predicate. Recall that NP Constraint violations are rather weak and Subject Island violations are rather strong, so one would expect that the (a) items would be systematically more acceptable than the (b) items. Chaves and Dery (2019) find that the acceptability difference between subject and object subextractions vanishes after eight exposures, at which point both item types are equally highly acceptable. Crucially, no such sharp acceptability increase is observed in unambiguously ungrammatical control items.

Chaves and Dery (2019) complement their offline findings with a self-paced reading experiment which shows that gap-filling inside subject phrases is similarly sensitive to the probabilities of the distribution of filler-gap dependencies. Chaves and Dery (2019) used a between-subject block design, whereby participants were randomly assigned to one of two groups (henceforth the 'Subject' group and the 'Object' group). In both groups, participants were exposed to two blocks of sentences, reading a total of forty-five pseudo-randomized sentences in the first block, and thirty pseudo-randomized sentences in the second block.

Participants in the Subject group read fifteen Subject Island violation sentences and thirty distractor sentences in the first block, while participants in the Object group read forty-five distractors in the first block. The second block was identical for both groups, and contained ten Subject Island 'violation' sentences and twenty distractors. In (20) we illustrate the Subject items that participants saw. The symbol '|' indicates the regions that were shown during the experiment. Note that the adverb (region 4) is consistent with a gapless parse because adverbs can modify an upcoming NP (e.g. in attested examples like *the infants of reportedly non-smoking mothers*, or in *the execution of allegedly innocent people*). It is the main verb region (region 5) that is incompatible with a gapless parse.

(20)   a. Which animal $_1$| does $_2$| the song of $_3$| reportedly $_4$| mimic $_5$| the Gray Catbird's sounds? $_6$|

       b. Which athlete $_1$| does $_2$| the manager of $_3$| clearly $_4$| resemble $_5$| Tiger Woods's agent? $_6$|

       c. Which company $_1$| do $_2$| the employees of $_3$| allegedly $_4$| reject $_5$| salary increases? $_6$|

Figure 6.1 shows mean residual reading times, where bars represent 95% confidence intervals. Of all six regions, only region 5 exhibited a significant effect ($\beta = 86.80$, $t = 2.07$,

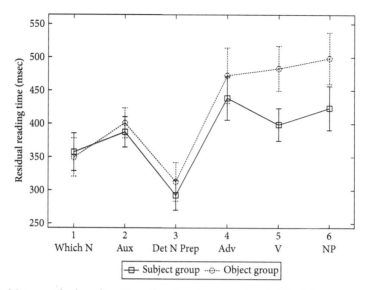

Figure 6.1 Mean residual reading times for all sentence regions in Block 2

$p = 0.04$), suggesting that participants in the Subject group (i.e. who saw fifteen Subject Island violation sentences in Block 1) read the region of interest of the Subject Island violations in Block 2 faster than participants in the Object group (i.e. who saw zero Subject Island violation sentences in Block 1).

The participants in the Subject group adjusted their expectations about subject-embedded gaps during their exposure to Block 1, and therefore were less surprised by such long-distance dependencies in Block 2 than participants in the Object group. Gap-filling in Subject Island environments seems to be modulated by malleable probabilistic expectations, as argued by Hofmeister, Casasanto, et al. (2013, 49), which comprehenders can revise, given sufficient exposure. Together with Experiment 1, these findings suggest that extraction from subjects is in principle construable by the parser, and grammatical. In what follows we report a replication of the sentence-acceptability study (Experiment 1) reported in Chaves and Dery (2019).

6.2.1.1 Methods

We analyzed data provided by sixty-nine self-reported native speakers from AMT. Unlike Chaves and Dery (2019), the experiment was directly run on AMT. We used the same twenty-two experimental items from Chaves and Dery (2019), each of which had two versions, as illustrated in (18–19). The declarative counterparts of the twenty-two items were normed to express equally highly plausible propositions. For example, the sentences in (18a,b) were converted into (21a,b) respectively, and participants were asked to rate the plausibility of the sentences.[3]

(21)   a. The value of the dollar often parallels the price of this stock.

        b. The value of this stock often parallels the price of the dollar.

---

[3] All items for all experiments can be downloaded from the URL referenced in §6.2.

This plausibility norming stage ensured that the propositions described by the items are equally felicitous to begin with. Hence, any difference in acceptability must come from extraction itself, not from other sources independent from extraction.

The twenty-two experimental items were counterbalanced across two lists using a Latin Square design so that each participant responded to only one version of each experimental item. Also, experimental items were interspersed among forty-four distractor items so that different participants saw items in different orders. A sample of the distractors is seen in (22) and (23), which were either object gaps or subject gaps, some of which were clause-embedded. Half of the distractors were ungrammatical, as in (23).

(22) a. Which cabinet does the stack of papers belong to according to the secretary?

b. Which type of music does the flyer say that the band of traveling musicians plays?

c. Which jury members does the judge reportedly consider to be problematic for the trial?

(23) a. *Which complaint does the tenant of the condo rarely hear at each of the caretakers?

b. *Which artifact does the Museum of Fine Arts wish purchases about the British Museum?

c. *Which boat does the report unexpectedly reveal that the soldiers were thinking?

The distractors were relatively homogeneous, as they all consisted of *which* interrogatives with an adverb and a clause-embedded gap. The gap could be either a complement or a subject, but the source of oddness—if any—always involved an incorrect word form (and/or the lack thereof). Unlike the original study, the grammatical distractors were not immediately followed by a yes/no comprehension question. However, this caused no substantial difference in the replication results.

As in the original study, participants were asked to judge how natural various sentences sound, by rating each one with a number from 1 (very unnatural) to 7 (very natural).

6.2.1.2 Results

Chaves and Dery (2019) found that the acceptability of the subject condition items was 3.99 ($SD = 1.69$), and that of the object condition 5.08 ($SD = 1.51$). The mean response for the grammatical distractors was 5.7 ($SD = 1.46$), and 2.67 ($SD = 1.59$) for the ungrammatical distractors. Similarly, we found that the acceptability of the subject condition items was also very low, 3.36 ($SD = 1.73$), and that of the object condition, 4.91 ($SD = 1.61$). The mean response for the grammatical distractors was 5.64 ($SD = 1.51$), and 2.81 ($SD = 1.54$) for the ungrammatical distractors.

Chaves and Dery (2019) report that a Linear Mixed-Effect Regression (LMER) model with gap location, (scaled and centered to minimize collinearity), presentation order (i.e. number of exposures), plausibility, and all possible interactions between the three factors as fixed factors revealed a main effect of gap location in which subject gaps were rated lower than object gaps ($\beta = -1.065, t = -7.69, p < 0.0001$), and a significant interaction between gap location and presentation order ($\beta = 0.061, t = 5.23, p < 0.0001$). This suggests that the acceptability of subject and object items changed during the experiment.

No significant effect of plausibility was found, nor of any interactions. Since no two participants saw the items in the same order, the changes in acceptability cannot be due to any particular item order. We found similar results, fitting the same models to our data. An LMER reveals a main effect of gap location in which subject gaps were rated lower than object gaps ($\beta = -1.496, t = -13.91, p < 0.0001$), and a significant interaction between gap location and presentation order ($\beta = 0.02, t = 3.08, p = 0.002$).

Simple effects analyses were conducted by Chaves and Dery (2019) for each condition, by fitting LMER models with (scaled and centered) presentation order as a fixed predictor. Presentation order was not significant for the object-gap condition ($\beta = 0.004, t = 0.58, p = 0.56$), and highly significant for the subject-gap condition ($\beta = 0.065, t = 7.84, p < 0.0001$). Separate models revealed that the acceptability of the ungrammatical distractors did not increase during the experiment ($\beta = -0.003, t = 1.41, p = 0.24$), but that of the grammatical distractors did ($\beta = 0.005, t = 1.98, p = 0.04$).

Our simple-effect models obtained almost exactly the same results. Presentation order was significant for the object-gap condition, but the effect size was small ($\beta = 0.012, t = 2.74, p < 0.006$). In contrast, the effect of presentation order for the subject-gap condition was much stronger ($\beta = 0.032, t = 6.76, p < 0.0001$). That is, per each unit of exposition the acceptability of the Object items increased by a factor of 0.012, whereas the Subject items increased by 0.032. Separate models revealed that the acceptability of the ungrammatical distractors increased only very weakly during the experiment ($\beta = 0.007, t = 2.021, p = 0.04$), and that of the grammatical distractors increased as well ($\beta = 0.01, t = 3.84, p < 0.001$). The results are illustrated in Figure 6.2, with regression lines for all conditions and distractors, with 95% confidence intervals.

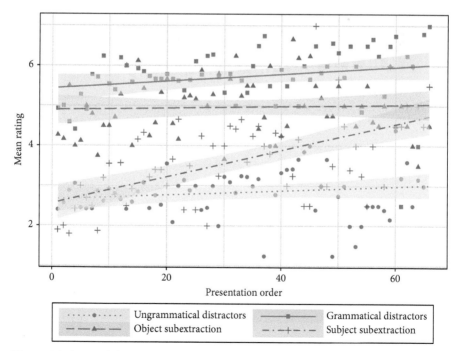

Figure 6.2 Acceptability across item types according to presentation order

Recall that no two participants saw the items in exactly the same order. Consequently, each dot in this graph corresponds to the average acceptability rating of items observed in the respective order indicated in the x axis. The graph reported in Chaves and Dery (2019) normalizes the order according to each condition, but Figure 6.2 does not, for clarity. The interested reader is invited to compare the two. In subsequent graphs we adopt Chaves and Dery's format, where presentation order is normalized across each of the conditions.

Since 1–7 Likert scale ratings are arguably ordinal in nature and not necessarily equidistant, then mixed-effect ordinal regression models would be more appropriate. Treating ordinal responses as continuous measures is in principle incorrect because the scale is not a ratio, but it can in practice be acceptable to apply linear regression, as long as it is reasonable to assume that the scale can be treated as interval data; e.g. the distances between individual response categories are meaningful/comparable. As a consequence, LMER models may not be entirely reliable. To avoid these concerns, we fit Bayesian cumulative logit multilevel regression models (BLRs) with a flexible threshold and weakly uniformative priors $\mathcal{N}(0, 10)$ for the presentation order predictor, using the BRMS package (Bürkner, 2017). The models had the same structure as above, i.e. (scaled and centered) presentation order as a fixed predictor, allowing for the intercept to be adjusted by items, subjects, and lists, in order to account for random effects. We checked the convergence of the models after fitting them with four chains and 4,000 iterations, half of which were the burn-in or warm-up phase. In order to assess convergence, we verified that the $\hat{R}$s were close to one, and we also visually inspected the chains. The results are shown in Table 6.1, along with the Credible Intervals (CrIs) of the estimated coefficient's posterior distribution. Again, the evidence suggests that the acceptability rating increases with presentation order were strongest in the Subject items, and weakest in the Ungrammatical distractors.

Table 6.1 Logit estimates, credible intervals, and posterior probability

Item type	β	SD	95% Crl	$P(\beta > 0)$
Subject	0.05	0.01	[0.04, 0.07]	1
Object	0.02	0.01	[0.01, 0.04]	1
Grammatical distractors	0.02	0	[0.01, 0.03]	1
Ungrammatical distractors	0.01	0	[0.00, 0.02]	0.97

The β coefficients express the log-odds of the acceptability rating increasing with one unit increase in presentation order. After exponentiation, we can say that as presentation order increases by one unit, the odds of an acceptability rating below a given threshold vs. the odds of an acceptability rating above that given threshold increase by 5.1% for Subject items, by 2% for Object items and Grammatical distractors, and by 1% for Ungrammatical distractors. Since the lower bound of the CrI for the ungrammatical distractors includes 0, it is not considered to be as strongly significant as the other estimates (Kruschke et al., 2012, 730). The last column indicates the probability that the coefficients are non-zero. In sum, the BLR results are overall consistent with those of the LMER models. Although an increase of 5% is small, it, of course, adds up significantly after a dozen exposures.

Crucially, Chaves and Dery (2019) found that by the end of their experiment there was no statistically significant difference in acceptability between the Subject and Object conditions. We extracted the acceptability ratings for the 80 experimental items in the last quarter of our experiment ($n =$38 for the object condition and $n = 42$ for the subject condition; overall mean $t = -0.95$, SD $= 0.01$). Next, we fitted an LMER model with gap location as a fixed predictor, allowing the random effects to have different slopes for the main factor, which only approached statistical difference ($t = -1.893, p = 0.07$). Through the selection of only these late presentations the sample size has been reduced considerably, increasing the chances of a significant difference not being found, even though one may exist. Chaves and Dery address this problem via bootstrapping (Wilcox, 2005; Larson-Hall and Herrington, 2010), and show that the results are robust. To be clear, it should be impossible for the Subject Island violations to vanish if they were due to syntactic or architectural constraints on human language. Rather, the evidence shows that comprehenders can adapt to unusual constructions, given enough exposure.

We accordingly sampled with replacement from the latter part of our experiment. We extracted 80 total data points at the end of the experiment (40 per condition) to create 670 data points (335 per condition). This process was repeated 100 times, and for each upsampled data set we ran an LMER model with gap location as a fixed predictor, allowing the random effects to have different slopes for the main factor. Like Chaves and Dery, we found no significant difference between subject and object conditions (mean $t = -1.71$, SD $= 0.1$).

6.2.1.3 Discussion

As in Chaves and Dery (2019), the results suggest that the acceptability contrast between extracting from NP complements and extracting from NP subjects is transient and can vanish if (i) the underlying propositions are equally plausible, and (ii) comprehenders are exposed to the two types of extraction in equal amounts. Repeated exposure to unusual structures can cause comprehenders to adapt and become better at processing such structures. The acceptability increase for the ungrammatical distractors is negligible, suggesting that the cause for their oddness is completely different than the cause of oddness for the Subject condition items. The fact that Chaves and Dery found no amelioration for the ungrammatical distractors can simply be due to noise, given the small effect size.

This configuration of results undercuts the concern that the rise in acceptability ratings stems from a task-related effect. If general task demands or features were to drive the observed effects, we would predict all conditions to pattern the same, which is clearly not the case. Rather, the findings are consistent with the hypothesis that the frequency increase of (highly pragmatically felicitous) sentences containing subject-internal gaps can lead the parser to revise its expectations about subject-internal gaps. If so, the oddness of Subject Island violations is at least in part due to processing difficulty caused by the inconsistency between a priori probabilistic expectations about gap locations and about the pragmatic role of subject-embedded referents relative to the subject referent (i.e. how relevant the subject-embedded referent can be for the main action expressed by the proposition).

6.2.2 Adaptation extraction from clausal subjects

The fact that increased exposure can have a significant effect in the processing and acceptability of subextraction from subject phrases raises the question of whether deeper extractions are similarly susceptible. In what follows we provide new experimental data suggesting that it is possible to ameliorate Sentential Subject Condition (SSC) violations, specifically if cues are added which make such constructions more canonical (i.e. more likely) and therefore more expected, and that this seems to facilitate extraction from clausal subjects, trumping the cost of making the construction longer and more complex.

Recall that Ross's (1967) SSC states that no phrase can move from a clause inside a subject phrase, as illustrated in (24a). Crucially, no such constraint is observed if the extracted phrase is embedded in a clausal complement, as in (24b).

(24)   a.   *[Who]$_i$ did [that Sharapova beat __$_i$] surprise everyone?
             (cf. *That Sharapova beat Serena surprised everyone*)

         b.   [Who]$_i$ did you say [that Sharapova beat __$_i$]?

But sentences with complex subjects are harder to process than sentences with complex complements (Kluender, 2004). For example, there is a trade-off between subject length and verb phrase length in early acquisition, so that the longer the subject, the shorter the verb phrase, and vice versa (Bloom, 1990). This trade-off does not change with age in spontaneous written production (Kemper, 1987). Children also tend to produce shorter lexical noun subjects than lexical noun objects, and pronouns are used more often in subject than in object position (Bloom, 1990). Similarly, elderly adults have far more difficulty repeating sentences with complex subjects than sentences with complex objects (Kemper, 1986), and similar difficulty is found in timed reading comprehension tasks (Kynette and Kemper, 1986), as well as in disfluencies in non-elderly adults (Clark and Wasow, 1998). Speech initiation times for sentences with complex subjects are also known to be longer than for sentences with simple subjects (Ferreira, 1991; Tsiamtsiouris and Cairns, 2009). Finally, sentences with center-embedding in subjects are harder to process than sentences with center-embedding in objects (Amy and Noziet, 1978; Eady and Fodor, 1981), and sentence-initial open-class words are harder to process than closed-class words (Garnsey, 1985; Kutas et al., 1988; Petten and Kutas, 1991). Indeed, the tendency to place complex phrases toward the end of sentences rather than toward the beginning is plausibly motivated by the pressure to create a temporally shorter strain on limited memory resources (Yngve, 1960; Hawkins, 1994; Wasow, 1997; Gibson, 1998), allowing the production system to buy time for the planning of more complex material (Wasow, 2002).

The fact that sentential subjects are difficult to process and are therefore rare can only result in lower acceptability when compounded with another source of complexity (a filler-gap dependency). In fact, the mere presence of a CP subject often results in lower acceptability in the presence of a licit filler-gap dependency in the complement phrase, as illustrated by the contrasts in (25) and (26). Davies and Dubinsky (2009, 115) argue that such acceptability contrasts are more likely to be the result of extra-grammatical factors than of grammatical conditions, given that not all extractions like (26b) are unacceptable, as already noted by Delahunty (1983, 382–7).[4]

---

[4] Incidentally, a similar effect can be seen for some extractions from non-clausal subjects, as shown by (i) and (ii). Extracting from the in situ subject position is less acceptable than extracting from the extraposed subject, according to Takahashi (1994), Lasnik and Park (2003), and Stepanov (2007).

i. *Who was [a picture of __] on the wall?
ii. Who was there [a picture of __] on the wall?

(25) a. ?*What does that he will come prove_?
      b. What does his coming prove_?
          (Lewis, 1993)

      c. *Who did that the food that John ordered tasted good please_?
      d. That the food that John ordered tasted good pleased me.
          (Cowper, 1976; Gibson, 1991)

(26) a. *Who did that John left early disappoint_?
      b. Who did it disappoint that John left early_?
          (Koster, 1978)

If CP subjects are difficult to process, mainly because comprehenders expect the first clause to be the main clause, then it follows that if the CP were embedded in an NP, the oddness should be partially mitigated simply because the subject phrase would no longer be a CP. Since the CP is now embedded inside an NP, the ambiguity caused by a sentence-initial complementizer is avoided, and the subject phrase becomes more canonical and more consistent with the expectations about English-speaking subjects. However, previous researchers have claimed that such embeddings do not yield more acceptable island violations, as seen in (27).

(27) a. *Who does [the claim that Mary likes_] upset Bill?
          (Lasnik and Saito, 1992, 42)

      b. *Who did [the fact that the candidate supported_] upset voters?
          (Phillips, 2006, 796)

      c. *What did [the fact that Ellen remembered_] surprise her children?
          (Phillips, 2013a, 67)

But informal consultations with native speakers indicate that there is some amelioration caused by embedding the gapped clause in an NP, as illustrated in (28). In fact, by making the *wh*-phrase more specific, the amelioration effect is much clearer. See, for example, (29).

(28) a. *Who did [that Bill kissed_] surprise you?
      b. ?Who did [the fact that Bill kissed_] surprise you?

(29) a. Which puzzle did the fact that nobody could solve_ astonish you the most?
      b. Which crime did the fact that nobody was accused of_ astonish you the most?
      c. Which question did the fact that none of us could answer_ surprise you the most?
      d. Which joke did the fact that nobody laughed at_ surprise you the most?

If this is correct, this suggests that expectations can trump structural complexity in certain situations, since more canonical (though more complex) structures are more acceptable than less canonical (though simpler) counterparts. Below, we demonstrate that although sentences like (29) are initially very low in acceptability, they undergo a sharp boost in acceptability relative to counterparts with non-embedded CP subjects and to their (grammatical) extraposed counterparts. This behavior again is consistent with the idea that speakers deploy probabilistic syntactic expectations about the distribution of filler-gap dependencies, and that those expectations can be revised so that unusual (i.e. unattested) filler-gap dependencies like those in (29) can be successfully processed, analogously to the frequency-sensitive adaptive behavior already discussed.

In what follows we provide new evidence that SSC violations can be ameliorated via repeated exposure, provided that the subject phrase has a more canonical NP structure, in comparison to a CP structure, even though the former is more complex than the latter.

6.2.2.1 Methods

Data from seventy-six AMT informants were analyzed, following the protocols of previous experiments. A total of twenty-four experimental items were constructed, each of which had three versions, as seen in (30) and (31). Participants were asked to judge how natural each sentence was, by giving it a number between 1 (very unnatural) and 5 (very natural).

(30) a. Which movie did it confuse you the most that nobody wanted to watch?
     (Baseline condition)

     b. Which movie did that nobody wanted to watch confuse you the most?
     (CP condition)

     c. Which movie did the fact that nobody wanted to watch confuse you the most?
     (NP condition)

(31) a. Which word did it irritate you the most that nobody could spell?
     (Baseline condition)

     b. Which word did that nobody could spell irritate you the most?
     (CP condition)

     c. Which word did the fact that nobody could spell irritate you the most?
     (NP condition)

The first condition involves a complement CP with an indisputably licit gap (baseline condition), the second involves a gapped subject CP (the CP condition), and the third and final condition involves a gapped CP embedded inside an NP (the NP condition). If gaps in finite subject-embedded environments act as barriers to extraction, as assumed by Engdahl (1983), Phillips (2006), and many others, then only the baseline should be rated as acceptable. However, if the oddness of such extractions is due to expectation-based processing difficulties caused in part by sentence-initial CPs and by subject-internal gaps, then it should be possible to mitigate that difficulty by disambiguating the complementizer by embedding the CP in an NP. In other words, we expect items in the NP condition to start with low acceptability but to eventually become as acceptable as the baseline.

The experimental items were counterbalanced across three lists using a Latin Square design so that each participant only responded to one version of each experimental item. The experimental items were interspersed among forty-eight distractor items, a sample of which is given in (32) and (33). Given that arguably at least half of our experimental items have low acceptability, only 25% of the distractors were ungrammatical, as illustrated in (33). The latter were made odd by use of a resumptive inside the island environment. Recall from §3.3.3 that complement resumptive pronouns in relative clause islands do not neutralize the island effect.

(32) a. Which box did that machine at the warehouse around the corner scratch the most?

b. Which issue did that student who never speaks in class insist on discussing the most?

c. Which lawyer did the assumption that nobody tampered with the evidence vex the most?

d. Which commission did the discovery that nobody replicated the experiment rattle the most?

(33) a. *Which joke did the gentleman at the end of the bar who told it amused you the most?

b. *Which bass guitar did the woman that bought it at auction impressed you the most?

6.2.2.2 Results

The mean responses for each of the stimulus types are shown in Table 6.2. Pair-wise t tests suggest that the acceptability of the Grammatical distractors was not statistically different from that of the NP items ($p = 0.14$, $t = -1.47$), while all other combinations yielded statistically significant differences. LMER models confirmed these results: there was no significant difference between the Grammatical distractors and the NP condition ($t = -1.74$, $p = 0.008$) but all other pairs were significantly different (e.g. Baseline condition vs. NP condition: $\beta = -0.4$, $t = -4.97$, $p < 0.0001$; CP condition vs. NP condition: $\beta = 0.79$, $t = 11.85$, $p < 0.0001$).

Table 6.2 Acceptability means per item type

Item type	Mean	SD
Baseline	3.56	1.11
Grammatical distractors	3.24	1.27
NP	3.16	1.12
CP	2.36	1.25
Ungrammatical distractors	2.06	1.05

However, a by-item analysis reveals that only five of the twenty-four NP items were judged to be significantly different from their Baseline counterparts (i.e. items #1, #7, #8, #19, #20 were all $p < 0.05$). Some items merely approached significance (i.e. #12, #14, #15, #17, #21 with $0.06 < p < 0.09$), whereas for all twelve remaining items the there was no evidence of statistical difference (p's > 0.1). The full range of variation is shown in Figure 6.3.

This extreme range of variation is difficult to explain in a purely syntactic account, since all examples had the same syntactic structure. Rather, these differences make sense if the proposition itself is a key factor for the processing of complex and unusual UDCs.

We then constructed a LMER model with order of experimental presentation as a fixed predictor in order to determine whether the acceptability of the experimental items increased as a function of presentation order. Each of the three experimental types was analyzed separately. All three models revealed that presentation order was a significant predictor, indicating that participants' acceptability judgments gradually increased in all

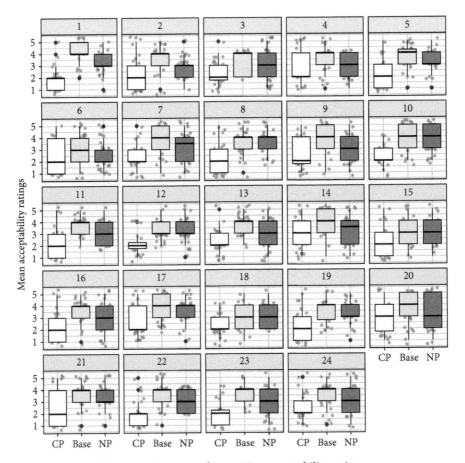

Figure 6.3 By-item subextraction acceptability ratings

experimental types (Baseline condition: $\beta = 0.01$, $t = 6.331$, $p < 0.0001$; CP condition: $\beta = 0.006$, $t = 3.33$, $p < 0.0001$; NP condition: $\beta = 0.009$, $t = 5.54$, $p < 0.0001$). The Ungrammatical distractors also showed minute improvement ($\beta = 0.003$, $t = 3.96$, $p < 0.0001$), as did the Grammatical distractors ($\beta = 0.005$, $t = 5.19$, $p < 0.0001$). Figure 6.4 shows the regression lines for all item types. Here we display the normalized presentation order across each of the conditions, not the raw (overall) presentation order.

Analogously to Experiment 1, we compared the acceptability of the NP Condition items that were seen by participants at the end of the experiment with an equal number of baseline items seen in the beginning of the experiment, by forming a subset of the data containing 126 responses for NP Condition items whose presentation orders were 17 or higher, as well as 122 responses for baseline items whose presentation orders were 1, 2, or 3. Mean response for the NP Condition items was 4.23 ($SD = 1.62$), and for the baseline items was 3.79 ($SD = 1.65$). We then fitted an LMER model with experimental condition as a fixed predictor, which revealed a significant difference in acceptability judgments as a function of experimental condition ($t = 2.42$, $p = 0.016$): the acceptability responses to the NP Condition items seen at the end of the experiment were significantly *higher* than the responses to the baseline items seen at the beginning of the experiment. Hence, there is no reason to believe that NP Condition items are illicit in any way. Rather, the fact that

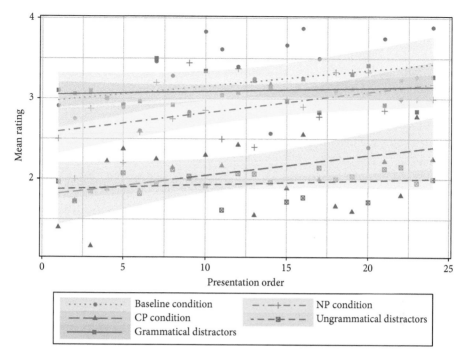

Figure 6.4 Acceptability across item types according to presentation order

they are extremely unusual may cause some initial difficulty but comprehenders are able to adapt and interpret such constructions as acceptable.

6.2.2.3 Discussion

Our results suggest that the difficulty in extracting from subject-embedded finite environments can be completely mitigated by increased frequency and by introducing syntactic cues that (i) avoid the processing problems created by the frequency-based parsing expectation that a sentence-initial clause is the matrix clause (Davies and Dubinsky, 2009), and (ii) remove the lexical ambiguity interference caused by the most frequent use of the word *that* in sentence-initial position (Gibson, 2006).

The fact that items improved with repeated exposure is consistent with an experience-based model in which increase of frequency leads to processing ease. Note also that the magnitude of increase is much larger in the SSC violations than in the ungrammatical distractors, suggesting that the oddness behind SSC effects is not as extreme as that of the oddness of the distractors. As in Experiment 1, the results indicate that the rise in ratings cannot be dismissed as a task-related effect, as this would predict all conditions to pattern the same, which is clearly not the case.

6.2.3 Relevance effects in object subextraction

If the semantic plausibility of a proposition plays a role in how felicitous it is to extract a referent from it, then there should be a positive correlation between sentence plausibility (as expressed by a declarative clause) and the extractability of a deeply embedded object. The more coherent the semantic components and the more prototypical their relations are, the more likely it is that the whole complex of frames be evoked as a complex unit, which in turn allows a wider range of referents to be deemed relevant to the main action, and therefore eligible for extraction. For example, if an NP-embedded PP is rather circumstantial and irrelevant for the situation described by the verb, then the proposition is not as plausible and it is less likely for the embedded referent to be part of the conventionalized component of the situational knowledge evoked by the predication.

Chaves and King (2020) (Experiment 2) approach this question by a norming stage in which speakers were asked to rate the plausibility of the situation described by sentences like those in (34), on a 1-5 Likert scale. The goal was to elicit a rating that correlates with how commonplace and prototypical the state of affairs described by the sentence intuitively is. There were a total of sixteen such sentences, interspersed with thirty-two distractors.

(34)   a. The kids heard stories about pictures of this artist.
       b. The farmers question the analysis of the impact of this pesticide.
       c. The editor has strict control over the publication of this content.
       d. The experts receive requests for articles about this topic.

After the norming stage, data from fifty-four additional AMT informants were collected, who were asked to rate how natural the sub-subextracted counterparts of (34) are, illustrated in (35), again using a 1–5 scale.

(35)   a. Who did the kids hear stories about pictures of?
       b. Who did the farmers question the analysis of the impact of?
       c. What does the editor have strict control over the publication of?
       d. What did the experts receive requests for articles about?

There was a total of sixteen sentences interspersed with thirty-two distractors, half ungrammatical, half grammatical. The latter were as usual followed by comprehension questions.

A simple regression model was fitted with the mean acceptability ratings per item as a dependent variable and the mean plausibility ratings per item from the questionnaire experiment as the independent variable. The model suggests that the topicality ratings were a strong linear predictor of the subextraction acceptability ratings ($\beta = 0.2$, $SD = 0.04$, $t = 4.07$, p = 0.001), with an adjusted R^2 value of 0.54. A Pearson test further suggests that the mean plausibility ratings for declarative items like (34) are correlated with the mean acceptability ratings for the deep subextractions counterparts in (35): $r = 0.66$, $p < 0.001$, as illustrated in Figure 6.5.[5]

Chaves and King (2020) fitted an Ordered Regression Model with the ORDINAL package (Christensen, 2018), with the same structure as the linear mixed-effect model above, again finding evidence of a positive correlation.

In sum, these results suggest a positive correlation between the plausibility of the proposition (as expressed by a declarative clause) and the extractability of a deeply object-embedded referent therein. The more coherent the semantic components and the more

---

[5] The outliers at the lower left of the graph has a minimal influence on the result, since its removal still allows for a strong correlation ($r = 0.76$, $p = 0.001$).

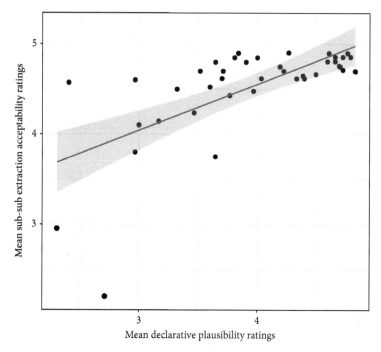

Figure 6.5 Sub-sub extraction acceptability vs. Declarative plausibility

prototypical their relations are, the more acceptable the extraction of one of those components is. The fact that there is significant variability across the items suggests that syntax is not the key factor responsible for UDC acceptability.

But Chaves and King (2020) go further, and attempt to detect the effect of relevance more directly (Experiment 1). If indeed some referents are more likely than others to be relevant for the main action that the sentence describes, then the degree to which they are recognized as such should correlate with the acceptability of extracting such referents. The logic is as follows. Although the declaratives in (36) are equally acceptable, the referent for *verdict* is intuitively more relevant for the utterance in (36a) than for that in (36b), because whether someone makes a comment or not crucially depends on the the comment's subject matter, whereas whether someone misreads a comment or not can depend on many other things besides the comment's subject matter.

(36)   a. Kayla posted a comment about the verdict.   (+Relevant)
       b. Kayla misread a comment about the verdict.   (−Relevant)

The mention of the comment's topic in (36a) is easy to contextualize, whereas the mention in (36b) is only felicitous in very specific contexts. To ensure that the +Relevant condition items were indeed more relevant for the proposition than the −Relevant condition items, Chaves and King (2020) conducted a norming experiment in which sixty participants were asked use a five-point Likert scale to judge how much they agreed with sentences like those in (37), created from the twenty original experimental items, by rating each one with a number from 1 (strongly disagree) to 5 (strongly agree).

(37)   a. How much does the topic of a comment matter when posting a comment?
       b. How much does the topic of a comment matter when misreading a comment?

Such questions are meant to provide a proxy of how relevant a referent is in the overall proposition, and show that this value is correlated with the acceptability of extracting that referent. A t-test revealed that the items in the +Relevant condition received higher ratings than those in the –Relevant condition ($t = -20.765$, $p < 0.001$). The overall mean rating for the former was 4.37 ($SD = 0.92$) and the overall mean for the latter was 2.94 ($SD = 1.43$). A by-item t-test analysis revealed that all item pairs were statistically different in the same direction, so that no –Relevant item received an average rating that was equal or superior to its +Relevant counterpart.

To ensure that any acceptability difference between item pairs like (36) was caused by extraction itself rather than by semantic or pragmatic differences between the item pairs, a second norming experiment was conducted with a different group of forty participants to measure the acceptability of the declarative counterparts of twenty items like those illustrated in (36), interspersed with forty distractor sentences. This task was thus designed to ensure that all non-extracted counterparts of the items were equally highly acceptable to begin with. The speakers were asked to rate the acceptability of these items on a Likert scale of 1 to 5.

Finally, the extracted counterparts of the twenty experimental items were constructed, as illustrated in (38), and sixty speakers were asked to rate their acceptability, again on a 5-point Likert scale.

(38)   a. What did Kayla post a comment about?   (+Relevant)
        b. What did Kayla misread a comment about?   (–Relevant)

A Pearson test also found a positive correlation between the by-item mean relevance ratings and the by-item mean subextraction acceptability ratings ($r = 0.75$, $p < 0.0001$). An LMER model was also fitted, where the mean subextraction acceptability ratings was the dependent variable, the mean relevance ratings by-item from the questionnaire experiment the independent variable, and the verb-object frequency a random effect. The results again suggest that the relevance ratings are correlated with the subextraction acceptability ratings ($\beta = 0.56$, $SD = 0.08$, $t = 7.04$, $p < 0.0001$), with an (adjusted) R^2 value of 0.55. Finally, Chaves and King (2020) also fitted an Ordered Regression Model, which again found evidence for a correlation between raw relevance ratings and raw extraction acceptability ratings. In Figure 6.6 the mean acceptability ratings for the subextraction items are pitted against the mean relevance ratings for the declarative counterparts.

The results suggest that the acceptability of object subextractions is contingent on an interplay between the verb and the extracted element, such that the more important the latter is for the proposition described by the utterance, the more acceptable the subextraction. This is consistent with extant pragmatic accounts of subextraction effects. The findings also suggest that not all subextractions are equally acceptable, ranging from very low acceptability (e.g. lowest acceptability means of 2.5) to high acceptability (e.g. highest acceptability means of 4.8). It is therefore unsurprising that some subextractions can be ameliorated with contextualization, and others less so. Figure 6.7 compares acceptability ratings with relevance ratings for each item in each condition.

The fact that subextractions are graded and span almost the full range of the scale is not compatible with syntactic accounts, as nothing in them predicts gradient acceptability,

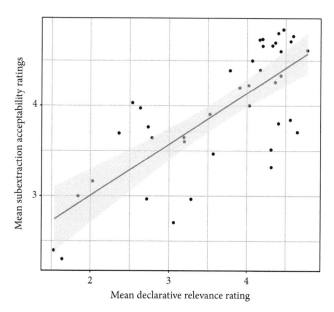

Figure 6.6 Subextraction acceptability vs. declarative relevance ratings

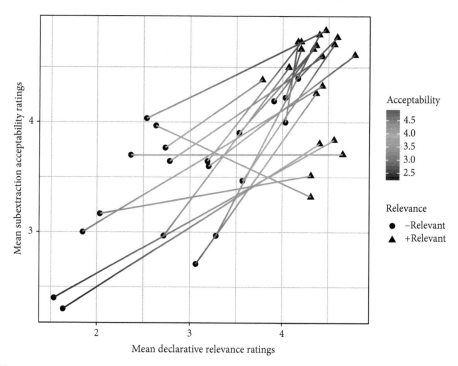

Figure 6.7 By-item acceptability ratings vs. relevance ratings

but is fully compatible with a pragmatic account, provided that the likelihood of an NP-embedded referent being relevant for the assertion is a matter of degree. In what follows we apply the logic used in the preceding experiment to Subject Island violations. Corey

Wright, a student at the University at Buffalo, assisted with the item design. We analyzed data provided by fifty AMT participants via IbexFarm.

6.2.3.1 Methods

A total of twenty experimental items were constructed, each of which had two versions, as seen in (39–41). The extracted referents in the –Relevant condition are (according to our intuitions) less important for the situation described by the sentence than the items in the +Relevant condition.

(39)   a. Which joke was the punchline of extremely offensive?
           (+Relevant)

       b. Which joke was the punchline of overheard by the teacher?
           (–Relevant)

(40)   a. Which book is the appendix of extremely comprehensive?
           (+Relevant)

       b. Which book is the appendix of oddly formatted?
           (–Relevant)

(41)   a. Which employee was the resignation of completely unexpected?
           (+Relevant)

       b. Which employee did the resignation of get saved as a PDF?
           (–Relevant)

To ensure that the +Relevant condition items were indeed more relevant than the –Relevant condition items, we conducted a second norming experiment in which a different group of fifty participants also recruited via AMT were asked to use a five-point Likert scale to answer a questionnaire, composed of sentences based on our twenty original experimental items. More specifically, the participants were asked to rate how much they agreed with statements like those in (42), where 1 = very little, 5 = very much.

(42)   a. Whether the punchline of a joke is [offensive / overheard by the teacher] depends on what the joke is.

       b. Whether the appendix of a textbook is [extremely comprehensive / oddly formatted] depends on what the textbook is.

       c. Whether the resignation of an employee [got saved as a PDF/ is completely unexpected] depends on who the employee is.

The twenty items were pseudo-randomized with forty distractor sentences and counterbalanced across two lists in a Latin Square design so that each participant only responded to one version of each experimental item. A sample of distractors is given in (43).

(43) a. Whether someone finds the outcome of a poll a bit unexpected depends on where the poll is.

    b. Whether residents are somewhat critical of their city's local government depends on what the city is.

    c. Whether a professor is rather surprised at the grades for an exam depends on where the exam is.

A t-test revealed that the items in the +Relevant condition received higher relevance ratings than those in the –Relevant condition (t = -17.34, p < 0.0001). The overall mean rating for the former was 3.99 (SD = 1.23) and the overall mean for the latter was 2.47 (SD = 1.51). A by-item t-test analysis revealed that only five item pairs were not statistically different across conditions. We removed these five item pairs from the final analysis.

    Finally, to ensure that any acceptability difference between the item pairs was caused by extraction itself rather than by semantic or pragmatic differences between the item pairs, a norming experiment was conducted to measure the acceptability of the declarative counterparts of the twenty items, as illustrated in (44). The goal of this task is to ensure that the non-extracted counterparts of the items were equally acceptable to begin with.

(44) a. The punchline of this joke was extremely offensive / overheard by the teacher.
    b. The appendix of this textbook is extremely comprehensive / oddly formatted.
    c. The resignation of this employee was saved as a PDF / was completely unexpected.

Accordingly, a different group of forty English speakers were asked to rate how natural the twenty declarative counterpart items sampled in (44) sounded, using a five-point Likert scale. The items were counterbalanced across two lists, interspersed with forty distractor sentences, and pseudo-randomized. All distractors were grammatical as illustrated in the sample in (45).

(45) a. The winner of the contest played a guitar solo on stage.
    b. The main suspect was sentenced to prison for assault.
    c. The delivery person placed this pie on that table.

The rating results indicate that both types of sentences were deemed highly acceptable: for each experimental item, the mean was above 4, with an overall mean of 4.21. The overall mean for +Relevant items was 4.24, and the overall mean for -Relevant items was 4.15. No statistical difference existed between the two conditions ($t = -1.39, p = 0.16$). Pairwise t-tests by-items analysis revealed that four item pairs exhibited a statistical difference, and for this reason we included the acceptability of the declarative counterparts as a factor in the mixed-effect models reported here.

    After the norming stage, the twenty subject subextraction items were counterbalanced across two lists using a Latin Square design so that each participant only responded to one version of each experimental item, as in the above experiments. The twenty experimental items were again interspersed among forty distractor items, a sample of which is seen in (46). Half of the distractors were ungrammatical because the final verb phrase has an illicit object. Participants were asked to judge how natural each sentence was by giving it a number from 1 (very unnatural) to 5 (very natural).

(46)　a.　*What did your friends at school in all likelihood enjoy to learn?
　　　b.　*Who did Lauren bake an incredibly delicious chocolate cake to?
　　　c.　What did the boy next door presumably climb the tree for?
　　　d.　What did the customer at the bar perhaps drink too much of?

We found five item pairs which did not exhibit the required difference in relevance ratings during the norming phase, and therefore discarded those items from the analysis.

6.2.3.2　Results

The data from the remaining fifteen item pairs were analyzed. The mean response for the +Relevant condition was 2.98 ($SD = 1.17$), and 2.85 ($SD = 1.09$) for the –Relevant condition. The mean response for the grammatical distractors was 4.01 ($SD = 1.01$) and 2.3 ($SD = 1.24$) for the ungrammatical distractors.

A LMER model with the mean subextraction acceptability ratings per item as a dependent variable and the mean relevance ratings per item from the questionnaire experiment as the independent variable (allowing for the intercept to vary with items and declarative acceptability ratings as random effects) suggests that the relevance ratings were correlated with the subextraction acceptability ratings ($\beta = 0.07$, $SD = 0.03$, $t = 2.38$, $p = 0.02$). A Pearson test found near-significant evidence of a weak correlation between the mean relevance ratings and the mean subextraction acceptability ($r = 0.34$, $p = 0.06$). A by-item inspection reveals that five items were not positively correlated, whereas the remaining items were, as illustrated in Figure 6.8.[6] Another factor in the weak correlation

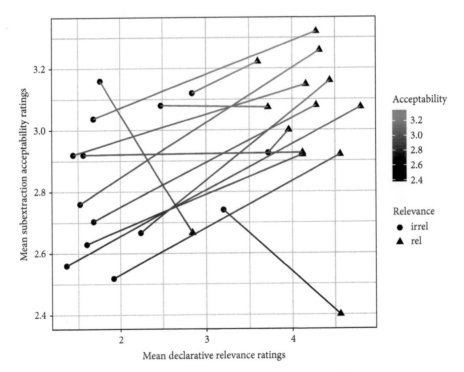

Figure 6.8 By-item subextraction acceptability ratings vs. relevance ratings

---

[6] One item was removed from the analysis because of a typo graphical error in the experimental stimuli.

is that the acceptability range for the subextractions was narrower than for the relevance ratings.

Finally, we also fitted a Cumulative BLRs model with the raw relevance ratings as ordered predictors of subextraction acceptability ratings, allowing the intercepts to vary with items and the acceptability of the declarative counterparts as random effects. The model used a flexible threshold and uniformative priors, converging after four chains and 4,000 iterations with $\hat{R}$ of one throughout. The log-odds coefficient for the relevance rating was $\beta = 0.08$ ($SD = 0$, CrI = $[0.07, 0.08]$, P($\beta > 0$) = 1), again providing some evidence for the presence of a weak correlation.

6.2.3.3 Discussion

Our results suggest that the more important the extracted referent is for the proposition described by the utterance, the more acceptable the subject subextraction. The effect is much weaker than in object subextraction, as one would expect, given the semantic and pragmatic constraints typically imposed on subjects; see §3.2.6. Subject phrases are typically reserved for topics, which causes a conflict between the discourse function of the extracted element and the discourse function of the subject phrase. Of course, not all subject phrases are equally biased to be assigned the same pragmatic function. This depends on the predication, the proposition, and the context.

Hence, it is not unexpected that the effect of relevance is harder to isolate in Subject Island violations, where there are additional pressures against subextraction as compared with NP Constraint violations. Other than this difference, the findings are similar in that not all subextractions are equally acceptable, ranging from very low acceptability to high acceptability, as can be seen in Figure 6.8. The existence of moderately and highly acceptable subextractions is exactly what we would expect if the Subject Island constraint effects are due to multiple factors, including relevance, contextualization difficulty, and violated expectations about where gaps are likely to be found in the sentence.

6.2.4 Event-based effects in phrasal adverbials

In the remaining experiments we turn our attention to extraction from adverbial phrases, and show that these too are graded, ranging from highly acceptable to highly unacceptable, and can improve dramatically with repeated exposure. The results are consistent with the view that Adjunct Island effects are contingent on the semantic link between the verb phrase and the adverbial phrase, as argued in §6.1.

The first experiment following is from previously unpublished work by Hofmeister (2011), with the goal of comparing how the acceptability of different kinds of constructions with different kinds of grammatical issues is affected by increased exposure. The results suggest that amelioration rates are different for different constructions, which makes sense in an exemplar-based conception of grammar. The two main takeaways concerning Adjunct Islands are as follows: first, Adjunct Island violations ameliorate only if the number of exposures is sufficiently high. This suggests that past research has failed to detect amelioration because of an insufficient number of exposures. Second, the results suggest that Adjunct Island violations range from highly acceptable to highly unacceptable. As in all other island phenomena surveyed so far, this again is consistent with the hypothesis that extractability from such island environments is contingent on the proposition itself, rather than strictly on its syntax.

6.2.4.1 Methods

We analyzed data from ninety-six informants (approximately forty per list), who had question comprehension accuracy above 75%. Two groups of participants read and judged the materials for this experiment. For four different data sets, the materials were distributed across experimental lists such that one group saw twice as many tokens as the other group, controlling for overall list length. In the island materials for this experiment, sentences with dependencies into Adjunct Islands were contrasted with non-island-violating sentences, as in (47). Every experimental item was followed by a comprehension question.

(47) a. Just a few years ago, Mosul was a city which terrorists would have thought twice before attacking.
        (Would terrorists have thought of attacking Mosul a few years ago? Y/N)

        [Adjunct Island condition]

      b. Just a few years ago, terrorists would have thought twice before attacking the city of Mosul.
        (Would terrorists have thought of attacking Mosul a few years ago? Y/N)

        [Non-island condition]

List 1 contained twenty-four such island items (twelve per condition), while List 2 had twelve (six per condition). Three additional material types were included in each experimental list, varying in terms of (i) complexity, (ii) grammatical vs. ungrammatical case marking, and (iii) grammatical vs. ungrammatical subject-verb agreement. In (48) we exemplify the materials that varied with respect to complexity: a right-branching structure is used in (48a) vs. a center-embedded structure in (48b). List 1 had twelve such items; List 2 had twenty-four.

(48) a. The rebels in the jungle captured the diplomat who pleaded with the villagers after they threatened to kill his family for not complying with their demands.
        (Was the diplomat captured by rebels? Y/N)   [Right-branching]

      b. The diplomat who the rebels who were in the jungle captured pleaded with the villagers after they threatened to kill his family for not complying with their demands.
        (Was the diplomat captured by rebels? Y/N)   [Center-embedded]

Another set of sentences differed in the case marking of an object pronoun (nominative vs. accusative), as shown in (49). List 1 carried twenty-four of these items, while List 2 had twelve. A third set contrasted agreement marking on a copula, as depicted in (50). List 1 had twelve, and List 2 had twenty-four.

(49) a. The psychologist who counseled Elizabeth instructed she that negative thoughts can be chased away by positive ones.
        (Did the therapist give Elizabeth advice about positive thinking? Y/N)

        [Case nom]

b. The psychologist who counseled Elizabeth instructed her that negative thoughts can be chased away by positive ones.
(Did the therapist give Elizabeth advice about positive thinking? Y/N) [Case acc]

(50) a. The advertisement on the skyscrapers was hard to read except from a long distance away.
(Was the ad easy to read? Y/N)   [S-V agreement match]

b. The advertisement on the skyscrapers were hard to read except from a long distance away.
(Was the ad easy to read? Y/N)   [S-V agreement mismatch]

Participants saw only one condition of each item, and all materials were pseudorandomized for presentation order. Each group of participants read and judged an equal number of total sentences in the experiment, using a 0–10 Likert scale.[7] The net effect is that each group of participants judged eighteen sentences with case or agreement problems. Moreover, of the seventy-two sentences each group rated, thirty-six were predicted to be relatively unacceptable, and thirty-six relatively acceptable.

6.2.4.2 Results

The mean acceptability ratings by data set and condition in Experiment 1 are shown in Table 6.3. Values in parentheses indicate standard errors. Both the sentences with case violations and those with nested dependencies triggered far lower judgments than sentences with Adjunct Island violations. In fact, the acceptability of Adjunct Island violations was fairly high, as was the acceptability of sentences with subject-verb agreement issues.

LMER models were fitted for the data in each set of materials. Each model contained a predictor for the item order of the relevant trial, relative to other items in the same condition. This item order term was centered in each model to minimize collinearity, as in prior experiments. The results reveal that judgments for Adjunct Island violations

Table 6.3 Mean acceptability ratings (0–10) by data set and condition

Data set	List		
		island	*non-island*
EXTRACTION	List1	6.72 (.11)	8.63 (.07)
	List2	6.38 (.16)	8.40 (.12)
		mismatch	*match*
S-V AGREE	List1	7.11 (.16)	8.47 (.1)
	List2	6.22 (.12)	8.49 (.09)
		nominative	*accusative*
CASE	List1	3.42 (.12)	7.94 (.07)
	List2	6.76 (.14)	7.88 (.12)
		center-embedded	*right-branching*
COMPLEXITY	List1	2.39 (.13)	5.81 (.15)
	List2	2.7 (.1)	5.66 (.11)

---

[7] According to Hofmeister (2011), a replication with a more typical Likert scale of 1–10 yielded quantitatively similar results.

Table 6.4 Model summary of fixed effects for List 1

Data set	Factor	Estimate	SD	t
Islands	DEPENDENCY[DEPENDENCY=1]	−0.326	0.051	−6.44
	ITEM ORDER	0.024	0.007	3.71
	DEPENDENCY[DEPENDENCY=1] × ITEM ORDER	0.013	0.007	2.05
Case	GRAMMATICALITY[NOM.=1]	−0.725	0.048	−14.97
	ITEM ORDER	0.011	0.006	1.94
	GRAMMATICALITY[NOM.=1] × ITEM ORDER	0.015	0.007	2.17
S-V agree	GRAMMATICALITY[MISMATCH=1]	−0.228	0.068	−3.36
	ITEM ORDER	−0.005	0.023	−0.23
	GRAMMATICALITY[MISMATCH=1] × ITEM ORDER	−0.005	0.016	−0.30
Complexity	COMPLEXITY[RIGHT-BRANCH=1]	0.568	0.048	11.81
	ITEM ORDER	0.046	0.020	2.35
	COMPLEXITY[RIGHT-BRANCH=1] × ITEM ORDER	−0.051	0.015	−3.53

rose with repeated exposure; however, this effect is only reliable given twelve repetitions. In fact, item order interacts with island condition in List 1 (= twelve repetitions per condition). As revealed by separate mixed-effect models per condition, this interaction reflects the fact that judgments for the island-violating condition increased significantly with exposure ($\beta = 0.038$; $SD = 0.012$; $t = 3.31$), unlike in the non-island-violating condition ($\beta = 0.012$; $SD = 0.008$; $t = 1.46$). The model summary for List 1 is in Table 6.4. Each model contains a predictor for the primary manipulation, item order, and their interaction. Bracketed material indicates the treatment level of the experimental manipulation whose corresponding statistics are shown.

A main effect of item order is observed for the data set with the case manipulation in List 1. Here, as in the case of the islands data set, judgments also rose over the course of twelve presentations of case violations ($\beta = 0.026$; $SD = 0.009$; $t = 3.08$), but not for sentences without such violations ($\beta = -0.003$; $SD = 0.006$; $t = -0.53$), leading to an interaction. The same main effect of item order recurs in List 2, although no interaction emerges in this case, as judgments in both conditions climb with item order (Nominative: $\beta = 0.071$; $SD = 0.036$; $t = 1.97$; Accusative: $\beta = 0.045$; $SD = 0.026$; t = 1.77). In both lists, agreement errors fail to yield higher judgments as item order increases: there are no significant main effects of item order or interactions of item order and condition. Conversely, across both lists, there is a parallel relationship between item order and sentences that vary in processing complexity: judgments for complex, nested sentences rise with repeated exposure (List 1: $\beta = 0.097$; $SD = 0.024$; $t = 4.08$; List 2: $\beta = 0.051$; $SD = 0.009$, $t = 5.41$), unlike judgments for right-branching sentences (List 1: $\beta = -0.007$; $SD = 0.025$; $t = -0.29$; List 2: $\beta = 0.012$; $SD = 0.010$; $t = 1.20$).

In List 2 (= six repetitions per condition), however, no main effect of item order is evident for Adjunct Islands, nor is there an interaction. Separate fits confirm that neither condition improves with only six repetitions (Adjunct Island: $\beta = 0.049$; $SE = 0.039$; $t = 1.29$; Non-Island: $\beta = 0.025$; $SD = 0.025$; $t = 1.01$). Had List 2 been the only source of evidence, the

Table 6.5 Model summary of fixed effects for List 2

Data set	Factor	Estimate	SD	t
Islands	DEPENDENCY[DEPENDENCY=1]	−0.335	0.062	−5.39
	ITEM ORDER	0.037	0.028	1.33
	DEPENDENCY[DEPENDENCY=1] × ITEM ORDER	0.014	0.018	0.76
Case	GRAMMATICALITY[NOM.=1]	−0.679	0.061	−11.16
	ITEM ORDER	0.057	0.022	2.59
	GRAMMATICALITY[NOM.=1] × ITEM ORDER	0.014	0.024	0.57
S-V agree	GRAMMATICALITY[MISMATCH=1]	−0.370	0.056	−6.65
	ITEM ORDER	−0.008	0.007	1.13
	GRAMMATICALITY[MISMATCH=1] × ITEM ORDER	−0.003	0.007	−0.50
Complexity	COMPLEXITY[RIGHT-BRANCH=1]	0.506	0.041	12.48
	ITEM ORDER	0.031	0.008	3.83
	COMPLEXITY[RIGHT-BRANCH=1] × ITEM ORDER	−0.019	0.007	−2.94

conclusion would most likely be that sentences with dependencies into Adjunct Islands do not become increasingly better with exposure, contrary to fact. The model summary for List 2 is shown in Table 6.5.

Beyond showing the utility of testing at high levels of repetition, the results here demonstrate that ungrammaticality per se is not sufficient to observe repeated exposure effects, even at relatively high levels of repetition. Judgments for multiple conditions remain quite stable, a configuration of results which undercuts any concern that the rise in ratings stems from a task-related effect. If general task demands or features drive the observed effects, then all conditions should pattern the same, which is clearly not the case in this experiment nor in any other experiment where amelioration was detected.

In addition to the fact that Adjunct Island violations were rated quite high, a by-items analysis on the full data set also reveals that there was a significant amount of variation across each sentence. The plots in Figure 6.9 illustrate the range of acceptability differentials.

Among the twenty-four Island Violation items, one-third received acceptability judgments that were not statistically different from their non-island counterparts (mean p value of 0.34, $SD = 0.2$). The remaining fifteen items were statistically less acceptable than the non-island controls (mean p value of 0.004, $SD = 0.01$). Similarly, different Adjunct Islands exhibited different degrees of amelioration due to repeated exposition. All this variability is difficult to explain if Adjunct Island violations are syntactically illicit, since all the sentences in this condition had the same structure. The results are completely expected if such extractions are syntactically licit but governed by semantic and pragmatic constraints, such as relevance and contextualization difficulty. We suspect that what matters is the degree to which the verbal phrase and the adverb cohere with each other, i.e. how prototypical the complex situation they describe is, given world-knowledge experience–in other words, to what extent the frame evoked by the main action is related to the semantics of the adverbial, so that the extracted referent is construed as relevant for the main action.

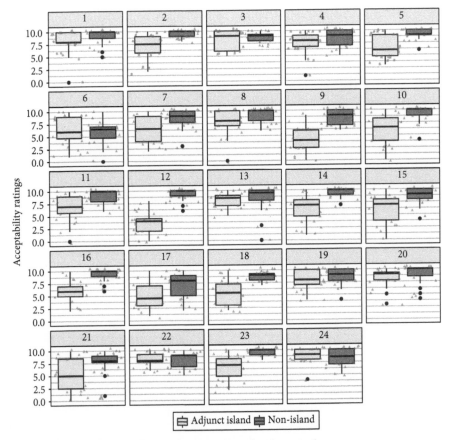

Figure 6.9 By-item acceptability ratings as compared with controls

6.2.4.3 Discussion

The results suggest that not all Adjunct Island violations are created equal, and range from acceptable to unacceptable and everything in between. This is consistent with the findings of Kohrt et al. (2018a, b) and indicates that the proposition itself plays a key role in the acceptability of such UDCs. The results also suggest that the effect that repeated exposure has on acceptability varies from construction to construction. While the island-violating cases were found to improve given only twelve exposures, judgments for sentences with case violations and nested dependencies rose reliably even with just six. This makes sense in the framework we have adopted; different assumptions about linguistic structure have different credibility, and therefore require different amounts of exposure to revise. Nonetheless, sentences with case violations and those with nested dependencies triggered far lower judgments than sentences with Adjunct Island violations, which suggests that the cause of the oddness of these constructions is not the same.

The only data set that showed no effect of item order involved a manipulation of subject-verb agreement. In the agreement error examples, however, all stimuli involve number attraction, e.g. 'The key to the cabinets are…' Such configurations are attested in real speech, and notoriously cause speakers to overlook the number mismatch between the head noun and the verb. If speakers overlook the oddness or correct the agreement error (consciously or not), this would explain the fact that these conditions received notably high ratings. The results again demonstrate that ungrammaticality per se does not lead to repeated exposure effects, even at relatively high levels of repetition. Judgments for multiple conditions remain quite stable. This configuration of results undercuts any concern that the rise in ratings stems from a task-related effect, which would predict that all conditions pattern the same, contrary to fact.

6.2.5 Event-based effects in tensed adverbial clauses

As discussed in §3.2.7.2, tensed Adjunct Islands are widely regarded as one of the strongest environments prohibiting extraction. Experimental studies have found that such interrogative Adjunct Island violations have low acceptability (Sprouse, 2007b; Sprouse et al., 2012, 2013, 2016), and do not ameliorate with repeated exposure (Hiramatsu, 1999; Snyder, 2000; Sprouse, 2009; Francom, 2009; Goodall, 2011; Snyder, 2017). Similarly, Braze (2002) found no evidence that repeated exposure had any effect on online processing of such UDCs. But there is good reason to believe that the generality of these null effects has been overstated. Not all Adjunct Island violations are created equal. Müller (2017) argues that extraction from tensed adjuncts in Swedish is constrained by the degree of syntactic integration of the adjunct clause, the internal syntax of the adjunct clause, and semantic coherence. Similar findings have been made for Norwegian (Bondevik, 2018). In our view, the same constraints are active in English: the interpretation of sentences with tensed Adjunct Island violations is influenced by the degree of semantic-pragmatic cohesion between the matrix and the adjunct. This would predict that different types of tensed adjuncts ameliorate at different rates. As Jin (2015) notes, tensed Adjunct Island effects align well with the interclausal semantic relations hierarchy in Van Valin (2005, 208, 209), in which conditionals are one of the weakest relations, followed by reason, concessive, and causative relations. Conditionals involve events that are more independent than those of causatives. At the opposite end of the spectrum Van Valin places indirect discourse connectors, manner modifiers, and means, which are highly dependent. We note that a similar hierarchy is proposed by Engdahl (1983, 9) concerning parasitic gap licensing: manner, temporal, and purpose adverbs are quite permeable to parasitic gaps, indirect discourse clauses are intermediate, and temporal, causal, and conditional clauses are the least permeable. We suspect the same pattern is true for resumptive pronoun use and acceptability.

Adjunct phrases are a classic syntactic environment for expressing presupposed or backgrounded information, and, as such, extraction from adjuncts should be difficult (Van Valin, 1994; Erteschik-Shir, 2006b, 2007; Goldberg, 2013). But this does not entail that all adjuncts are equally likely to express non-at-issue information, and so there should be some variability within each type of adjunct violation as well.

6.2.5.1 Methods
We analyzed data from one hundred and nineteen self-reported native speakers with IP addresses originating from the United States, recruited via AMT. The experiment was run using IbexFarm. The goal of this experiment was to test whether temporal, conditional, and causal Tensed Adjunct Island violations ameliorate with increased repeated exposure.[8]

---

[8] The temporal items contained *when*, *while*, *before*, and *after* adverbials. As in all other experiments discussed in this chapter, all experimental items can be downloaded from the URL referenced in §6.2.

There were twenty-four experimental items, distributed and counterbalanced across three conditions as illustrated in (51). Informal consultations with native speakers were conducted in an attempt to arrive at items in which the declarative counterparts of these items expressed 'typical' situations.

(51) a. Who did Sue blush when /because/if she saw?   [Temporal/Causal/Conditional]
      b. What did Tom get mad when/because/if Phil forgot to say?   [Temporal/Causal/Conditional]
      c. What would Mia be impressed when/because/if Robin cleaned?   [Temporal/Causal/Conditional]

Thus, each participant saw the Adjunct Island violation items interspersed with thirty-six filler phrases; half of the latter were ungrammatical, as in (52) and (53). The latter grammatical fillers were immediately followed by a comprehension question, as shown. All items were pseudo-randomized to ensure that no two participants saw them in the same order. Half of the distractors contained proper names.

(52) a. *Who does the union identify as having most recently fired from?
      b. *What did Daniel explicitly warn against doing for?

(53) a. What wrongdoing did Mia accidentally confess to during the wedding rehearsal?
          Q: The maid of honor was a victim of wrongdoing during the rehearsal. T/F

      b. What did the editor recommend should be revised?
          Q: The person in charge decided that something was not good enough. T/F

Participants were asked to judge how natural each sentence was, by giving it a rating from 1 (very unnatural) to 5 (very natural). The one hundred and nineteen participants obtained a mean comprehension question accuracy of 86%. Other participants were removed from the analysis for having comprehension-question accuracy levels below 75% accuracy.

6.2.5.2 Results
The overall acceptability of the tensed Adjunct Island violations was low (2.58, $SD = 1.26$), as was the acceptability of the ungrammatical distractors (2.19, $SD = 1.11$). The acceptability of the grammatical controls was, as expected, much higher (4.16, $SD = 1.05$). Within each condition, the results were as shown in Table 6.6.

Table 6.6 Mean and median acceptability ratings per condition

Adjunct	Mean	Median	SD
Conditional	2.92	3	1.3
Temporal	2.42	2	1.27
Causal	2.09	2	1.07

A within-items inspection revealed a wide range of acceptability patterns, as Figure 6.10 illustrates. The aggregate grammatical distractors are shown as 'G' and the aggregate

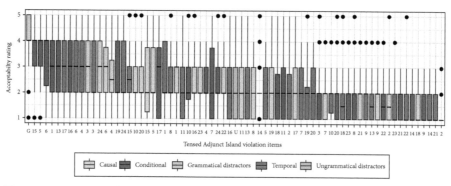

Tensed Adjunct Island violation items

Causal Conditional Grammatical distractors Temporal Ungrammatical distractors

Figure 6.10 Acceptability ratings per item and item type

ungrammatical distractors as 'U'. The conditional items clustered at the high end of the scale, causal items at the end, and temporal in the middle.

Such a distribution of acceptability ratings is unexpected for any purely syntactic account of islands that we are aware of, but fully consistent with accounts in which semantic-pragmatic cohesiveness of the two propositions plays a role in Adjunct Island violations effects, like Müller (2017). Furthermore, the range of acceptability ratings is unexpected as well, since some are fairly high in acceptability and others fairly low.

In order to rule out the hypothesis that these contrasts are caused by anything other than the UDC itself, we conducted a norming sentence acceptability experiment with the declarative counterparts of the stimuli, as illustrated in (54).

(54) a. Sue blushed when she saw someone.   [Temporal]
      b. Tom got mad because Phil forgot to say something.   [Causal]
      c. Mia would be impressed if Robin cleaned something.   [Conditional]

The items were interspersed with grammatical and ungrammatical declarative distractors, and a different set of informants were asked to rate the sentences on a scale of 1 to 5. Overall mean acceptability was 4.34 ($SD = 0.88$), and the by-condition results were as follows: Causal (4.54, $SD = 0.64$), Conditional (4.02, $SD = 0.99$), Temporal (4.65, $SD = 0.71$). An LMER model with the island acceptability ratings as a dependent variable and the adjunct type and the declarative ratings as interacting factors revealed no significant effects (all $p > 0.37$). Moreover, independent LMER models for each adjunct type showed that the declarative ratings do not predict island acceptability ratings (Conditional: $t = 0.32, p = 0.76$, Causal: $t = -0.61, p = 0.57$, Temporal: $t = 1.21, p = 0.26$).

To probe for the effect of repeated exposure within each condition, independent LMER models were fitted, with acceptability as the dependent variable and presentation order as the predictor, with participants, items, and reading time as random variables. All conditions exhibited significant amelioration as Table 6.7 shows. BLR models revealed the same pattern.

Because the stimuli were pseudo-randomized, different participants saw different items in different orders. Although the effect sizes are small, they can in principle have a dramatic effect over longer series of exposures. Recall that repeated exposure should not cause amelioration of these islands according to syntactic account according to the null effects

Table 6.7 LMER results by Tensed Adjunct violation type

Adjunct Type	Intercept	β	SD	t	p
Conditional	2.92	0.007	0.002	2.77	0.005*
Temporal	2.44	0.009	0.002	3.72	<0.005*
Causal	2.26	0.012	0.002	4.58	<0.0001*

found in previous experiments (Hiramatsu, 1999; Snyder, 2000, 2017; Braze, 2002; Sprouse, 2009; Francom, 2009; Goodall, 2011).

To further probe the ameliorating effect of exposure per item, we extracted the experimental observations for the last quarter of the experiment, containing 212 Causal item observations, 196 Conditional item observations, 210 Temporal item observations, 648 Grammatical distractor observations, and 648 Ungrammatical distractor observations. As Figure 6.11 suggests, by the end of the experiment the top five items became highly acceptable, and as acceptable as the grammatical controls (p's > 0.08).

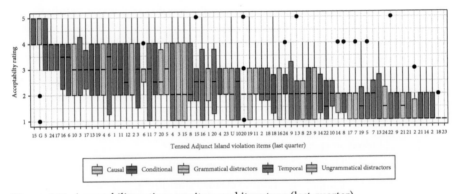

Figure 6.11 Acceptability ratings per item and item type (last quarter)

Let us return to the main experiment. Phillips (2006, 806, 807) assumes that acceptability judgments above 3 on a 5-point Likert scale indicate grammatically. Such a decision is somewhat arbitrary, as it depends on the choice of grammatical controls, but if we apply this rule of thumb to the present experiment, then five conditional tensed Adjunct Island violations are acceptable, with an overall mean of over 3, as shown in (55); cf. with Figure 6.10. These results argue strongly against syntactic explanations and favor gradient, experience-based approaches in which the proposition itself (including the semantic and pragmatic relation between the matrix and the subordinate) plays a role.

(55) a. Who would Amy be really happy if she could speak to?   (#15; 3.48)
      b. What would Jill get very angry if she missed?   (#5; 3.45)
      c. What would Allison get really upset if she forgot?   (#6; 3.4)
      d. What would John be impressed if Robin cleaned?   (#1; 3.13)
      e. What would Richie get grumpy if he were told to do?   (#13; 3.02)

All of these items involve psychological predicates which subcategorize for the cause of the state (e.g. *Amy is happy to speak to you, Amy is happy about speaking to you*, etc.).

In the terms of the Frame Semantics account we discussed in §5.2.1, the cause of the psychological state is a (non-core) event participant. Therefore, the semantics of the *if* clause not too difficult to integrate because it expresses information that the psychological predicate readily evokes: being really happy is strongly contingent on a cause for that state, being very angry is strongly contingent on a cause for that state, and so on.

In addition, the two events that each sentence in (55) describes cohere particularly well, i.e. people are often happy to speak with certain other people, people are often angered by others' forgetfulness, etc. The content of the conditional clause is crucial for the event described by the matrix predicate in all of these items. If it instead expresses circumstantial information, then the utterances are less felicitous. Compare with the sample of temporal items in (56), and their respective mean acceptability ratings.

(56) a. Who did Dan sound very excited when he talked about?   (#17; 2.89)
      b. What did Emily get really sad when she lost?   (#3; 2.75)
      c. Who did Sam feel terrible after he accidentally hit?   (#24; 2.59)
      d. What did Mia fall asleep while she was watching?   (#8; 2.4)

The situation of someone sounding very excited is more contingent on the cause for the excitement than on a particular utterance time. Similarly, someone getting really sad is more contingent on a cause for the sadness then on a particular moment in time, and so on. The graded acceptability judgments we have found make sense if relevance and coherence are key factors in the acceptability of Adjunct Islands.

6.2.5.3 Discussion

Our findings are consistent with claims in the literature that some tensed Adjunct Constraint violations may in fact be acceptable (Grosu, 1981; Deane, 1991; Kluender, 1998), and with evidence that comprehenders attempt to fill gaps in tensed Adjunct Islands (Kohrt et al., 2020). Although Tensed Adjunct Islands are notoriously strong extraction domains, our experimental results indicate that their acceptability ratings are heterogeneous, which in turn suggests that there are multiple factors in play. A syntactic explanation for this gradient acceptability is unlikely, since the strength of the island effect is graded and seems to hinge on the semantic nexus between the matrix and the modifier (Kohrt et al., 2018a, b), or in our terms, between the main predication and the (non-core) frame argument. The degree to which such clauses are islands arguably depends on the nature of the complex proposition that the two clauses describe together, as proposed by Jin (2015) and Müller (2017), drawing from independent work by Engdahl (1983, 9) and Van Valin (2005, 208, 209) about how some inter-clausal connections are semantically 'tighter' than others.

6.3 Summary

The experimental evidence presented in this chapter suggests that the acceptability of certain island violations is contingent on the prior experience that speakers have with the main situation type described by the proposition itself, and the particular syntactic construction in which it is conveyed. Highly coherent and prototypical complex structures more easily lend themselves to licensing extraction from otherwise deeply embedded positions, and comprehenders can adapt to the frequency of the input in order to overcome the processing difficulty caused when the input is unusual and inconsistent with their prior experience.

Acceptability ratings thus range from acceptable to unacceptable, suggesting that the plausibility of the proposition itself, the degree to which the extracted phrase plays a role in the main action, and the frequency of such UDCs create a malleable acceptability cline. For example, in ideal conditions subextraction from subject phrases becomes as acceptable as extraction from object phrases, provided that comprehenders are exposed to a sufficient number of exemplars for them to adapt to such unusual extractions. This should be impossible if extraction from subjects is banned by the syntax of such UDCs, since all items have the same syntactic structure.

Our findings indicate that modern syntactic theory has overstated the role that configurational syntax plays in explaining island phenomena, in particular with respect to CED effects. The data show that such islands are to some extent governed by extragrammatical factors, such as the amount of information that the main predication evokes (the background frame), as Deane (1991) originally proposed, drawing from Erteschik-Shir (1981), Kuno (1987), and others. The extracted referent must be relevant important enough for the main state of affairs that the sentence describes, i.e. for the background frame at the center of attention. Thus, if a given referent is part of the frame information that a predication evokes, or more indirectly, part of the information that is evoked by strongly associated frames linked by world knowledge, then it can be deemed sufficiently important to be singled out via extraction in a UDC. In contrast, referents that bear no clear relation to the main action described by the utterance are more likely to be deemed circumstantial or irrelevant, and therefore cannot be felicitously singled out for extraction because of a Gricean Maxim violation. Hence, acceptability differences most likely stem from the proposition itself, the world knowledge it evokes, and the degree to which the extracted referent matters for the main state of affairs that the utterance conveys, as per the EVENT PARTICIPANT SALIENCE CONDITION and the RELEVANCE PRESUPPOSITION CONDITION.

The present approach does not require stipulations to explain the behavioral phenomena. It has long been recognized that speakers make crucial use of background knowledge (frames) to make sense of discourse (Goffman, 1974; Rumelhart, 1975; Fillmore, 1977; Schank and Abelson, 1977; Lakoff, 1987; Langacker, 1987; Sanford and Garrod, 1981, 1998), and there is growing evidence that repeated linguistic exposure can lead to adaptation in a wide range of constructions and linguistic domains (Fine et al., 2013; Wells et al., 2009; Fine and Jaeger, 2016; Bridgwater et al., 2019; Prasad and Linzen, 2020; Malone and Mauner, 2020). In Chapter 7 we show how an experience-based conception of UDCs can be made consistent with the declarative construction-based theory of grammar described in Chapter 5.

7

The acquisition of UDCs

According to Chomsky (1965) and much subsequent work, the human capacity for language is principally biological, determined by **Universal Grammar** (UG), which is generally taken to consist of the attributes and principles common to all human languages, and is assumed to explain why language acquisition is possible. This **Poverty of the Stimulus** (POS) argument states that children are not exposed to rich enough data within their linguistic environments to acquire every feature of their language, which therefore indicates that humans are born with some amount of linguistic knowledge. This stance is usually referred to as **nativism**.

The acquisition of island effects is a classic argument for the existence of innate linguistic knowledge: since island violations are ungrammatical, they are not included in the speech that children hear, and so it follows that something internal to the child must contribute this knowledge about which kinds of extractions are licit. Yang et al. (2017) refer to this process as 'language growth', given the assumption that certain parameters are biologically in place to guide the acquisition process (White, 2003; Lust, 2006; Guasti, 2017). The time course and growth of the grammar take place owing to the interdependence of some of these parameters, i.e. properties of grammatical knowledge that represent default elements of language whose setting is determined by exposure to sufficient input.

No explicit nativist models of acquisition have ever been proposed, however, partially because it is unclear what UG effectively consists of. Indeed, the notion of UG has evolved over time, and its role has undergone significant reduction. For example, parameters were once argued to be a core component of UG but are now considered by some to be external (Boeckx, 2014a, 2016; Wiltschko, 2014; Eguren et al., 2016). Chomsky et al. (2019), in particular, reduce the content of UG to fundamental operations such as MERGE and AGREE. It is not clear how such an impoverished view of UG can effectively solve the POS problem, but the upshot of keeping UG minimal is that it more plausibly could have evolved via genetic mutation (Hauser et al., 2002). This is a controversial hypothesis, however (Pinker and Jackendoff, 2005; Jackendoff, 2017). In particular, there is no evidence of recent selection in the FOXP2 gene in human evolution (Atkinson, Audesse, et al., 2018), indicating that this gene cannot be responsible for UG.

An alternative perspective about language is one that assumes no innate morphosyntactic linguistic endowment (Bybee, 1985, 2010; Bod, 1992, 2008; Goldberg, 1995, 2006; Croft, 2001; MacWhinney, 2005, 2013; Tomasello, 2000, 2003). This more empiricist or domain-general and emergentist view is skeptical of POS arguments and instead argues that the acquisition of grammars emerges through exposure and usage, eschewing the necessity of genetically predetermined linguistic knowledge. The acquisition of grammar, including UDCs, all proceeds in incremental fashion, from simple to more complex knowledge (Pullum and Scholz, 2002; Tomasello, 2003; Cameron-Faulkner et al., 2003; Diessel, 2004; Abbot-Smith and Behrens, 2006; Clark and Lappin,

Unbounded Dependency Constructions: Theoretical and Experimental Perspectives. Rui P. Chaves and Michael T. Putnam,
Oxford University Press (2020). © Rui P. Chaves and Michael T. Putnam.
DOI: 10.1093/oso/9780198784999.001.0001

2011; Ambridge et al., 2014; Tomasello, 2000). Domain-general approaches are heavily usage-based and exclusively input-driven, and conceptually quite minimalist.[1] In such a view, cross-linguistic patterns are best explained as the result of historical, functional, and cognitive pressures, not exclusively connected with genetics (Dryer, 1997; Croft, 2001; Hawkins, 2004; Newmeyer, 2005; Culicover and Jackendoff, 2005; Goldberg, 2006; Haspelmath, 2007; Hawkins, 2014; Goldberg, 2019). The frequency with which particular forms and elements of grammar are encountered and their utility lead to their eventual **entrenchment** in the grammar. The development of complex sentences originates from simple non-embedded sentences, and children's early complex sentences are lexically specific constructions that are associated with concrete expressions (Diessel, 2004, 175). Thus, linguistic competence emerges from language use (Langacker, 1987, 2000; MacWhinney, 1987, 2013; Bybee, 1985, 2010; Tomasello, 1992, 2003; Elman et al., 1996; Hopper, 2001; Christiansen and Chater, 2016).

Contrary to the situation in the nativist camp, there are several empiricist grammar induction models; see Clark and Lappin (2011), Bod (2009), and Perfors et al. (2011) for examples and reviews. Da Costa and Chaves (2020) find evidence that general-purpose Transformer-based neural language models like OpenAI's GPT-2 (Radford et al., 2019) are remarkably good at processing (even very long) UDCs without any special UDC training, faring much better than Recurrent Neural Networks (Chowdhury and Zamparelli, 2018; Wilcox et al., 2018). In other words, even though GPT-2's training objective is simply to be good at predicting the next word in any given English sentence at large, without particular focus on UDCs, it acquired a significant amount of information about the morphosyntax of filler-gap dependencies. Such models are imperfect and linguistically impoverished, of course, but impressive none the less.

That said, all extant models of grammatical acquisition, including connectionist models assume the existence of some innate capacity for language acquisition, in one form or another (Briscoe, 2000). It is, therefore, possible to speak of UG in a highly conservative sense (Ackerman and Webelhuth, 1998; Tomasello, 2000; Hauser et al., 2002; Jackendoff, 2002, 2017; Chomsky et al., 2019), as a label for the difference in cognitive linguistic capacity between humans and non-human animals. In this chapter we turn our attention to behavioral evidence concerning acquisition of UDCs and island phenomena. Here we provide a general overview of the trajectory of the acquisition of UDCs in normal developing L1, focusing on the emergence of UDCs from one-word constructions to multi-clausal constructions and island effects. We show that the gradual and frequency-based developmental evidence is consistent with an exemplar-based approach that contains rich morphosyntactic, semantic, and pragmatic information along the lines of the empiricist perspective.

---

[1] The only genetic difference between humans and chimpanzees, as far as the brain is concerned, has to do with cortical synaptogenesis: whereas brain cell division extends to five years in humans, it lasts less than a year in chimpanzees and macaques (Liu et al., 2012). The fact that the only human-specific genes that concern the brain simply govern the number of rounds of cell division during fetal brain development suggests that the sheer number of extra neural layers and connections in the human brain and their developmental timing may be the key factors for the linguistic and cognitive differences between humans and chimps.

7.1 L1 acquisition

As early as seven months of age, children are able to recognize patterns in sequences generated in natural and artificial grammars (Marcus et al., 1999), and sensitivity to discontinuous elements starts to emerge one year later (Santelmann and Jusczyk, 1998). It is also at this age that successive single-word utterances are first produced, ushering in the beginning of complex word combinations (i.e. **chunks**), with embedded structures and first signs of long-distance dependencies appearing around age two (Bloom, 1973). As grammars grow beyond these initial one-word constructions, certain developmental errors begin to emerge in the speech of children. The pattern of these developments is not random; cross-linguistic evidence points to a sequence of particular errors. This consistent trajectory of acquisition takes place in spite of the fact that child-directed speech consists of variable input, often including non-canonical constructions.

In what follows we first focus on how L1 acquisition proceeds from simple **initial structures** consisting of one-word or two-word utterances like *What('s) that?* into more complex UDCs. We then discuss Subject-Auxiliary Inversion, a classic POS phenomenon that interacts with interrogative UDCs, and discuss how it can be acquired piecemeal, drawing from the frequencies of the input. We then consider more complex filler-gap dependencies across clausal boundaries and island constraints, showing how the extant developmental evidence is consistent with an exemplar-based and incremental development.

7.1.1 Initial structures

The developmental stages of questions, especially those involving *wh*-words, are relatively uncontroversial (Clancy, 1989; Roeper and de Villiers, 2011). Cross-linguistic evidence supports the observation that the *wh*-words *what* and *where* are commonly acquired first, presumably reflecting their relative utility to young and developing learners:

(1) what/where < who < how/why < when
     (Clancy, 1989)

The initial structures attested in L1 English grammars consist of individual *wh*-words (i.e. *Dat?*), and polar yes/no questions (i.e. *Doggy?*). Yes/no-questions (YNQs) initially appear in intonationally marked constructions. This one-word stage of the acquisition of questions is also marked by a large number of constructions that begin with *what* and *where*. It is also common that the first verb they appear with is the copula *be*:

(2) a. Whereda N?
     b. Whereda [Name]?
     c. Where N?/Where's N?
        (Tomasello, 1992)

Such utterances are some of the first complex structures that are produced. The seminal study of Klima and Bellugi (1966) found regularities in developmental stages in the acquisition of negation and *wh*-questions in L1 English children. The data produced by the three children in Brown (1973) further suggests that these outputs originated primarily from two formulaic expressions: *What NP (doing)?* and *Where NP (going)?* Similar results were found by Fletcher (1985) and Clancy (1989), among many others. Cameron-Faulkner et al. (2003), in particular, found that half of the utterances in a sample of child-directed speech began with one of fifty-two simple constructions, such as *Look at the N* or *Where's the N?* Many of the remaining constructions were repeated in daily routines (feeding, bathing, dressing, etc.), making them frequent before specific nouns (e.g. *Wash your* before *hands*, *Have a* before *bath*). Crucially, such constructions are also used when adults introduce children to unfamiliar words, e.g. *That's a N, Those are N, This is called a N* (Clark and Wong, 2002; Estigarribia and Clark, 2007), and plausibility plays a key role in helping learners extract information about syntactic categories and structure (Mintz et al., 2002; Mintz, 2003; Weisleder and Waxman, 2010). The extant behavioral evidence suggests that children rely on distributional patterns and chunks to draw generalizations from early on (Saffran, Aslin, et al., 1996; Saffran, Newport, et al., 1996; Swingley and Aslin, 2002; Arnon and Clark, 2011), and can use information about the kinds of subjects that verbs take to arrive at syntactic generalizations (Goodman et al., 1998). All that the child needs to realize is that a particular sequence of phonemes is associated with a (pragmatic) intention. Drawing from Green (2011, 389), we illustrate the structure and meaning of a one-word construction in Figure 7.1. This one-word utterance *Dat?* consists solely of a lexical element that is paired with the intention of eliciting the addressee to provide information about the name of a contextually salient referent. See Jackendoff and Wittenberg (2014) for a related account.

At this stage, lexical entries lack semantic content as well as morphosyntactic information, i.e. parts of speech, case, agreement, and argument structure. The expression *Dat?* is understood purely in pragmatic terms. There exists no distinction between lexical and phrasal signs. All that exists at this stage is phonological and pragmatic information (as specified here by the feature CNTXT). The BACKGRD feature describes a *want* event, indicating that this linguistic expression is uttered when the ACTOR/SPEAKER desires something from the GOAL/ADDRESSEE. The value of the C-INDS (*contextual-indices*) feature specify which individuals in the speech act relate to the intention that is expressed.

As more elaborate representations of both linguistic and non-linguistic knowledge become available, the learner eventually discovers that words can be combined with each other to yield predictable and novel utterances. Then, morphosyntactic and semantic

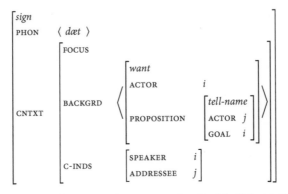

Figure 7.1 Initial interrogative construction *Dat?* (= 'What is that?')

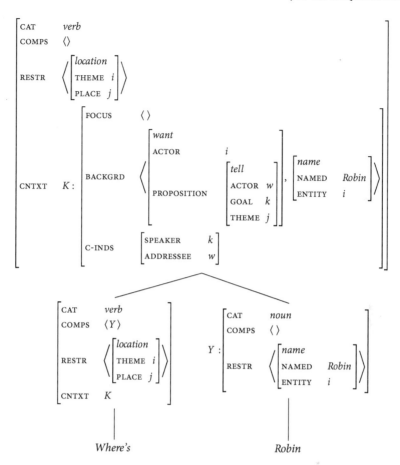

Figure 7.2 Simple interrogative *Where's Robin?*

categories are formed according to the input, which allow for finer-grained distinctions and some amount of compositionality. For example, *Where's* will be able to combine with a wide range of nominal expressions, reliably describing an information request about the location of that nominal's referent. Thus, a construction like *Where's X* may at some point correspond to a structure where *What's* selects a proper name complement, as in Figure 7.2, adapted from Green (2011, 390). This utterance means 'person i is named Robin and is at location j, tell me what j is'.

These constructions are typically accompanied by certain errors, such as lack or auxiliary inversion (3a,b) and double auxiliary forms (3c).

(3) a. Why his feet are cold?
         [*wh*-question without inversion]

     b. Why Ann and Dave bought this?
         [missing auxiliary, wrong finite verb form]

     c. What's "delusions" is?
         [double auxiliary form]
         (Green, 2011)

In fact, when auxiliary verbs are produced, they are seldom produced in the position they appear in adult English. In the next section we take a closer look at the incremental emergence of Subject-Auxiliary Inversion (SAI) in developing L1 English grammars, and then its connection to UDCs.

7.1.2 Subject-auxiliary inversion

Piattelli-Palmarini (1980, 40) claimed that although children make many errors during language learning, they do not produce errors such as *Is the man who here is tall?*, where the auxiliary in the relative clause is fronted rather than the auxiliary in the main verb phrase, i.e. *Is the man who is here tall?* The experimental results in this domain, like those of Crain and Nakayama (1987), seemed to confirm this claim, and suggested that subjects interpret sentences like (4a) as (4b), not as (4c).

(4) a. Can eagles that fly eat?
     b. = Is it the case that eagles that fly can eat?
     c. ≠ Is it the case that eagles that can fly eat?
         (Berwick and Chomsky, 2008)

Ambridge et al. (2008) pointed out several design flaws in Crain and Nakayama (1987), and described elicited production studies showing that children do in fact produce the supposedly nonexistent type of sentences. In forming polar interrogatives of sentences with two instances of 'can', around 20% of children's responses involved either doubling the auxiliary (*Can the boys who can run fast can jump high?*) or exactly the type of error that Chomsky claimed never occurs, e.g. *Can the boy who run fast can jump high?* The results were similar with sentences involving two occurrences of 'is' (*Is the boy who washing the elephant is tired?*). Ambridge et al. (2008) concludes that the data do not provide any support for the claim that structure dependence is an innate constraint, and that it is possible that children form a structure-dependent grammar on the basis of exposure to input that exhibits this property. Moreover, 62% of the responses in Crain and Nakayama (1987) contained other kinds of errors, and older children tested by Ambridge et al. (2008) still produced 52.6% incorrect questions. Such evidence suggests that the acquisition of complex questions is a rather slow process that requires accumulation of much evidence.

In construction-based theories, SAI is not derived from an underlying non-inverted clause. Rather, the same lexical entry for an auxiliary verb can be instantiated in a standard VP construction or in a SAI construction; see §5.2.2. All the child must learn, as far as syntax is concerned, is that a sentence-initial auxiliary is followed by its subject and its complement. As noted by Sag et al. (2020), there is ample evidence for this, especially when the auxiliary agrees with the subject, as in (5).[2]

[2] In particular, it should be very clear to learners that what follows the auxiliary *be* is a subject and then a complement, since the form of the verb agrees with the subject, and the range of possible complements is exactly the same as in non-inverted clauses.

(5)   a. Has/*Have Kim gone home?
      b. Have/*Has the boys gone home?
      c. Is/*are Kim going home?

From simple examples a learner can note that polar interrogatives involve an auxiliary followed by its subject and its complement. From HPSG's perspective, for example, learning to produce SAI constructions amounts to learning that such constructions begin with an auxiliary verb that selects the subsequent expressions. This simply requires that (i) the child correctly recognizes auxiliary verbs (which can be done on the basis of positive evidence) and (ii) that the child can produce/recognize arguments that are independently syntactically licit. Once the learner is able to perform these tasks, more complex examples will pose no difficulty, regardless of whether the learner has experienced such complex examples or not. Thus, SAI poses no discernible challenges to incremental acquisition. Indeed, a range of computational modeling results suggest that SAI can be learned by CFGs from the data alone, such as Lewis and Elman (2001), Clark and Eyraud (2006), Reali and Christiansen (2007), Bod (2009), McCoy et al. (2018), and Warstadt and Bowman (2020). For more discussion, see Pullum and Scholz (2002), Scholz and Pullum (2006), Estigarribia (2007, 14–16), and Clark and Lappin (2011, ch. 2).

   Estigarribia (2010) proposes a specific incremental process that developing L1 grammars go through in order to master canonical SAI construction. By focusing on 8,770 children and 10,122 YNQs produced by five children and their parents in the CHILDES database, Estigarribia (2010) notes that the data set includes non-canonical forms like those in (6), produced both by adults in child-directed speech and by the children.

(6)   a. Hear it popping? (Abe's mother, 2; 8.1)
      b. Throw it away now? (Adam's mother, 2; 10.2)
      c. That your tablet? (Eve's mother, 2; 3.23)
      d. Think that's a panda bear? (Shem's mother, 2; 10.25)
      e. He talking? (Adam's mother, 2; 11.28)
      f. You think he's in the garage? (Shem's mother, 2; 3.2)
      g. Nana buy you lots of pretty dresses? (Sarah's mother, 2; 7.12)
      h. That taste pretty good? (Eve's mother, 2; 3.22)
         (Estigarribia, 2010, 73)

Crucially, the questions in (6) are fragmentary; some are reduced questions where the initial auxiliary is missing, whereas in others the auxiliary and object are missing, with none of the parents reaching the canonical benchmark of 90% accuracy of SAI production, which is standardly assumed to be a measure of 'completed' acquisition (Brown, 1973). As a matter of fact, canonical YNQs represent less than half of the input children received (33–47%) in the selection of data analyzed in this study.

   Estigarribia (2010) thus proposes that the acquisition of YNQs in English proceeds via a **facilitation path**, where developing L1 grammars initially produce the simplest (fragment) structural units, which increase in complexity. At a later stage, the auxiliary is added to the structure. Along this facilitated acquisitional path, fragments are hypothesized to appear first and be dominant, then subjects are consistently present in the fragments, and finally aux-initial structures become dominant (see Stromswold, 1990 and Rowland and Pine, 2000 for additional evidence). We illustrate how such a path may proceed below, using the HPSG formalism adopted to far. First, verbs and complements are used as clauses, as in Figure 7.3 (semantics and pragmatics omitted).

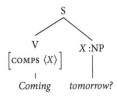

Figure 7.3 YNQ fragment representation (initial stage)

In a subsequent stage, the subject is overtly expressed, perhaps at first in a flat structure that does not recognize the VP, as in Figure 7.4.

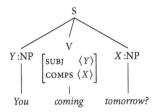

Figure 7.4 YNQ fragment representation (intermediate stage I)

Of course, ultimately VPs must be formed in order to allow adult-like complex structures like (7). In (7a) we have a coordination of VPs under the scope of negation and an adverb that requires two events, and in (7b,c) we have the preposing of the VP complement of an auxiliary verb.

(7) a. You can't simultaneously [_{VP} [_{VP} drink a bottle of wine] and [_{VP} drive a car]]!
     b. Mary wanted to move to London and [_{VP} move to London]_e she did __e.
     c. [_{VP} SING THE MELODY]_e I most certainly can __e, but not while playing the piano.

Once VPs are acquired, YNQs become more adult-like, as in Figure 7.5.

Finally, the auxiliary is added to the construction so that it selects both its (inverted) subject and a VP that subcategorizes for the same NP, as in Figure 7.6. Multiple SAI constructions become grammaticalized, each with very different semantic and pragmatic properties; see §5.2.2.

A particularly attractive feature of this hypothesis is that simpler classes of forms never completely cease to be produced, but are only replaced in frequency. Although Estigarribia (2010) finds individual variability in the children's speech behavior in the CHILDES database, the overall trajectory is consistent with his analysis. Further evidence for an incremental exemplar-driven process comes from evidence showing that children initially fail to apply SAI in *wh*-questions even after they have mastered the same operation with YNQs:

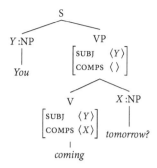

Figure 7.5 YNQ fragment representation (intermediate stage II)

(8) a. Can I sing?
　　b. *What I can sing?
　　(Roeper and de Villiers, 2011)

Lexical sensitivity also appears to be the guiding factor determining the sequence of acquisition (Borer and Wexler, 1992; Roeper and de Villiers, 1994; Tomasello, 2003), which is as expected in an exemplar-/usage-based model.

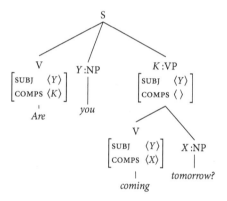

Figure 7.6 YNQ fragment representation (final stage)

7.1.3 Cross-clausal UDCs

Immediately before age 3, UDCs that cross clausal boundaries begin to emerge in production. Research by Thornton (1990) and Thornton and Crain (1994) extensively examined the production of these constructions in L1 grammars. Using a storyboard elicitation task, Thornton (1990) interviewed twenty-one English-speaking children from ages 2 to 6. While most children produced adult-like instances of long-distance subject and object extraction, they also produced various non-adult structures. Thirteen children produced the subject and object questions with the presence of the complementizer *that* (9a), but ten formed questions that included an additional overt *wh*-word at the edge of the subordinate clause (9b, c).

(9) a. What do you think that Ninja Turtles like to eat? (3.11)
     b. What do you think what Cookie Monster eats? (5.5)
     c. Who do you think what babies drink ... to grow big? (3.3)
        (Thornton, 1990)

These findings were replicated in a study by van Kempen (1997), who investigated the speech of two Dutch children. In spontaneous production, one of the children continued to produce these non-adult-like structures up until age 7. See also McDaniel et al. (1995) for a study that shows that children judge medial-*wh*-questions as acceptable. The *wh*-word that appears in the intermediate clause is almost always the same one that appears in the matrix.

It is tempting to view such data as reflecting the extraction pathway, analogously to the use of multiple *wh*-phrases in German (McDaniel, 1989); see §4.2.1 for relevant examples and discussion. This is the interpretation pursued by Thornton (1990) and Thornton and Crain (1994). An alternative is put forth by Dąbrowska et al. (2009): medial *wh*-errors result from the juxtaposition of two independent questions (e.g. *What do you think?* and *What is in the box?*). Children make use of the chunk *What do you think X?*, which is the dominant form that these long-distance structures appear in. If so, then the *wh*-phrase is used more as a device to signal a content question than as a device to signal the extraction pathway. Indeed, Thornton (1990) notes that the 'subordinate' clause is always finite. Children initially produce sentences with medial-*wh* and medial gaps in subject and object questions, but eventually they restrict the use of medial-*wh* to subject extraction. See Lutken et al. (2020) for recent experimental evidence that such errors are the result of children's immature sentence production ability, not immature grammatical knowledge. Van Valin (1998, §5) also notes that *wh*-objects are less marked than *wh*-subjects: whereas the former involve unmarked narrow focus, the latter involve marked narrow focus. This sheds light on why extraction involving object-*wh* extraction appears before (or roughly at the same time as) subject-*wh* extraction, even though the extraction pathway for the latter is structurally 'simpler' (Van Valin, 1994, 1998; Stromswold, 1995).

7.1.4 Parsing strategies in children

Successful language comprehension involves three essential elements. First, it requires *accuracy*, with each word introducing a new set of requirements that must be satisfied (e.g. thematic relations, morphosyntactic agreement, scope, etc.). Another element is **reanalysis**: incremental parsing involves temporary ambiguities, which often must be revised and corrected. This is a difficult task for adults (Ferreira and Henderson, 1991), let alone for children. Extant research suggests that reanalysis is very difficult for children (Trueswell et al., 1999; Choi and Trueswell, 2010; Kidd et al., 2011), and that children appear to be less successful than adults in integrating multiple cues in order to arrive at an alternative parse (Snedeker and Trueswell, 2004; Weighall, 2008; Engelhardt, 2014); see Snedeker and Huang (2009) for a summary of existing literature.

There is some evidence that developmental L1 grammars actively attempt to fill gaps (Love, 2007; Omaki et al., 2014; Lassotta et al., 2015), but none of these previous studies provided a fine time course measure to investigate whether or not adult-like predictions are being generated. Atkinson, Wagers, et al. (2018), building upon research initially carried out in Atkinson (2016), compared child *wh*-corpus data from the CHILDES Treebank (Pearl and Sprouse, 2013) with adult spoken language from the CallHome corpus (Kingsbury et al., 1997) and with data elicited from a Question-after-Story paradigm (Sussman and Sedivy, 2003; Omaki, 2010). Forty English-speaking children (age range 5.0–7.0; $M = 5.10$) participated in this study, with exactly half ($n = 20$) being in the 5-year-old group, and the other half ($n = 20$) in the 6-year-old group. Atkinson, Wagers, et al. (2018) developed stimuli such as the following to investigate if children incrementally generate similar syntactic predictions when compared with adults:

(10)   Can you tell me what Emily was eating the cake with_?

In (10) there are two competing gap positions: one at the direct-object gap position (*. . . what Emily was eating_?*), and the other at the prepositional object-gap position. The comparison of the child and adult corpus data revealed that there is little difference between adults and children with regard to filler-gap regularities involving direct-object and prepositional-object gaps, with an overwhelming preference for direct object (85%) over prepositional object (15%) gaps. Using a visual world paradigm with eye-tracking to measure the online performance, Atkinson, Wagers, et al. were able to measure how children (and adults) incrementally assign interpretations to such temporarily ambiguous questions.

These results suggest an important difference between the 5- and 6-year-old participants; while the 6-year-old group showed a bias for active dependency formation at the earliest region (i.e. the verb region) just like the adults, the 5-year-old informants did not display the same bias. Atkinson, Wagers, et al. (2018) hypothesize that these findings suggest that adult-like active formation of filler-gap dependencies begins to emerge around age 6. Since children of this age generally possess adult-like syntactic knowledge (Hamburger and Crain, 1982; de Villiers and Roeper, 1995; Gagliardi et al., 2016), these observed differences can be understood as a reflection of parsing strategies and return us to the challenging question of the relation of parser and grammar across the lifespan discussed in §4.4. Atkinson's (2016) and Atkinson, Wagers, et al.'s (2018) findings correlate with Dąbrowska et al.'s (2009) findings concerning the average age at which medial *wh*-errors decrease. Although incremental parsing in developing L1 grammars exhibits many core attributes also observed in adult-like performance, children struggle with comprehension tasks involving reanalysis and gap prediction until age 6. This suggests that the mechanism that processes UDCs is unlikely to be an innate linguistic mechanism, since it does not seem to aid children in the initial stages of L1 acquisition. On the contrary, the step-wise nature of acquisition is more consistent with the development of constructions via exemplars. As Clahsen and Felser (2018) conclude, grammatical knowledge is most likely gradient rather than purely categorical.

Finally, island effects seem to appear as early as age 3.0 in various languages like German and French (Weissenborn et al., 1995), Dutch, Italian, Spanish, and Greek (Baauw, 2002), and Arabic (Al-Abdulkarim et al., 1997; Al-Abdulkarim, 2001). Investigating the properties of island constraints in developmental grammars is tricky, and quite often the absence of islands in production is accepted as credible evidence of (innate) grammatical constraints at work. This is not necessarily true, of course (Lohmann and Tomasello, 2003; Ambridge and Lieven, 2011). First, it is possible that islands have not been acquired, but the task simply failed to prompt children to produce them (a null effect). Second, even after islands are acquired, nothing forces us to conclude that innate pressures are in play. The child may have simply learned the relevant constraints that limit extraction, grammatical or otherwise. As discussed in §3.1, there is also significant cross-linguistic variation in island phenomena (Jurka et al., 2011; Kush et al., 2013; Sprouse et al., 2016; Fukuda et al., 2018; Kush et al., 2018), likely reflecting different processing heuristics, different information packaging constraints, different syntax-phonology patterns, and different grammaticalization patterns (Engdahl, 1986; Van Valin, 1994; Arnon et al., 2007; Hawkins, 2014).

7.2 Exemplar-based construction grammar

We now sketch a model of language acquisition based on the construction-based grammatical framework that we have adopted in this chapter. The result is an **exemplar-based** or **usage-based** conception of grammar along the same lines as what is advocated by Bybee (2010, 2013), Traugott and Trousdale (2014), and Diessel (2015), among others. We draw close inspiration from Bod (1992) and Bod (2008), which has been adapted to HPSG by Linardaki (2006), and Arnold and Linardaki (2007). However, we will assume that the grammar itself consists of lexical and phrasal chunks. In this reconceptualization, the HPSG constructional rules discussed in Chapter 5 are nothing but idealized and abstract representations of a myriad of chunks of grammatical structure that comprise speakers' grammars (Klein and Manning, 2005).

We define chunks as linguistic representations of a given size, constrained by cognitive limitations, which are committed to working memory during exposure to linguistic input, associated with a communicative function, and categorized morphosyntactically according to their distribution. As Verhagen et al. (2019) show, linguistic variation across individuals in familiarity ratings of complex expressions (across time) suggest linguistic representations consist of a continually updating set of exemplars that include a large amount of detail concerning linguistic and extra-linguistic properties. The result is a model in which there are many different tree chunks, of different complexity, and with different frequencies, which can be deployed during incremental language processing as grammar rules. The advantage of such a perspective is that it brings us descriptively closer to the implementational level, in David Marr's terminology (see §4.4.1.1), and as such opens the way to modeling probabilistic incremental sentence processing and acquisition without particularly complex computational modeling.

There are different views of how grammars are formed in emergentist approaches (Elman et al., 1996; Langacker, 2000; Tomasello, 2003; Goldberg, 2006, 2019; Bybee, 2010; MacWhinney, 2013; Christiansen and Chater, 2016; Culicover, 2020), but a common thread is as follows. Learners begin by exploiting very low-level statistical regularities in the input in order to chunk it (Saffran, Aslin, et al., 1996; Saffran, Newport, et al., 1996; Swingley and Aslin, 2002; Arnon and Clark, 2011). This gives rise to one-word constructions like those discussed in §7.1.2, where a sound–form–meaning correspondence is formed. Speakers are able to form chunks on a single exposure, at least long enough that a subsequent instance might be encountered so that the memory can be strengthened; see Bybee (2010) and Goldberg (2019, ch. 4). Memory traces that are reactivated become more entrenched, and therefore easier to activate. This explains why inflected or derived word forms with high frequency are directly memorized. As Bannard and Matthews (2008) show, 2- and

3-year-olds are faster and better at repeating higher-frequency phrases compared to lower-frequency ones, even though the two strings were equally plausible and matched on all other frequency measures. This chunking behavior persists into adulthood: Alegre and Gordon (1999) and various others found frequency effects for regularly inflected words, suggesting that such word forms are memorized. There is also a growing body of historical evidence suggesting that more complex forms are memorized (Bybee, 2006; Traugott and Trousdale, 2014). The advantage of this redundancy is that the processing of frequently occurring words is more efficient (Corrigan et al., 2009).

The utility of a linguistic representation most likely plays a role in whether it is consolidated into memory as a chunk. It is now known that utility is important in memory consolidation and learning in general, not just in language, over and above frequency (Ballard, 2015, §2.7). For example, it has been demonstrated that dopamine, which is behaviorally related to novelty and reward prediction, modulates synapse plasticity. See, for example, Legenstein et al. (2008) for a cognitively motivated reward-based learning theory. To give an anecdotal example, anyone who has interacted with 3-year-old children knows that they do not need a half a dozen exposures to the word *chocolate* in order to learn it. One exposure is enough, provided that the child is also given some chocolate to eat. Words that are associated with highly desirable goals or traumatic events are quickly committed to memory, presumably given their high utility value. More broadly, the very act of being able to predict upcoming events and expressions can cause a linguistic representation to have high utility, and to motivate its consolidation into memory as a chunk.

In subsequent stages of language acquisition, multiword chunks of greater complexity are recognized, and admitted to the repository of exemplar chunks. Eventually, chunks that are similar give rise to more abstract chunks, serving as generalizations. Development proceeds from invariant formulas through increasingly general formulaic frames to abstract templates (Dąbrowska, 2004, 200). Such a perspective is consistent with evidence showing that adults and children alike are sensitive to the distributional properties of multiword sequences (Bannard and Matthews, 2008; Arnon and Snider, 2010; Arnon and Clark, 2011), and that multiword chunks appear to be linguistic units in their own right (Christiansen and Arnon, 2017; Arnon et al., 2017). More broadly, speakers make probabilistic predictions about a wide range of linguistic modalities, such as upcoming lexical items (Kutas and Hillyard, 1984; Altmann and Kamide, 1999; DeLong et al., 2005; Creel et al., 2008; Arai and Keller, 2013; Melnick et al., 2011), lexical categories (Tabor et al., 1997; Gibson, 2006; Levy and Keller, 2013), syntactic structures (Staub and Clifton, 2006; Lau et al., 2006; Levy, 2008; Levy et al., 2012; Omaki and Lidz, 2015; Bridgwater et al., 2019), semantics (Altmann and Kamide, 1999; Federmeier and Kutas, 1999; Kamide et al., 2003), and pragmatics (Ni et al., 1996; Mak et al., 2008; Roland et al., 2012).

Learners can construct unseen chunks, perhaps by combining extant chunks into new ones, or by generalizing over different chunks as exposure accumulates, via analogy (Goldberg, 2006; Bybee, 2010; Alishahi and Stevenson, 2008; Bod, 2009). Some forms of generalization may themselves be emergent. Perhaps all that is stored is concrete exemplars, and novel uses (i.e. rule-like behavior) result from partial instantiation of extant exemplars. Alternatively, it is possible that complex chunks partially decay in memory, and give rise to more abstract templates. Recall that our chunks are complex bundles of phonological, morphosyntactic, semantic, and pragmatic information, which we model in Chapter 5 as feature structures. If such feature bundles are memorized as a function of their relative frequency or utility, then it is conceivable that some features decay from memory faster than others that get more frequently reactivated, and that, as a consequence, some chunks will be rich with specific information and others will be more underspecified and rule-like. As Goldberg (2019) points out, memory is lossy, and lossy memories may cluster together, forming families of partially specified chunks (i.e. constructions).

Complex phrasal chunks, rich in semantics and pragmatics, are plausibly represented in a distributed manner, across overlapping neural pathways. Linguistic patterns that are common get reactivated frequently and lead to frequency effects. Likewise, linguistic patterns with high utility have a good chance of being consolidated in more permanent forms of memory than others that are rarer, and less useful. An exemplar-based grammar can thus emerge from the natural dynamics of the neural substrate: via repetition, categorization, and generalization, partially specified and probabilistic phrasal chunks may be arrived at, rich in form and meaning. An exemplar approach such as the one sketched in this chapter could yield rule-like chunks like the one in Figure 7.7, based on Linardaki (2006). In this chunk, the value of the GAP feature is shared between the mother and the daughters. Owing to space limitations, the semantics, phonology, and pragmatics are omitted, but it should be clear that such information is present, and can likewise be partially underspecified.

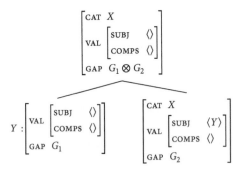

Figure 7.7 A rule-like phrasal chunk

The end result is a grammar model that consists of chunks, some rule-like, others less so. Some subtree chunks will contain different constraints on GAP values, with various degrees of generality. In some cases, certain nodes will be associated with [GAP ⟨⟩] constraints, leading to the expectation that no gap can be found in that phrase. In other cases, the GAP value may be underspecified but required to be list-joined with other GAP values. The abstract rules discussed in §5.2 can, therefore, be recast in terms of numerous simpler partially specified chunks. For example, instead of the Argument Realization construction one may have various partially specified lexical constructions like determining which members of ARG-ST are in SUBJ, COMPS, and GAP.

Some chunks can be quite large, if their communicative utility warrants it. Suppose, for instance, that the UDC pattern 'X NP *like!*' in Figure 7.8 is highly frequent, and therefore is chunked and resists memory decay. Note how the direct object and the filler phrase are only partially instantiated (shaded, for perspicuity) prior to their combination with the respective arguments. Again, semantics and pragmatics is omitted here, for ease of exposition. Such a usage-based model is consistent with the fact that some types of unacceptable sentences (including some island violations) ameliorate and are processed faster if comprehenders are exposed to multiple occurrences of such UDC patterns, as

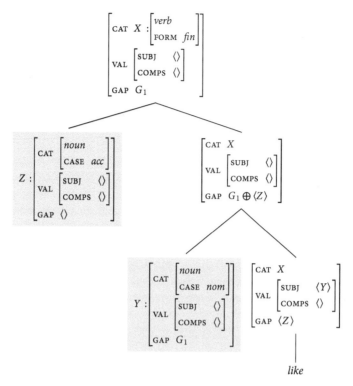

Figure 7.8 A complex UDC chunk

discussed in Chapter 6. See also Dąbrowska (2008) for other relevant experiments and discussion. The number of exposures seems to be a crucial factor. Whereas Sprouse (2009), Crawford (2011), and Hiramatsu (2000) found no amelioration for their Subject Island violations after only four or five exposures, Hiramatsu (2000) found an effect with seven exposures, and Chaves and Dery (2014) with ten. Analogously, Hofmeister (2015) detected acceptability increase for untensed Adjunct Islands only after eight exposures, but shorter exposures failed to detect any amelioration. Other short-exposure studies similarly found no amelioration in untensed Adjunct Islands (Hiramatsu, 1999; Sprouse, 2009; Francom, 2009; Goodall, 2011; Snyder, 2017), nor reduced reading time (Braze, 2002). In Snyder (2000), the amelioration was marginally significant ($p = 0.07$) after nine exposures, and Sprouse (2009) similarly found weak evidence for amelioration ($p = 0.08$) at six exposures. These results suggest to us that comprehenders can adapt to unusual filler-gap patterns, and become better at processing them once they overcome the violated expectations about where gaps are likely located; cf. the ERP data from Michel (2014, ch. 7), which reveals the importance of real-time prediction for the online processing of islands. This is fully consistent with Surprisal Theory (Hale, 2001; Levy, 2008), which holds that more cognitive effort is required to process input that is less expected. The relation between surprisal and processing effort has been experimentally validated (Boston, 2012; Demberg and Keller, 2008; Roark et al., 2009; Smith and Levy, 2008), and there is also evidence for a correlation between sentence acceptability and probability (Keller, 2003; Lau et al., 2015; Manning, 2003).

7.3 Summary

Our overview of the general properties and sequence of acquisition supports a usage-based view in which the growth of a grammar proceeds from simple units to more complex ones, exploiting the frequency of simple as well as complex exemplars (Bannard and Matthews, 2008; Arnon and Clark, 2011). There appears to be an initial disassociation between the acquisition of grammatical knowledge and online parsing strategies (Dąbrowska et al., 2009; Atkinson, 2016; Atkinson, Wagers, et al., 2018). Although children also employ some version of the active filler strategy, this does not appear to be a default setting that fully assists children in the initial stages of L1 acquisition; hence it is not an innate mechanism that aids younger children in acquisition.

Studying the development of sentence processing mechanisms in tandem with emerging linguistic competence is essential in achieving an enriched understanding of how these related processes differ and mutually benefit one another at various stages of development (Valian, 1990; Fodor, 1998; Truswell, 2007; Omaki, 2010; Omaki et al., 2014). Clahsen and Felser (2018) propose that an effective way to consider modeling this state of affairs is by assuming that grammatical knowledge is gradient rather than purely categorical (Bod, 1992, 2008; Hale, 2001, 2006; Levy, 2008; Smolensky et al., 2014; Goldrick et al., 2016; Clahsen and Felser, 2018), which is a position in line with the grammatical approach we have presented. We therefore arrive at a exemplar- and chunk-based account of grammar development composed of rich information that is probabilistic in nature, and shaped by experience. Much more work is needed to fully flesh out these ideas, needless to say, but we hope our contribution can be of use in such an endeavor.

8

Conclusion

There has certainly been much progress in our understanding of UDCs since Ross (1967), but there is also very little that has been conclusively resolved, and much that is still not well understood. Regardless of what the future holds, any theory of UDCs must account for the fact that there are many UDC families, each with its own syntactic, semantic, pragmatic, and phonological idiosyncrasies, which can interact and interweave in a myriad of ways. In particular, UDCs allow several types of filler-gap dependencies (e.g. convergent, cumulative, and chaining), which have posed and continue to pose problems for movement-based accounts.. Various families of island phenomena were also identified, which are not easily explained by a single unifying constraint, let alone a syntactic one. Rather, different types of islands most likely result from different combinations of grammatical and extra-grammatical factors, often tied to the particular type of UDC. Thus, many island phenomena are not cross-constructionally active, and vanish in particular UDCs precisely because such constructions introduce very different pragmatic constraints on the proposition and on the extracted referent.

We have argued, based on Erteschik-Shir (1981), Kuno (1987), and others that all UDCs have in common a pragmatic function: to draw attention to a distinguished event participant that is particularly relevant for the main action conveyed by the utterance. By and large, in our opinion most types of island phenomena are at least in part due to this event participant not being connected to the main action, and therefore its extraction is not felicitous on Gricean grounds (Van Valin, 2005, 288). In addition to Relevance, we have argued along with other authors that semantic-pragmatic contradictions, contextualization difficulty, the syntax-semantics interface, the syntax-phonological interface, and processing difficulty all play different roles in explaining different kinds of islands.

Our review of extant theories and formal models of grammar in Chapters 2 and 3 focused on some of the key strengths and weaknesses in modeling UDCs. In particular, we found that reliance on a unified operation like MOVE to account for filler-gap phenomena in a bottom-up model faces serious theoretical, empirical, and psycholinguistic difficulties. There are issues with how UDCs in general are supposed to be modeled, even setting aside more complex cases like convergent, cumulative, and chaining dependencies. Moreover, the treatment of island phenomena in movement-based approaches faces challenges, since island phenomena appear to be due to a constellation of factors that cannot easily be reduced to syntactic constraints.

Declarative, constraint-based, and non-movement alternatives to linguistic theory are demonstrably more suitable for capturing a much wider range of observable properties of UDCs, whilst being more consistent with the behavioral facts of incremental sentence processing than mainstream movement-based approaches. We discussed how such constraint- and construction-based models can be reconceptualized as exemplar-based models of grammar, where exposure to linguistic structure is responsible for bringing about

Unbounded Dependency Constructions: Theoretical and Experimental Perspectives. Rui P. Chaves and Michael T. Putnam,
Oxford University Press (2020). © Rui P. Chaves and Michael T. Putnam.
DOI: 10.1093/oso/9780198784999.001.0001

rule-like chunks consisting of rich representations that express generalizations of varying degree, in a distributed way. Finally, we considered the roles of frequency, utility, and lossy memory consolidation in modulating the emergence of partially specified complex chunks. Our hope is that the exemplar-based and constructional model of grammar discussed in this work can inspire better algorithmic-level approximations to implementational-level descriptions of UDC phenomena.

The experimental evidence from Chapter 6 supports the idea that frequency and pragmatic constraints are at work in various (relevance-based) island phenomena. In particular, we found evidence that background knowledge (frames) plays a role in such island effects, as originally suggested by Deane (1991), and that comprehenders can adapt to unexpected structures to the point where the island effect vanishes in ideal circumstances. The experimental results challenge the classic view of Subject and Adjunct islands as purely structural constraints. Not only is the expressed proposition key to explaining the acceptability clines caused by extraction, but also such islands can be made to weaken via some form of adaptation, an exposure-based phenomenon independently observed in various other constructions (Wells et al., 2009; Fine et al., 2013; Fine and Jaeger, 2016; Prasad and Linzen, 2020; Bridgwater et al., 2019; Malone and Mauner, 2020).

Experimental and linguistic research will continue to shape and change our understanding of linguistic phenomena and the relationship between grammar and the mind. This research program will likely lead to a reassessment of a number of longstanding claims that have held to date and, in some cases, to the revision and elimination of many of them. Such practice is simply the sign of progress in active scientific inquiry. In science, no one truly ever has the last word on any given topic, and as we hope to have emphasized throughout this book, much important research remains to be carried out. We hope that this work can be useful to those who want to further the understanding of extraction phenomena and that our discussion has showcased the relevance and importance of formal theories of grammar and their integration with models of language processing.

References

Abbot-Smith, Kirsten and Behrens, Heike. 2006. How known constructions influence the acquisition of other constructions: The German passive and future constructions. *Cognitive Science* 30(6), 995–1026.

Abeillé, Anne, Bonami, Olivier, Godard, Danièle, and Tseng, Jesse. 2004. The Syntax of French N' Phrases. In Stefan Müller (ed.), *Proceedings of the HPSG-2004 Conference, Center for Computational Linguistics, Katholieke Universiteit Leuven*, pages 6–26, Stanford: CSLI Publications.

Abeillé, Anne and Borsley, Robert D. 2008. Comparative correlatives and parameters. *Lingua* 118(8), 1139–57.

Abeillé, Anne, Hemforth, Barbara, Winckel, Elodie, and Gibson, Edward. 2018. A construction-conflict explanation of the subject-island constraint, *31th Annual CUNY Conference on Human Sentence Processing*, pages 565–6, Davis, CA: University of California.

Abeillé, Anne, Hemforth, Barbara, Winckel, Elodie, and Gibson, Edward. 2020. Extraction from subjects: differences in acceptability depend on the discourse function of the construction. *Cognition*, 204, 104293.

Abels, Klaus. 2012. *Phases: An essay on cyclicity in syntax* Berlin: Mouton de Gruyter.

Abney, Steven P. 1997. Stochastic attribute-value grammars. *Computational Linguistics* 23(4), 597–618.

Abrusán, Márta. 2007. Contradiction and Grammar: The Case of Weak Islands PhD dissertation, Massachusetts Institute of Technology.

Abrusán, Márta. 2011. Presuppositional and Negative Islands: A Semantic Account. *Natural Language Semantics* 19, 257–321.

Abrusán, Márta. 2014. *Weak island semantics*. Oxford: Oxford University Press.

Abrusán, Márta and Spector, Benjamin. 2011. A Semantics for Degree Questions Based on Intervals: Negative Islands and Their Obviation. *Journal of Semantics* 28(1), 107–47.

Ackerman, Farrell and Webelhuth, Gert. 1998. *A theory of predicates*. Stanford, CA: CSLI Publications.

Ackerman, Lauren, Frazier, Michael, and Yoshida, Masaya. 2018. Resumptive Pronouns Can Ameliorate Illicit Island Extractions. *Linguistic Inquiry* 49(4), 847–59.

Aho, Alred V. and Ullman, Jeffrey D. 1972. *The Theory of Parsing, Translation, and Compiling. Volume I: Parsing* Upper Saddle River, NJ: Prentice-Hall.

Al-Abdulkarim, Lamya M. 2001. Complex wh-questions and universal grammars: new evidence from the acquisition of negative barriers. PhD thesis, University of Massachusetts, Amherst, MA.

Abdulkarim, Lamya, Roeper, Thomas, and de Villiers, Jill G. 1999. Negative islands in language acquisition. In B. Hollebrandse (ed.), *New perspectives on language acquisition*, pages 187–96, University of Massachusetts Occasional Papers (UMOP) 22. Amherst, MA: GLSA.

Alegre, Maria and Gordon, Peter. 1999. Frequency effects and the representational status of regular inflections. *Journal of Memory and Language* 40, 41–61.

Alexopoulou, Theodora and Keller, Frank. 2007. Locality, Cyclicity and Resumption: At the Interface between the Grammar and the Human Sentence Processor. *Language* 83(1), 110–60.

Alishahi, Afra and Stevenson, Suzanne. 2008. A computational model of early argument structure acquisition. *Cognitive Science* 32(5), 789–834.

Allen, Cynthia L. 1980. *Topics in diachronic English syntax*. New York & London: Garland Publishing, Inc.

Allwood, Jens. 1976. The complex NP constraint as a non-universal rule and some semantic factors influencing the acceptability of Swedish sentences which violate the CNPC. In Justine Stillings (ed.), *University of Massachusetts Occasional Papers in Linguistics, Volume II*, pages 1–20, Amherst, MA: University of Massachusetts, Amherst, MA.

Alotaibi, Mansour and Borsley, Robert D. 2013. Gaps and Resumptive Pronouns in Modern Standard Arabic. In Stefan Müller (ed.), *Proceedings of the 20th International Conference on Head-Driven Phrase Structure Grammar*, pages 6–26, Stanford, CA: CSLI Publications.

Alsina, Alex. 2008. A theory of structure-sharing: Focusing on long-distance dependencies and parasitic gaps. In Miriam Butt and Tracy Holloway King (eds), *Proceedings of LFG08*, pages 5–25, Stanford: CA: CSLI Publications.

Altmann, Gerry T. M. and Kamide, Yuki. 1999. Incremental interpretation at verbs: Restricting the domain of subsequent reference. *Cognition* 73, 247–64.

Ambar, Manuela and Veloso, Rita. 2001. On the nature of wh-phrases-word order and wh-in-situ Evidence from Portuguese, French, Hungarian and Tetum. In Yves D'hulst, Johan Rooryck, and Jan Schroten (eds), *Romance Languages and Linguistic Theory 1999: Selected Papers from 'Going Romance' 1999 (Current Issues in Linguistic Theory)*, pages 1–38, Amsterdam: John Benjamins.

Ambridge, Ben and Goldberg, Adele E. 2008. The island status of clausal complements: Evidence in favor of an information structure explanation. *Cognitive Linguistics* 19(3), 357–89.

Ambridge, Ben and Lieven, Elena V. M. 2011. *Child language acquisition: Contrasting theoretical approaches*. Cambridge: Cambridge University Press.

Ambridge, Ben, Pine, Julian Mark, and Lieven, Elena V. 2014. Child language acquisition: Why universal grammar doesn't help. *Language* 90(3), e53–e90.

Ambridge, Ben, Rowland, Caroline, and Pine, Julian. 2008. Is structure dependence an innate constraint? New experimental evidence from children's complex-question production. *Cognitive Science* 32, 222–55.

Amy, Gérard and Noziet, Georges. 1978. Memory requirements and local ambiguities of parsing strategies. *Journal of Psycholinguistic Research* 20(3), 233–50.

Anderson, Carol. 1983. Generating coordinate structures with asymmetric gaps. In Costas P. Canakis, Grace P. Chan, and Jeannette Marshall Denton (eds), *Chicago Linguistic Society*, volume 19, pages 3–14, Chicago: Chicago Linguistic Society.

Andersson, Lars-Gunnar. 1982. What is Swedish an exception to? Extractions and island constraints. In Elisabet Engdahl and Eva Ejerhed (eds), *Readings on Unbounded Dependencies in Scandinavian Languages*, pages 33–46, Stockholm: Almqvist and Wiksell International.

Aoshima, Sachiko, Phillips, Colin, and Weinberg, Amy. 2004. Processing filler-gap dependencies in a head-final language. *Journal of Memory and Language* 51(1), 23–54.

Aoun, Joseph, Hornstein, Norbert, Lightfoot, David, and Weinberg, Amy. 1987. Two types of locality. *Linguistic Inquiry* 18(4), 537–77.

Aoun, Joseph, Hornstein, Norbert, and Sportiche, Dominique. 1981. Some aspects of wide scope quantification. *Journal of Linguistic Research* 1(3), 69–95.

Arai, Manabu and Keller, Frank. 2013. The use of verb-specific information for prediction in sentence processing. *Language and Cognitive Processes* 4(28), 525–60.

Ariel, Marc. 2001. Accessibility theory: An overview. In T. Sanders, J. Schilperoord, and W. Spooren (eds), *Text representation: Linguistic and psycholinguistic aspects* volume 8, pages 29–87, Amsterdam: John Benjamins.

Arnold, Doug and Borsley, Robert D. 2008. Non-restrictive Relative Clauses, Ellipsis and Anaphora. In Stefan Müller (ed.), *The Proceedings of the 15th International Conference on Head-Driven Phrase Structure Grammar*, pages 325–45, Stanford, CA: CSLI Publications.

Arnold, Doug and Linardaki, Evita. 2007. A Data-oriented parsing model for HPSG. In Anders Søgaard and Petter Haugereid (eds), *2nd International Workshop on Typed Feature Structure Grammars* (TFSG'07), pages 1–9, Tartu, Estonia, May 24–6. Center for Sprogteknologi, Kobenhavens Universitet, Working Papers, Report No. 8, ISN1600-339X. Available at http://cst.dk/anders/publ/tfsg/proceedings07.pdf, accessed June 7, 2020.

Arnon, Inbal and Clark, Eve V. 2011. Why *brush your teeth* is better than *teeth* – children's word production is facilitated in familiar sentence-frames. *Language Learning and Development* 7, 107–29.

Arnon, Inbal, McCauley, Stuart C., and Christiansen, Morten H. 2017. Digging up the building blocks of language: Age-of-Acquisition effects for multiword phrases. *Journal of Memory and Language*, 265–80.

Arnon, Inbal and Snider, Neal. 2010. More than words: Frequency effects for multi-word phrases. *Journal of Memory and Language* 62(1), 67–82.

Arnon, Inbal, Snider, Neal, Hofmeister, Philip, Jaeger, T. Florian, and Sag, Ivan Andrew. 2007. Cross-Linguistic Variation in a Processing Account: The Case of Multiple Wh-Questions. In Roslyn Burns, Chundra Cathcart, Emily Cibelli, Kyung-Ah Kim, and Elise Stickles (eds), *Proceedings of Berkeley Linguistics Society 32*, pages 23–35, Berkeley, CA: Berkeley Linguistics Society.

Asher, Nicholas and Lascarides, Alex. 2003. *Logics of conversation*. Cambridge: Cambridge University Press.

Assmann, Anke, Heck, Fabian, Hein, Johannes, Keine, Stefan, and Mueller, Gereon. 2010. Does chain hybridization in Irish support movement-based approaches to long-distance dependencies? In Stefan Müller (ed.), *Proceedings of the 17th International Conference on Head-Driven Phrase Structure Grammar*, Stanford, CA: CSLI Publications.

Asudeh, Ash. 2004. Resumption as Resource Management PhD thesis, Stanford University.

Asudeh, Ash. 2011. Towards a unified theory of resumption. In Alain Rouveret (ed.), *Resumptive Pronouns at the Interfaces*, pages 121–87, Amsterdam: John Benjamins.

Asudeh, Ash. 2012. *The logic of pronominal resumption*. Oxford: Oxford University Press.

Atkinson, Elizabeth Grace, Audesse, Amanda Jane, Palacios, Julia Adela, Bobo, Dean Michael, Webb, Ashley Elizabeth, Ramachandran, Sohini, and Henn, Brenna Mariah. 2018. No Evidence for Recent Selection at FOXP2 among Diverse Human Populations. *Cell* 174(6), 1424–35.e15.

Atkinson, Emily. 2016. Active dependency completion in adults and children: Representations and adaptation. PhD thesis, Johns Hopkins University.

Atkinson, Emily, Wagers, Matthew W., Lidz, Jeffrey, Phillips, Colin, and Omaki, Akira. 2018. Developing incrementality in filler-gap dependency processing. *Cognition* 179, 132–49.

Baauw, Sergio. 2002. *Grammatical features and the acquisition of reference: A comparative study of Dutch and Spanish*. Outstanding dissertations in linguistics, New York: Garland.

Bach, Emmon and Horn, George G. 1976. Remarks on 'Conditions on transformations'. *Linguistic Inquiry* 7, 265–99.

Bachrach, Asaf and Katzir, Roni. 2008. Right-Node Raising and Delayed Spell-Out. In Kleanthes K. Grohmann (ed.), *InterPhases: Phase-Theoretic Investigations of Linguistic Interfaces*, pages 284–316, Oxford; Oxford University Press.

Bailey, Karl K. D. and Ferreira, Fernanda. 2003. Disfluencies influence syntactic parsing. *Journal of Memory and Language* 49, 183–200.

Bailyn, Josef. 1992. LF movement of anaphora and the acquisition of embedded clauses in Russian. *Language Acquisition* 2, 307–36.

Baker, Carl L. 1970. Notes on the description of English questions: The role of an abstract question morpheme. *Foundations of Language* 6, 197–219.

Baker, Mark. 2001. *The atoms of language*. New York: Basic Books.

Baldridge, Jason. 2002. Lexically Specified Derivational Control in Combinatory Categorial Grammar. PhD dissertation, University of Edinburgh.

Balewski, Idan Blank Zuzanna, Mahowald, Kyle, and Fedorenko, Evelina. 2016. Syntactic processing is distributed across the language system. *Neuroimage* 127, 307–23.

Ballard, Dana H. 2015. *Brain Computation as Hierarchical Abstraction*. Computational Neuroscience Series, Cambridge, MA: MIT Press.

Baltin, Mark. 1982. A landing site theory of movement rules. *Linguistic Inquiry* 13(1), 1–38.

Bannard, Colin and Matthews, Danielle. 2008. Stored word sequences in language learning: the effect of familiarity on children's repetition of four-word combinations. *Psychological Science* 19, 241–8.

Bar-Hillel, Yehoshua. 1954. Logical syntax and semantics. *Language* 30(2), 230–7.

Barlett, Frederc. 1932. *Remembering: A Study in Experimental and Social Psychology*. Cambridge: Cambridge University Press.

Bartels, Christine. 1999. *The Intonation of English Statements and Questions*. New York: Garland.

Bates, Douglas, Mächler, Martin, Bolker, Benjamin M., and Walker, Steven C. 2014. Fitting Linear Mixed-Effects Models Using lme4, https://cran.r-project.org/web/packages/lme4/vignettes/lmer.pdf, accessed August 20, 2020.

Bender, Emily and Flickinger, Dan. 1999. Peripheral constructions and core phenomena. In Gert Webelhuth, Andreas Kathol, and Jean-Pierre Koenig (eds), *Lexical and Constructional Aspects of Linguistic Explanation*, Stanford, CA: CSLI Publications.

Bergen, Benjamin K. and Chang, Nancy. 2005. Embodied Construction Grammar in simulation-based language understanding. In J.-O. Östman and Mirjam Fried (eds), *Construction Grammar(s): Cognitive grounding and theoretical extensions*, pages 147–0, Amsterdam: John Benjamins.

Berwick, Robert C. and Chomsky, Noam. 2008. 'Poverty of the Stimulus' Revisited: Recent Challenges Reconsidered. In B. C. Love, K. McRae, and V. M. Sloutsky (eds), *30th Annual Meeting of the Cognitive Science Society*, pages 383–4, Austin, TX: Cognitive Science Society.

Berwick, Robert C and Chomsky, Noam. 2016. *Why only us: Language and evolution*. Cambridge, MA: MIT Press.

Berwick, Robert C., Friederici, Angela D., Chomsky, Noam, and Bolhuis, Johan J. 2013. Evolution, Brain, and the Nature of Language. *Trends in Cognitive Sciences* 17(2), 89–98.

Berwick, Robert C. and Weinberg, Amy S. 1984. *The grammatical basis of linguistic performance*. Cambridge, MA: MIT Press.

Bever, Thomas G. 1974. The ascent of the specious; or, There's a lot we don't know about mirrors. In David Cohen (ed.), *Explaining Linguistic Phenomena*, pages 173–200, Washington DC: Hemisphere. i

Bianchi, Valentina and Chesi, Cristiano. 2014. Subject islands, reconstruction, and the flow of the computation. *Linguistic Inquiry* 45(4), 525–69.

Biezma, Maria. 2019. Presupposing Questions. In M. Teresa Espinal et al. (eds), *Proceedings of Sinn und Bedeutung*, Volume 23, pages 143–61, Barcelona: Universitat Autònoma de Barcelona.

Bird, Steven. 1995. *Computational Phonology: A Constraint-Based Approach*. Studies in Natural Language Processing, Cambridge: Cambridge University Press.

Blevins, James P. and Sag, Ivan A. 2012. Phrase Structure Grammar. In Marcel den Dikken (ed.), *The Cambridge Handbook of Generative Syntax*, pages 202–25, Cambridge: Cambridge University Press.

Bloom, Leonard. 1973. *One word at a time: the use of single word utterances before syntax*. The Hague: Mouton de Gruyter.

Bloom, Lois. 1990. Subjectless sentences in child language. *Linguistic Inquiry* 21(4), 491–504.

Boas, Hans and Sag, Ivan A. (eds). 2012. *Sign-Based Construction Grammar* Stanford, CA: CSLI Publications.

Bock, Katheryn J. 1989. Closed-class immanence in sentence production. *Cognition* 31, 163–86.

Bod, Rens. 1992. A Computational Model of Language Performance: Data Oriented Parsing. In Alexander Gelbukh (ed.), *14th International Conference on Computational Linguistics, COLING 1992, Nantes, France, August 23–28, 1992*, https://www.aclweb.org/anthology/C92-3126.pdf, accessed August 21, 2020.

Bod, Rens. 2008. The Data-Oriented Parsing Approach: Theory and Application. In John Fulcher and Lakhmi C. Jain (eds), *Computational Intelligence: A Compendium*, pages 307–48, Berlin and Heidelberg: Springer.

Bod, Rens. 2009. From Exemplar to Grammar: A Probabilistic Analogy-Based Model of Language Learning. *Cognitive Science* 33(5), 752–93.

Boeckx, Cedric. 2003. *Islands and Chains. Resumption as Stranding*. Amsterdam: John Benjamins.

Boeckx, Cedric. 2008. Islands. *Language and Linguistics Compass* 2(1), 151–67.

Boeckx, Cedric. 2012. *Syntactic islands*. Cambridge: Cambridge University Press.

Boeckx, Cedric. 2014a. *Elementary syntactic structures: Prospects of a feature-free syntax*. Cambridge: Cambridge University Press.

Boeckx, Cedric. 2014b. What Principles and Parameters got wrong. In M. Carme Picallo (ed.), *Linguistic Variation in the Minimalist Framework*, pages 155–78, Oxford: Oxford University Press.

Boeckx, Cedric. 2016. Considerations pertaining to the nature of logodiversity. In Luis Eguren, Olga Fernández Soriano, and Amaya Mendikoetxea (eds), *Rethinking Parameters*, pages 64–104, Oxford: Oxford University Press.

Boeckx, Cedric and Grohmann, Kleanthes K. 2007. Remark: Putting phases in perspective. *Syntax* 10(2), 204–22.

Boeckx, Cedric and Grohmann, Kleanthes K. (eds). 2013. *The Cambridge handbook of biolinguistics.* Cambridge: Cambridge University Press.

Boland, Julie E. 1993. The role of verb argument structure in sentence processing: Distinguishing between syntactic and semantic effects. *Journal of Psycholinguistic Research* 22, 133–52.

Boland, Julie E., Tanenhaus, Michael K., Garnsey, Susan M., and Carlson, Greg N. 1995. Verb argument structure in parsing and interpretation: Evidence from wh-questions. *Journal of Memory and Language* 43, 413–32.

Bolhuis, Johan J., Tattersall, Ian, Chomsky, Noam, and Berwick, Robert C. 2014. How could language have evolved? *PLoS Biology* 12(8), e1001934.

Bolinger, Dwight. 1972. *What did John keep the car that was in? *Linguistic Inquiry* 3, 109–14.

Bolinger, Dwight. 1978. Asking more than one thing at a time. In Henry Hiz (ed.), *Questions*, pages 107–50, Dordrecht: Springer.

Bolinger, Dwight. 1992. The role of accent in extraposition and focus. *Studies in Language* 16, 265–324.

Bonami, Olivier and Crysmann, Berthold. 2013. Morphotactics in an Information-Based Model of Realizational Morphology. In Stefan Müller (ed.), *Proceedings of the 20th International Conference on Head-Driven Phrase Structure Grammar*, pages 27–47, Stanford, CA: CSLI Publications.

Bonami, Olivier and Delais-Roussarie, Elisabeth. 2006. Metrical Phonology in HPSG. In Stefan Müller (ed.), *Proceedings of the 13th International Conference on Head-Driven Phrase Structure Grammar*, pages 39–59, Stanford, CA: CSLI Publications.

Bondevik, Ingrid. 2018. Investigating the universality of adjunct islands through formal acceptability experiments—A comparative study of English and Norwegian. Masters' thesis, Norwegian University of Science and Technology.

Borer, Hagit. 1984. Restrictive relatives in modern Hebrew. *Natural Language & Linguistic Theory* 2(2), 219–60.

Borer, Hagit and Wexler, Ken. 1992. Bi-unique relations and the maturation of grammatical principles. *Natural Language & Linguistic Theory* 10(2), 147–89.

Bornkessel-Schlesewsky, Ina and Schlesewsky, Matthias. 2013. Reconciling time, space and function: a new dorsal–ventral stream model of sentence comprehension. *Brain and Language* 125(1), 60–76.

Borsley, Robert D. 1994. In defence of coordinate structures. *Linguistics Analysis* 24, 218–426.

Borsley, Robert D. 2005. Against ConjP. *Lingua* 4(115), 461–82.

Borsley, Robert D. 2006. Syntactic and lexical approaches to unbounded dependencies. *Essex Research Reports in Linguistics* 49, 31–57.

Borsley, Robert D. 2010. An HPSG approach to Welsh unbounded dependencies. In Stefan Müller (ed.), *Proceedings of the 17th International Conference on Head Driven Phrase Structure Grammar*, pages 80–100, Stanford, CA: CSLI Publications.

Borsley, Robert D. 2011. Constructions, functional heads and comparative correlatives. *Empirical Issues in Syntax and Semantics* 8, 7–26.

Borsley, Robert D. 2012. Don't move! *Iberia* 4(1), 110–39.

Bošković, Željko. 2017. Extraction from Complex NPs and Detachment. In M. Everaert and H. C. van Riemsdijk (eds), *The Blackwell Companion to Syntax, Volume 2, 2nd edn*, pages 1541–66, Malden, MA: Blackwell.

Bosque, Ignacio and Gallego, Ángel J. 2014. Reconsidering Subextraction: Evidence from Spanish. *Borealis—An International Journal of Hispanic Linguistics* 3(2), 223–58.

Boston, Marisa Ferrara. 2012. A Computational Model of Cognitive Constraints in Syntactic Locality. PhD dissertation, Cornell University.

Bouma, Gosse, Malouf, Robert, and Sag, Ivan A. 2001. Satisfying Constraints on Extraction and Adjunction. *Natural Language & Linguistic Theory* 19(1), 1–65.

Brame, Michael K. 1978. *Base generated syntax.* Seattle, WA: Noit Amrofer.

Branigan, Holly and Pickering, Martin J. 2017. An experimental approach to linguistic representation. *Behavioral and Brain Sciences* 40, 1–61.

Braze, Forrest D. 2002. Grammaticality, acceptability, and sentence processing: A psycholinguistic study. PhD thesis, University of Connecticut.

Brennan, Jonathan R. and Pylkkänen, Liina. 2017. MEG Evidence for Incremental Sentence Composition in the Anterior Temporal Lobe. *Cognitive Science* 41, 1515–31.

Bresnan, Joan. 1977. Variables in the Theory of Transformations. In Adrian Akmajian, Peter W. Culicover, and Thomas Wasow (eds.), *Formal Syntax*, pages 157–96, New York: Academic Press.

Bresnan, Joan. 1978. A realistic transformational grammar. In Morris Halle, Joan Bresnan, and George A. Miller (eds), *Linguistic theory and psychological reality*, pages 1–59, Cambridge, MA: MIT Press.

Bresnan, Joan. 1991. Locative Case vs. Locative Gender. In Laurel A. Sutton, Christopher Johnson, and Ruth Shields (eds), *Proceedings of the Seventeenth Annual Meeting of the Berkeley Linguistics Society*, pages 53–66, Berkeley, CA: Berkeley Linguistics Society.

Bresnan, Joan. 1995. Linear Order, Syntactic Rank, and Empty Categories: On Weak Crossover. In Mary Dalrymple, Ronald Kaplan, John T. Maxwell III, and Annie Zaenen (eds), *Formal Issues in Lexical-Functional Grammar* pages 241–74, Stanford, CA: CSLI Publications.

Bresnan, Joan. 2001. *Lexical-functional Syntax*. Oxford: Blackwell.

Bresnan, Joan. 2007. Is syntactic knowledge probabilistic? Experiments with the English dative alternation. In Sam Featherston and Wolfgang Sternefeld (eds), *Roots: Linguistics in search of its evidential base*, page 75–96, Berlin: Mouton de Gruyter.

Bridgwater, Emma, Kyröläinen, Aki-Juhani, and Kuperman, Victor. 2019. The influence of syntactic expectations on reading comprehension is malleable and strategic: An eye-tracking study of English dative alternation. *Canadian Journal of Experimental Psychology/Revue canadienne de psychologie expérimentale* 73(3), 179–92.

Briscoe, Ted. 2000. Grammatical acquisition: Inductive bias and coevolution of language and the language acquisition device. *Language* 76(2), 245–96.

Brody, Michael. 1995. *Lexico-Logical Form: A radically minimalist theory*. Cambridge, MA: MIT Press.

Brothers, Trevor, Swaab, Tamara, and Traxler, Matthew J. 2017. Goals and strategies influence lexical prediction during sentence comprehension. *Journal of Memory and Language* 93, 203–13.

Brown, Roger. 1973. *A first language: The early stages*. Cambridge, MA: Harvard University Press.

Browne, Eppes Wayles. 1972. Conjoined Question Words and a Limitation on English Surface Structures. *Linguistic Inquiry* 3, 223–6.

Browning, Marguerite A. 1989. ECP≠ CED. *Linguistic Inquiry* 20, 481–91.

Bryant, John Edward. 2008. Best-Fit Constructional Analysis PhD dissertation, University of California at Berkeley.

Brysbaert, Marc, Stevens, Michaël, Mandera, Pawel, and Keuleers, Emmanuel. 2016. How many words do we know? Practical estimates of vocabulary size dependent on word definition, the degree of language input and the participant's age. *Frontiers in Psychology* 7, 1116.

Bürkner, Paul-Christian. 2017. brms: An R package for Bayesian multilevel models using Stan. *Journal of Statistical Software* 80(1), 1–28.

Bybee, Joan L. 1985. *Morphology: A study of the relation between meaning and form*, Volume 9. Amsterdam: John Benjamins.

Bybee, Joan L. 2006. From usage to grammar: The mind's response to repetition. *Language* 82, 711–33.

Bybee, Joan L. 2010. *Language, usage and cognition*. Cambridge: Cambridge University Press.

Bybee, Joan L. 2013. Usage-based theory and exemplar representation. In T. Hoffmann and G. Trousdale (eds), *The Handbook of Construction Grammar*, pages 49–69, Oxford: Oxford University Press.

Cable, Seth. 2010. *The grammar of Q: Q-particles, wh-movement, and pied-piping* Oxford: Oxford University Press.

Calcagno, Mike. 1999. Some Thoughts on Tough Movement. In Valia Kordoni (ed.), *Tübingen Studies in Head-Driven Phrase Structure Grammar*, Arbeitsberichte des SFB 340, No. 132, pages 198–230, Tübingen: Universität Tübingen.

Calude, Andreea. 2008. *Cleft Constructions in Spoken English*. Berlin: VDM Verlag.

Cameron-Faulkner, Thea, Lieven, Elena, and Tomasello, Michael. 2003. A construction based analysis of child directed speech. *Cognitive Science* 27(6), 843–73.

Canac Marquis, Réjean. 1996. The distribution of *à* and *de* in tough constructions in French. In Karen Zagona (ed.), *Grammatical theory and Romance languages*, pages 35–46, Amsterdam: John Benjamins.

Cann, Ronnie, Kaplan, Tami, and Kempson, Ruth. 2005. Data at the grammar-pragmatics interface: the case of resumptive pronouns in English. *Lingua* 115, 1551–77.

Caponigro, Ivano and Polinsky, Maria. 2011. Relative embeddings: A Circassian puzzle for the syntax/semantics interface. *Natural Language & Linguistic Theory* 29(1), 71–122.

Caponigro, Ivano and Sprouse, Jon. 2007. Rhetorical questions as questions. In E. Puig-Waldmüller (ed.), *Proceedings of Sinn und Bedeutung 11*, pages 121–33, Barcelona: Universitat Pompeu Fabra.

Carnap, Rudolf. [1934]1968. *Logische Syntax der Sprache*. Dordrecht: Springer.

Carpenter, Bob. 1992. *The Logic of Typed Feature Structures*. Cambridge: Cambridge University Press.

Carpenter, Bob. 1997. *Type-Logical Semantics*. Cambridge, MA: MIT Press.

Carpenter, Bob, Gelman, Andrew, Hoffman, Matthew D., Lee, Daniel, Goodrich, Ben, Betancourt, Michael, Brubaker, Marcus, Guo, Jiqiang, Li, Peter, and Riddell, Allen. 2017. Stan: A probabilistic programming language. *Journal of Statistical Software* 76(1)1–32.

Carroll, John. 1994. Relating Complexity to Practical Performance in Parsing with Wide-coverage Unification Grammars. In *Proceedings of the 32nd Annual Meeting on Association for Computational Linguistics*, ACL '94, pages 287–94, Stroudsburg, PA: Association for Computational Linguistics.

Cattell, Ray. 1978. On the source of interrogative adverbs. *Language* 54, 61–77.

Cattell, Ray. 1979. On Extractability from Quasi-NPs. *Linguistic Inquiry* 10, 168–72.

Cecchetto, Carlo and Donati, Caterina. 2015. *(Re) labeling*. Cambridge, MA: MIT Press.

Chacón, Dustin A. 2019a. How to Make a Pronoun Resumptive. In Richard Stockwell, Maura O'Leary, Zhongshi Xu, and Z. L. Zhou (eds), *Proceedings of the 36th West Coast Conference on Formal Linguistics*, pages 99–108, Los Angeles, CA: Cascadilla Proceedings Project.

Chacón, Dustin A. 2019b. Minding the gap?: Mechanisms underlying resumption in English. *Glossa: A Journal of General Linguistics* 4(1), 68.

Chafe, Wallace L. 1994. *Discourse, consciousness, and time: the flow and displacement of conscious experience in speaking and writing*. Chicago, IL: University Chicago Press.

Chapman, Cassandra and Kučerová, Ivona. 2016. Structural and semantic ambiguity of why-questions: An overlooked case of weak islands in English. In Patrick Farrell (ed.), *Proceedings of the Linguistics Society of America* 1, pages 1–15, Washington DC: Linguistics Society of America.

Chaves, Rui P. 2007. Coordinate Structures—Constraint-based Syntax-Semantics Processing. PhD dissertation, University of Lisbon.

Chaves, Rui P. 2012a. Conjunction, cumulation and *respectively* readings. *Journal of Linguistics* 48(2), 297–344.

Chaves, Rui P. 2012b. On the grammar of extraction and coordination. *Natural Language and Linguistic Theory* 30(2), 465–512.

Chaves, Rui P. 2013. An expectation-based account of subject islands and parasitism. *Journal of Linguistics* 2(49), 285–327.

Chaves, Rui P. 2014. On the disunity of Right Node Raising phenomena: Extraposition, Ellipsis, and Deletion. *Language* 4(90), 834–86.

Chaves, Rui P. 2018. Freezing as a probabilistic phenomenon. In Jutta Hartmann, Marion Knecht, Andreas Konietzko, and Susanne Winkler (eds.), *Freezing—Theoretical Approaches and Empirical Domains*, pages 403–29, Berlin and Boston, MA: Mouton de Gruyter.

Chaves, Rui P. 2019. Construction Grammar. In András Kertész, Edith Sik, and Csilla Rákosi (eds), *Current approaches to syntax—a comparative handbook*, Comparative Handbooks of Linguistics series, pages 49–96, Berlin and Boston, MA: Mouton de Gruyter.

Chaves, Rui P. 2020. What Don't RNN Language Models Learn about Filler-Gap Dependencies? In *3rd Annual Meeting of the Society for Computation in Linguistics*, Vol. 3 Article 4: 20–30.

Chaves, Rui P. and Dery, Jeruen E. 2014. Which subject islands will the acceptability of improve with repeated exposure? In R. E. Santana-LaBarge (ed.), *31st West Coast Conference on Formal Linguistics*, pages 96–106, Somerville, MA: Cascadilla Proceedings Project.

Chaves, Rui P. and Dery, Jeruen E. 2019. Frequency effects in Subject Islands. *Journal of Linguistics*, 55(3), 475–521.

Chaves, Rui P. and King, Adriana. 2020. A usage-based account of subextraction effects. *Journal of Cognitive Linguistics* 30(4), 719–50.

Chaves, Rui P. and Paperno, Denis. 2007. On The Russian Hybrid Coordination Construction. In Stefan Müller (ed.), *Proceedings of the 14th International Conference on Head-Driven Phrase Structure Grammar*, pages 46–64, Stanford, CA: CSLI Publications.

Chen, Evan, Gibson, Edward, and Wolf, Florian. 2005. Online syntactic storage costs in sentence comprehension. *Journal of Memory and Language* 52, 144–69.

Cheng, Lisa. 1991. On the typology of WH-questions. PhD thesis, Massachusetts Institute of Technology.

Cheng, Lisa Lai-Shen. 2009. Wh-in-situ, from the 1980s to Now. *Language and Linguistics Compass* 3(3), 767–91.

Cheng, Lisa Lai-Shen and Rooryck, Johan. 2000. Licensing wh-in-situ. *Syntax* 3(1), 1–19.

Chesi, Cristiano. 2004. Phases and cartography in linguistic computation: Toward a cognitively motivated computational model of linguistic competence PhD thesis, Università degli Studi di Siena.

Chesi, Cristiano. 2007. An introduction to Phase-based Minimalist Grammars: why move is Top-Down from Left-to-Right. *Studies in Linguistics* 1, 49–90.

Chesi, Cristiano. 2015. On directionality of phrase structure building. *Journal of Psycholinguistic Research* 44(1), 65–89.

Choi, Youngon and Trueswell, John C. 2010. Children's (in)ability to recover from garden paths in a verb-final language: Evidence for developing control in sentence processing. *Journal of Experimental Child Psychology* 106(1), 41–61.

Chomsky, Noam. 1955. Logical syntax and semantics: Their linguistic relevance. *Language* 31(1), 36–45.

Chomsky, Noam. 1956. Three models for the description of language. *IRE Transactions on information theory* 2(3), 113–24.

Chomsky, Noam. 1957. *Syntactic Structures*. The Hague: Mouton de Gruyter.

Chomsky, Noam. 1964. *Current issues in linguistic theory*. The Hague: Mouton de Gruyter.

Chomsky, Noam. 1965. *Aspects of the Theory of Syntax*. Cambridge, MA: MIT Press.

Chomsky, Noam. 1973. Conditions on transformations. In Stephen Anderson and Paul Kiparsky (eds), *A Festschrift for Morris Halle*, pages 232–86, New York: Holt, Reinhart & Winston.

Chomsky, Noam. 1975. *The Logical Structure of Linguistic Theory*. Chicago: University of Chicago Press.

Chomsky, Noam. 1977. On Wh-Movement. In Adrian Akmajian, Peter W. Culicover, and Thomas Wasow (eds), *Formal Syntax*, pages 71–132, New York: Academic Press.

Chomsky, Noam. 1981. *Lectures on Government and Binding*. Dordrecht: Foris.

Chomsky, Noam. 1982. *Concepts and Consequences of the Theory of Government and Binding*. Cambridge, MA: MIT Press.

Chomsky, Noam. 1986a. *Barriers*. Cambridge, MA: MIT Press.

Chomsky, Noam. 1986b. *Knowledge of Language: Its Nature, Origin, and Use* New York: Praeger.

Chomsky, Noam. 1989. Some notes on economy of derivation and representation. *MIT Working Papers in Linguistics* 10, 43–74.

Chomsky, Noam. 1993. A minimalist program for linguistic theory. In K. Hale and S. J. Keyser (eds), *The view from Building 20*, pages 1–52, Cambridge, MA: MIT Press.

Chomsky, Noam. 1995. *The Minimalist Program*. Cambridge, MA: MIT Press.

Chomsky, Noam. 1998. *On Language*. New York: New York Press.

Chomsky, Noam. 2000a. Minimalist inquiries: the framework. In R. Martin, D. Michaels, and J. Uriagereka (eds), *Step by Step*, pages 89–155, Cambridge, MA: MIT Press.

Chomsky, Noam. 2000b. *New horizons in the study of language and mind*. Cambridge: Cambridge University Press.

Chomsky, Noam. 2001. Derivation by phase. In M. Kenstowicz (ed.), *Ken Hale: a life in language*, pages 1–50, Cambridge, MA: MIT Press.

Chomsky, Noam. 2004. Beyond explanatory adequacy. In Adriana Belletti (ed.), *Structures and beyond*, pages 104–31, Oxford: Oxford University Press.

Chomsky, Noam. 2005. Three Factors in Language Design. *Linguistic Inquiry* 36, 1–22.

Chomsky, Noam. 2008. On Phases. In Robert Freidin, David Michaels, Carlos P. Otero, and Maria Luisa Zubizarreta (eds.), *Foundational Issues in Linguistic Theory: Essays in Honor of Jean-Roger Vergnaud*, pages 133–65, Cambridge, MA: MIT Press.

Chomsky, Noam. 2010. Restricting Stipulations: Consequences and Challenges. Talk given at the University of Stuttgart, March 24.

Chomsky, Noam. 2013. Problems of projection. *Lingua* 130, 33–49.

Chomsky, Noam. 2016. *Language and Mind* Cambridge: Cambridge University Press.

Chomsky, Noam, Gallego, Ángel J., and Ott, Dennis. 2019. Generative Grammar and the Faculty of Language: Insights, Questions, and Challenges. *Catalan Journal of Linguistics*, Special Issue, 229–61, https://revistes.uab.cat/catJL/issue/view/sp2019, accessed August 18, 2020.

Chomsky, Noam and Miller, George A. 1963. Introduction to the formal analysis of natural languages. In Robert R. Bush R. Duncan Luce, and Eugene Galanter (eds), *The Handbook of Mathematical Psychology*, Volume 2, pages 269–321, New York: Wiley.

Chowdhury, Shammur Absar and Zamparelli, Roberto. 2018. RNN simulations of grammaticality judgments on long-distance dependencies. In Emily M. Bender, Leon Derczynski, and Pierre Isabelle (eds), *Proceedings of the 27th International Conference on Computational Linguistics*, pages 133–44, Santa Fe, NM: ACL.

Christensen, Rune Haubo Bojesen. 2018. Ordinal: Regression Models for Ordinal Data, R package version 2018.8-25, https://cran.r-project.org/ web/packages/ordinal/ordinal.pdf, accessed August 20, 2020.

Christiansen, Morten H. and Arnon, Inbal. 2017. More Than Words: The Role of Multiword Sequences in Language Learning and Use. *Topics in Cognitive Science*, 9(3), 542–51.

Christiansen, Morten H and Chater, Nick. 2016. *Creating language: Integrating evolution, acquisition, and processing*. Cambridge, MA: MIT Press.

Chung, Sandra. 1982. Unbounded dependencies in Chamorro grammar. *Linguistic Inquiry* 13, 39–77.

Chung, Sandra. 1994. Wh-agreement and 'referentiality' in Chamorro. *Linguistic Inquiry* 25, 1–44.

Chung, Sandra and McCloskey, James. 1983. On the interpretation of certain island facts in GPSG. *Linguistic Inquiry* 14, 703–14.

Cinque, Guglielmo. 1990. *Types of A̅-Dependencies* Cambridge, MA: MIT Press.

Cinque, Guglielmo. 1999. *Adverbs and Functional Heads: A cross-linguistic perspective*. Oxford: Oxford University Press.

Citko, Barbara. 2005. On the Nature of Merge: External Merge, Internal Merge, and Parallel Merge. *Linguistic Inquiry* 36, 475–97.

Citko, Barbara. 2011. *Symmetry in Syntax: Merge, Move and Labels*. Cambridge: Cambridge University Press.

Clahsen, Harald and Felser, Claudia. 2018. Some notes on the shallow structure hypothesis. *Studies in Second Language Acquisition* 40(3), 693–706.

Clancy, Patricia M. 1989. Form and function in the acquisition of Korean wh-questions. *Journal of Child Language* 16(2), 323–47.

Clark, Alexander and Eyraud, Rémi. 2006. Learning Auxiliary Fronting with Grammatical Inference. In Lluis Marquez and Dan Klein, (program chairs), *Proceedings of the Tenth Conference on Computational Natural Language Learning*, CoNLL-X '06, pages 125–32, Stroudsburg, PA: Association for Computational Linguistics.

Clark, Alexander and Fijalkow, Nathanaël. 2020. Consistent Unsupervised Estimators for Anchored PCFGs, *Transactions of the Association for Computational Linguistics*, 8, 409–22.

Clark, Alexander and Lappin, Shalom. 2011. *Linguistic Nativism and the Poverty of the Stimulus*. Oxford: Wiley-Blackwell.

Clark, Eve and Kelly, Barbara F. 2006. *Constructions in acquisition* Stanford, CA: CSLI Lecture Notes.

Clark, Eve V and Wong, Andrew D-W. 2002. Pragmatic directions about language use: Offers of words and relations. *Language in Society* 31(2), 181–212.

Clark, Herbert H. and Wasow, Thomas. 1998. Repeating words in spontaneous speech. *Cognitive Psychology* 37, 201–42.

Clausen, David R. 2011. Informativity and Acceptability of Complex Subject Islands. Poster presented at the 24th Annual CUNY Sentence Processing Conference, Stanford, CA.

Clements, George N. 1984. Binding domains in Kikuyu. *Studies in the Linguistic Sciences* 14, 37–56.

Clements, George N., McClosey, James, Maling, Joan, and Zaenen, Annie. 1983. String-vacuous rule application. *Linguistic Inquiry* 14, 1–17.

Clifton, Charles, Fanselow, Gisbert, and Frazier, Lyn. 2006. Amnestying Superiority Violations: Processing Multiple Questions. *Linguistic Inquiry* 37(1), 51–68.

Collins, Chris. 1994. Economy of derivation and the generalized proper binding condition. *Linguistic Inquiry* 25, 45–61.

Collins, Chris. 2005. A smuggling approach to the passive in English. *Syntax* 8(2), 81–120.

Collins, Chris and Stabler, Edward. 2016. A Formalization of Minimalist Syntax. *Syntax* 19(1), 43–78.

Collins, Peter C. 1991. Pseudoclefts and cleft constructions: A thematic and informational interpretation. *Linguistics* 29(3), 481–520.

Cooper, Robin. 1983. *Quantification and Syntactic Theory*. Dordrecht; Reidel Publications.

Copestake, Ann, Flickinger, Daniel, Sag, Ivan A., and Pollard, Carl. 2005. Minimal Recursion Semantics: An Introduction. *Journal Research on Language & Computation* 3(4), 281–332.

Copestake, Ann, Lascarides, Alex, and Flickinger, Dan. 2001. An Algebra for Semantic Construction in Constraint-based Grammars. In *Proceedings of the 39th Annual Meeting of the Association for Computational Linguistics (ACL/EACL 2001)*, pages 132–9, Toulouse: Association for Computational Linguistics.

Corrigan, Roberta, Moravcsik, Edith A., Ouali, Hamid, and Wheatley, Kathleen M. (eds). 2009. *Formulaic language. Volumes I–II*. Amsterdam: John Benjamins.

Corver, Norbert. 1990. *The Syntax of Left Branch Extractions* PhD dissertation, Katholieke Universiteit Brabant, Tilburg.

Corver, Norbert. 2014. Recursing in Dutch. *Natural Language & Linguistic Theory* 32(2), 423–57.

Cowart, Wayne. 1997. *Experimental syntax: Applying objective methods to sentence judgments*. Thousand Oaks, CA: Sage.

Cowper, Elizabeth A. 1976. Constraints on sentence complexity: a model for syntactic processing PhD dissertation, University of California, Irvine, CA.

Crain, Stephen and Fodor, Janet Dean. 1985. How can grammars help parsers? In David Dowty, Lauri Karttunen, and Arnold M. Zwicky (eds), *Natural language parsing: psycholinguistic, computational, and theoretical perspectives*, pages 94–128, Cambridge: Cambridge University Press.

Crain, Stephen and Nakayama, Mineharu. 1987. Structure Dependence in Grammar Formation. *Language* 63(3), 522–43.

Crawford, Jean. 2011. Using Syntactic Satiation Effects to Investigate Subject Islands. In Jaehoon Choi et al. (eds), *WCCFL 29 Proceedings*, pages 38–45, Somerville, MA: Cascadilla Press.

Creel, Sarah C., Aslin, Richard N., and Tanenhaus, Michael K. 2008. Heeding the voice of experience: The role of talker variation in lexical access. *Cognition* 106, 633–64.

Cresti, Diana. 1995. Extraction and reconstruction. *Natural Language Semantics* 3(1), 79–122.

Croft, William. 2001. *Radical construction grammar: Syntactic theory in typological perspective*. Oxford: Oxford University Press.

Croft, William. 2003. *Typology and universals*, 2nd edn. Cambridge: Cambridge University Press.

Crysmann, Berthold. 2012. Resumption and Islandhood in Hausa. In Philippe de Groote and Mark-Jan Nederhof (eds), *Formal Grammar. 15th and 16th International Conference on Formal Grammar, FG 2010 Copenhagen, Denmark, August 2010, FG 2011 Lubljana, Slovenia, August 2011*, volume 7395, Dordrecht: Springer.

Crysmann, Berthold. 2016. An underspecification approach to Hausa resumption. In Doug Arnold, Miriam Butt, Berthold Crysmann, Tracy Holloway King, and Stefan Müller (eds), *Proceedings of the Joint 2016 Conference on Head-driven Phrase Structure Grammar and Lexical Functional Grammar, Polish Academy of Sciences, Warsaw, Poland*, pages 194–214, Stanford, CA: CSLI Publications.

Culicover, Peter W. 1971. Syntactic and Semantic Investigations. PhD thesis, MIT.

Culicover, Peter W. 1993. Evidence against ECP accounts of the that-t effect. *Linguistic Inquiry* 24(3), 557–61.

Culicover, Peter W. 1999. *Syntactic Nuts: Hard Cases in Syntax*. Volume 1 of Foundations of Syntax. Oxford: Oxford University Press.

Culicover, Peter W. 2001. Parasitic gaps: A history. In *Parasitic Gaps*, pages 3–68, Cambridge, MA: MIT Press.

Culicover, Peter W. 2013. *Grammar & Complexity: Language at the interface of competence and performance.* Oxford: Oxford University Press.

Culicover, Peter W. 2020. The Origin of Languages: Universals, Conceptual Structure and Constructional Typology, MS.

Culicover, Peter W. and Jackendoff, Ray. 1997. Semantic subordination despite syntactic coordination. *Linguistic Inquiry* 28, 195–217.

Culicover, Peter W. and Jackendoff, Ray. 1999. The view from the periphery: The English comparative correlative. *Linguistic Inquiry* 30, 543–71.

Culicover, Peter W. and Jackendoff, Ray. 2005. *Simpler Syntax.* Oxford: Oxford University Press.

Culicover, Peter W. and Postal, Paul M. 2001. *Parasitic Gaps.* Cambridge, MA: MIT Press.

Culicover, Peter W. and Winkler, Susanne. 2018. Freezing: Between grammar and processing. In Jutta Hartmann, Marion Knecht, Andreas Konietzko, and Susanne Winkler (eds), *Freezing: Theoretical Approaches and Empirical Domains*, pages 353–86, Berlin and Boston, MA: Mouton de Gruyter.

Culicover, Peter W. and Winkler, Susanne. 2019. Parasitic gaps aren't parasitic, or, The Case of the Uninvited Guest, MS. Ohio State University and University of Tübingen.

Dąbrowska, Ewa. 2004. *Language, mind, and brain: Some psychological and neurologial constraints on theories of grammar* Edinburgh: Edinburgh University Press.

Dąbrowska, Ewa. 2008. Questions with long-distance dependencies: A usage-based perspective. *Cognitive Linguistics* 19(3), 391–425.

Dąbrowska, Ewa, Rowland, Caroline, and Theakston, Anna. 2009. The acquisition of questions with long-distance dependencies. *Cognitive Linguistics* 20(3), 571–97.

Da Costa, Jillian K. and Chaves, Rui P. 2020. Assessing the ability of Transformer-based Neural Models to represent structurally unbounded dependencies. In *3rd Annual Meeting of the Society for Computation in Linguistics*, Vol. 3, Article 20, 189–98.

Dalrymple, Mary. 2001. *Lexical functional grammar.* Leiden: Brill.

Dalrymple, Mary, Kaplan, Ronald, and King, Tracy Holloway. 2008. The Absence of Traces: Evidence from Weak Crossover. In Annie Zaenen, Jane Simpson, Tracy Holloway King, Jane Grimshaw, Joan Maling, and Christopher Manning (eds), *Architectures, Rules, and Preferences: Variations on Themes by Joan W. Bresnan*, pages 85–102, Stanford, CA: CSLI Publications.

Dalrymple, Mary, Kaplan, Ronald, Maxwell John T., III, and Zaenen, Annie. 1995. Nonlocal dependencies. In Mary Dalrymple, Ronald Kaplan, John T. Maxwell III, and Annie Zaenen (eds), *Formal Issues in Lexical-Functional Grammar*, pages 131–5, Stanford, CA: CSLI Publications

Davies, Mark. 2008. The Corpus of Contemporary American English: 450 million words, 1990-present, http://corpus.byu.edu/coca/.

Davies, William D. and Dubinsky, Stanley. 2003. On Extraction from NPs. *Natural Language & Linguistic Theory* 21(1), 1–37.

Davies, William D. and Dubinsky, Stanley. 2009. On the Existence (and Distribution) of Sentential Subjects. In Donna B. Gerdts, John C. Moore, and Maria Polinsky (eds), *Hypothesis A/Hypothesis B. Linguistic Explorations in Honor of David M. Perlmutter*, pages 111–28, Cambridge, MA: MIT Press.

Davis, Anthony. 2001. *Linking by Types in the Hierarchical Lexicon.* Stanford, CA: CSLI Publications.

Deane, Paul D. 1991. Limits to Attention: A Cognitive Theory of Island Phenomena. *Cognitive Linguistics* 2(1), 1–63.

Deane, Paul D. 1992. *Grammar in Mind and Brain.* Berlin and Boston, MA: Mouton de Gruyter.

Delahunty, Gerald P. 1983. But Sentential Subjects Do Exist. *Linguistic Analysis* 12, 379–98.

DeLong, Katherine A., Urbach, Thomas P., and Kutas, Marta. 2005. Probabilistic word pre-activation during language comprehension inferred from electrical brain activity. *Nature Neuroscience* 8(8), 1117–21.

Demberg, Vera and Keller, Frank. 2008. Data from eye-tracking corpora as evidence for theories of syntactic processing complexity. *Cognition* 109(2), 193–210.

Den Dikken, Marcel. 2009. Arguments for successive-cyclic movement through SpecCP: a critical review. *Linguistic Variation Yearbook* 9(1), 89–126.

Den Dikken, Marcel. 2018. *Dependency and directionality.* Cambridge: Cambridge University Press.

de Villiers, Jill and Roeper, Thomas. 1995. Relative clauses are barriers to wh-movement for young children. *Journal of Child Language* 22(2), 389–404.

de Vries, Mark. 2009. On Multidominance and Linearization. *Biolinguistics* 3(4), 344–403.

Diesing, Molly. 1990. Verb Movement and the Subject position in Yiddish. *Natural Language and Linguistic Theory* 8, 41–79.

Diessel, Holger. 2004. *The acquisition of complex sentences* Cambridge: Cambridge University Press.

Diessel, Holger. 2015. Usage-based construction grammar. In Ewa Dabrowska and Dagmar Divjak (eds), *Handbook of Cognitive Linguistics*, pages 295–321, Berlin: Mouton de Gruyter.

Dillon, Brian and Hornstein, Norbert. 2013. On the structural nature of island constraints. In Jon Sprouse and Norbert Hornstein (eds), *Experimental Syntax and island effects*, pages 208–20, Cambridge: Cambridge University Press.

Do, Monica L. and Kaiser, Elsi. 2017. The Relationship between Syntactic Satiation and Syntactic Priming: A First Look. *Frontiers in Psychology* 8, 1851.

Dobashi, Yoshihito. 2010. Computational efficiency in the syntax–phonology interface. *The Linguistic Review* 27(3), 241–60.

Dobashi, Yoshihito. 2014. Prosodic Domains and the Syntax-Phonology Interface. In Andrew Carnie, Dan Siddiqi, and Yosuke Sato (eds), *The Routledge Handbook of Syntax*, pages 365–87, London: Routledge.

Doron, Edit. 1982. On the syntax and semantics of resumptive pronouns. *Texas Linguistics Forum* 19, 1–48.

Dryer, Matthew S. 1997. Are grammatical relations universal? In Joan L. Bybee, John Haiman, and Sandra Thompson (eds), *Essays on Language Function and Language Type: Dedicated to T. Givon*, pages 115–43, Amsterdam: John Benjamins.

Dryer, Matthew S. 2012. On the position of interrogative phrases and the order of complementizer and clause. In Thomas Graf, Denis Paperno, Anna Szabolcsi, and Jos Tellings (eds), *Theories of Everything. In Honor of Ed Keenan. UCLA Working Papers 17*, pages 72–9, Los Angeles, CA: UCLA.

Dubey, Amit, Sturt, Patrick, and Keller, Frank. 2005. Parallelism in coordination as an instance of syntactic priming: Evidence from corpus-based modeling. In *Proceedings of the Human Language Technology Conference and the Conference on Empirical Methods in Natural Language Processing*, pages 827–34, Vancouver: Association for Computational Linguistics.

Duffield, Cecily Jill and Michaelis, Laura A. 2011. Why subject relatives prevail: Constraints versus constructional licensing. *Language and Cognition* 3(2), 171–208.

Dwivedi, Veena D. 2013. Interpreting quantifier scope ambiguity: evidence of heuristic first, algorithmic second processing. *PloS One* 8(11 e81461).

Dwivedi, Veena D., Phillips, Natalie A., Einagel, Stephanie, and Baum, Shari. 2008. The neurophysiology of scope ambiguity. In Susie Jones (ed.), *Proceedings of the Canadian Linguistics Association*, 15 pp, Vancouver: Association canadienne de linguistique/Canadian Linguistics Association.

Eady, Stephen J. and Fodor, Janet Dean. 1981. Is center embedding a source of processing difficulty? Paper presented at the Linguistics Society of America Annual Meeting, New York.

Edelman, Shimon and Christiansen, Morten H. 2003. How seriously should we take Minimalist syntax? *Trends in Cognitive Sciences* 7(2), 60–1.

Eguren, Luis, Soriano, Olga Fernández, and Mendikoetxea, Amaya (eds). 2016. *Rethinking parameters*. Oxford: Oxford University Press.

Elman, Jeffrey L., Bates, Elizabeth A., Johnson, Mark H., Karmiloff-Smith, Annette, Parisi, Domenico, and Plunkett, Kim. 1996. *Rethinking Innateness. A connectionist perspective on development*. Cambridge, MA: MIT Press.

Emonds, Joseph E. and Faarlund, Jan Terje. 2014. *English: The Language of the Vikings*. Olomouc: Palacký University.

Engdahl, Elisabet. 1980. Wh-constructions in Swedish and the relevance of subjacency. In J. T. Jensen (ed.), *Cahiers Linguisticques d'Ottawa: Proceedings of the Tenth Meeting of the North East Linguistic Society*, pages 89–108, Ottawa: University of Ottawa Department of Linguistics.

Engdahl, Elisabet. 1982. Restrictions on unbounded dependencies in Swedish. In Elisabet Engdahl and Eva Ejerhed (eds), *Readings on Unbounded Dependencies in Scandinavian Languages*, pages 151–74, Stockholm: Almqvist and Wiksell International.

Engdahl, Elisabet. 1983. Parasitic gaps. *Linguistics and Philosophy* 6, 3–34.

Engdahl, Elisabet. 1986. *Constituent Questions*. Synthese Language Library. Dordrecht: Reidel.

Engdahl, Elisabet. 2013. Strange things happen on extraction paths. Technical Report, Institutionen för svenska språket, Göteborgs universitet Series/Report no.: GU-ISS, Gothenburg: Institutionen för svenska språket, Göteborgs universitet.

Engdahl, Elisabet and Vallduví, Enric. 1996. Information Packaging in HPSG. In Claire Grover and Enric Vallduví (eds), *Edinburgh Working Papers in Cognitive Science* volume 12, pages 1–32, Edinburgh: Centre for Cognitive Science, University of Edinburgh.

Engelhardt, Paul E. 2014. Children's and adolescents' processing of temporary syntactic ambiguity: An eye movement study. *Child Development Research* 2014, Art 475315, https://www.hindawi.com/journals/cdr/2014/475315/, accessed August 18, 2020.

Erlewine, Michael Yoshitaka. 2016. Anti-locality and optimality in Kaqchikel Agent Focus. *Natural Language & Linguistic Theory* 34(2), 429–79.

Erteschik-Shir, Nomi. 1973. On the Nature of Island Constraints. PhD dissertation, Cambridge, MA: MIT.

Erteschik-Shir, Nomi. 1977. *On the Nature of Island Constraints*. Bloomington, IN: Indiana University Linguistics Club.

Erteschik-Shir, Nomi. 1979. Discourse constraints on dative movement. In T. Givón (ed.), *Syntax and Semantics 12: Discourse and Syntax*, pages 441–67, New York: Academic Press.

Erteschik-Shir, Nomi. 1981. More on extractability from quasi-NPs. *Linguistic Inquiry* 12, 665–70.

Erteschik-Shir, Nomi. 1992. Resumptive pronouns in islands. In Helen Goodluck and Michael Rochemont (eds), *Island Constraints*, pages 89–108, Norwell, MA: Kluwer Academic Publishers.

Erteschik-Shir, Nomi. 1997. *The Dynamics of Focus Structure*. Cambridge: Cambridge University Press.

Erteschik-Shir, Nomi. 2006a. Bridge phenomena. In Martin Everaert, Henk Van Riemsdijk, Rob Goedemans, and Bart Hollebrandse (eds), *The Blackwell Companion to Syntax*, Volume 5, pages 284–94, Oxford: Blackwell.

Erteschik-Shir, Nomi. 2006b. What's What? In Gisbert Fanselow, C. Fery, M. Schlesewsky, and R. Vogel (eds), *Gradience in Grammar*, pages 317–35, Oxford: Oxford University Press.

Erteschik-Shir, Nomi. 2007. *Information Structure: The Syntax-Discourse Interface*. Oxford: Oxford University Press.

Erteschik-Shir, Nomi and Lappin, Shalom. 1979. Dominance and the functional explanation of island phenomena. *Theoretical Linguistics* 6, 41–86.

Estigarribia, Bruno. 2007. Asking questions: language variation and language acquisition. PhD dissertation, Stanford University.

Estigarribia, Bruno. 2010. Facilitation by variation: Right-to-Left learning of English yes/no questions. *Cognitive Science* 34(1), 68–93.

Estigarribia, Bruno and Clark, Eve V. 2007. Getting and maintaining attention in talk to young children. *Journal of Child Language* 34(4), 799–814.

Fadlon, Julie, Morgan, Adam M., Meltzer-Asscher, Aya, and Ferreira, Victor S. 2019. It depends: Optionality in the production of filler-gap dependencies. *Journal of Memory and Language* 106, 40–76.

Falk, Yehuda N. 2011. Multiple-gap constructions. In Miriam Butt and Tracy Holloway King (eds), *Proceedings of LFG11*, pages 194–214, Stanford, CA: CSLI Publications.

Featherston, Sam. 2001. *Empty categories in sentence processing*. Amsterdam: John Benjamins.

Federmeier, Kara D. 2007. Thinking ahead: The role and roots of prediction in language comprehension. *Psychophysiology* 44, 491–505.

Federmeier, Kara D. and Kutas, Marta. 1999. A rose by any other name: Long-term memory structure and sentence processing. *Journal of Memory and Language* 41, 469–95.

Fedorenko, Evelina and Gibson, Edward. 2010. Adding a Third Wh-phrase Does Not Increase the Acceptability of Object-initial Multiple-wh-questions. *Syntax* 13(3), 183–95.

Feldman, Jerome, Dodge, Ellen, and Bryant, John. 2009. Embodied Construction Grammar. In Bernd Heine and Heiko Narrog (eds), *The Oxford Handbook of Linguistic Analysis*, pages 121–46, Oxford: Oxford University Press.

Felser, Claudia. 2004. Wh-copying, phases, and successive cyclicity. *Lingua* 114(5), 543–74.

Ferreira, Fernanda. 1991. Effects of length and syntactic complexity on initiation times for prepared utterances. *Journal of Memory and Language* 30(2), 210–33.

Ferreira, Fernanda. 2005. Psycholinguistics, formal grammars, and cognitive science. *Linguistic Review* 22, 365–80.

Ferreira, Fernanda and Henderson, John M. 1991. Recovery from misanalyses of garden-path sentences. *Journal of Memory and Language* 31, 725–45.

Ferreira, Fernanda and Henderson, John M. 1993. Basic reading processes during syntactic analysis and reanalysis. *Canadian Journal of Psychology: Special Issue on Reading and Language Processing* 47, 247–75.

Ferreira, Fernanda and Patson, Nikole D. 2007. The 'good enough' approach to language comprehension. *Language and Linguistics Compass* 1(1–2), 71–83.

Ferreira, Fernanda and Swets, Benjamin. 2005. The production and comprehension of resumptive pronouns in relative clause 'island' contexts. In Anne Cutler (ed.), *Twenty-first century psycholinguistics: Four cornerstones*, pages 263–78, Mahwah, NJ: Lawrence Erlbaum.

Fiebach, Christian, Schlesewsky, Matthias, and Friederici, Angela. 2002. Separating syntactic memory costs and syntactic integration costs during parsing: the processing of German wh-questions. *Journal of Memory and Language* 47(2), 250–72.

Fiengo, Robert. 1980. *Surface Structure: The Interface of Autonomous Components*. Cambridge, MA: Harvard University Press.

Fiengo, Robert. 2007. *Asking Questions: Using Meaningful Structures to Imply Ignorance*. Oxford: Oxford University Press.

Fiengo, Robert and Higginbotham, James. 1981. Opacity in NP. *Linguistic Analysis* 7(4), 395–421.

Fillmore, Charles J. 1977. The case for case reopened. In P. Cole (ed.), *Grammatical Relations* (Syntax and Semantics 8), pages 58–81, New York: Academic Press.

Fillmore, Charles J. 1982. Frame semantics. In Linguistic Society of Korea (ed.), *Linguistics in the Morning Calm*, pages 111–37, Seoul: Hanshin.

Fillmore, Charles J. 1985. Syntactic Intrusions and the Notion of Grammatical Construction. In *Proceedings of the Eleventh Annual Meeting of the Berkeley Linguistics Society*, pages 73–86, Berkeley, CA: Berkeley Linguistics Society.

Fillmore, Charles J. 1999. Inversion and constructional inheritance. In G. Webelhuth, J.-P. Koenig, and A. Kathol (eds), *Lexical and Constructional Aspects of Linguistic Explanation*, pages 113–28, Stanford, CA: CSLI Publications.

Fillmore, Charles J. 2009. Berkeley Construction Grammar. In T. Hoffmann and G. Trousdale (eds), *The Oxford Handbook of Construction Grammar* pages 111–32, Oxford: Oxford University Press.

Fillmore, Charles J., Johnson, Christopher, R., and Petruck, Miriam R. L. 2003. Background to Framenet. *International Journal of Lexicography* 16(3), 235–50.

Fillmore, Charles J. and Kay, Paul. 1996. Construction Grammar Coursebook, MS, University of California Berkeley.

Fillmore, Charles J., Kay, Paul, and O'Connor, Catherine. 1988. Regularity and Idiomaticity in Grammatical Constructions: The Case of let alone. *Language* 64, 501–38.

Fine, Alex B. and Jaeger, Florian T. 2016. The role of verb repetition in cumulative structural priming in comprehension. *Journal of Experimental Psychology: Learning, Memory, and Cognition* 42(9), 1362–76.

Fine, Alex B., Jaeger, Florian T., Farmer, Thomas A., and Qian, Ting. 2013. Rapid expectation adaptation during syntactic comprehension. *PLoS ONE* 8(10), e77661, https://journals.plos.org/plosone/article/citation?id=10.1371/journal.pone.0077661, accessed August 19, 2020.

Fletcher, Paul. 1985. *A child's learning of English*. Malden, MA: Blackwell-Wiley.

Fodor, Janet Dean. 1978. Parsing strategies and constraints on transformations. *Linguistic Inquiry* 9, 427–73.

Fodor, Janet Dean. 1979. *Superstrategy: Sentence Processing*. Mahwah, NJ: Lawrence Erlbaum.

Fodor, Janet Dean. 1983. Phrase Structure Parsing and the Island Constraints. *Linguistics and Philosophy* 6, 163–223.

Fodor, Janet Dean. 1992. Islands, Learnability and the Lexicon. In Helen Goodluck and Michael Rochemont (eds), *Island Constraints: Theory, Acquisition and Processing*, pages 109–80, Dordrecht: Kluwer.

Fodor, Janet Dean. 1998. Learning to parse? *Journal of Psycholinguistic Research* 27(2), 427–73.

Fodor, Janet Dean. 2002a. Prosodic disambiguation in silent reading. In M. Hirotani (ed.), *NELS 32*, pages 113–32, Amherst, MA: GLSA Publications.

Fodor, Janet Dean. 2002b. Psycholinguistics cannot escape prosody. In Bernard Bel and Isabelle Marlien (eds), *Proceedings of the SPEECH PROSODY 2002 Conference*, pages 83–8, Aix-en Provence: International Speech Communication Association.

Fodor, Janet Dean and Nickels, Stefanie. 2011. Prosodic phrasing as a source of center-embedding difficulty. Poster presented at the 2nd Experimental and Theoretical Approaches to Prosody Conference. McGill University, Canada.

Fodor, Janet Dean and Sag, Ivan Andrew. 1982. Referential and quantificational indefinites. *Linguistics and Philosophy* 5, 355–400.

Foley, William A. and Van Valin, Robert D., Jr. 1984. *Functional syntax and universal grammar.* Cambridge: Cambridge University Press.

Fong, Sandiway. 2014. Unification and Efficient Computation in the Minimalist Program. In Francis Lowenthal and Laurent Lefebvre (eds), *Language and Recursion*, pages 129–38, Dordrecht: Springer.

Fox, Barbara A. and Thompson, Sandra A. 1990. A discourse explanation of the grammar of relative clauses in English conversation. *Language* 66(2), 297–316.

Fox, Danny. 2000. *Economy and semantic interpretation.* Cambridge, MA: MIT Press.

Fox, Danny and Hackl, Martin. 2006. The universal density of measurement. *Linguistics and Philosophy* 29, 537–86.

Fox, Danny and Lasnik, Howard. 2003. Successive-cyclic movement and island repair: The difference between sluicing and VP-ellipsis. *Linguistic Inquiry* 34(1), 143–54.

Fox, Danny and Nissenbaum, Jon. 2004. Condition A and scope reconstruction. *Linguistic Inquiry* 35(3), 475–85.

Francez, Nissim and Wintner, Shuly. 2012. *Unification Grammars.* Cambridge: Cambridge University Press.

Francom, Jerid. 2009. Experimental syntax: exploring the effect of repeated exposure to anomalous syntactic structure: evidence from rating and reading tasks. PhD thesis, University of Arizona.

Frank, Stefan L., Trompenaars, Thijs, and Vasishth, Shravan. 2015. Cross-linguistic differences in processing double-embedded relative clauses: Working-memory constraints or language statistics? *Cognitive Science* 40, 554–78.

Frazier, Lyn. 1985. Syntactic complexity. In David Dowty, Lauri Karttunen, and Arnold Zwicky (eds), *Natural language processing: Psychological, computational and theoretical perspectives*, pages 129–89, Cambridge: Cambridge University Press.

Frazier, Lyn. 1987. Syntactic processing: evidence from Dutch. *Natural Language and Linguistic Theory* 5, 519–59.

Frazier, Lyn and Clifton, Charles. 1989. Successive cyclicity in the grammar and the parser. *Language and Cognitive Processes* 4(2), 93–126.

Frazier, Lyn and Flores d'Arcais, Giovanni B. 1989. Filler driven parsing: A study of gap filling in Dutch. *Journal of Memory and Language* 28(3), 331–44.

Frazier, Lyn and Rayner, Keith. 1982. Making and correcting errors during sentence comprehension: Eye movements in the analysis of structurally ambiguous sentences. *Cognitive Psychology* 14(2), 178–210.

Friederici, Angela D. 2009. Pathways to language: fiber tracts in the human brain. *Trends in Cognitive Sciences* 13(4), 175–81.

Fujii, Tomohiro and Takita, Kensuke. 2007. Wh-adverbials in-situ, their island(in)sensitivity and the role of demonstratives in wh-in-situ licensing. *Nanzan Linguistics Special Issue* 3, 107–26.

Fukuda, Shin, Nakao, Chizuru, Omaki, Akira, and Polinsky, Maria. 2018. Revisiting subject-object asymmetry: subextraction in Japanese. In Theodore Levin and Ryo Masuda (eds), *Proceedings of the 10th Workshop on Altaic Formal Linguistics*, MIT Working Papers in Linguistics, Cambridge, MA: MIT Press.

Gagliardi, Annie, Mease, Tara M., and Lidz, Jeffrey. 2016. Discontinuous development in the acquisition of filler-gap dependencies: Evidence from 15- and 20-month-olds. *Language Acquisition* 23(3), 234–60.

Gahl, Susanne and Garnsey, Susan Marie. 2004. Knowledge of grammar, knowledge of usage: Syntactic probabilities affect pronunciation variation. *Language* 80(4), 748–75.

Gallego, Angel and Uriagereka, Juan. 2007. A critique of phase extension, with a comparison to phase sliding. *Theoretical Linguistics* 33(1), 65–74.

Garnsey, Susan. 1985. *Function words and content words: Reaction time and evoked potential measures of word recognition*. University of Rochester Cognitive Science Tech. Rep. No. URCS 29, Rochester, NY: University of Rochester.

Garnsey, Susan M., Tanenhaus, Michael K., and Chapman, Robert M. 1989. Evoked potentials and the study of sentence comprehension. *Journal of Psycholinguistic Research* 18(1), 51–60.

Gawron, Jean Mark and Kehler, Andrew. 2003. Respective Answers to Coordinated Questions. In R. Young and Y. Zhou (eds), *Semantics and Linguistic Theory 13 (SALT 13)*, pages 91–108, Ithaca, NY: Cornell University.

Gawron, Jean Mark and Kehler, Andrew. 2004. The Semantics of Respective Readings, Conjunction and Filler-Gap Dependencies. *Linguistics and Philosophy* 27, 169–207.

Gazdar, Gerald. 1981. Unbounded Dependencies and Coordinate Structure. *Linguistic Inquiry* 12(2), 155–84.

Gazdar, Gerald, Klein, Ewan, Pullum, Geoffrey K., and Sag, Ivan A. 1985. *Generalized Phrase Structure Grammar*. Oxford: Blackwell.

George, Leland Maurice. 1980. Analogical generalization in natural language syntax. PhD thesis, MIT.

Georgopoulos, Carol. 1985. Variables in Palauan syntax. *Natural Language & Linguistic Theory* 3, 59–94.

Georgopoulos, Carol. 1991. *Syntactic Variables: Resumptive Pronouns and A' Binding in Palauan*. Dordrecht: Kluwer.

Gibson, Edward. 1991. A computational theory of human linguistic processing: Memory limitations and processing breakdown Phd dissertation, Carnegie Mellon University.

Gibson, Edward. 1998. Linguistic complexity: locality of syntactic dependencies. *Cognition* 68, 1–76.

Gibson, Edward. 2000. The Dependency Locality Theory: a distance-based theory of linguistic complexity. In Yasuhi Miyashita, Alec P. Marantz, and Wayne O'Neil (eds), *Image, language, brain*, pages 95–126, Cambridge, MA: MIT Press.

Gibson, Edward. 2006. The interaction of top-down and bottom-up statistics in the resolution of syntactic category ambiguity. *Journal of Memory and Language* 54, 363–8.

Gibson, Edward and Hickok, Gregory. 1993. Sentence processing with empty categories. *Language and Cognitive Processes* 8(2), 147–61.

Gibson, Edward and Thomas, James. 1999. Memory Limitations and Structural Forgetting: The Perception of Complex Ungrammatical Sentences as Grammatical. *Language and Cognitive Processes* 14(3), 225–48.

Gieselman, Simone, Kluender, Robert, and Caponigro, Ivano. 2011. Pragmatic processing factors in Negative Island Contexts. In Dina Bailey and Victoria Teliga (eds), *Proceedings of WECOL 2010: Western Conference On Linguistics*, pages 65–76, Fresno, CA: California State University.

Gilligan, Gary Martin. 1987. A cross-linguistic approach to the pro-drop parameter. PhD dissertation, UCLA.

Ginzburg, Jonathan. 1995. Resolving Questions, I & II. *Linguistics and Philosophy* 18(5/6), 459–527, 567–609.

Ginzburg, Jonathan and Sag, Ivan A. 2000. *Interrogative Investigations: the form, meaning and use of English interrogative constructions*. Stanford, CA: CSLI Publications.

Givón, Talmy. 1979. *On Understanding Grammar* New York: Academic Press.

Godard, Danièle. 1988. *La Syntaxe des relatives en français*. Paris: Éditions du Centre National de la Recherche Scientifique.

Godard, Danièle. 1992. Extraction Out of NP in French. *Natural Language and Linguistic Theory* 10, 233–77.

Goffman, Erving. 1974. *Frame analysis: An essay on the organization of experience* London: Harper and Row.

Goldberg, Adele E. 1995. *Constructions: A Construction Grammar Approach to Argument Structure*. Chicago, IL: University of Chicago Press.

Goldberg, Adele E. 2006. *Constructions at Work: the nature of generalization in Language*. Oxford: Oxford University Press.

Goldberg, Adele E. 2013. Backgrounded constituents cannot be extracted. In Jon Sprouse and Norbert Hornstein (eds), *Experimental Syntax and Island Effects*, pages 221–38, Cambridge: Cambridge University Press.

Goldberg, Adele E. 2019. *Explain me this: creativity, competition and the partial productivity of constructions*. Princeton, NJ: Princeton University Press.

Goldrick, Matthew, Putnam, Michael, and Schwarz, Lara. 2016. Coactivation in bilingual grammars: A computational account of code mixing. *Bilingualism: Language and Cognition* 19(5), 857–76.

Goldsmith, John. 1981. The Structure of wh-Questions in Igbo. *Linguistic Analysis* 7(4), 367–93.

Goldsmith, John. 1985. A Principled Exception to the Coordinate Structure Constraint. In Randolph Graczyk and Caroline Wiltshire (eds), *Papers from the Twenty-First Annual Regional Meeting of the Chicago Linguistic Society*, pages 133–43, Chicago, IL: Chicago Linguistic Society.

Goodall, Grant. 1987. *Parallel Structures in Syntax: Coordination, Causatives, and Restructuring*. Cambridge: Cambridge University Press.

Goodall, Grant. 2011. Syntactic satiation and the inversion effect in English and Spanish *wh-* questions. *Syntax* 14, 29–47.

Goodall, Grant and Michel, Dan. 2013. Finiteness and the nature of island constraints. In Nobu Goto, Koichi Otaki, Atsushi Sato, and Kensuke Takita (eds), *Proceedings of GLOW in Asia IX 2012: The Main Session*, pages 187–97, Tsu: Mie University.

Goodman, Judith C., McDonough, Laraine, and Brown, Natasha B. 1998. The role of semantic context and memory in the acquisition of novel nouns. *Child Development* 69(5), 1330–44.

Gorrell, Paul. 1993. Evaluating the direct association hypothesis: A reply to Pickering and Barry (1991). *Language and Cognitive Processes* 8(2), 129–46.

Green, Georgia M. 2011. Modeling grammar growth: Universal Grammar with innate principles or parameters. In Robert D. Borsley and Kersti Börjars (eds), *Non-transformational syntax: Formal and explicit models of grammar*, pages 378–403, Malden, MA: Blackwell-Wiley.

Gregory, Michelle L. and Michaelis, Laura A. 2001. Topicalization and Left Dislocation: A Functional Opposition Revisited. *Journal of Pragmatics* 33, 1665–706.

Grice, Paul H. 1975. Logic and Conversation. In P. Cole and J. Morgan (eds.), *Syntax and Semantics, vol.3*, pages 51–8, New York: Academic Press.

Gries, Stefan T. 2002. Preposition stranding in English: predicting speakers' behaviour. In Vida Samiian (ed.), *Proceedings of the Western Conference on Linguistics*, volume 12, pages 230–41, Fresno, CA: California State University.

Gries, Stefan T. 2005. Syntactic priming: A corpus-based approach. *Journal of Psycholinguistic Research* 35(4), 365–99.

Grodzinsky, Yosef. 1986. Language deficits and the theory of syntax. *Brain and Language* 27, 135–59.

Grodzinsky, Yosef. 2000. The neurology of syntax: Language use without Broca's area. *Behavioral and Brain Sciences* 23(1), 1–21.

Grosu, Alexander. 1973. On the Nonunitary Nature of the Coordinate Structure Constraint. *Linguistic Inquiry* 4, 88–92.

Grosu, Alexander. 1981. *Approaches to island phenomena*. Amsterdam, Oxford: North-Holland.

Grosu, Alexander. 1985. Subcategorization and parallelism. *Theoretical Linguistics* 12, 231–40.

Grover, Claire. 1995. Rethinking Some Empty Categories: Missing Objects and Parasitic Gaps in HPSG. PhD thesis, University of Essex.

Gruberg, Nicholas, Ostrand, Rachel, Momma, Shota, and Ferreira, Victor S. 2019. Syntactic entrainment: The repetition of syntactic structures in event descriptions. *Journal of Memory and Language* 107, 216–32.

Guasti, Maria Teresa. 2017. *Language acquisition: The growth of grammar* Cambridge, MA: MIT Press.

Guilliot, Nicolas. 2006. A Top-Down Analysis for Reconstruction. *Lingua* 116, 1888–914.

Haegeman, Liliane. 1984. Parasitic gaps and adverbial clauses. *Journal of Linguistics* 20(2), 229–32.

Haegeman, Liliane, Jiménez-Fernández, Ángel L., and Radford, Andrew. 2013. Deconstructing the Subject Condition: Cumulative constraint violation and tolerance thresholds. *The Linguistic Review* 31(1), 73–150.

Hagoort, Peter. 2003. Interplay between syntax and semantics during sentence comprehension: Erp effects of combining syntactic and semantic violations. *Journal of Cognitive Neuroscience* 15, 883–99.

Hagoort, Peter. 2005. On Broca, brain, and binding: a new framework. *Trends in Cognitive Sciences* 9, 416–23.

Hagstrom, Paul Alan. 1998. Decomposing questions. PhD thesis, Massachusetts Institute of Technology.

Haig, John H. 1996. Subjacency and Japanese grammar: A functional account. *Studies in Language*, 20(1), 53–92.

Hale, John T. 2001. A probabilistic Earley parser as a psycholinguistic model. In *Proceedings of NAACL-2001*, pages 159–66, Pittsburgh, PA: Association for Computational Linguistics, Carnegie Mellon University.

Hale, John T. 2006. Uncertainty about the Rest of the Sentence. *Cognitive Science* 30(4), 643–72.

Hale, John T. 2014. *Automaton Theories of Human Sentence Comprehension* Stanford, CA: CSLI Publications.

Hamburger, Henry and Crain, Stephen. 1982. Relative acquisition. In Stan A. Kuczaj (ed.), *Language Development (Vol. 1: Syntax and Semantics)*, pages 245–72, Hillsdale, NJ: Lawrence Erlbaum.

Han, Chung-hye, Elouazizi, Noureddine, Galeano, Christina, Görgülü, Emrah, Hedberg, Nancy, Hinnell, Jennifer, Jeffrey, Meghan, min Kim, Kyeong, and Kirby, Susannah. 2012. Processing strategies and resumptive pronouns in English. In Nathan Arnett and Ryan Bennett (eds), *Proceedings of the 30th West Coast Conference on Formal Linguistics*, pages 153–61, Somerville, MA: Cascadilla Press.

Hankamer, Jorge. 1973. Unacceptable ambiguity. *Linguistic Inquiry* 4, 17–28.

Hankamer, Jorge and Sag, Ivan A. 1976. Deep and Surface Anaphora. *Linguistic Inquiry* 7(3), 391–428.

Hardt, Daniel. 1999. VPE as a proform: Some consequences for binding. *Empirical Issues in Formal Syntax and Semantics* 2, 215–32.

Harris, Zellig S. 1951. *Methods in Structural Linguistics*. Chicago, IL: University of Chicago Press.

Harris, Zellig S. 1957. Co-occurrence and transformation in linguistic structure. *Language* 33, 283–340, reprinted in Harris (1981), 143–210.

Harris, Zellig S. 1981. Co-Occurrence and Transformation in Linguistic Structure. In H. Hiż (ed.), *Papers on Syntax*. Synthese Language Library (Text and Studies in Linguistics and Philosophy), volume 14, pages 143–210, Dordrecht: Springer.

Hartman, Jeremy. 2011. (Non-)intervention in A-movement: Some cross-constructional and cross-linguistic considerations. *Linguistic Variation* 11(2), 121–48.

Harwood, F. W. 1955. Axiomatic syntax: The construction and evaluation of a syntactic calculus. *Language* 31(3), 409–13.

Haspelmath, Martin. 2007. Pre-established categories don't exist: consequences for language description and typology. *Linguistic Typology* 11(1), 119–32.

Hauser, Marc D., Chomsky, Noam, and Fitch, W. Tecumseh. 2002. The faculty of language: What is it, who has it, and how did it evolve? *Science* 298(5598), 1569–79.

Häussler, Jana, Grant, Margaret, Fanselow, Gisbert, and Frazier, Lyn. 2015. Superiority in English and German: Cross-Language Grammatical Differences? *Syntax* 18(3), 235–65.

Häussler, Jana and Juzek, Tom. 2017. Hot Topics Surrounding Acceptability Judgment Tasks. In Sam Featherston, Robin Hörning, Reinhild Steinberg, Birgit Umbreit, and Jennifer Wallis (eds), *Proceedings of Linguistic Evidence* 2016, University of Tübingen, https://publikationen.uni-tuebingen.de/xmlui/handle/10900/77638, accessed August 19, 2020.

Hawkins, John A. 1994. *A performance theory of order and constituency*. Cambridge: Cambridge University Press.

Hawkins, John A. 2004. *Efficiency and Complexity in Grammars*. Oxford: Oxford University Press.

Hawkins, John A. 2014. *Cross-linguistic variation and efficiency*. Oxford: Oxford University Press.

Heestand, Dustin, Xiang, Ming, and Polinsky, Maria. 2011. Resumption still does not rescue islands. *Linguistic Inquiry* 42(1), 138–52.

Hegarty, Michael. 1990. On adjunct extraction from complements. In Lisa Lai-Shen Cheng and Hamida Demirdash (eds), *MIT Working Papers in Linguistics 13*, pages 101–24, Cambridge, MA: MIT Press.

Heim, Irene. 1982. The semantics of definite and indefinite NPs. PhD thesis, University of Massachusetts at Amherst.

Hendriks, Petra. 1995. Comparatives and Categorial Grammar. PhD thesis, University of Groningen.

Henry, Alison. 1995. *Belfast English and Standard English: Dialect Variation and Parameter Setting*. Oxford: Oxford University Press.

Heycock, Caroline. 2006. Embedded root phenomena. In Martin Everaert and Henk van Riemsdijk (eds), *The Blackwell Companion to Syntax*, pages 174–209, Oxford: Blackwell.

Hicks, Glyn. 2009. Tough-constructions and their derivation. *Linguistic Inquiry* 40(4), 535–66.

Higgins, Francis Roger. 1973. On J. Emond's analysis of Extraposition. *Syntax and Semantics* 2, 149–95.

Hiramatsu, Kazuko. 1999. Subject and adjunct island asymmetries: Evidence from syntactic satiation. In Sonya Bird, Andrew Carnie, Jason D. Haugen, and Peter Norquest (eds), *Proceedings of the West Coast Conference on Formal Linguistics 18*, pages 183–92, Somerville, MA: Cascadilla Press.

Hiramatsu, Kazuko. 2000. Accessing Linguistic Competence: Evidence from Children's and Adults' Acceptability Judgments. PhD thesis, University of Connecticut.

Hobbs, Jerry R. 1979. Coherence and Coreference. *Cognitive Science* 3(1), 67–90.

Hobbs, Jerry R., Stickel, Mark E., Appelt, Douglas E., and Martin, Paul. 1993. Interpretation as abduction. *Artificial Intelligence* 63(1), 69–142.

Hofmeister, Philip. 2011. Representational complexity and memory retrieval in language comprehension. *Language and Cognitive Processes* 3(26), 376–405.

Hofmeister, Philip. 2015. Experience-driven acceptability effects, MS.

Hofmeister, Philip, Casasanto, Laura Staum, and Sag, Ivan A. 2012. How do individual cognitive differences relate to acceptability judgments? A reply to Sprouse, Wagers, and Phillips. *Language* 88(2), 390–400.

Hofmeister, Philip, Casasanto, Laura Staum, and Sag, Ivan A. 2013. Islands in the grammar? Standards of Evidence. In Jon Sprouse and Norbert Hornstein (eds), *Experimental Syntax and islands effects*, pages 42–63, Cambridge: Cambridge University Press.

Hofmeister, Philip, Culicover, Peter W., and Winkler, Susanne. 2015. Effects of processing on the acceptability of 'frozen' extraposed constituents. *Syntax* 18, 464–83.

Hofmeister, Philip, Jaeger, T. Florian, Arnon, Inbal, Sag, Ivan A., and Snider, Neal. 2013. The source ambiguity problem: Distinguishing the effects of grammar and processing on acceptability judgments. *Language and Cognitive Processes* 28(1–2), 48–87.

Hofmeister, Philip, Jaeger, T. Florian, Sag, Ivan A., Arnon, Inbal, and Snider, Neal. 2007. Locality and Accessibility in Wh-Questions. In Sam Featherston and Wolfgang Sternefeld (eds), *Roots: Linguistics in Search of its Evidential Base*, pages 185–206, Berlin: Mouton de Gruyter.

Hofmeister, Philip and Norcliffe, Elisabeth. 2013. Does resumption facilitate sentence comprehension? In Philip Hofmeister and Elisabeth Norcliffe (eds), *The Core and the Periphery: data-driven perspectives on syntax inspired by Ivan A. Sag*, pages 225–46, Stanford, CA: CSLI Publications.

Hofmeister, Philip and Sag, Ivan A. 2010. Cognitive Constraints and Island Effects. *Language* 86(2), 366–415.

Höhle, Tilman N. 1999. An Architecture for Phonology. In Robert D. Borsley and Adam Przepiórkowski (eds), *Slavic in Head-Driven Phrase Structure Grammar*, Studies in Constraint-Based Lexicalism, pages 61–90, Stanford, CA: CSLI Publications.

Hooper, Joan B. and Thompson, Sandra. 1973. On the applicability of Root Transformations. *Linguistic Inquiry* 4, 465–98.

Hopper, Paul J. 2001. Grammatical constructions and their discourse origins: prototype or family resemblance. In Martin Pütz and Susanna Niemeier (eds), *Applied Cognitive Linguistics: Theory, Acquisition, and Language Pedagogy*, pages 109–30, Berlin: Mouton de Gruyter.

Horn, Laurence. 1972. On the Semantic Properties of Logical Operators in English PhD dissertation, University of California, LA.

Hornstein, Norbert. 2000. *Move! A minimalist theory of construal*, volume 10. Malden, MA: Wiley-Blackwell.

Hornstein, Norbert. 2009. *A Theory of Syntax: Minimal Operations and Universal Grammar*. Cambridge: Cambridge University Press.

Hornstein, Norbert. 2019. The Stupendous Success of the Minimalist Program. In András Kertész, Edith Sik, and Csilla Rákosi (eds), *Current approaches to syntax: a comparative handbook*, Comparative Handbooks of Linguistics series, pages 187–214, Berlin and Boston, MA: Mouton de Gruyter.

Horvath, Julia. 1992. The anti c-command and case-compatibility in the licensing of parasitic chains. *The Linguistic Review* 9, 183–218.

Huang, Cheng-Teh James. 1982. Logical relations in Chinese and the theory of grammar. PhD thesis, MIT.

Huang, Phoebe K. 1977. Wh-fronting and Related Processes. PhD thesis, University of Connecticut, Storrs.

Huck, Geoffrey J. and Na, Younghee. 1990. Extraposition and focus. *Language* 66, 51–77.

Huddleston, Rodney 2002. Comparative Constructions. In Rodney Huddleston and Geoffrey K. Pullum (eds), *The Cambridge Grammar of the English Language*, pages 1097–170, Cambridge University Press.

Huddleston, Rodney and Pullum, Geoffrey K. 2002a. *The Cambridge Grammar of the English Language* Cambridge University Press.

Huddleston, Rodney, Pullum, Geoffrey K., and Peterson, Peter. 2002b. Relative clause constructions and unbounded dependencies. In Rodney Huddleston and Geoffrey K. Pullum (eds), *The Cambridge Grammar of the English Language*, pages 1033–96. Cambridge: Cambridge University Press.

Hudson, Richard. 1996. The difficulty of (so-called) self-embedded structures. *UCL Working Papers in Linguistics*, 8, 283–314.

Hudson, Richard. 2007. *Language Networks: The New Word Grammar*. Oxford: Oxford University Press.

Hukari, Thomas E. and Levine, Robert D. 1987. Parasitic Gaps, Slash Termination and the C-Command Condition. *Natural Language & Linguistic Theory* 5(2), 197–222.

Hukari, Thomas E. and Levine, Robert D. 1991. On the disunity of unbounded dependency constructions. *Natural Language and Linguistic Theory* 9, 97–144.

Hukari, Thomas E. and Levine, Robert D. 1995. Adjunct Extraction. *Journal of Linguistics* 31(2), 195–226.

Hukari, Thomas E. and Levine, Robert D. 1996. Phrase Structure Grammar: The Next Generation. *Journal of Linguistics* 32, 465–96.

Hunter, Tim. forthcoming. Formal Methods in Experimental Syntax. In Jon Sprouse (ed.), *The Oxford Handbook of Experimental Syntax*, Oxford: Oxford University Press.

Hunter, Tim and Dyer, Chris. 2013. Distributions on Minimalist Grammar Derivations. In András Kornai and Marco Kuhlmann (eds), *Proceedings of the 13th Meeting on the Mathematics of Language (MoL 13)*, pages 1–11, Sofia: Association for Computational Linguistics.

Jackendoff, Ray. 1992. Parts and Boundaries. In Beth Levin and Steven Pinker (eds), *Lexical and Conceptual Semantics (Cognition Special Issues)*, pages 9–45, Cambridge, MA: Blackwell.

Jackendoff, Ray. 2002. *Foundations of Language: Brain, Meaning, Grammar, Evolution*. Oxford: Oxford University Press.

Jackendoff, Ray. 2017. In defense of theory. *Cognitive Science* 41, 185–212.

Jackendoff, Ray and Culicover, Peter W. 1972. A reconsideration of dative movement. *Foundations of Language* 7, 397–412.

Jackendoff, Ray and Wittenberg, Eva. 2014. What you can say without syntax: A hierarchy of grammatical complexity. In Frederick J. Newmeyer and Laurel B. Preston (eds), *Measuring grammatical complexity*, pages 65–82, Oxford: Oxford University Press.

Jacobs, Joachim. 2001. The dimensions of topic-comment. *Linguistics* 4(39), 641–82.

Jacobson, Pauline. 2008. Direct compositionality and variable free semantics: the case of antecedent contained ellipsis. In Kyle Johnson (ed.), *Topics in Ellipsis*, pages 30–68, Cambridge: Cambridge University Press.

Jiménez-Fernández, Ángel L. 2009. On the Composite Nature of Subject Islands: A Phase-Based Approach. *SKY Journal of Linguistics* 22, 91–138.

Jin, Dawei. 2015. Coherence relation and clause linkage: Towards a discourse approach to adjunct islands in Chinese. *Studies in Language* 392, 424–58.

Jin, Dawei. 2016. The Semantics-Pragmatics Interface and Island Constraints in Chinese. PhD thesis, University of Buffalo.

Johannessen, Janne Bondi. 1998. *Coordination*. Oxford: Oxford University Press.

Johnson, David E. and Lappin, Shalom. 1999. *Local constraints vs. economy*. Stanford, CA: CSLI Publications.

Johnson-Laird, Philip N. 1983. *Mental models* Cambridge, MA: Harvard University Press.

Jurafsky, Daniel. 1996. A probabilistic model of lexical and syntactic access and disambiguation. *Cognitive Science* 2(20), 137–94.

Jurafsky, Daniel. 2003. Probabilistic Modeling in Psycholinguistics: Linguistic Comprehension and Production. In Rens Bod, Jennifer Hay, and Stefanie Jannedy (eds), *Probabilistic Linguistics*, pages 39–96, Cambridge, MA: MIT Press.

Jurka, Johannes, Nakao, Chizuru, and Omaki, Akira. 2011. It's not the end of the CED as we know it: revisiting German and Japanese subject islands. In Mary Byram Washburn, Katherine McKinney-Bock, Erika Varis, Ann Sawyer, and Barbara Tomaszewicz (eds), *Proceedings of the 28th West Coast Conference on Formal Linguistics*, pages 124–32, Somerville, MA: Cascadilla Proceedings Project.

Kaan, Edith, Harris, Anthony, Gibson, Edward, and Holcomb, Phillip. 2000. The P600 as an index of syntactic integration difficulty. *Language and Cognitive Processes* 15(2), 159–201.

Kamide, Yuki, Scheepers, Christoph, and Altmann, Gerry T. M. 2003. Integration of syntactic and semantic information in predictive processing: Crosslinguistic evidence from German and English. *Journal of Psycholinguistic Research* 32(1), 37–55.

Kandybowicz, Jason. 2006. Comp-trace Effects Explained Away. In Donald Baumer, David Montero, and Michael Scanlon (eds), *Proceedings of the 25th West Coast Conference on Formal Linguistics*, pages 220–8, Somerville, MA: Cascadilla Press.

Kandybowicz, Jason. 2009. Comp-trace Effects and the Syntax–Phonology Interface. In Jacqueline Bunting, Sapna Desai, Robert Peachey, Christopher Straughn, and Zuzana Tomková (eds), *Proceedings of CLS 42 (Volume 1: The Main Session)*, pages 103–15, Chicago, IL: Chicago Linguistics Society.

Kaplan, Ronald M. and Bresnan, Joan. 1982. Lexical-Functional Grammar: a formal system for grammatical representation. In Joan Bresnan (ed.), *The Mental Representation of Grammatical Relations*, pages 173–281, Cambridge, MA: MIT Press, reprinted in Mary Dalrymple, Ronald Kaplan, John Maxwell, and Annie Zaenen, (eds), *Formal Issues in Lexical-Functional Grammar*, pages 29–130. Stanford: CSLI Publications.

Kaplan, Ronald M. and Maxwell, John T. 1988. Constituent Coordination in Lexical-Functional Grammar. In *Proceedings of COLING 88*, pages 303–5, Budapest, Hungary, reprinted in 1995 (eds) Mary Dalrymple, Ronald Kaplan, John T. Maxwell III, and Annie Zaenen, (eds), *Formal Issues in Lexical-Functional Grammar* pp. 199–210. Stanford, CA: CSLI Publications.

Kaplan, Ronald M. and Zaenen, Annie. 1989. Long-distance dependencies, constituent structure, and functional uncertainty. In M. Baltin and A. Kroch (eds), *Alternative Conceptions of Phrase Structure*, Chicago, IL: Chicago University Press.

Kathol, Andreas. 2001. Non-existence of parasitic gaps in German. In Peter W. Culicover and Paul M. Postal (eds), *Parasitic gaps*, pages 315–38, Cambridge, MA: MIT Press.

Katz, Jerrold J. and Postal, Paul M. 1964. *Toward an Integrated Theory of Linguistic Description*. Cambridge, MA: MIT Press.

Kay, Paul. 1989. Contextual operators: respective, respectively, and vice versa. In Kira Hall, Michael Meacham, and Richard Shapiro (eds), *Proceedings of the Fifteenth Annual Meeting of the Berkeley Linguistics Society*, pages 181–92, Berkeley, CA: Berkeley Linguistics Society, Inc.

Kay, Paul. 1992. At least. In A. Lehrer and E. F. Kittay (eds), *Frames, Fields, and Contrasts*, pages 309–31, Mahwah, NJ: Lawrence Erlbaum.

Kay, Paul. 2000. Comprehension deficits of Broca's aphasics provide no evidence for traces. *Behavioral and Brain Sciences* 23(1), 37–8.

Kay, Paul. 2002. An informal sketch of a formal architecture for construction grammar. *Grammars* 5, 1–19.

Kay, Paul and Fillmore, Charles J. 1999. Grammatical Constructions and Linguistic Generalizations: the *What's X Doing Y?* Construction. *Language* 75(1), 1–33.

Kayne, Richard. 1981. ECP Extensions. *Linguistic Inquiry* 12, 93–133.

Kayne, Richard. 1983. Connectedness. *Linguistic Inquiry* 14, 223–49.

Kayne, Richard. 1984. *Connectedness and Binary Branching*. Dordrecht: Foris.

Kayne, Richard and Pollock, Jean-Yves. 1978. Stylistic Inversion, Successive Cyclicity, and Move NP in French. *Linguistic Inquiry* 9, 93–133.

Keenan, Edward and Comrie, Bernard. 1977. Noun Phrase Accessibility and Universal Grammar. *Linguistic Inquiry* 8(1), 63–99.

Keer, Edward. 1999. Anti-* that-trace Effects in Norwegian and Optimality Theory. *Nordic Journal of Linguistics* 22(2), 183–203.

Keffala, Bethany. 2013. Resumption and gaps in English relative clauses: Relative acceptability. In Chundra Cathcart, I-Hsuan Chen, Greg Finley, Shinae Kang, Clare S. Sandy, and Elise Stickles (eds), *Proceedings of the 37th Annual Meeting of the Berkeley Linguistics Society*, pages 140–54, Berkeley, CA: Berkeley Linguistics Society.

Kehler, Andrew. 2002. *Coherence, Reference, and the Theory of Grammar*. Stanford, CA: CSLI Publications.

Kehler, Andrew, Kertz, Laura, Rohde, Hannah, and Elman, Jeffrey L. 2008. Coherence and Coreference Revisited. *Journal of Semantics* 25(1), 1–44.

Keine, Stefan and Poole, Ethan. 2017. Intervention in tough-constructions revisited. *The Linguistic Review* 34(2), 295–329.

Keller, Frank. 2003. A Probabilistic Parser as a Model of Global Processing Difficulty. In Richard Alterman and David Kirsh (eds), *Proceedings of the 25th Annual Conference of the Cognitive Science Society*, pages 646–51, Boston, MA: Cognitive Science Society.

Kemper, Susan. 1986. Imitation of complex syntactic constructions by elderly adults. *Applied Psycholinguistics* 7, 277–88.

Kemper, Susan. 1987. Life-span changes in syntactic complexity. *Journal of Gerontology* 42(3), 323–8.

Kertz, Laura. 2013. Verb phrase ellipsis: The view from information structure. *Language* 89(3), 390–428.

Keshet, Ezra. 2008. Only the strong: Restricting situation variables. *Semantics and Linguistic Theory*, 18, 483–95.

Keshev, Maayan and Meltzer-Asscher, Aya. 2019. A processing-based account of subliminal wh-island effects. *Natural Language & Linguistic Theory* 37(2), 621–57.

Keshev, Maayan and Meltzer-Asscher, Aya. 2020. The effects of syntactic pressures and pragmatic considerations on predictive dependency formation. *Language, Cognition and Neuroscience* 35(2), 256–72.

Kidd, Evan, Stewart, Andrew J., and Serratrice, Ludovica. 2011. Children do not overcome lexical biases where adults do: The role of the referential scene in garden-path recovery. *Journal of Child Language* 38(1), 222–34.

Kim, Soo-Yeon and Susumu Kuno. 2013. A note on sluicing with implicit indefinite correlates. *Natural Language Semantics* 21, 315–332.

Kind, Jonathan W. and Kutas, Marta. 1995. Who did what and when? Using word- and clause-level ERPs to monitor working memory usage in reading. *Journal of Cognitive Neuroscience* 7(3), 376–95.

Kingsbury, Paul, Strassel, Stephanie, McLemore, Cynthia, and MyIntyre, Robert. 1997. *CALLHOME American English Transcripts LDC97T14*. Technical Report, Philadelphia, PA: Linguistic Data Consortium.

Kishimoto, Hideki. 2005. Wh-in-situ and movement in Sinhala questions. *Natural Language & Linguistic Theory* 23(1), 1–51.

Kitagawa, Yoshihisa and Fodor, Janet Dean. 2006. Prosodic influence on syntactic judgments. In Gisbert Fanselow, C. Fery, M. Schlesewsky, and R. Vogel (eds), *Gradience in Grammar*, pages 336–54, Oxford: Oxford University Press.

Kitahara, Hisatsugu. 1995. Target α: Deducing strict cyclicity from derivational economy. *Linguistic Inquiry* 26(1), 47–77.

Kitahara, Hisatsugu. 1997. *Elementary operations and optimal derivations*. Cambridge, MA: MIT Press.

Klein, Dan and Manning, Chris. 2005. Natural language grammar induction with a generative constituent-context model. *Pattern Recognition* 38, 1407–19.

Klein, Ewan and Sag, Ivan A. 1985. Type-driven translation. *Linguistics and Philosophy* 8, 163–201.

Klima, Edward and Bellugi, Ursula. 1966. Syntactic regularities in the speech of children. In J. Lyons and R. J. Wales (eds), *Psycholinguistic papers*, pages 183–208, Edinburgh: Edinburgh University Press.

Kluender, Robert. 1992. Deriving island constraints from principles of predication. In Helen Goodluck and Michael Rochemont (eds), *Island Constraints: Theory, Acquisition and Processing*, pages 223–58, Dordrecht: Kluwer.

Kluender, Robert. 1998. On the distinction between strong islands and weak islands: a processing perspective. In Peter W. Culicover and Louise McNally (eds), *Syntax and Semantics 29: The Limits of Syntax*, pages 241–79, New York: Academic Press.

Kluender, Robert. 2004. Are subject islands subject to a processing account? In B. Schmeiser, V. Chand, A. Kelleher, and A. Rodriguez (eds), *Proceedings of the WCCFL 23*, pages 101–25, Somerville, MA: Cascadilla Press.

Kluender, Robert and Kutas, Marta. 1993a. Bridging the gap: Evidence from ERPs on the processing of unbounded dependencies. *Journal of Cognitive Neuroscience* 5(2), 196–214.

Kluender, Robert and Kutas, Marta. 1993b. Subjacency as a processing phenomenon. *Language and Cognitive Processes* 8, 573–633.

Kobele, Gregory M., Retoré, Christian, and Salvati, Sylvain. 2007. An automata theoretic approach to minimalism. In James Rogers and S. Kepser (eds), *Proceedings of the Workshop: Model-theoretic syntax at 10*, pages 73–82, Dublin: Trinity College.

Koenig, Jean-Pierre. 1999. *Lexical Relations*. Stanford, CA: CSLI Publications.

Koenig, Jean-Pierre and Davis, Anthony. 2006. The KEY to lexical semantic representations. *Journal of Linguistics* 42, 71–108.

Koenig, Jean-Pierre, Mauner, Gail, and Bienvenue, Breton. 2003. Arguments for adjuncts. *Cognition* 89(2), 67–103.

Kohrt, Annika, Sorensen, Trey, and Chacón, Dustin A. 2018a, b. Syntax Predicts, Semantics Revises: Filler-gap Dependencies into Adjunct Clauses Poster presented at the 31st Annual CUNY Sentence Processing Conference, Davis, CA: University of California.

Koenig, Jean-Pierre and Michelson, Karin. 2015. Invariance in argument realization: The case of Iroquoian. *Language* 91(1), 1–47.

Kohrt, Annika, Sorensen, Trey, and Chacón, Dustin A. 2018b. The real-time status of semantic exceptions to the adjunct island constraint. In Trevor Driscoll (ed.), *Proceedings of WECOL 2018: Western Conference on Linguistics*, pages 197–225, Fresno, CA: Department of Linguistics, California State University.

Kohrt, Annika, Sorensen, Trey, O'Neill, Peter, and Chacón, Dustin A. 2020. Inactive gap formation: An ERP study on the processing of extraction from adjunct clauses. In Patrick Farrell (ed.), *Proceedings of the Linguistic Society of America*, pages 807–21, New Orleans, LA: Linguistic Society of America.

Konieczny, Lars. 1996. *Human sentence processing : a semantics-oriented parsing approach*. Freiburg: University of Freiburg.

Konieczny, Lars and Hemforth, Barbara. 1994. Incremental parsing with lexicalized grammars. In G. Strube (ed.), *Current research in Cognitive Science at the Center for Cognitive Science, Vol. IIG-Berichte 1/94*, pages 33–54, Freiburg: Albert-Ludwigs Universität, Institut für Informatik und Gesellschaft.

Koopman, Hilda and Sportiche, Dominique. 1986. A note on long extraction in Vata and the ECP. *Natural Language & Linguistic Theory* 4(3), 357–74.

Koopman, Hilda and Sportiche, Dominique. 1991. The position of subjects. *Lingua* 85(2–3), 211–58.

Koster, Jan. 1978. Why subject sentences don't exist. In S. Jay Keyser (ed.), *Recent transformational studies in European languages*, pages 53–64, Cambridge, MA: MIT Press.

Koster, Jan. 1987. *Domains and dynasties: The radical autonomy of syntax*, volume 30. Berlin: Mouton de Gruyter.

Kothari, Anubha. 2008. Frequency-based Expectations and Context Influence Bridge Quality. In M. Grosvald and D. Soares (eds), *Proceedings of WECOL 2008: Western Conference on Linguistics*, pages 136–49, Fresno, CA: California State University.

Kounios, John and Holcomb, Phillip J. 1994. Concreteness effects in semantic processing: ERP evidence supporting dual-coding theory. *Journal of Experimental Psychology: Learning, Memory, and Cognition* 20(4), 804–23.

Kravtchenko, Ekaterina, Polinsky, Maria, and Xiang, Ming. 2009. Are all subject islands created equal? Poster presented at the 22nd CUNY conference on Human Sentence Processing. Davis, CA: University of California.

Krifka, Manfred. 1992. A compositional semantics for multiple focus constructions. In J. Jacobs (ed.), *Informationsstruktur und Grammatik*, pages 17–53, Opladen: Westdeutscher Verlag.

Kroch, Anthony. 1981. On the role of resumptive pronouns in amnestying island constraint violations. In Robert A. Hendrick, Carrie S. Masek, and Mary Frances Miller (eds), *Papers from the 17th Regional Meeting of the Chicago Linguistic Society*, pages 125–35, Chicago, IL: University of Chicago.

Kroch, Anthony. 1998. Amount quantification, referentiality, and long *wh*-movement. In Alexis Dimitriadis, Hikyoung Lee, Christine Moisset, and Alexander Williams (eds), *University of Pennsylvania Working Papers in Linguistics*, volume 5(2), Article 3, Philadelphia, PA: University of Pennsylvania.

Kruschke, John K., Aguinis, Herman, and Joo, Harry. 2012. The time has come: Bayesian methods for data analysis in the organizational sciences. *Organizational Research Methods* 15(4), 722–52.

Kubota, Yusuke and Lee, Jungmee. 2015. The Coordinate Structure Constraint as a discourse-oriented principle: Further evidence from Japanese and Korean. *Language* 91(3), 642–75.

Kubota, Yusuke and Levine, Robert D. 2016a. The syntax-semantics interface of 'respective' predication: A unified analysis in Hybrid Type-Logical Categorial Grammar. *Natural Language & Linguistic Theory* 34(3), 911–73.

Kubota, Yusuke and Levine, Robert D. 2016b. Gapping as hypothetical reasoning. *Natural Language and Linguistic Theory* 34(1), 107–56.

Kubota, Yusuke and Levine, Robert D. 2020. *Coordination and Ellipsis: a type-logical approach*. Cambridge, MA: MIT Press.

Kuhn, Jonas. 1996. An Underspecified HPSG Representation for Information Structure. In Jun-ichi Tsuji (ed.), *Proceedings of Coling-96. 16th International Conference on Computational Linguistics (COLING96). Copenhagen, Denmark, August 5–9, 1996*, pages 670–5, Somerset, NJ: Association for Computational Linguistics.

Kuno, Susumu. 1972. Functional sentence perspective: a case study from Japanese and English. *Linguistic Inquiry* 3, 299–320.

Kuno, Susumu. 1973. Constraints on internal clauses and sentential subjects. *Linguistic Inquiry* 4, 363–86.

Kuno, Susumu. 1976. Subject, theme, and the speaker's empathy: A reexamination of relativization phenomena. In Charles N. Li (ed.), *Subject and topic*, pages 417–44, New York: Academic Press.

Kuno, Susumu. 1987. *Functional syntax: anaphora, discourse and empathy*. Chicago, IL and London: University of Chicago Press.

Kuno, Susumu and Takami, Ken-Ichi. 1993. *Grammar and discourse principles: functional syntax and GB theory*. Chicago, IL, and London: University of Chicago Press.

Kuno, Susumu and Takami, Ken-ichi. 1997. Remarks on negative islands. *Linguistic Inquiry* 28, 553–76.

Kuroda, Shige-Yuki. 1965. Generative Grammatical Studies in the Japanese Language. PhD dissertation, MIT, Cambridge, MA.

Kush, Dave, Lohndal, Terje, and Sprouse, Jon. 2018. Investigating variation in island effects: a case study of Norwegian *wh*-extraction. *Natural Language and Linguistic Theory* 36(3), 743–79.

Kush, David, Omaki, Akira, and Hornstein, Norbert. 2013. Microvariation in Islands? In Jon Sprouse and Norbert Hornstein (eds), *Experimental Syntax and Island Effects*, pages 239–64, Cambridge: Cambridge University Press.

Kutas, Marta, Besson, Mireille, and Petten, Cyma Van. 1988. Event-related potential asymmetries during the reading of sentences. *Electroencephalography and Neurophysiology* 69, 218–33.

Kutas, Marta and Hillyard, Steven A. 1984. Brain potentials during reading reflect word expectancy and semantic association. *Nature* 5947(307), 161–3.

Kuznetsova, Alexandra, Brockhoff, Per Bruun, and Christensen, Rune Haubo Bojesen. 2015. *Package 'lmerTest'*. Technical Report, University of Bergen, https://cran.r-project.org/web/packages/lmerTest/lmerTest.pdf, accessed August 20, 2020.

Kynette, Donna and Kemper, Susan. 1986. Aging and the loss of grammatical forms: a cross-sectional study of language performance. *Language and Communication* 6, 65–72.

Labelle, Marie. 2007. Biolinguistics, the Minimalist Program, and psycholinguistic reality. *Snippets* 14, http://www.ledonline.it/snippets/, accessed May 21, 2020.

Lakoff, George. 1969. Presuppositions and relative grammaticality. *Journal of Philosophical Linguistics* 1(1), 103–16.

Lakoff, George. 1971. On Generative Semantics. In Danny D. Steinberg and Leon A. Jacobovits (eds), *Semantics: An Interdisciplinary Reader*, pages 232–96, Cambridge: Cambridge University Press.

Lakoff, George. 1986. Frame Semantic Control of the Coordinate Structure Constraint. In Chicago Linguistic Society (ed.), *Papers from the 22nd Regional Meeting of the Chicago Linguistic Society*, pages 152–67, Chicago, IL: Chicago Linguistic Society.

Lakoff, George. 1987. *Women, Fire, and Dangerous Things: What Categories Reveal about the Mind*. Chicago, IL: University of Chicago Press.

Lambrecht, Knud. 1988. There was a farmer had a dog: Syntactic amalgams revisited. In Berkeley Linguistics Society (ed.), *Annual Meeting of the Berkeley Linguistics Society*, volume 14, pages 319–39, Berkeley, CA: Berkeley Linguistics Society.

Lambrecht, Knud. 1994. *Information Structure and Sentence Form: topic, focus, and the Mental Representation of Discourse Referents*. Cambridge: Cambridge University Press.

Lambrecht, Knud and Michaelis, Laura A. 1998. Sentence Accent in Information Questions: Default and Projection. *Linguistics and Philosophy* 21(5), 477–544.

Langacker, Ronald W. 1987. *Foundations of Cognitive Grammar, Volume 1: Theoretical Prerequisites*. Stanford, CA: CSLI Publications.

Langacker, Ronald W. 2000. A dynamic usage-based model. In M. Barlow and S. Kemmer (eds), *Usage based models of language*, pages 1–64, Stanford, CA: CSLI Publications.

Langendoen, D. Terence. 2003. Merge. In Andrew Carnie, Mary Willie, and Heidi Harley (eds), *Formal Approaches to Function in Grammar: In Honor of Eloise Jelinek*, pages 307–18, Amsterdam: John Benjamins.

Larson, Bradley. 2012. A dilemma with accounts of right node raising. *Linguistic Inquiry* 43(1), 143–50.

Larson-Hall, Jenniver and Herrington, Richard. 2010. Improving Data Analysis in Second Language Acquisition by Utilizing Modern Developments in Applied Statistics. *Applied Linguistics* 31, 368–90.

Lasnik, Howard. 2000. When can you save the structure by destroying it? In M. Kim and U. Strauss (eds), *Proceedings of the North Eastern Linguistic Society 31*, pages 301–20, Amherst, MA: GLSA Publications.

Lasnik, Howard and Park, Myung-Kwan. 2003. The EPP and the subject condition under sluicing. *Linguistic Inquiry* 34, 649–60.

Lasnik, Howard and Saito, Mamoru. 1984. On the nature of proper government. *Linguistic Inquiry* 15, 235–89.

Lasnik, Howard and Saito, Mamoru. 1992. *Move α: conditions on its application and output*. Cambridge, MA: MIT Press.

Lassotta, Romy, Omaki, Akira, and Franck, Julie. 2015. Developmental changes in misinterpretation of garden-path-wh-questions in French. *The Quarterly Journal of Experimental Psychology* 69(5), 1–26.

Lau, Ellen, Stroud, Clare, Plesch, Silke, and Phillips, Colin. 2006. The role of structural prediction in rapid syntactic analysis. *Brain and Language* 1(98), 74–88.

Lau, Jey Han, Clark, Alexander, and Lappin, Shalom. 2015. Unsupervised Prediction of Acceptability Judgments. In Chengqing Zong and Michael Strub (eds), *Proceedings of the 53rd Annual Conference of the Association of Computational Linguistics, Beijing*, pages 1618–28, Beijing: Association for Computational Linguistics.

Lee-Goldman, Russell. 2011. Context in Constructions. PhD dissertation, University of California, Berkeley.

Legenstein, Robert, Pecevski, Dejan, and Maass, Wolfgang. 2008. A Learning Theory for Reward-Modulated Spike-Timing-Dependent Plasticity with Application to Biofeedback. *PLOS Computational Biology* 4(10), 1–27.

Leiken, Kimberly, McElree, Brian, and Pylkkänen, Liina. 2015. Filling Predictable and Unpredictable Gaps, with and without Similarity-Based Interference: Evidence for LIFG Effects of Dependency Processing. *Frontiers in Psychology* 6, 1739.

Levin, Nancy and Prince, Ellen F. 1986. Gapping and Clausal Implicature. *Papers in Linguistics* 19, 351–64.

Levine, Robert D. 2001a. The extraction riddle: just what are we missing? *Journal of Linguistics* 37, 145–74.

Levine, Robert D. 2001b. Tough complementation and the extraclausal propagation of argument descriptions. In Dan Flickinger and Andreas Kathol (eds), *Proceedings of the 7th International Conference on Head-Driven Phrase Structure Grammar*, pages 325–44, Stanford, CA: CSLI Publications, http://cslipublications.stanford.edu/HPSG/1/, accessed May 21, 2020.

Levine, Robert D. 2004. The syntax of extraction: derivation or constraint satisfaction? In Olivier Bonami and Patricia Cabredo Hofherr (eds), *Empirical Issues in Syntax and Semantics*, pages 159–77, Paris: Colloque de Syntaxe et Sémantique à Paris.

Levine, Robert D. 2017. *Syntactic Analysis: An HPSG-based Approach* Cambridge: Cambridge University Press.

Levine, Robert D. and Hukari, Thomas E. 2006. *The unity of unbounded dependency constructions*. Stanford, CA: CSLI Publications.

Levine, Robert D., Hukari, Thomas E., and Calcagno, Michael. 2001. Parasitic gaps in English: some overlooked cases and their theoretical implications. In Peter W. Culicover and Paul M. Postal (eds), *Parasitic Gaps*, pages 181–222, Cambridge, MA: MIT Press.

Levine, Robert D. and Sag, Ivan A. 2003. Some empirical issues in the grammar of extraction. In Stefan Müller (ed.), *Proceedings of the HPSG-2003 Conference, Michigan State University, East Lansing*, pages 236–56, Stanford, CA: CSLI Publications.

Levy, Roger. 2008. Expectation-based syntactic comprehension. *Cognition* 3(106), 1126–77.

Levy, Roger, Fedorenko, Evelina, Breen, Mara, and Gibson, Ted. 2012. The processing of extraposed structures in English. *Cognition* 12(1), 12–36.

Levy, Roger and Keller, Frank. 2013. Expectation and locality effects in German verb-final structures. *Journal of Memory and Language* 2(68), 199–222.

Lewis, John D. and Elman, Jeffrey L. 2001. Learnability and the Statistical Structure of Language: Poverty of Stimulus Arguments Revisited. In Barbora Skarabela, Sarah Fish, and Anna H.-J. Do (eds), *Proceedings of the 26th annual Boston University conference on language development*, pages 359–70, Somerville, MA: Cascadilla Press.

Lewis, Richard L. 1993. An architecturally-based theory of Human sentence comprehension. PhD dissertation, Carnegie Mellon University.

Lewis, Richard L. and Vasishth, Shravan. 2005. An activation-based model of sentence processing as skilled memory retrieval. *Cognitive Science* 29, 1–45.

Lewis, Richard L., Vasishth, Shravan, and Dyke, Julie A. Van. 2006. Computational principles of working memory in sentence comprehension. *Trends in Cognitive Science* 10(10), 447–54.

Lewis, Shevaun, Larson, Bradley, and Kush, David. 2012. What and when can you fill a gap with something? Poster presented at the 25th Annual CUNY Sentence Processing Conference, CUNY, New York City.

Lewis, Shevaun and Phillips, Colin. 2015. Aligning grammatical theories and language processing models. *Journal of Psycholinguistic Research* 44(1), 27–46.

Li, Yen-Hui. 1990. *Order and Constituency in Mandarin Chinese*. Dordrecht: Kluwer.

Linardaki, Evita. 2006. Linguistic and Statistical Extensions of Data Oriented Parsing. PhD dissertation, University of Essex.

Link, Godehard. 1983. The logical analysis of plurals and mass terms: a lattice-theoretical approach. In R. Bäuerle, C. Schwarze, and A. von Stechow (eds), *Meaning, Use and Interpretation of Language*, pages 302–23, Berlin: Mouton de Gruyter.

Liu, Xiling, Somel, Mehmet, Tang, Lin, Yan, Zheng, Jiang, Xi, Guo, Song, Yuan, Yuan, He, Liu, Oleksiak, Anna, Zhang, Yan, Yuhui Hu, Na Li, Chen, Wei, Qiu, Zilong, Pääbo, Svante, and Khaitovich, Philipp. 2012. Extension of cortical synaptic development distinguishes humans from chimpanzees and macaques. *Genome Research* 22(4), 611–22.

Liu, Yingtong, Ryskin, Rachel, Futrell, Richard, and Gibson, Edward. 2019. Verb frequency explains the unacceptability of factive and manner-of-speaking islands in English. In Ashok Goel, Colleen Seifert, and Christian Freksa (eds), *Proceedings of the 41st Annual Meeting of the Cognitive Science Society*, pages 685–91, Montreal: Cognitive Science Society.

Lohmann, Heidemarie and Tomasello, Michael. 2003. The role of language in the development of false belief understanding: a training study. *Child Development* 74, 1130–44.

Loss, Sara S. and Wicklund, Mark. 2020. Is English resumption different in appositive relative clauses? *Canadian Journal of Linguistics/Revue canadienne de linguistique* 65(1), 25–51. doi:10.1017/cnj.2019.19.

Love, Tracy E. 2007. The Processing of Non-canonically Ordered Constituents in Long Distance Dependencies by Pre-school Children: a Real-time Investigation. *Journal of Psycholinguistic Research* 36(3), 191–206.

Lust, Barbara. 2006. *Child Language: Acquisition and Growth*. Cambridge: Cambridge University Press.

Lutken, Jane, Legendre, Géraldine, and Omaki, Akira 2020. Syntactic Creativity Errors in Children's Wh-Questions, *Cognitive Science*, 44(7), e12849.

McCawley, James D. 1964. Qualitative and quantitative comparison. Paper read at annual meeting, Linguistic Society of America, republished in his *Grammar and Meaning* (1973), pages 1–14. Tokyo: Taishukan and Neyong Academic Press.

McCawley, James D. 1968. Concerning the base component of a transformational grammar. *Foundations of Language* 4(1), 55–81, reprinted in his *Meaning and Grammar* (1976), 35–58. New York: Academic Press.

McCawley, James D. 1981. The syntax and semantics of English relative clauses. *Lingua* 53, 99–149.

McCawley, James D. 1998. *The Syntactic Phenomena of English*. Chicago, IL: University of Chicago Press, second edition.

McCloskey, James. 1979. *Transformational syntax and model theoretic semantics: a case study in modern Irish*. Dordrecht: Reidel.

McCloskey, James. 2002. Resumption, Successive Cyclicity, and the Locality of Operations. In S. Epstein and D. Seeley (eds), *Derivation and Explanation*, pages 184–226, Oxford, UK/Cambridge, MA: Blackwell Publishers.

McCoy, R. Thomas, Frank, Robert, and Linzen, Tal. 2018. Revisiting the poverty of the stimulus: hierarchical generalization without a hierarchical bias in recurrent neural networks. In Timothy T. Rogers, Marina Rau, Jerry Zhu, and Chuck Kalish (eds), *Proceedings of the 40th Annual Conference of the Cognitive Science Society*, pages 2093–8, Austin, TX: Cognitive Science Society.

McDaniel, Dana. 1989. Partial and multiple wh-movement. *Natural Language and Linguistic Theory* 7, 565–604.

McDaniel, Dana, Chiu, Bonnie, and Maxfield, Thomas L. 1995. Parameters for wh-movement types: Evidence from child language. *Natural Language and Linguistic Theory* 13, 709–53.

McDaniel, Dana and Cowart, Wayne. 1999. Experimental evidence for a minimalist account of English resumptive pronouns. *Cognition* 70(2), B15–B24.

MacDonald, Maryellen C. 1994. Probabilistic constraints and syntactic ambiguity resolution. *Language and Cognitive Processes* 9(2), 157–201.

MacDonald, Maryellen C., Pearlmutter, Neal J., and Seidenberg, Mark S. 1994. The lexical nature of syntactic ambiguity resolution. *Psychological Review* 101(4), 676–703.

McKee, Cecile and McDaniel, Dana. 2001. Resumptive Pronouns in English Relative Clauses. *Language Acquisition* 9(2), 113–56.

MacWhinney, Brian. 1987. The competition model. In Brian MacWhinney (ed.), *Mechanisms of language acquisition*, pages 249–308, Hillsdale, NJ: LEA.

MacWhinney, Brian. 2005. A unified model of language acquisition. In J. F. Kroll and A. M. B. de Groot (eds), *Handbook of bilingualism: Psycholinguistic approaches*, pages 49–67, Oxford: Oxford University Press.

MacWhinney, Brian. 2013. The logical of the unified model. In Susan M. Gass and Alison Mackey (eds), *Handbook of cognitive linguistics and second language acquisition*, pages 341–71, New York: Routledge.

Mair, Christian. 1990. *Infinitival Complement Clauses in English: A Study of Syntax in Discourse*. Cambridge: Cambridge University Press.

Mak, Willem M., Vonk, Wietske, and Schriefers, Herbert. 2008. Discourse structure and relative clause processing. *Memory & Cognition* 36, 170–81.

Maling, Joan. 1989. Adverbials and structural case in Korean. In Susumu Kunu, Ik-Hwan Lee, John Whitman, Syng-Yun Bak, Young-Se Kang, and Young Joo Kim (eds), *Harvard Studies in Korean Linguistics III*, pages 297–308, Cambridge, MA: Department of Linguistics, Harvard University.

Maling, Joan. 1993. Of Nominative and Accusative: The Hierarchical Assignment of Grammatical Case in Finnish. In Anders Holmberg and Urpo Nikanne (eds), *Case and Order Functional Categories in Finnish Syntax*, pages 51–76, Dordrecht: Mouton de Gruyter.

Maling, Joan and Zaenen, Annie. 1982. A Phrase Structure Account of Scandinavian Extraction Phenomena. In Pauline Jacobson and G. K. Pullum (eds), *The Nature of Syntactic Representation*, volume 15, pages 229–82 Dordrecht: Springer.

Malone, Avery and Mauner, Gail. 2018. What do readers adapt to in syntactic adaptation? In Fernanda Ferreira, David Corina, John Henderson, Debra Long, Gwendolyn Rehrig, Tamara Swaab, and Matthew Traxler (eds), *Poster session presented at the 31st Annual CUNY Sentence Processing Conference*, Davis, CA: University of California.

Malone, Avery and Mauner, Gail. 2020. Syntactic Adaptation to Multiple Constructions Independent of Task Adaptation, MS.

Manning, Christopher D. 2003. Probabilistic Syntax. In Rens Bod, Jennifer Hay, and Stefanie Jannedy (eds), *Probabilistic Linguistics*, pages 289–341, Cambridge, MA: MIT Press.

Manning, Christopher D., Sag, Ivan A. and Iida, Masayo. 1999. The Lexical Integrity of Japanese Causatives. In Robert D. Levine and Georgia Green (eds), *Studies in Contemporary Phrase Structure Grammar"*, pages 39–79, Cambridge: Cambridge University Press.

Marcus, Gary F., Vijayan, Sujith, Bandi-Rao, Shoba, and Vishton, Peter M. 1999. Rule learning by seven-month-old infants. *Science* 283(5398), 77–80.

Marcus, Mitchell, Santorini, Beatrice, and Marcinkiewicz, Mary Ann. 1993. Building a large annotated corpus of English: the Penn Treebank. *Computational Linguistics* 19, 313–30.

Marr, David. 1982. *Vision: A Computational Investigation into the Human Representation and Processing of Visual Information*. New York: Freeman.

Martin, Andrea E. and McElree, Brian. 2008. A content-addressable pointer mechanism underlies comprehension of verb-phrase ellipsis. *Journal of Memory and Language* 58(3), 879–906.

Martin, Andrea E. and McElree, Brian. 2009. Memory operations that support language comprehension: Evidence from verb-phrase ellipsis. *Journal of Experimental Psychology: Learning, Memory, and Cognition* 35(5), 1231.

Martin, Andrea E. and McElree, Brian. 2011. Direct-access retrieval during sentence comprehension: evidence from sluicing. *Journal of Memory and Language* 64(4), 327–43.

Martins, Pedro Tiago and Boeckx, Cedric. 2019. Language evolution and complexity considerations: The no half-Merge fallacy. *PLOS Biology* 17(11), 1–7.

Matchin, William. 2014. Investigations of the syntax-brain relationship. PhD thesis, University of California Irvine.

Matchin, William, Hammerly, C., and Lau, Ellen. 2017. The role of the IFG and pSTS in syntactic prediction: Evidence from a parametric study of hierarchical structure in fMRI. *Cortex* 88, 106–23.

Matchin, William, Almeida, Diogo, Sprouse, Jon, and Hickok, Gregory. 2018. Semantic processing triggered by subject island violations (but not phrase structure violations): evidence from fMRI. Poster presented at the 18th Conference on Human Sentence Processing, Davies, CA: University of California.

Matchin, William and Hickok, Gregory. 2019. The cortical organization of syntax. *Cerebral Cortex* 30(3), 1481–98.

Mathieu, Eric. 2016. The wh parameter and radical externalization. In Luis Eguren, Olga Fernández Soriano, and Amaya Mendikoetxea (eds), *Rethinking Parameters*, pages 252–328, Oxford: Oxford University Press.

Matushansky, Ora. 2005. Going through a phase. *MIT working papers in linguistics* 49, 157–81.

May, Robert. 1985. *Logical Form: its structure and derivation*. Cambridge, MA: MIT Press.

Mellow, J. Dean. 2004. Connectionism, HPSG signs and SLA representations: Specifying principles of mapping between form and function. *Second Language Research* 20(2), 131–65.

Melnick, Robin, Jaeger, T. Florian, and Wasow, Thomas. 2011. Speakers employ fine-grained probabilistic knowledge. In Patrick Farrell (ed.), *85th Annual Meeting of the Linguistic Society of America*. Pittsburgh, PA: Linguistics Society of America.

Menn, Lise. 1974. Assertions not made by the main clause of a sentence. *Studies in the Linguistic Sciences: University of Illinois* 4(1), 132–43.

Merchant, Jason. 2001. *The syntax of silence: Sluicing, islands, and the theory of ellipsis*. Oxford: Oxford University Press.

Merchant, Jason. 2004. Resumptivity and non-movement. *Studies in Greek linguistics* 24, 471–81.

Metusalem, Ross, Kutas, Marta, Urbach, Thomas, Hare, Mary, McRae, Ken, and Elman, Jeffrey L. 2012. Generalized event knowledge activation during online sentence comprehension. *Journal of Memory and Language* 66, 545–67.

Meurers, Detmar W. 1999. Raising Spirits (and assigning them case). *Groninger Arbeiten zur germanistischen Linguistik* 43, 173–226.

Michaelis, Jens. 2001. On Formal Properties of Minimalist Grammars. PhD thesis, Universität Potsdam.

Michaelis, Laura A. 2003. Headless Constructions and Coercion by Construction. In Elaine J. Francis and Laura A. Michaelis (eds), *Mismatch: Form-Function Incongruity and the Architecture of Grammar* pages 259–310, Stanford, CA: CSLI Publications.

Michaelis, Laura A. 2012. Making the Case for Construction Grammar. In Hans Boas and Ivan A. Sag (eds), *Sign-Based Construction Grammar*, pages 31–69, Stanford, CA: CSLI Publications.

Michaelis, Laura, A. and Feng, Hanbing. 2015. What is this, Sarcastic Syntax? *Constructions and Frames* 7, 148–80.

Michaelis, Laura, and Francis, Hartwell. 2007. Lexical subjects and the conflation strategy. In N. Hedberg and R. Zacharski (eds), *Topics in the Grammar-Pragmatics Interface: Papers in honor of Jeanette K. Gundel*, Amsterdam: John Benjamins.

Michel, Daniel. 2014. Individual Cognitive Measures and Working Memory Accounts of Syntactic Island Phenomena PhD thesis, University of California, San Diego, CA.

Miller, Philip. 2001. Discourse constraints on (non)extraposition from subject in English. *Linguistics* 39(4), 683–701.

Miller, Philip and Pullum, Geoffrey K. 2013. Exophoric VP Ellipsis. In Philip Hofmeister and Elisabeth Norcliffe (eds), *The Core and the Periphery: data-driven perspectives on syntax inspired by Ivan A. Sag*, pages 167–220, Stanford, CA: CSLI Publications.

Minsky, Marvin. 1975. A framework for representing knowledge. In P. H. Winston (ed.), *The psychology of computer vision*, pages 211–77, New York: McGraw-Hill.

Mintz, Toben H. 2003. Frequent frames as a cue for grammatical categories in child directed speech. *Cognition* 90(1), 91–117.

Mintz, Toben H., Newport, Elissa L., and Bever, Thomas G. 2002. The distributional structure of grammatical categories in speech to young children. *Cognitive Science* 26(4), 393–424.

Miyao, Yusuke and Tsujii, Jun'ichi. 2005. Probabilistic Disambiguation Models for Wide-Coverage HPSG Parsing. In Kevin Knight, Hwee Tou Ng, and Kemal Oflazer (eds), *Proceedings of the 43rd*

Annual Meeting of the Association for Computational Linguistics, pages 83–90, Ann Arbor, MI: Association for Computational Linguistics.

Miyao, Yusuke and Tsujii, Jun'ichi. 2008. Feature forest models for probabilistic HPSG parsing. *Computational Linguistics* 34(1), 35–80.

Moltmann, Friederike. 1992. Coordination and Comparatives. PhD dissertation, MIT, Cambridge, MA.

Momma, Shota and Phillips, Colin. 2018. The relationship between parsing and generation. *Annual Review of Linguistics* 4, 233–54.

Moore-Cantwell, Claire. 2013. Syntactic predictability influences duration. *Proceedings of Meetings on Acoustics ICA2013*, 19(1), 060206.

Moortgat, Michael. 1988. *Categorial Investigations*. Dordrecht: Foris.

Morgan, Adam Milton and Wagers, Matthew W. 2018. English Resumptive Pronouns Are More Common Where Gaps Are Less Acceptable. *Linguistic Inquiry* 49(4), 861–76.

Morrill, Glynn. 1994. *Type Logical Grammar*. Dordrecht: Kluwer.

Müller, Christiane. 2017. Extraction from Adjunct Islands in Swedish. *Norsk Lingvistisk Tidsskrift* 35(1), 67–85.

Müller, Gereon. 2010. On deriving CED effects from the PIC. *Linguistic Inquiry* 41(1), 35–82.

Müller, Gereon. 2011. *Constraints on displacement: A phase-based approach* Amsterdam: John Benjamins.

Müller, Horst M., King, Jonathan W., and and Kutas, Marta. 1997. Event related potentials elicited by spoken relative clauses. *Cognitive Brain Research* 5(3), 193–203.

Müller, Stefan. 2017. Head-Driven Phrase Structure Grammar, Sign-Based Construction Grammar, and Fluid Construction Grammar: Commonalities and differences. *Constructions and Frames* 9, 139–74.

Müller, Stefan, Abeillé, Anne, Borsley, Robert D., and Koenig, Jean-Pierre (eds). 2020. *Head-Driven Phrase Structure Grammar: The handbook*. Berlin: Language Science Press.

Munn, Alan. 1993. Topics in the Syntax and Semantics of coordinate structures PhD dissertation, University of Maryland.

Munn, Alan. 1998. ATB movement without identity. In Jennifer Austin and Aaron Lawson (eds), *Proceedings of the 14th Eastern States Conference on Linguistics (ESCOL-97)*, pages 150–60, Ithaca, NY: CLC Publications.

Munn, Alan. 1999. On the identity requirement of ATB extraction. *Natural Language Semantics* 7, 421–5.

Na, Younghee and Huck, Geoffrey. 1992. On Extracting from Asymmetrical Structures. In Diane Brentari, Gary N. Larson, and Lynn A. MacLeod (eds), *The Joy of Grammar*, pages 251–74, Amsterdam: John Benjamins.

Nakanishi, Hiroko, Miyao, Yusuke, and Ichi, Jun. 2005. Probabilistic models for disambiguation of an HPSG-based chart generator. In Harry Bunt and Robert Malouf (eds), *Proceedings of the Ninth International Workshop on Parsing Technology*, pages 93–102, Vancouver: Association for Computational Linguistics.

Nanni, Debbie. 1978. The EASY class of adjectives in English. PhD dissertation, University of Massachusetts at Amherst.

Nanni, Debbie. 1980. On the surface syntax of constructions with easy-type adjectives. *Language* 56(3), 568–91.

Napoli, Donna Jo. 1983. Comparative Ellipsis: A Phrase Structure Analysis. *Linguistic Inquiry* 14(4), 675–94.

Ness, Tal and Meltzer-Asscher, Aya. 2019. When is the verb a potential gap site? The influence of filler maintenance on the active search for a gap. *Language, Cognition and Neuroscience* 34(7), pages 1–13.

Neumann, Günter. 1998. Interleaving Natural Language Parsing and Generation through Uniform Processing. *Artificial Intelligence* 99, 121–63.

Newmeyer, Frederick J. 1998. *Language Form and Language Function* Cambridge, MA: MIT Press.

Newmeyer, Frederick J. 2004. Against a parameter-setting approach to typological variation. *Linguistic Variation Yearbook* 4, 181–234.

Newmeyer, Frederick J. 2005. *Possible and Probable Languages: A Generative Perspective on Linguistic Typology*. Oxford: Oxford University Press.

Newmeyer, Frederick J. 2006. Newmeyer's rejoinder to Roberts & Holmberg on parameters, http://ling.auf.net/lingBuzz/000248.

Newmeyer, Frederick J. 2016. Nonsyntactic Explanations of Island Constraints. *Annual Review of Linguistics* 2(1), 187–210.

Ni, Weijia, Crain, Stephen, and Shankweiler, Donald. 1996. Sidestepping garden paths: Assessing the contributions of syntax, semantics and plausibility in resolving ambiguities. *Language & Cognitive Processes* 11(3), 283–334.

Nicol, Janet, Fodor, Janet, and Swinney, David. 1994. Using cross-modal lexical decision tasks to investigate sentence processing. *Journal of Experimental Psychology: Learning, Memory and Cognition* 20, 1229–38.

Nicol, Janet and Pickering, Martin J. 1993. Processing syntactically ambiguous sentences: Evidence from semantic priming. *Journal of Psycholinguistic Research* 22, 207–37.

Nicol, Janet and Swinney, David. 1989. The role of structure and co-reference assignment during sentence comprehension. *Journal of Psycholinguistic Research* 18, 5–19.

Nieto-Castañón, Alfonso and Fedorenko, Eveline. 2012. Subject-specific functional localizers increase sensitivity and functional resolution of multi-subject analyses. *Neuroimage* 63(3), 1646–69.

Nishigauchi, Taisuke. 1990. *Quantification in the Theory of Grammar*, volume 37. Dordrecht: Springer.

Nunes, Jairo. 1995. The copy theory of movement and linearization of chains in the Minimalist Program. PhD thesis, University of Maryland.

Nunes, Jairo. 2001. Sideward movement. *Linguistic Inquiry* 32(2), 303–44.

Nunes, Jairo. 2004. *Linearization of Chains and Sideward Movement*. MIT Press, Cambridge, MA.

Nunes, Jairo and Uriagereka, Juan. 2000. Cyclicity and extraction domains. *Syntax* 3, 20–43.

Nykiel, Joann. 2010. Competence, performance and extra prepositions. *Journal of English Linguistics* 38, 143–66.

Oepen, Stephan, Flickinger, Dan, Toutanova, Kristina, and Manning, Christopher D. 2004. LinGO Redwoods: A Rich and Dynamic Treebank for HPSG. *Research on Language and Computation* 4(2), 575–96.

Omaki, Akira. 2010. Commitment and Flexibility in the Developing Parser. PhD thesis, University of Maryland, College Park.

Omaki, Akira and Lidz, Jeffrey. 2015. Linking Parser Development to Acquisition of Syntactic Knowledge. *Language Acquisition* 22(2), 158–92.

Omaki, Akira, White, Imogen Davidson, Goro, Takuya, Lidz, Jeffrey, and Phillips, Colin. 2014. No Fear of Commitment: Children's Incremental Interpretation in English and Japanese Wh-Questions. *Language Learning and Development* 10(3), 206–33.

Osborne, Timothy, Putnam, Michael, and Groß, Thomas. 2012. Catenae: Introducing a novel unit of syntactic analysis. *Syntax* 15(4), 354–96.

Oshima, David Y. 2007. On factive Islands: pragmatic anomaly vs. pragmatic infelicity. In Takashi Washio, Ken Satoh, Hideaki Takeda, and Akihiro Inokuchi (eds), *Proceedings of the 20th Annual Conference on New frontiers in Artificial Intelligence*, JSAI'06, pages 147–61, Berlin, Heidelberg: Springer-Verlag.

Pan, Victor Junnan. 2014. Wh-ex-situ in Mandarin Chinese: Mapping between Information Structure and Split CP. *Linguistic Analysis* 39, 371–415.

Park, Jayeon and Sprouse, Jon. 2017. ERP responses to two types of subject island violations and constructions with substantially similar processing dynamics. Poster presented at the 9th Annual Society for the Neurobiology of Language Conference.

Park, Sang-Hee. 2019. Gapping: A Constraint-Based Syntax-Semantics Interface. PhD thesis, University of Buffalo.

Parker, Dan. 2017. Processing multiple gap dependencies: Forewarned is forearmed. *Journal of Memory and Language* 97, 175–86.

Pasch, Renate, Brauße, Ursula, Breindl, Eva, and Waßner, Ulrich Hermann. 2003. *Handbuch der deutschen Konnektoren: linguistische Grundlagen der Beschreibung und syntaktische Merkmale der deutschen Satzverknüpfer (Konjunktionen, Satzadverbien und Partikeln)*, volume 1. Berlin: Mouton de Gruyter.

Pearl, Lisa and Sprouse, Jon. 2013. Syntactic Islands and Learning Biases: Combining Experimental Syntax and Computational Modeling to Investigate the Language Acquisition Problem. *Language Acquisition* 20(1), 23–68.

Pereira, Fernando C. N. and Warren, David H. D. 1983. Parsing as deduction. In *Proceedings of the 21st Annual Meeting of the Association for Computational Linguistics*, pages 137–44, Cambridge, MA: Association for Computational Linguistics.

Perfors, Amy, Tenenbaum, Joshua B., and Regier, Terry. 2011. The learnability of abstract syntactic principles. *Cognition* 118(3), 306–38.

Perlmutter, David M. 1968. Deep and surface structure constraints in syntax. PhD thesis, Massachusetts Institute of Technology.

Perlmutter, David M. 1971. *Deep and surface structure constraints in syntax*. New York: Holt, Rinehart and Winston.

Perrault, C. Raymond. 1984. On the Mathematical Properties of Linguistic Theories. *Computational Linguistics* 10(3–4), 165–76.

Pesetsky, David. 1982. Paths and Categories. PhD thesis, Massachusetts Institute of Technology.

Pesetsky, David. 1987. Wh-in-situ: Movement and unselective binding. *The representation of (in) definiteness* 98, 98–129.

Pesetsky, David. 2000. *Phrasal movement and its kin*. Cambridge, MA: MIT Press.

Pesetsky, David. 2019. Complementizer-trace effects. In Martin Everaert and Henk van Riemsdijk (eds), *A Companion to Syntax*, 2nd edn, Oxford: Blackwell.

Peters, P. Stanley and Ritchie, Robert W. 1973. On the generative power of transformational grammars. *Information Sciences* 6, 49–83.

Petrov, Slav, Barrett, Leon, Thibaux, Romain, and Klein, Dan. 2006. Learning Accurate, Compact, and Interpretable Tree Annotation. In Nicoletta Calzolari, Claire Cardie, and Pierre Isabelle (eds), *Proceedings of the 21st International Conference on Computational Linguistics*, pages 433–40, Stroudsburg, PA: Association for Computational Linguistics.

Petten, Cyma Van and Kutas, Marta. 1991. Influences of semantic and syntactic context on open and closed class words. *Memory and Cognition* 19, 95–112.

Phillips, Colin. 1996. Order and Structure. PhD dissertation, Massachusetts Institute of Technology.

Phillips, Colin. 2006. The real-time status of island phenomena. *Language* 82, 795–823.

Phillips, Colin. 2013a. On the nature of island constraints. I: Language processing and reductionist accounts. In Jon Sprouse and Norbert Hornstein (eds), *Experimental syntax and island effects* pages 64–108, Cambridge: Cambridge University Press.

Phillips, Colin. 2013b. Some arguments and non-arguments for reductionist accounts of syntactic phenomena. *Language and Cognitive Processes* 28, 156–87.

Phillips, Colin. 2017. Parser-grammar relations: We don't understand everything twice. In Montserrat Sanz, Itziar Laka, and Michael K. Tanenhaus (eds), *Language down the Garden Path: The Cognitive and Biological Basis for Linguistic Structures*, pages 294–315, Oxford: Oxford University Press.

Phillips, Colin, Kazanina, Nina, and Abada, Shani H. 2005. ERP effects of the processing of syntactic long-distance dependencies. *Cognitive Brain Research* 22(3), 407–28.

Phillips, Colin and Lewis, Shevaun. 2013. Derivational order in syntax: evidence and architectural consequences. *Studies in Linguistics* 6, 11–47.

Phillips, Colin and Wagers, Matthew. 2007. Relating structure and time in linguistics and psycholinguistics. In M. Gareth Gaskell (ed.), *The Oxford handbook of psycholinguistics*, pages 739–56, Oxford: Oxford University Press.

Phillips, Colin, Wagers, Matthew W., and Lau, Ellen F. 2011. Grammatical Illusions and Selective Fallibility in Real-Time Language Comprehension. In Jeffrey Runner (ed.), *Experiments at the Interfaces. Syntax & Semantics, vol. 37*, pages 153–86, Bingley, UK: Emerald Publications.

Piattelli-Palmarini, Massimo. 1980. *Language and Learning: The Debate between Jean Piaget and Noam Chomsky*. Cambridge, MA: Harvard University Press.

Pickering, Martin J. 1993. Direct association and sentence processing: A reply to Gorrell and to Gibson and Hickok. *Language and Cognitive Processes* 8(2), 163–96.

Pickering, Martin J. 1994. Processing local and unbounded dependencies: A unified account. *Journal of Psycholinguistic Research* 23(4), 323–52.

Pickering, Martin J. and Barry, Guy. 1991. Sentence Processing without Empty Categories. *Language and Cognitive Processes* 6, 229–59.

Pickering, Martin J., Barton, Stephen, and Shillcock, Richard. 1994. Unbounded dependencies, island constraints and processing complexity. In Charles Clifton, Lyn Frazier, and Keith Rayner (eds), *Perspectives on sentence processing*, pages 199–224, London: Lawrence Erlbaum.

Pickering, Martin J. and Garrod, Simon C. 2013. An integrated theory of language production and comprehension. *Behavioral and Brain Sciences* 36(4), 329–47.

Pickering, Martin J. and Traxler, Matthew J. 2003. Evidence against the use of subcategorisation frequency in the processing of unbounded dependencies. *Language and Cognitive Processes* 18(4), 469–503.

Pinker, Steven and Bloom, Paul. 1990. Natural language and natural selection. *Behavioral and Brain Sciences* 13(4), 707–84.

Pinker, Steven and Jackendoff, Ray. 2005. The faculty of language: what's special about it? *Cognition* 95(2), 201–36.

Pires, Acrisio and Taylor, Heather Lee. 2009. The syntax of wh-in-situ and common ground. In M. Elliot, J. Kirby, O. Sawada, E. Staraki, and S. Yoon (eds), *Proceedings from the Panels of the Forty-third Annual Meeting of the Chicago Linguistic Society*, pages 201–15, Chicago, IL: Chicago Linguistic Society.

Polinsky, Maria, Gallo, Carlos Gómez, Graff, Peter, Kravtchenko, Ekaterina, Morgan, Adam Milton, and Sturgeon, Anne. 2013. Subject islands are different. In Jon Sprouse and Norbert Hornstein (eds), *Experimental Syntax and island effects*, pages 286–309, Cambridge: Cambridge University Press.

Pollard, Carl. 1996. The nature of constraint-based grammar. In *Pacific Asia Conference on Language information, and Computation*, pages 1–18, Seoul: Kyung Hee University.

Pollard, Carl and Sag, Ivan A. 1987. *Information-Based Syntax and Semantics; Volume One: Fundamentals* CSLI Lecture Notes No.13. Stanford, CA: CSLI Publications.

Pollard, Carl and Sag, Ivan A. 1994. *Head-driven phrase structure grammar* Chicago, IL: University of Chicago Press and Stanford, CA: CSLI.

Post, Emil L. 1943. Formal reductions of the general combinatorial decision problem. *American Journal of Mathematics* 65(2), 197–215.

Post, Emil L. 1947. Recursive unsolvability of a problem of Thue. *The Journal of Symbolic Logic* 12(1), 1–11.

Postal, Paul M. 1971. *Cross-over phenomena*. New York: Holt, Rinehart and Winston.

Postal, Paul M. 1993. Parasitic Gaps and the Across-the-board Phenomenon. *Linguistic Inquiry* 24, 735–54.

Postal, Paul M. 1998. *Three investigations of extraction*. Cambridge, MA: MIT Press.

Postal, Paul M. 2004. *Skeptical Linguistic Essays*. Oxford and New York: Oxford University Press.

Postal, Paul M. and Pullum, Geoffrey K. 1982. The contraction debate. *Linguistic Inquiry* 13, 122–38.

Postal, Paul M. and Ross, John R. 1971. ¡Tough movement sí, tough deletion no! *Linguistic Inquiry* 2, 544–6.

Prasad, Grusha and Linzen, Tal. 2020. Do self-paced reading studies provide evidence for rapid syntactic adaptation? https://psyarxiv.com/9ptg4/, accessed May 21, 2020.

Price, Patty, Ostendorf, Mari, Shattuck-Hufnagel, Stefanie, and Fong, Cynthia. 1991. The use of prosody in syntactic disambiguation. *Journal of Acoustical Society of America* 90, 2956–70.

Prince, Ellen F. 1981. Topicalization, Focus-Movement, and Yiddish-Movement: a pragmatic differentiation. In Danny K. Alford, Karen Ann Hunold, Monica A. Macaulay, Jenny Walter, Claudia Brugman, Paula Chertok, Inese Civkulis, and Marta Tobey (eds), *Proceedings of the Seventh Annual Meeting of the Berkeley Linguistics Society*, pages 249–64, Berkeley, CA: Berkeley Linguistics Society.

Prince, Ellen F. 1984. Topicalization and Left-Dislocation: A Functional Analysis. *Annals of the New York Academy of Sciences* 433(1), 213–25.

Prince, Ellen F. 1990. Syntax and discourse: A look at resumptive pronouns. In Kira Hall, Jean-Pierre Koenig, Michael Meacham, Sondra Reinman, and Laurel A. Sutton (eds), *Proceedings of the Sixteenth Annual Meeting of the Berkeley Linguistics Society: Parasession on the Legacy of Grice*, pages 482–97, Berkeley, CA: University of California, Berkeley Linguistics Society.

Prince, Ellen F. 1997. On kind-sentences, resumptive pronouns, and relative clauses. In Gregory R. Guy, Crawford Faeagin, Deborah Schiffrin, and John Baugh (eds), *Towards a social science of language: Papers in honor of William Labov, Vol. 2: Social interaction and discourse structures*, pages 223–36, Amsterdam: John Benjamins.

Prince, Ellen F. 1998. On the limits of syntax, with reference to Left-Dislocation and Topicalization. In Peter W. Culicover and Louise McNally (eds), *The Limits of Syntax*, volume 29 of *Syntax and Semantics*, pages 281–302, San Diego, CA: Academic Press.

Przepiórkowski, Adam. 1999. On Case Assignment and 'Adjuncts as Complements'. In Gert Webelhuth, Jean-Pierre Koenig, and Andreas Kathol (eds), *Lexical and Constructional Aspects of Linguistic Explanation*, pages 231–45, Stanford, CA: CSLI Publications.

Pullum, Geoffrey K. 1997. The morpholexical nature of English to-contraction. *Language* 73(1), 79–102.

Pullum, Geoffrey K. and Scholz, Barbara C. 2002. Empirical assessment of stimulus poverty arguments. *The Linguistic Review* 19, 9–50.

Pullum, Geoffrey K. and Zwicky, Arnold M. 1997. Licensing of prosodic features by syntactic rules: The key to auxiliary reduction. Paper presented at Annual Meeting of the Linguistic Society of America. [Abstract available at www-csli.stanford.edu/zwicky/LSA97.abst.pdf].

Pustejovsky, James. 1985. Studies in Generalized Binding PhD dissertation, University of Massachusetts, Amherst.

Putnam, Michael T. and Stroik, Thomas. 2009. Traveling without moving: the conceptual necessity of Survive-minimalism. In Michael T. Putnam (ed.), *Towards a derivational syntax*, pages 3–20, Amsterdam and Philadelphia, PA: John Benjamins.

Pylkkänen, Liina. 2019. The neural basis of combinatory syntax and semantics. *Science* 366(6461), 62–6.

Quinn, Deirdre, Abdelghany, Hala, and Fodor, Janet Dean. 2000. More evidence of implicit prosody in silent reading: French, English and Arabic relative clauses. Poster presented at the 13th Conference on Human Sentence Processing, La Jolla, CA.

Rackowski, Andrea and Richards, Norvin. 2005. Phase edge and extraction: A Tagalog case study. *Linguistic Inquiry* 36(4), 565–99.

Radford, Alec, Wu, Jeff, Child, Rewon, Luan, David, Amodei, Dario, and Sutskever, Ilya. 2019. Language Models are Unsupervised Multitask Learners, https://github.com/openai/gpt-2, accessed May 21, 2020.

Radford, Andrew. 1981. *Transformational Syntax: A student's guide to Chomsky's Extended Standard Theory*. Cambridge: Cambridge University Press.

Radford, Andrew. 1988. *Transformational Grammar: A First Course* Cambridge: Cambridge University Press.

Radford, Andrew. 2009. *Analysing English Sentences* Cambridge: Cambridge University Press.

Radford, Andrew. 2019. *Relative Clauses: Structure and Variation in Everyday English*. Cambridge: Cambridge University Press.

Radford, Andrew and Felser, Claudia. 2011. On preposition copying and preposition pruning in wh- clauses in English. *Essex Research Reports in Linguistics* 60(4), 1–35.

Ramchand, Gillian and Svenonius, Peter. 2014. Deriving the functional hierarchy. *Language Sciences* 46, 152–74.

Rasmussen, Nathan and Schuler, William. 2017. Left-Corner Parsing with Distributed Associative Memory Produces Surprisal and Locality Effects. *Cognitive Science* 42(4), 1009–42.

Reali, F. and Christiansen, M. H. 2007. Processing of relative clauses is made easier by frequency of occurrence. *Journal of Memory and Language* 57, 1–23.

Reape, Michael. 1996. Getting things in order. In Harry Bunt and Arthur van Horck (eds), *Discontinuous Constituency* Natural Language Processing Series, number 6, pages 209–53, Berlin and New York: Mouton de Gruyter.

Reinhart, Tanya. 1981. Pragmatics and linguistics: an analysis of sentence topics. *Philosophica* 27(1), 53–94.

Reinhart, Tanya. 1983. *Anaphora and Semantic Interpretation*. London: Croom Helm.

Reinhart, Tanya. 1998. Wh-in-situ in the framework of the Minimalist Program. *Natural Language Semantics* 6(1), 29–56.

Reitter, David, Keller, Frank, and Moore, Johanna D. 2006a. Computational modelling of structural priming in dialogue. In Robert C. Moore, Jeff A. Bilmes, Jennifer Chu-Carroll, and Mark Sanderson (eds), *Proceedings of the Human Language Technology Conference of the North American Chapter of the Association for Computational Linguistics*, pages 121–4, New York: Association for Computational Linguistics.

Reitter, David, Keller, Frank, and Moore, Johanna D. 2006b. Priming of syntactic rules in task-oriented dialogue and spontaneous conversation. In Ron Sun (ed.), *Proceedings of the 28th Annual Conference of the Cognitive Science Society*, pages 685–90, Vancouver: eScholarship.

Reitter, David and Moore, Johanna D. 2014. Alignment and task success in spoken dialogue. *Journal of Memory and Language* 76, 29–46.

Repp, Sophie. 2009. *Negation in Gapping*. Oxford: Oxford University Press.

Resnik, Philip. 1992. Left-corner Parsing and Psychological Plausibility. In Antonio Zampolli (ed.), *Proceedings of the 14th Conference on Computational Linguistics: Volume 1* COLING '92, pages 191–7, Nantes: Association for Computational Linguistics.

Reyle, Uwe. 1993. Dealing with ambiguities by underspecification: Construction, representation and deduction. *Journal of Semantics* 10(2), 123–79.

Rezac, Milan. 2006. On tough-movement. In Cedric Boeckx (ed.), *Minimalist essays*, pages 288–325, Amsterdam: John Benjamins.

Richards, Marc D. 2011. Deriving the Edge: What's in a Phase? *Syntax* 14(1), 74–95.

Richards, Norvin. 1999. Dependency formation and directionality of tree construction. In V. Lin, C. Krause, B. Bruening, and K. Arregi (eds.), *MITWPL 34: Papers on Morphology and Syntax, Cycle Two*, pages 67–105, Cambridge, MA: MIT Press.

Richards, Norvin. 2001. *Movement in Language: interactions and architectures* Oxford and New York: Oxford University Press.

Richards, Norvin. 2010. *Uttering trees*. Cambridge, MA: MIT Press.

Richards, Norvin. 2016. *Contiguity theory*. Cambridge, MA: MIT Press.

Richter, Frank and Sailer, Manfred. 2004. Basic Concepts of Lexical Resource Semantics. In Arnold Beckmann and Norbert Preining (eds), *ESSLLI 2003: Course Material I*, volume 5 of *Collegium Logicum*, pages 87–143. Vienna: Kurt Gödel Society.

Richter, Stephanie and Chaves, Rui P. 2020. Investigating the Role of Verb Frequency in Factive and Manner-of-speaking Islands. In Stephanie Denison, Michael Mack, Yang Xu, and Blair Armstrong (eds), *Proceedings of the 42nd Annual Virtual Meeting of the Cognitive Science Society*, Toronto, pp. 7.

Riehemann, Susanne Z. 1998. Type-Based Derivational Morphology. *Journal of Comparative Germanic Linguistics* 2, 49–77.

Ritchart, Amanda, Goodall, Grant, and Garellek, Marc. 2016. Prosody and the That-Trace Effect: An Experimental Study. In Kyeong-min Kim, Pocholo Umbal, Trevor Block, Queenie Chan, Tanie Cheng, Kelli Finney, Mara Katz, Sophie Nickel-Thompson, and Lisa Shorten (eds), *33rd West Coast Conference on Formal Linguistics*, pages 320–8, Somerville, MA: Cascadilla Proceedings Project.

Rizzi, Luigi. 1982. *Violations of the wh-island constraint and the Subjacency Condition*. Issues in Italian Syntax, Studies in Generative Syntax 11, Dordrecht: Foris.

Rizzi, Luigi. 1990. *Relativized Minimality*. Cambridge, MA: MIT Press.

Rizzi, Luigi. 1997. The fine structure of the left periphery. In Liliane Haegeman (ed.), *Elements of Grammar: Handbook of Generative Syntax*, pages 281–337, Dordrecht: Springer.

Rizzi, Luigi. 2007a. On Some Properties of Criterial Freezing. *CISCL Working Papers on Language and Cognition* 1, 145–58.

Rizzi, Luigi. 2007b. On the form of chains: Criterial positions and ECP effects. In Lisa Lai-Shen Cheng and N. Corver (eds), *WH-movement: Moving on*, pages 97–133, Cambridge, MA: MIT Press.

Rizzi, Luigi. 2013. Notes on cartography and further explanation. *International Journal of Latin and Romance Linguistics* 25(1), 197–226.

Rizzi, Luigi. 2015. Cartography, Criteria and Labelling. In U. Shlonsky (ed.), *Beyond Functional Sequence: The Cartography of Syntactic Structures*, volume 10, pages 314–38, Oxford: Oxford University Press.

Roark, Brian, Bachrach, Asaf, Cardenas, Carlos, and Pallier, Christopher. 2009. Deriving lexical and syntactic expectation-based measures for psycholinguistic modeling via incremental top-down parsing. In Philipp Koehn and Rada Mihalcea (eds), *Proceedings of the 2009 conference on empirical methods in natural language processing*, pages 324–33, Singapore: Association for Computational Linguistics.

Roberts, Craige. 1996. Information Structure in Discourse. In Jae Hak Yoon and Andreas Kathol (eds), *Ohio Working Papers in Semantics 49*, pages 91–136, Columbus, OH: Ohio State University.

Roberts, Craige. 2012. Information structure in discourse: Towards an integrated formal theory of pragmatics. *Semantics and Pragmatics* 5(6), 1–69.

Roeper, Thomas and de Villiers, Jill. 1994. Lexical links in the wh-chain. *Syntactic theory and first language acquisition: Cross-Linguistic Perspectives* 2, 357–90.

Roeper, Thomas and de Villiers, Jill. 2011. The acquisition path for wh-questions. In Jill de Villiers and Thomas Roeper (eds), *Handbook of generative approaches to language acquisition*, pages 189–246, Dordrecht: Springer.

Rogalsky, Corianne, Almeida, Diogo, Sprouse, Jon, and Hickok, Gregory. 2015. Sentence processing selectivity in Broca's area: evident for structure but not syntactic movement. *Language, Cognition and Neuroscience* 30(10), 1326–38.

Rogalsky, Corianne and Hickok, Gregory. 2011. The role of Broca's area in sentence comprehension. *Journal of Cognitive Neuroscience* 23(7), 1664–80.

Rogers, James and Pullum, Geoffrey K. 2011. Aural pattern recognition experiments and the subregular hierarchy. *Journal of Logic, Language and Information* 20, 329–42.

Rohde, Hannah. 2006. Rhetorical questions as redundant interrogatives. In Eric Bakovic, Shin Fukuda, George Gibbard, and Chi-ju Hsieh (eds), *San Diego Linguistics Papers, Vol. 2*, pages 134–68, San Diego, CA: University of California.

Roland, Douglas, Mauner, Gail, O'Meara, Carolyn, and Yun, Hongoak. 2012. Discourse expectations and relative clause processing. *Journal of Memory and Language* 66, 479–508.

Romero, Maribel. 1998. Focus and reconstruction effects in wh-phrases. PhD thesis, University of Massachusetts, Amherst.

Ross, John R. 1967. Constraints on Variables in Syntax. PhD dissertation, Massachusetts Institute of Technology, Cambridge, MA. [Published in 1986 as *Infinite Syntax!* Norwood, NJ: Ablex Publishing].

Ross, John R. 1984. Inner Islands. In Berkeley Linguistics Society (ed.), *Proceedings of BLS 10, University of California, Berkeley*, pages 258–65, Berkeley, CA: Berkeley Linguistics Society.

Ross, John Robert. 1969. Guess Who? In Robert Binnick, Alice Davison, Georgia Green, and Jerry Morgan (eds), *Papers from the 5th Regional Meeting of the Chicago Linguistic Society*, pages 252–86, Chicago, IL: Chicago Linguistics Society.

Rowland, Caroline and Pine, Julian. 2000. Subject–auxiliary inversion errors and wh-question acquisition:'What children do know?' *Journal of Child Language* 27(1), 157–81.

Rullmann, Hotze. 1995. Maximality in the semantics of wh-constructions. PhD dissertation, University of Massachusetts Amherst, GLSA.

Rumelhart, David E. 1975. Notes on a schema for stories. In D. G. Brown and A. Collins (eds), *Representation and understanding: Studies in cognitive science*, New York: Academic Press.

Ruppenhofer, Josef and Michaelis, Laura A. 2014. Frames and the interpretation of omitted arguments in English. In Stacey Katz Bourns and Lindsy L. Myers (eds.), *Perspectives on Linguistic Structure and Context: Studies in honor of Knud Lambrecht*, pages 57–86, Amsterdam: John Benjamins.

Ruys, Eddy. 1993. The scope of indefinites. PhD thesis, Universiteit Utrecht.

Sabbagh, James. 2007. Ordering and Linearizing Rightward Movement. *Natural Language and Linguistic Theory* 25(2), 349–401.

Sabel, Joachim. 2002. A minimalist analysis of syntactic islands. *Linguistic Review* 19(3), 271–315.

Sadock, Jerrold M. 1972. Speech act idioms. In Paul M. Peranteau (ed.), *Papers from the Eighth Regional Meeting of the Chicago Linguistic Society*, pages 329–39, Chicago, IL: Chicago Linguistic Society.

Saffran, Jenny R., Aslin, Richard N., and Newport, Elissa L. 1996. Statistical learning by 8-month-old infants. *Science* 274(5294), 1926–8.

Saffran, Jenny R., Newport, Elissa L., and Aslin, Richard N. 1996. Word segmentation: The role of distributional cues. *Journal of Memory and Language* 35(4), 606–21.

Sag, Ivan A. 1992. Taking Performance Seriously. In Carlos Martin-Vide (ed.), *VII Congreso de Lenguajes Naturales y Lenguajes Formales*. Barcelona: Promociones y Publicaciones.

Sag, Ivan A. 1997. English relative clause constructions. *Journal of Linguistics* 33(2), 431–84.

Sag, Ivan A. 2000. Another argument against *wh*-trace. Jorge Hankamer Webfest, web.archive.org/web/20110720081732/http://ling.ucsc.edu/Jorge/sag.html, accessed August 19, 2020.

Sag, Ivan A. 2010. English filler-gap constructions. *Language* 86(3), 486–545.

Sag, Ivan A. 2012. Sign-Based Construction Grammar: An informal synopsis. In Hans Boas and Ivan A. Sag (eds), *Sign-Based Construction Grammar*, pages 69–202, Stanford, CA: CSLI Publications.

Sag, Ivan A., Chaves, Rui P., Abeillé, Anne, Estigarribia, Bruno, Flickinger, Dan, Kay, Paul, Michaelis, Laura A., Müller, Stefan, Pullum, Geoffrey K., Van Eynde, Frank, and Wasow, Thomas. 2020. Lessons from the English Auxiliary System. *Journal of Linguistics* 56(1), 87–155.

Sag, Ivan A. and Fodor, Janet Dean. 1995. Extraction without traces. In Raul Aranovich, William Byrne, Susanne Preuss, and Martha Senturia (eds), *Proceedings of the Thirteenth West Coast Conference on Formal Linguistics*, pages 365–84, Stanford, CA: CSLI.

Sag, Ivan A., Gazdar, Geral, Wasow, Thomas, and Weisler, Steven. 1985. Coordination and how to distinguish categories. *Natural Language and Linguistic Theory* 3, 117–71.

Sag, Ivan A. and Hankamer, Jorge. 1984. Toward a Theory of Anaphoric Processing. *Linguistics and Philosophy* 7, 325–45.

Sag, Ivan A., Hofmeister, Philip, and Snider, Neal. 2009. Processing complexity in subjacency violations: the complex noun phrase constraint. In Malcolm Elliott, James Kirby, Osamu Sawada, Eleni Staraki, and Suwon Yoon (eds), *Proceedings of the 43rd Annual Meeting of the Chicago Linguistic Society (2007)*, volume 43, pages 215–29, Chicago, IL: Chicago Linguistic Society.

Sag, Ivan A. and Nykiel, Joann. 2011. Remarks on sluicing. In Stefan Müller (ed.), *Proceedings of the 18th International Conference on Head-Driven Phrase Structure Grammar*, University of Washington, pages 188–208, Stanford, CA: CSLI Publications.

Sag, Ivan A. and Pollard, Carl. 1991. An Integrated Theory of Complement Control. *Language* 67(1), 63–113.

Sag, Ivan A. and Wasow, Thomas. 2011. Performance-Compatible Competence Grammar. In Robert Borsley and Kersti Börjars (eds), *Non-Transformational Syntax: Formal and explicit models of grammar*, pages 359–77, Cambridge, MA: Wiley-Blackwell.

Sag, Ivan A. and Wasow, Thomas. 2015. Flexible processing and the design of grammar. *Journal of Psycholinguistic Research* 44(1), 47–63.

Sag, Ivan A., Wasow, Thomas, and Bender, Emily M. 2003. *Syntactic Theory: A formal introduction. 2nd Edition*. Stanford, CA: CSLI Publications.

Sakas, William and Fodor, Janet Dean. 2001. The structural triggers learner. In Stefano Bertolo (ed.), *Language acquisition and learnability*, pages 172–233, Cambridge: Cambridge University Press.

Salzmann, Martin, Häussler, Jana, Bader, Markus, and Bayer, Josef. 2013. That-trace effects without traces. An experimental investigation. In Stefan Keine and Shayne Sloggett (eds), *Proceedings of the 42nd Annual Meeting of the North East Linguistic Society* pages 149–62, Amherst, MA: GLSA, Department of Linguistics, University of Massachusetts.

Sanford, Anthony J. and Garrod, Simon C. 1981. *Understanding written language: Explorations of comprehension beyond the sentence* Chichester: John Wiley & Sons.

Sanford, Anthony J. and Garrod, Simon C. 1998. The role of scenario mapping in text comprehension. *Discourse Processes* 26, 159–90.

Santelmann, Lynn M. and Jusczyk, Peter W. 1998. Sensitivity to discontinuous dependencies in language learners: Evidence for limitations in processing space. *Cognition* 69, 105–34.

Santi, Andrea and Grodzinsky, Yosef. 2007a. Taxing working memory with syntax: Bihemispheric modulations. *Human Brain Mapping* 28(11), 1089–97.

Santi, Andrea and Grodzinsky, Yosef. 2007b. Working memory and syntax interact in Broca's area. *Neuroimage* 37(1), 8–17.

Santorini, Beatrice. 2007. (Un?)expected movement, University of Pennsylvania, https://www.ling.upenn.edu/ beatrice/examples/movement.html, accessed January 2, 2012.

Sauerland, Uli. 1999. Erasibility and interpretation. *Syntax* 2, 161–88.

Sauerland, Uli and Elbourne, Paul D. 2002. Total reconstruction, PF movement, and derivational order. *Linguistic Inquiry* 33(2), 283–319.

Schank, Roger C. and Abelson, Robert P. 1977. *Scripts, Plans, Goals and Understanding: an Inquiry into Human Knowledge Structures*. Hillsdale, NJ: Lawrence Erlbaum.

Scholz, Barbara C. and Pullum, Geoffrey K. 2006. Irrational nativist exuberance. In Robert Stainton (ed.), *Contemporary Debates in Cognitive Science*, pages 59–80, Oxford: Basil Blackwell.

Schütze, Carson T. 1996. *The empirical base of linguistics: grammaticality judgments and linguistic methodology*. Chicago, IL: University of Chicago Press.

Schwanenflugel, Paula J. 1991. Why are abstract concepts hard to understand? In Paula J. Schwanenflugel (ed.), *The Psychology of Word Meanings*, pages 223–50, Hillsdale, NJ: Lawrence Erlbaum.

Schwarz, Bernhard and Simonenko, Alexandra. 2018. Factive islands and meaning-driven unacceptability. *Natural Language Semantics* 26(3–4), 253–79.

Selkirk, Elisabeth. 1984. *Phonology and Syntax: The Relation between Sound and Structure*. Cambridge, MA: MIT Press.

Sells, Peter. 1984. Syntax and semantics of resumptive pronouns. PhD thesis, University of Massachusetts at Amherst.

Seuren, Pieter A. M. 2004. *Chomsky's Minimalism*. Oxford: Oxford University Press.

Shieber, Stuart M. 1986. *An Introduction to Unification-Based Approaches to Grammar*. Stanford, CA: CSLI Publications.

Shimojo, Mitsuaki. 2002. Functional theories of island phenomena: the case of Japanese. *Studies in Language* 26, 67–123.

Shimojo, Mitsuaki. 2020. Extraction restrictions in complex sentences. In Robert D. Van Valin Jr. (ed.), *The Cambridge Handbook of Role and Reference Grammar*, page 26, Cambridge: Cambridge University Press.

Shlonsky, Ur. 1992. Resumptive pronouns as a last resort. *Linguistic Inquiry* 23(3), 443–68.

Shlonsky, Ur. 2010. The cartographic enterprise in syntax. *Language and Linguistics Compass* 4(6), 417–29.

Shlonsky, Ur. 2015. *Beyond Functional Sequence: The Cartography of Syntactic Structures*. Oxford: Oxford University Press.

Smith, Nathaniel J. and Levy, Roger. 2008. Optimal processing times in reading: A formal model and empirical investigation. In B. C. Love, K. McRae, and V. M. Sloutsky (eds), *Proceedings of the thirtieth annual conference of the Cognitive Science Society*, pages 595–600. University of California: escholarship.

Smith, Neil. 1989. *The Twitter Machine. Reflections on language*. Oxford: Blackwell.

Smolensky, Paul, Goldrick, Matthew, and Mathis, Donald. 2014. Optimization and quantization in gradient symbol systems: a framework for integrating the continuous and the discrete in cognition. *Cognitive Science* 38(6), 1102–38.

Snedeker, Jesse and Huang, Yi Ting. 2009. Sentence processing. In Edith L. Bavin and Letitia R. Naigles (eds), *The Cambridge handbook of child language*, pages 321–37, Cambridge: Cambridge University Press.

Snedeker, Jesse and Trueswell, John C. 2004. The developing constraints on parsing decisions: The role of lexical-biases and referential scenes in child and adult sentence processing. *Cognitive Psychology* 49(3), 238–99.

Snyder, William. 2000. An experimental investigation of syntactic satiation effects. *Linguistic Inquiry* 31, 575–82.

Snyder, William. 2017. On the nature of syntactic satiation, MS.

Snyder, William. forthcoming. Satiation. In Grant Goodall (ed.), *The Cambridge Handbook of Experimental Syntax*, Cambridge: Cambridge University Press.

Song, Sanghoun. 2017. *Modeling Information Structure in a Cross-linguistic Perspective*. Berlin: Language Science Press.

Song, Sanghoun and Bender, Emily M. 2012. Individual Constraints for Information Structure. In Stefan Müller (ed.), *Proceedings of the 19th International Conference on Head-Driven Phrase Structure Grammar, Chungnam National University, Daejeon*, pages 329–47, Stanford, CA; CSLI Publications.

Spevac, Samuel C., Falandays, J. Benjamin, and Spivey, Michael J. 2018. Interactivity of language. *Language and Linguistics Compass* 12(7), e12282.

Sportiche, Dominique. 1988. A theory of floating quantifiers and its corollaries for constituent structure. *Linguistic Inquiry* 19(3), 425–49.

Sprouse, Jon. 2007a. Continuous Acceptability, Categorical Grammaticality, and Experimental Syntax. *Biolinguistics* 1, 118–29.

Sprouse, Jon. 2007b. A program for experimental syntax: Finding the relationship between acceptability and grammatical knowledge PhD dissertation, University of Maryland.

Sprouse, Jon. 2009. Revisiting Satiation: evidence for an equalization response strategy. *Linguistic Inquiry* 40(2), 329–41.

Sprouse, Jon, Caponigro, Ivano, Greco, Ciro, and Cecchetto, Carlo. 2016. Experimental syntax and the variation of island effects in English and Italian. *Natural Language & Linguistic Theory* 34(1), 307–44.

Sprouse, Jon and Hornstein, Norbert (eds). 2013. *Experimental Syntax and island effects*. Cambridge: Cambridge University Press.

Sprouse, Jon, Schütze, Carson T., and Almeida, Diogo. 2013. A comparison of informal and formal acceptability judgments using a random sample from *Linguistic Inquiry* 2001–10. *Lingua* 134, 219–48.

Sprouse, Jon, Wagers, Matt, and Phillips, Colin. 2012. A test of the relation between working memory capacity and syntactic island effects. *Language* 88(1), 82–123.

Stabler, Edward. 1997. *Derivational Minimalism, Logical Aspect of Computational Linguistics*. Dordrecht: Springer.

Stabler, Edward. 2013. Two models of minimalist, incremental syntactic analysis. *Topics in Cognitive Science* 5(3), 611–33.

Stabler, Edward and Keenan, Edward L. 2003. Structural similarity within and among languages. *Theoretical Computer Science* 293(2), 345–63.

Stack, Caoimhe M. Harrington, James, Ariel N., and Watson, Duane G. 2018. A failure to replicate rapid syntactic adaptation in comprehension. *Memory and Cognition* 46(6), 864–77.

Staub, Adrian. 2007. The parser doesn't ignore intransitivity, after all. *Journal of Experimental Psychology: Learning, Memory, and Cognition* 33(3), 550–69.

Staub, Adrian and Clifton, Charles. 2006. Syntactic prediction in language comprehension: Evidence from either . . . or. *Journal of Experimental Psychology: Learning, Memory, and Cognition* 32(2), 425–36.

Steedman, Mark. 1985. Dependency and coordination in Dutch and English. *Language* 61, 523–68.

Steedman, Mark. 1996. *Surface structure and interpretation* Cambridge, MA: MIT Press.

Steedman, Mark. 2001. *The Syntactic Process*. Cambridge, MA: MIT Press.

Steedman, Mark. 2002. Plans, Affordances, and Combinatory Grammar. *Linguistics and Philosophy* 25(5–6), 723–53.

Steels, Luc and Beule, Joachim De. 2006. Unify and Merge in Fluid Construction Grammar. In Paul Vogt, Yuuga Sugita, Elio Tuci, and Chrystopher L. Nehaniv (eds), *Symbol Grounding and Beyond: Proceedings of the Third International Workshop on the Emergence and Evolution of Linguistic Communication*, Lecture Notes in Computer Science, pages 197–223, Berlin and Heidelberg: Springer.

Stepanov, Arthur. 2007. The end of CED? Minimalism and extraction domains. *Syntax* 10(1), 80–126.

Stepanov, Arthur and Georgopoulos, Carol. 1995. Structure building and the conceptual interface: An analysis of Russian long-distance wh-questions. In M. Lindseth and S. Franks (eds), *FASL 5*, pages 275–94, Ann Arbor, MI: Michigan Slavic Publications.

Stowe, Laurie A. 1986. Parsing WH-constructions: Evidence for online gap location. *Language and Cognitive Processes* 1, 227–45.

Stowe, Laurie A., Tanenhaus, Michael K., and Carlson, Gregory N. 1991. Filling gaps online: use of lexical and semantic information in sentence processing. *Language and Speech* 34, 319–40.

Stroik, Thomas S. 2009. Locality in minimalist syntax volume 51. Cambridge, MA: MIT Press.

Stroik, Thomas S. and Putnam, Michael T. 2013. *The structural design of language* Cambridge: Cambridge University Press.

Stromswold, Karin J. 1990. Learnability and the acquisition of auxiliaries. PhD thesis, Massachusetts Institute of Technology.

Stromswold, Karin J. 1995. The acquisition of subject and object wh-questions. *Language Acquisition* 4, 5–48.

Strunk, Jan and Snider, Neal. 2013. Subclausal locality constraints on relative clause extraposition. In Gert Webelhuth, Manfred Sailer, and Heike Walker (eds), *Rightward Movement in a Comparative Perspective*, pages 99–144, Amsterdam: John Benjamins.

Sussman, Rachel S. and Sedivy, Julie C. 2003. The time-course of processing syntactic dependencies: Evidence from eye movements during spoken narratives. *Language and Cognitive Processes* 18, 143–63.

Swaab, Tamara, Baynes, Kathleen and Knight, Robert T. 2003. Separable effects of priming and imageability on word processing: An ERP study. *Brain Research: Cognitive Brain Research* 15, 99–103.

Swingley, Daniel and Aslin, Richard N. 2002. Lexical neighborhoods and the word-form representations of 14-month-olds. *Psychological Science* 13(5), 480–4.

Szabolcsi, Anna. 2006. Strong vs. weak islands. In Martin Everaert and Henk van Riemsdijk (eds), *The Blackwell Companion to Syntax, Volume 4*, pages 479–531, Oxford: Wiley-Blackwell.

Szabolcsi, Anna and Zwarts, Frans. 1993. Weak Islands and an Algebraic Semantics for Scope Taking. *Natural Language Semantics* 1, 235–84.

Szmrecsanyi, Benedikt. 2005. Creatures of habit: A corpus-linguistic analysis of persistence in spoken English. *Corpus Linguistics and Linguistic Theory* 1, 113–49.

Tabor, Whitney and Hutchins, Sean. 2004. Evidence for self-organized sentence processing: digging-in effects. *Journal of Experimental Psychology: Learning, Memory, and Cognition* 30(2), 431–50.

Tabor, Whitney, Juliano, C., and Tanenhaus, Michael K. 1997. Parsing in a dynamical system: An attractor-based account of the interaction of lexical and structural constraints in sentence processing. *Language and Cognitive Processes* 2–3(12), 211–71.

Takahashi, Daiko. 1994. Minimality of movement. PhD thesis, University of Connecticut.

Takami, Ken-Ichi. 1988. Preposition stranding: arguments against syntactic analyses and an alternative functional explanation. *Lingua* 76, 299–335.

Takami, Ken-Ichi. 1992. *Preposition stranding: from syntactic to functional analyses*. Berlin: Mouton de Gruyter.

Tanenhaus, Michael K. and Carlson, Greg N. 1990. Comprehension of deep and surface verb phrase anaphors. *Language and Cognitive Processes* 5(4), 257–80.

Tanenhaus, Michael K., Carlson, Greg, and Trueswell, John C. 1989. The role of thematic structures in interpretation and parsing. *Language and Cognitive Processes* 4, 211–4.

Tanenhaus, Michael K., Spivey-Knowlton, Michael J., Eberhard, Kathleen M., and Sedivy, Julie C. 1995. Integration of visual and linguistic information in spoken language comprehension. *Science* 268(5217), 1632–34.

Taraldsen, Knut Tarald. 1978. The scope of wh movement in Norwegian. *Linguistic Inquiry* 9, 623–40.

Taraldsen, Knut Tarald. 1982. Extraction from relative clauses in Norwegian. Readings on Unbounded Dependencies in Scandinavian Languages. In Elisabet Engdahl and Eva Ejerhed (eds), *Readings on unbounded dependencies in Scandinavian languages*, pages 205–21, Stockholm: Almqvist and Wiksell International.

Taylor, Ann, Marcus, Mitchell, and Santorini, Beatrice. 2003. The Penn treebank: an overview. In Anne Abeillé (ed.), *Treebanks*, pages 5–22, Dordrecht: Springer.

Taylor, Heather Lee. 2007. Movement from IF-clause adjuncts. In Anastasia Conroy, Conroy Jing, Chunyuan Nakao, and Eri Takahashi (eds), *University of Maryland Working Papers in Linguistics (UMWPiL)*, volume 15, pages 192–206, College Park, MD: Department of Linguistics, University of Maryland.

Thompson, Sandra A. 2002. 'Object complements' and conversation: Towards a realistic account. *Studies in Language* 26, 125–64.

Thomson, Henry. 1975. The cycle: a formal statement. In Robin E. Grossman, L. James San, and Timothy J. Vance (eds.), *Papers from the Eleventh Regional Meeting, Chicago Linguistic Society* pages 589–603, Chicago, IL: Chicago Linguistic Society.

Thornton, Rosiland J. 1990. Adventures in long-distance moving: The acquisition of complex wh-question. PhD thesis, University of Connecticut, Storrs.

Thornton, Rosiland J. and Crain, Stephen. 1994. Successful cyclic movement. In Teun Hoekstra and Bonnie Schwartz (eds), *Language acquisition studies in generative grammar*, pages 215–52, Amsterdam: John Benjamins.

Tollan, Rebecca and Heller, Daphna. 2016. Elvis Presley on an island: *wh* dependency formation inside complex NPs. In *Proceedings of NELS 46*, page 2, Montreal: North East Linguistic Society.

Tomasello, Michael. 1992. *First verbs: A case study of early grammatical development*. Cambridge: Cambridge University Press.

Tomasello, Michael. 2000. First steps toward a usage-based theory of language acquisition. *Cognitive Linguistics* 11(1–2), 61–82.

Tomasello, Michael. 2003. *Constructing a language: A usage-based approach to child language acquisition*. Cambridge, MA: MIT Press.

Tonhauser, Judith, Beaver, David I., and Degen, Judith. 2018. How Projective is Projective Content? Gradience in Projectivity and At-issueness. *Journal of Semantics* 35(3), 495–542.

Torr, John, Stanojević, Milos, Steedman, Mark, and Cohen, Shay B. 2019. Wide-Coverage Neural A* Parsing for Minimalist Grammars. In Anna Korhonen, David Traum, and Lluís Màrquez (eds) *Proceedings of the 57th Annual Meeting of the Association for Computational Linguistics*, pages 2486–505, Florence: Association for Computational Linguistics.

Torrego, Esther. 1984. On inversion in Spanish and some of its effects. *Linguistic Inquiry* 15(1), 103–29.

Toutanova, Kristina, Manning, Christopher D., Flickinger, Dan, and Oepen, Stephan. 2005. Stochastic HPSG Parse Disambiguation using the Redwoods Corpus. *Research on Language and Computation* 3(1), 83–105.

Townsend, David J. and Bever, Thomas G. 2001. *Sentence comprehension: The integration of habits and rules*. Cambridge, MA: MIT Press.

Traugott, Elizabeth Closs and Trousdale, Graeme. 2014. *Constructionalization and Constructional Changes*. Oxford: Oxford University Press.

Traxler, Matthew J. and Pickering, Martin J. 1996. Plausibility and the processing of unbounded dependencies: an eye-tracking study. *Journal of Memory and Language* 35, 454–75.

Trueswell, John C. and Kim, Albert E. 1998. How to prune a garden path by nipping it in the bud: Fast priming of verb argument structure. *Journal of Memory and Language* 1(39), 102–23.

Trueswell, John C, Sekerina, Irina, Hill, Nicole M., and Logrip, Marian L. 1999. The kindergarten-path effect: Studying online sentence processing in young children. *Cognition* 73(2), 89–134.

Truswell, Robert. 2007. Tense, Events, and Extraction from Adjuncts. *Proceedings of the 43rd Annual Meeting of the Chicago Linguistic Society* 43(2), 233–47.

Truswell, Robert. 2011. *Events, Phrases and Questions*. Oxford: Oxford University Press.

Tseng, Jesse. 2008. The representation of syllable structure in HPSG. In Stefan Müller (ed.), *The Proceedings of the 15th International Conference on Head-Driven Phrase Structure Grammar*, pages 234–52, Stanford, CA: CSLI Publications.

Tsiamtsiouris, Jim and Cairns, Helen Smith. 2009. Effects of syntactic complexity and sentence-structure priming on speech initiation time in adults who stutter. *Journal of Speech, Language, and Hearing Research* 52(6), 1623–39.

Tsoulas, George and Yeo, Norman. 2017. Scope assignment: From wh-to QR. *Glossa: A Journal of General Linguistics* 2(1), 1–33.

Tutunjian, Damon and Boland, Julie E. 2008. Do We Need a Distinction between Arguments and Adjuncts? Evidence from Psycholinguistic Studies of Comprehension. *Language and Linguistics Compass* 2(4), 631–46.

Uriagereka, Juan. 1988. On Government. PhD thesis, University of Connecticut, Storrs.

Uriagereka, Juan. 1999. Minimal restrictions on Basque movements. *Natural Language & Linguistic Theory* 17(2), 403–44.

Vaillette, Nathan. 2002. Irish Gaps and Resumptive Pronouns in HPSG. In Frank van Eynde, Lars Hellan, and Dorothee Beermann (eds), *Proceedings of the HPSG-2001 Conference, Norwegian University of Science and Technology, Trondheim*, pages 284–99, Stanford, CA: CSLI Publications.

Valian, Virginia. 1990. Logical and psychological constraints on the acquisition of syntax. In Lynn Frazier and Jill de Villiers (eds), *Language processing and language acquisition*, pages 119–45, Dordrecht: Kluwer Academic.

VandenBos, Gary R. 2010. *Publication manual of the American Psychological Association*, 6th edn. Washington DC: American Psychological Association.

Van der Auwera, Johan. 1984. That COMP-fusions. In Claudia Brugman and Monica Macaulay (eds), *Annual Meeting of the Berkeley Linguistics Society*, volume 10, pages 660–73.

Van Eynde, Frank. 2003. On the Notion 'Determiner'. In Stefan Müller (ed.), *Proceedings of the HPSG-2003 Conference, Michigan State University, East Lansing*, pages 391–6, Stanford, CA: CSLI Publications.

Van Eynde, Frank. 2004. Pied piping is a Local Dependency. In Stefan Müller (ed.), *Proceedings of the HPSG-2004 Conference, Center for Computational Linguistics, Katholieke Universiteit Leuven*, pages 313–34, Stanford, CA: CSLI Publications.

Van Eynde, Frank. 2006. NP-internal agreement and the structure of the noun phrase. *Journal of Linguistics* 42(1), 139–86.

Van Eynde, Frank. 2015. *Predicative Constructions: From the Fregean to a Montagovian Treatment* Studies in Constraint-based Lexicalism, Stanford, CA: CSLI Publications.

van Kempen, Jacqueline. 1997. First steps in wh-movement. PhD thesis, University of Utrecht.

van Schijndel, Marten, Schuler, William, and Culicover, Peter W. 2014. Frequency Effects in the Processing of Unbounded Dependencies. In Paul Bello, Marjorie McShane, Marcello Guarini, and Brian Scassellati (eds), *Proceedings of CogSci 2014*, pages 1658–63, Quebec: Cognitive Science Society.

Van Valin, Robert D., Jr. 1986. Pragmatics, island phenomena, and linguistic competence. In A. M. Farley, P. T. Farley, and K.-E. McCullough (eds), *Papers from the Parasession on Pragmatics and Grammatical Theory*, volume 22(2), pages 223–33, Chicago, IL: Chicago Linguistic Society.

Van Valin, Robert D., Jr. 1987. The Role of Government in the Grammar of Head-Marking Languages. *International Journal of American Linguistics* 53(4), 371–97.

Van Valin, Robert D., Jr. 1994a. Extraction Restrictions, Competing Theories and the Argument from the Poverty of the Stimulus. In Susan D. Lima, Roberta L. Corrigan, and Gregory K. Iverson (eds), *The Reality of Linguistic Rules*, pages 243–59, Amsterdam and Philadelphia, PA: John Benjamins.

Van Valin, Robert D., Jr. 1994b. Toward a functionalist account of so-called extraction constraints. In B. Devriendt, L. Goossens, and J. van der Auwera (eds), *Complex structures: A functionalist perspective*, pages 26–60, Berlin: Mouton de Gruyter.

Van Valin, Robert D., Jr. 1998. The acquisition of wh-questions and the mechanisms of language acquisition. In M. Tomasello (ed.), *The new psychology of language*, pages 221–49, Hillsdale, NJ: Lawrence Erlbaum.

Van Valin, Robert D., Jr. 2005. *Exploring the Syntax-Semantics Interface*. Cambridge: Cambridge University Press.

Van Valin, Robert D., Jr. 2006. Semantic macroroles and language processing. In Ina Bornkessel, Matthias Schlesewsky, Bernard Comrie, and Angela D. Friederici (eds), *Semantic role universals and argument linking: Theoretical, typological and psycholinguistic perspectives*, pages 263–302, Berlin and New York: Mouton de Gruyter.

Van Valin, Robert D., Jr. and LaPolla, Randy J. 1997. *Syntax: Structure, meaning, and function*. Cambridge: Cambridge University Press.

Velleman, Daniel, Beaver, David, Onea, Edgar, Bumford, Dylan, Destruel, Emilie, and Coppock, Elizabeth. 2012. It-clefts are IT (Inquiry Terminating) Constructions. In Anca Chereches (ed.), *Semantics and Linguistic Theory 22 (SALT 22)*, pages 441–60, Chicago, IL: University of i Chicago.

Verhagen, Arie. 2006. On subjectivity and 'long distance Wh-movement'. In Angeliki Athanasiadou, Costas Canakis, and Bert Cornillie (eds), *Subjectification: Various paths to subjectivity*, pages 323–46, Berlin: Mouton de Gruyter.

Verhagen, Véronique, Mos, Maria, Schilperoord, Joost, and Backus, Ad. 2019. Variation is information: Analyses of variation across items, participants, time, and methods in metalinguistic judgment data. *Linguistics*. 0024-3949, 1–45.

Vicente, Luis. 2016. ATB extraction without coordination. In Christopher Hammerly and Brandon Prickett (eds), *Proceedings of the Forty-Sixth Annual Meeting of the North East Linguistic Society*, pages 257–70, Amherst, MA: Department of Linguistics, University of Massachusetts.

Villata, Sandra, Rizzi, Luigi, and Franck, Julie. 2016. Intervention effects and relativized minimality: New experimental evidence from graded judgments. *Lingua* 179, 76–96.

Vosse, Theo and Kempen, Gerard. 2000. Syntactic structure assembly in human parsing: A computational model based on competitive inhibition and lexicalist grammar. *Cognition* 75, 105–43.

Wagers, Matt, Borja, Manuel F., and Chung, Sandra. 2015. The real-time comprehension of wh-dependencies in a wh-agreement language. *Language* 91(1), 109–44.

Wagers, Matt and Phillips, Colin. 2009. Multiple dependencies and the role of the grammar in real-time comprehension. *Journal of Linguistics* 45, 395–433.

Wanner, Eric and Maratsos, Michael. 1978. An ATN approach to comprehension. In Morris Hale, Joan Bresnan, and George A. Miller (eds), *Linguistic theory and psychological reality*, pages 119–61, Cambridge, MA: MIT Press.

Ward, Gregory, Birner, Betty, and Huddleston, Rodney 2002. Information Packaging. In Rodney Huddleston and Geoffrey K. Pullum (eds), *The Cambridge Grammar of the English Language*, pages 1363–448. Cambridge: Cambridge University Press.

Ward, Gregory and Prince, Ellen F. 1991. On the topicalization of indefinite NPs. *Journal of Pragmatics* 16(2), 167–77.

Warren, Tessa and Gibson, Edward. 2002. The influence of referential processing on sentence complexity. *Cognition* 85, 79–112.

Warren, Tessa and Gibson, Edward. 2005. Effects of NP type and in reading cleft sentences in English. *Language and Cognitive Processes* 20, 751–67.

Warstadt, Alex, and Bowman, Samuel R. 2020. Can neural networks acquire a structural bias from raw linguistic data? in *Proceedings of the 42nd Annual Virtual Meeting of the Cognitive Science Society*, Toronto, pp. 7.

Wartenburger, Isabell, Heekeren, Hauke R., Burchert, Frank, Bleser, Ria De, and Villringer, Arno. 2003. Grammaticality judgments on sentences with and without movement of phrasal constituents: an event-related fMRI study. *Journal of Neurolinguistics* 16(4), 301–14.

Wasow, Thomas. 1997. Remarks on grammatical weight. *Language Variation and Change* 9, 81–105.

Wasow, Thomas. 2002. *Postverbal Behavior*. Stanford, CA: CSLI Publications.

Wasow, Thomas. 2020. Processing. In Stefan Müller, Anne Abeillé, Robert D. Borsley, and Jean-Pierre Koenig (eds.), *Head-Driven Phrase Structure Grammar: The Handbook* Berlin: Language Science Press.

Watanabe, Akira. 1992. Subjacency and S-structure movement of wh-in-situ. *Journal of East Asian Linguistics* 1(3), 255–91.

Watson, Duane and Gibson, Edward. 2004. The relationship between intonational phrasing and syntactic structure on language production. *Language and Cognitive Processes* 19, 713–55.

Webelhuth, Gert. 2012. The Distribution of that-Clauses in English: An SBCG Account. In Hans Boas and Ivan A. Sag (eds), *Sign-Based Construction Grammar*, pages 203–27, Stanford, CA: CSLI Publications.

Wechsler, Stephen. 1995. Preposition Selection outside the Lexicon. In Raul Aranovich, William Byrne, Susanne Preuss, and Martha Senturia (eds), *Proceedings of the Thirteenth West Coast Conference on Formal Linguistics*, pages 416–31, Stanford, CA: CSLI Publications.

Wechsler, Stephen and Lee, Yae-Sheik. 1996. The Domain of Direct Case Assignment. *Natural Language and Linguistic Theory* 13(3), 629–64.

Wechsler, Stephen and Zlatic, Larisa. 2003. *The Many Faces of Agreement: Morphology, Syntax, Semantics, and Discourse Factors in Serbo-Croatian Agreement*. Stanford, CA: CSLI Publications.

Weighall, Anna R. 2008. The kindergarten path effect revisited: Children's use of context in processing structural ambiguities. *Journal of Experimental Child Psychology* 99(2), 75–95.

Weisleder, Adriana and Waxman, Sandra R. 2010. What's in the input? Frequent frames in child-directed speech offer distributional cues to grammatical categories in Spanish and English. *Journal of Child Language* 37(5), 1089–108.

Weissenborn, Juergen, Roeper, Tom, and de Villiers, Jill. 1995. Wh-acquisition in French and German. *Recherches Linguistiques* 24, 125–55.

Wells, Justine, Christiansen, Morten H., Race, David S., Acheson, Daniel J., and MacDonald, Maryellen. 2009. Experience and sentence processing: Statistical learning and relative clause comprehension. *Cognitive Psychology* 58, 250–71.

Wells, Rulon S. 1948. Immediate Constituents. *Language* 23, 81–117, [Reprinted in M. Joos (ed.) (1958). *Readings in Linguistics I*, pages 186–207. Chicago, IL: University of Chicago Press].

Wexler, Kenneth and Culicover, Peter W. 1980. *Formal Principles of Language Acquisition*. Cambridge, MA: MIT Press.

White, Lydia. 2003. *Second language acquisition and universal grammar*. Cambridge: Cambridge University Press.

Whitman, Philip Neal. 2004. Semantics and pragmatics of English verbal dependent coordination. *Language* 80(3), 403–34.

Whitman, Philip Neal. 2006. Linguistically Lost, https://literalminded.wordpress.com/2006/10/23/linguistically-lost/{#}more-276, accessed May 12, 2020.

Wilcock, Graham. 2005. Information Structure and Minimal Recursion Semantics. In Antti Arppe, Lauri Carlson, Krister Lindén, Jussi Piitulainen, Mickael Suominen, Martti Vainio, Hanna Westerlund, and Anssi Yli-Jyrä (eds), *Inquiries into Words, Constraints and Contexts: Festschrift for Kimmo Koskenniemi on his 60th Birthday*, CSLI Studies in Computational Linguistics ONLINE, pages 268–77, Stanford, CA: CSLI Publications.

Wilcox, Ethan, Levy, Roger P., Morita, Takashi, and Futrell, Richard. 2018. What do RNN Language Models Learn about Filler-Gap Dependencies? In Ellen Riloff, David Chiang, Julia Hockenmaier, and Jun'ichi Tsujii (eds.), *Proceedings of the 2018 Empirical Methods in Natural Language Processing (and forerunners) (EMNLP) Workshop BlackboxNLP: Analyzing and Interpreting Neural Networks for NLP*, pages 211–21, Brussels: Association for Computational Linguistics.

Wilcox, Rand. 2005. *Introduction to Robust Estimation and Hypothesis Testing* San Francisco, CA: Elsevier.

Wilder, Chris. 1998. Transparent Free Relatives. In Artemis Alexiadou, Nanna Fuhrhop, Paul Law, and Ursula Kleinhenz (eds), *Zentrum Allgemeine Sprache (ZAS) Papers in Linguistics 10*, pages 191–9, Berlin: ZAS.

Williams, Edwin. 1978. Across-the-board Rule Application. *Linguistic Inquiry* 19, 31–43.

Wilson, Stephen M. and Saygın, Ayşe Pınar. 2004. Grammaticality Judgment in Aphasia: Deficits Are Not Specific to Syntactic Structures, Aphasic Syndromes, or Lesion Sites. *Journal of Cognitive Neuroscience* 16(2), 238–52.

Wiltschko, Martina. 2014. *The universal structure of categories: Towards a formal typology*. Cambridge: Cambridge University Press.

Winter, Yoad. 2001. *Flexibility Principles in Boolean Semantics: coordination, plurality and scope in natural language*. Cambridge, MA: MIT Press.

Wu, Jian-Xin. 1999. Syntax and semantics of quantification in Chinese. PhD thesis, University of Maryland at College Park.

Yang, Charles, Crain, Stephen, Berwick, Robert C., Chomsky, Noam, and Bolhuis, Johan J. 2017. The growth of language: Universal Grammar, experience, and principles of computation. *Neuroscience & Biobehavioral Reviews* 81, 103–19.

Yatabe, Shûichi. 2007. Evidence for the Linearization-Based Theory of Semantic Composition. In Stefan Müller (ed.), *Proceedings of the 14th International Conference on Head-Driven Phrase*

Structure Grammar, Stanford Department of Linguistics and CSLI's LinGO Lab, pages 323–43, Stanford, CA: CSLI Pub lications.

Yngve, Victor. 1960. A model and an hypothesis for language structure. *Proceedings of the American Philosophical Society* 104, 444–66.

Yoshida, Masaya. 2003. The Specificity Condition: PF-Condition or LF-Condition? In G. Garding and M. Tsujimura (eds.), *Proceedings of the West Coast Conference of Formal Linguistics (WCCFL) 22*, pages 547–60, Somerville, MA: Cascadilla Press.

Yoshida, Masaya, Lee, Jiyeon, and Dickey, Michael Walsh. 2013. The island (in)sensitivity of sluicing and sprouting. In Jon Sprouse and Norbert Hornstein (eds), *Experimental Syntax and Island Effects*, pages 360–76, Cambridge: Cambridge University Press.

Ytrestøl, Gisle. 2011. CuteForce: Deep Deterministic HPSG Parsing. In Harry Bunt, Joakim Nivre, and Özlem Çetinoglu (eds), *Proceedings of the 12th International Conference on Parsing Technologies*, pages 186–97, Dublin: Association for Computational Linguistics.

Zaenen, Annie. 1983. On syntactic binding. *Linguistic Inquiry* 14(3), 469–504.

Zaenen, Annie, Engdahl, Elisabet, and Maling, Joan M. 1981. Resumptive pronouns can be syntactically bound. *Linguistic Inquiry* 12(4), 679–82.

Zahn, Daniela and Scheepers, Christoph. 2011. Task effects in resolving RC attachment ambiguities. Poster presented at the 24th Conference on Human Sentence Processing, Stanford University, CA.

Zhang, Niina Ning. 2007. The Syntactic Derivations of Two Paired Dependency Constructions. *Lingua* 117(12), 2134–58.

Zhang, Yi and Kordoni, Valia. 2008. Robust Parsing with a Large HPSG Grammar. In Nicoletta Calzolari (Conference Chair), Khalid Choukri, Bente Maegaard, Joseph Mariani, Jan Odijk, Stelios Piperidis, and Daniel Tapias (eds), *Proceedings of the Sixth International Conference on Language Resources and Evaluation LREC*, pages 1888–93, Marrakesh: European Language Resources Association (ELRA).

Zhang, Yi and Krieger, Hans-Ulrich. 2011. Large-Scale Corpus-Driven PCFG Approximation of an HPSG. In Harry Bunt, Joakim Nivre, and Özlem Çetinoglu (eds), *Proceedings of the 12th International Conference on Parsing Technologies*, pages, 198–208, New Brunswick, NJ: Association for Computational Linguistics.

Zwicky, Arnold. 1986. The unaccented pronoun constraint in English. In Arnold Zwicky (ed.), *Interfaces, Volume 32 of Ohio State University Working Papers in Linguistics*, pages 100–14, Columbus, OH: Ohio State University Department of Linguistics.

Zwicky, Arnold. 2002. I wonder what kind of construction that this example illustrates. In David Beaver, Luis D. Casillias Martínez, Brady Z. Clark, and Stefan Kaufmann (eds), *The Construction of Meaning*, pages 219–48, Stanford, CA: CSLI Publications.

Zwicky, Arnold and Zwicky, Ann. 1973. How Come and What For. In Braj B. Kachru, Robert B. Lees, Yakov Malkiel, Angelina Pietrangeli, and Sol Saporta, (eds), *Papers in Honor of Henry and Renée Kahane*, Urbana, IL: University of Illinois Press.

Index

OXFORD SURVEYS IN SYNTAX AND MORPHOLOGY

General Editor
Robert D Van Valin, Jr,
Heinrich-Heine University and the University at Buffalo,
State University of New York

Advisory Editors
Guglielmo Cinque, University of Venice; Daniel Everett, Illinois State University;
Adele Goldberg, Princeton University; Kees Hengeveld, University of Amsterdam;
Caroline Heycock, University of Edinburgh; David Pesetsky, MIT; Ian Roberts,
University of Cambridge; Masayoshi Shibatani, Rice University; Andrew Spencer,
University of Essex; Tom Wasow, Stanford University